THE
EXECUTIVE'S
Lifetime Library
of
MODEL SPEECHES
for
Every Situation

THE
EXECUTIVE'S
Lifetime Library
of
MODEL SPEECHES
for
Every Situation

ROGER SHELBY

SHARPE PROFESSIONAL
An imprint of M.E. Sharpe, INC.

Library of Congress Cataloging-in-Publication Data

Shelby, Roger.
The executive's lifetime library of model speeches for every situation / Roger Shelby.
p.   cm.
Includes index.
ISBN 0-7656-0063-3 (hardcover : alk. paper)
1. Speeches, addresses, etc.   2. Business communication. I. Title.
PN6122.S58 1999   98-37094
815.008′09265   dc21
CIP

Printed in the United States of America

The paper used in this publication meets the minimum requirements of
American National Standard for Information Sciences—
Permanence of Paper for Printed Library Materials,
ANSI Z 39.48-1984.

BM (c)   10   9   8   7   6   5   4   3   2   1

ABOUT THE AUTHOR

Roger Shelby is an Atlanta-based writer specializing in business communication, marketing topics, and corporate history. A former university professor and publishing executive, Shelby has served as an adviser to top federal officials, has delivered speeches to a variety of service organizations, and has worked as a speech writer and consultant to customer service training organizations, the sales forces of major corporations, and to motivational speakers. He is president of a consulting firm serving cultural institutions and publishers.

ACKNOWLEDGMENTS

Books don't just happen. They happen because people make them happen. This book represents a collection of some twenty years of testing many of the words and speeches. Sincere thanks to all those exemplary public speakers in the business community who shared their advice, ideas, and speech-making experience over the years.

The inclusion of speeches by some of today's most important business leaders has greatly enhanced this book. For generously contributing their speeches, I thank Warren Bennis, Distinguished Professor of Business, Marshall School of Business, University of Southern California, Los Angeles; former Secretary of State Warren Christopher; President Bill Clinton; Earnest W. Deavenport, Jr., Chairman and CEO, Eastman Chemical Company; Lodewijk J.R. de Vink, President and COO, Warner-Lambert Company; Robert J. Eaton, Chairman and CEO, Chrysler Corporation; Richard Lidstad, Vice President for Human Resources, Minnesota Mining and Manufacturing Company; Dana G. Mead, Chairman and CEO, Tenneco, Inc., Eckhard Pfeiffer, President and CEO, Compaq Computer Corporation; James N. Sullivan, Vice Chairman, Chevron Corporation; Dominic Tarantino, former Chairman, Price Waterhouse World Firm; and Thomas W. White, President, GTE Telephone Operations.

—Roger Shelby

WHAT THIS BOOK WILL DO FOR YOU

The title of this book, *The Executive's Lifetime Library of Model Speeches for Every Situation,* tells you that it is a book about speeches and speech making. But, really, this is a book about time. For its principal assumption is that time is valuable to you and you just don't have much of it to spend, let alone waste. You are being called upon more than ever to communicate effectively. Frequently, you are called on to communicate to groups—that is, to make a speech or give an informal talk. Maybe you greet such a call as an opportunity, or maybe you see it as a dreaded demand. Either way, where will you find the time to put together an effective speech?

This tool will help.

The Executive's Lifetime Library of Model Speeches for Every Situation is a flexible resource of over 200 ready-to-use speeches and outlines (if you prefer to deliver a speech from an outline rather than a script) for your own customized use. Here you will find the most practical kind of help available: not abstract discussions of "how to give a speech" or a set of pep talks assuring you that "you can do it," but a generous selection of model speeches you can use more or less verbatim (just fill in the specifics that apply to your situation), or to inspire and guide you and trigger your own creativity.

With this book you can give useful, thought-provoking speeches and informal talks to a wide variety of audiences, ranging from trade organizations, to employees, to civic groups, to colleagues, to legislators, and to the press.

The core of this book is a series of **model speeches** classified according to virtually any business purpose or situation. Each model speech includes the type of speech, or occasion and principal topics, **Key Use of Speech, Style of Speech, Audience, and Time** it takes to give the speech. Each speech is liberally laced with speech **Tips** that emphasize structure and the techniques of persuasion. Accompanying many speeches are brief **Outlines** that can be used for speech presentations. **Directives** are included for modifying specific ideas to fit your own speech purpose. Finally, this book includes a selection of major contemporary speeches by CEOs and other business leaders, so that you can assess for yourself the state of the speech-making art in the world of commerce.

Whether you use these speeches word for word or modify them for your situation, this book makes it easy to create effective, interesting speeches. In the process, you will save valuable *time* in the preparation.

TABLE OF CONTENTS
Instant Speech Finder

Contents	Use this speech to . . .	Page
About the Author		v
Acknowledgments		vii
What This Book Will Do for You		ix
Announcements, Explanations of Events		**1**
001 Change in Location	*Inform employees of impending move*	3
002 Change in Medical Benefits	*Explain changes in medical benefits and reinforce the idea of common cause*	5
003 Change in Retirement Benefits	*Emphasize important changes in retirement benefits*	9
004 Change to Outsourcing *(also see Model Speech 048)*	*Justify the need to outsource a function formerly performed in house*	12
005 Departure of Employee *(also see Model Speech 045)*	*Express gratitude to a departing employee and reinforce team cohesiveness*	14
006 Downsizing *(also see Model Speech 133)*	*Explain a corporate downsize, address rumors, and put the event in perspective*	17
007 Introduction of New Sales Campaign	*Generate excitement about a new sales campaign*	21
008 Loss of a Major Customer	*Avoid panic or loss of morale*	25
009 Mergers and Acquisitions *(also see Model Speech 137)*	*Focus on the future*	27
010 New Major Customer	*Explain significance of new customer*	29

011 New Plant or Facility *Proclaim the construction of a new plant* 31
*(also see Model
Speech 025)*

012 Reaction to a Crisis/ *Establish leadership in a time of crisis* 33
Emergency

EXAMPLE: "CRISIS MANAGEMENT: PREVENTION AND PREPARATION," BY 35
JAMES N. SULLIVAN, VICE CHAIRMAN OF THE BOARD, CHEVRON
CORPORATION

013 Reorganization *Explain and instill enthusiasm in the* 41
reorganization

Awards, Congratulations **43**

014 Academic Distinction *Acknowledge employee achievement* 45

015 Civic Achievement *Present an award on behalf of the company* 47
Award

016 Cost-Saving Suggestion *Thank an employee for a cost-saving suggestion* 50

017 Employee Achievement *Explain the significance of the honoree's* 52
Award *achievement*

018 Exceptional Employee *Congratulate an employee* 54
Performance *(also see
Model Speech 084)*

019 Meeting or Exceeding *Congratulate a team or department for meeting* 57
Production Goals *production goals*

020 Meeting or Exceeding *Congratulate a team or department for meeting* 59
Sales Goals *sales goals*

021 Meeting or Exceeding *Congratulate a team or department for meeting* 61
Other Goals *a significant goal*

022 Safety Improvement *Congratulate a safety improvement suggestion* 63
Suggestion *(also see* *and encourage safety awareness*
Model Speech 102)*

Celebrations (*also see "Commemorations"*) **65**

023 Citizenship *Recognize the naturalization of a citizen* 67

024 Engagement/Wedding *Celebrate the announcement of an employee's* 69
engagement

025   Opening of New Facility   *Celebrate the opening of a new corporate facility*   71
        *(also see Model Speech
        011)*

Chairperson   **73**

026   Announcement of   *Provide focus when setting the agenda*   75
        Program Schedule

027   Introduction of   *Compliment a speaker briefly*   77
        Speaker(s)

028   Recognition of   *Introduce a distinguished guest and significance*   78
        Distinguished   *to the occasion*
        Guest(s)

Commemorations (*also see "Celebrations"*)   **79**

029   Anniversary of Company   *Praise an anniversary milestone and avoid*   81
                                tedious details

030   Birthday of Colleague or   *Express good wishes*   84
        Employee

031   Employment Anniversary   *Pay tribute to an employment anniversary*   86

032   Historical Building   *Enliven a commemorative speech that celebrates*   89
                            a historical building

033   Significant Event in the   *Create shared "corporate" myths and traditions*   91
        Past

034   Tragedy in the Past   *Remember a tragic death of an employee*   93

035   Gift/Endowment   *Celebrate a corporate gift to an educational*   96
                        institution and present challenges

036   Scholarship Program   *Inaugurate, express pride, and stress benefits in*   101
                            the scholarship program

037   Memorial   *Express grief for the tragedy*   105

Competition   **107**

038   Domestic, How to Exceed   *Encourage competition by looking within the*   109
                                organization

039   Foreign, How to Exceed   *Outline a program for competitiveness in the*   113
                                world marketplace

040 New Product as a Means   *Build excitement about a new product*   116
     to Beat Competition
     *(also see Model Speech
     127)*

Dedications   **119**

041 Dedication of New   *Point out benefits of the new building and*   121
     Facility   *express gratitude to employees*

042 Dedication of Memorial   *Express significance, pride, and bring the*   124
                                   subject of the memorial to life

Farewells   **127**

043 Benediction   *Wish those you are leaving well*   129

044 Company Moving Out   *Recount positive things company has done for* 130
     of Town   *the community*

045 Employee Leaving on   *Express best wishes to a departing employee* 132
     Favorable Note *(also
     see Model Speech
     005)*

     EXAMPLE: PRESIDENT CLINTON'S SPEECH ON THE RESIGNATION OF   134
     WARREN CHRISTOPHER

     EXAMPLE: SECRETARY OF STATE WARREN CHRISTOPHER'S RESIGNATION   137
     SPEECH

046 Retirement   *Thank employees and comment on future plans* 139
                                   in a positive manner

     EXAMPLE: "REFLECTIONS ON RETIREMENT," BY WARREN BENNIS,   141
     DISTINGUISHED PROFESSOR OF BUSINESS, UNIVERSITY OF SOUTHERN
     CALIFORNIA

Financial Reports, Meeting About   **147**

047 Financial Report to   *Outline performance*   149
     Executives and
     Managers

048 Financial Report to   *Emphasize the future*   151
     Financial Analysts
     *(also see Model
     Speech 004)*

049 Financial Report to   *Review the year's highlights and plans for next*   154
     Stockholders   *year*

Funerals   **157**

050 Eulogy   *Amplify the unique qualities of the deceased*   159

Gifts   **161**

051 Appreciation of Gift   *Express sincere gratitude for a gift*   163
     Received

052 Presentation of Gift   *Present a gift to an employee for an achievement*   164

Goals, Corporate *(also see Model Speeches 090, 091)*   **165**

053 Plans to Expand in an   *Present a plan for growth in good times*   167
     Expanding Economy
     *(also see Model Speech
     135)*

054 Plans to Ride Through   *Present a plan for operating in a poor economy*   170
     Recession

055 Plan to Ensure Quality   *Present a quality-control program*   174
     *(also see Model Speech
     099)*

Government Regulation   **177**

056 Bureaucratic Overkill   *Appeal to community organizations for a reform*   179
                                  in government bureaucracy

057 Environmental Regula-   *Appeal to community organizations for a*   182
     tion: The Good and the   *balance in environmental regulation*
     Ridiculous *(also see
     Model Speech 106)*

058 Market Price, Regulation   *Communicate to industry leaders an unpopular*   186
                                  viewpoint

059 Product Safety Regulation   *Promote product safety regulation*   188

060 Work-site Safety   *Convey to employees full support of safety*   193
     Regulation   *regulations*

Graduation   **195**

061 Academic Graduation   *Congratulate and inspire a graduation class*   197

062 Employee Training Program — *Express the value the company places on those employees who graduated from the corporate training program* — 201

EXAMPLE: "THE ULTIMATE KNOWLEDGE-BASED PRODUCT—YOU: DEVELOPING QUALITIES TO DRIVE YOUR OWN CAREER" BY DOMINIC TARANTINO, FORMER CHAIRMAN, PRICE WATERHOUSE WORLD FIRM — 203

History of Company — **211**

063 Products and Services — *Give historical perspective of the company* — 213

064 People and Labor Relations — *Give historical perspective in relation to the company's employees* — 217

Holiday Celebrations — **221**

065 New Year's Day — *Reflect on the successes of the past year and express warm wishes for the new year* — 223

066 Memorial Day — *Celebrate the seriousness of this holiday* — 224

067 Fourth of July — *Describe how this holiday is significant to the individual* — 226

068 Veterans' Day — *Give additional meaning to this holiday* — 228

069 Thanksgiving — *Acknowledge the importance of this holiday* — 231

070 Christmas and Chanukah — *Express warm and sincere wishes for the season* — 232

Informal Events — **233**

071 Company Picnic/Sports Event — *Impart the reason for holding an annual event* — 235

072 Holiday Season — *Give a warm and friendly toast* — 236

Introductions — **237**

073 New Employee — *Introduce and welcome a new employee* — 239

074 New Executive Manager — *Introduce and welcome a new manager* — 241

Legislative Affairs — **243**

075 Testimony Before Investigation Committee — *Present formal testimony covering a company pilot program* — 245

076   Testimony in Support   *Present formal testimony that could impact the*   249
          of a Bill   *future of an industry*

Media   **253**

077   Interview, Print   *Provide direct, informative statements when*   255
                                    interviewed for a publication

078   Interview, TV or   *Create a suitable interview for broadcast*   258
          Radio

079   News Conference   *Make a clear, unmistakable statement for a news*   260
                                    conference

Motivating Employees   **263**

080   Call to Action   *Communicate a clear, desired, and specific*   265
                                    action

          EXAMPLE: "THE QUALITIES OF SUCCESS: LEADERSHIP, DIVERSITY,   268
          COMMUNITY SERVICE, AND CAREER DEVELOPMENT," BY RICHARD
          LIDSTAD, VICE PRESIDENT FOR HUMAN RESOURCES, MINNESOTA MINING
          AND MANUFACTURING COMPANY

081   Challenges to Meet   *Inspire employees to meet a difficult challenge*   273

          EXAMPLE: "INTEGRATED HEALTH CARE: THE PATIENT IS WAITING," BY   275
          LODEWIJK J.R. DE VINK, PRESIDENT AND CHIEF OPERATING OFFICER,
          WARNER-LAMBERT COMPANY

082   Collaboration and   *Express the necessity of teamwork between*   283
          Cooperation Between   *departments*
          Departments

083   Employee Commitment   *Encourage employees to excel and solve*   286
                                    problems creatively

084   Customer Service   *Explain and define the role of customer service*   291
          Importance *(also*   *in the next millennium*
          see Model Speech
          018)

085   Decision-Making Skills   *Enhance and improve decision-making skills*   295
          (also see Model Speech
          134)

086   Determination and   *Encourage and inspire all employees to*   298
          Perseverance   *persevere*

087   Education   *Encourage employees to take advantage of*   300
                                       corporate educational development
                                       programs

      EXAMPLE: "WORKING IN INTERESTING TIMES," BY THOMAS W. WHITE,   303
      PRESIDENT, GTE TELEPHONE OPERATIONS

088   Ethics   *Avoid preaching but communicate the*   310
                                       company's view on values and integrity

089   Excellence   *Inspire excellence, with emphasis on research* 313
                                       and development

090   Goal Attainment *(also*   *Define goals and inspire employees to achieve* 315
      see "Goals,   *them*
      Corporate")

091   Goal Setting *(also see*   *Plan your work, and work your plan*   317
      "Goals, Corporate")

092   Imagination and   *Encourage brainstorming and using imagination* 319
      Creativity   *constructively and productively*

093   Increase Productivity   *Motivate and illustrate ways to be more*   323
                                       productive

094   Leadership   *Define your meaning of leadership to*   328
                                       managers/supervisors

095   Mission of Company   *Communicate to employees your company's*   332
                                       mission

096   Optimism Is Contagious   *Encourage managers/supervisors to be positive* 333

097   Procrastination   *Motivate employees to get things done*   335
      Avoidance

098   Public Image   *Motivate employees to think of ways to improve* 338
      Improvement   *a company's image*

099   Quality Improvement   *Set quality improvement goals*   340

100   Risk Taking   *Inspire managers to take risks*   342

101   Safety   *Inform employees that practicing safety is good* 344
                                       business

102   Teamwork *(also see*   *Urge employees to solve problems as a team*   346
      Model Speech 022)

Policies   **349**

103 Affirmative Action and   *Explain the company's policy on affirmative*   351
     EEO   *action and EEO*

104 Employee Development   *Persuade employees to take advantage of the*   353
                                firm's policy on employee development

105 Employee Empowerment   *Urge employees to become more involved*   355

106 Environmental Protection   *Enlighten employees on the company's*   357
     (also see Model Speech   *environmental policy*
     057)

     EXAMPLE: "STANDING AT THE EDGE OF HISTORY: SUSTAINABLE   361
     DEVELOPMENT AND THE CHEMICAL INDUSTRY," BY EARNEST W.
     DEAVENPORT, JR., CHAIRMAN AND CEO, EASTMAN CHEMICAL
     COMPANY

107 Foreign Manufacturing   *Formalize company policy for establishing*   366
     Facility   *foreign facilities*

108 Free Speech   *Explain corporate policy on public statements*   370

109 Growth   *Lay a foundation for the company's policy on*   372
                                growth

110 Labor Contracts   *Announce and define new policy on contract*   374
                                labor

111 Outsourcing *(also*   *Announce and define new policy on outsourcing*   376
     see Model Speech
     004)

112 Promotion   *Motivate managers to develop and promote*   378
                                staff

113 Recycling   *Inform employees and managers of corporate*   383
                                policy on recycling

Political Affairs   **385**

114 Support of Political   *Introduce a political candidate*   387
     Candidate

115 Support of a Single   *Seek support of a referendum important to an*   388
     Referendum   *industry*

Public Relations   391

116   Business Associations or Chambers of Commerce   *Enlighten and inform a business association or chamber of commerce about the challenge of change*   393

117   Civic Associations   *Take a leadership role over a community issue*   397

118   Service Clubs   *Prevail upon a civic group on a critical matter affecting business*   401

119   Trade Associations (Customers)   *Create goodwill when asked to speak to a customer's trade association*   405

120   Trade Associations (Suppliers)   *Create goodwill when asked to speak to a supplier's trade association*   408

121   Trade Associations (Industry Competitors)   *Create goodwill when asked to speak to a trade association made up of industry competitors*   412

    EXAMPLE: "FINDING SOMEONE TO SUE: REGAINING CONTROL OF THE TORT LAW," BY ROBERT J. EATON, CHAIRMAN AND CEO, CHRYSLER CORPORATION   416

Sales and Marketing   425

122   Advertising on Radio   *Play up to sales and marketing staff the new radio advertising campaign*   427

123   Customer Satisfaction   *Advocate good customer service practice to stay competitive*   431

124   Developing Brand Loyalty   *Reaffirm to sales staff the need to develop brand loyalty*   435

125   Developing New Markets   *Motivate sales staff to push new markets*   437

126   Developing Export Markets   *Announce to sales staff the plan to penetrate export markets*   439

127   New Product *(also see Model Speech 040)*   *Introduce a new product to sales staff*   441

Sales and Marketing Support   443

128   Support of Sales Campaign   *Encourage customer service employees to support sales*   445

129 Treatment of
     Customers
     Inspire behavior that creates customer
     satisfaction   447

130 Upholding Image of
     Company
     Express pride in the company image   451

Solicitations   **455**

131 Charitable Gifts   *Raise money for charity* 457

132 Donation of Labor for   *Encourage volunteering*   459
     Charity

Strategies   **463**

133 Downsizing Program   *Disclose a plan to downsize* 465
     Strategy *(also see Model*
     Speech 006)

134 Decision-Making Process *Call for a streamlined decision-making process* 467
     Strategy *(also see Model*
     Speech 085)

135 Growth Strategy *(also see* *Apprise stockholders of a new growth strategy* 469
     Model Speech 053)*

136 Hedging Strategy   *Explain to managers a change in the* 471
                             introduction of a new product

137 Mergers and Acquisitions *Announce a proposed acquisition* 473
     Strategy *(also see Model*
     Speech 009)

138 Reinventing Business   *Paint an exciting picture of how business is* 475
                             reinventing itself

139 Reinventing Government *Propose a new approach to government,* 478
                             especially as it relates to business

140 Research and   *Create excitement about a new R&D strategy* 483
     Development

141 Spin-off Strategy   *Create excitement about a spin-off strategy* 488

142 Strategic Planning   *State the need for a strategic plan and involve* 490
                             managers in creating such a plan

143 Turnaround Strategy   *Outline a turnaround and recovery strategy* 494

Technology   497

144 Communications   *Outline the opportunities and challenges of*   499
     Technology   *communications technology*

     EXAMPLE: "THE PC PLATFORM: COMPUTERS NOW AFFECT EVERY AGE   502
     GROUP AND ROOM OF YOUR HOME," BY ECKHARD PFEIFFER, PRESIDENT
     AND CEO, COMPAQ COMPUTER CORPORATION

145 Computer Utilization   *Establish ground rules for computer usage to*   510
                             employees

146 Desktop Publishing   *Make a presentation to small business owners on* 512
                             the advantages of using desktop publishing

147 Electronic Commuting   *Address members of a trade or professional*   516
     (Telecommuting)   *group on the growth of an your company's*
                             policy on telecommuting

148 Electronic Libraries   *Address members of a professional or*   521
                             educational group on the knowledge revolution
                             and the future of electronic information
                             distribution

     EXAMPLE: "GROWTH AND THE ROAD TO CYBERSPACE," BY DANA G.   525
     MEAD, CHAIRMAN AND CEO, TENNECO, INC.

149 Internet Successes and *Deliver an informal talk on the art of using the* 533
     Failures   *internet*

150 Machines Replacing   *Address students on the impact of technology on* 538
     Humans   *the job market*

     EXAMPLE: "TAMING THE TECHNOLOGICAL MONSTER," BY DOMINIC   540
     TARANTINO, CHAIRMAN, FORMER PRICE WATERHOUSE WORLD FIRM

Training Employees   549

151 Corporate Ethics   *Orient new employees on the company's policy*   551
                             concerning ethics

152 Introduction to Technical *Orient employees on the company's new*   553
     Training Program   *technical training program*

Index   557

Announcements, Explanations of Events

Openings

——*Are you ready for some good news?*

——*I am pleased to announce a program that is important to all of us.*

Closings

——*Thank you for your attention. I look forward to working with you on this exciting project.*

——*Please remember the key dates I have mentioned . . .*

MODEL SPEECH 001:
Change in Location

Key Use of Speech: To announce a corporate relocation.

Style of Speech: Informative, authoritative, team-building.

Audience: Company employees.

Time: 5 to 6 minutes.

→ Tip: A bantering tone can establish a pleasant, nonthreatening bond with your audience.

I was going to speak to you this morning wearing my hard hat. That's been a valuable piece of equipment around here lately. The rumors have been flying so thick and fast that there's a real risk of getting beaned by one of them if you venture out into the corridors unprotected.

The flying rumors concern our moving out of these offices.

Let me put an end to those rumors.

We *are* moving.

Now the rumors are no longer rumors, but fact.

→ Tip: The speaker details the reasons for the move. Providing reasons for an action goes a long way toward securing willing compliance and cooperation.

Here are some other facts: XYZ Industries has grown from **[number]** employees when we moved into this facility in **[year]** to **[number]** employees today. Now, we all like each other very much and we function beautifully as a team, but it's been getting so tight in here that sometimes I feel like taking a rush-hour subway ride just to get away from the crowds.

It's time to find more room.

A second fact: We have just signed a lease for space at **[new location]**. Our square footage there is **[number]**, compared with **[number]** here. That's a **[percentage amount]** increase.

→ Tip: Wherever possible, quantify information. Let your audience see for themselves the positive impact of the move.

A third fact: For some of you, the new location will mean a longer commute. For others, it will be more convenient. However, all of us will enjoy better access to public transportation. **[The speaker**

3

reviews the transit situation at the new location.] Parking is available in an adjacent lot. Spaces will be assigned on the basis of seniority; however, there are more spaces than we currently have, so that situation will also be an improvement.

Fact four: We plan to take occupancy of the new space on **[date]**. That's only **[number]** months off, which means we have some planning to do now.

While everyone will be given an opportunity to tour the new facility, and while all managers and supervisors will be consulted on questions of space allocation, I am forming a Relocation Committee to address such operations as facilities planning and the logistics of the move. Our liaison person with that committee will be **[name]**. Bring your questions and concerns to him; he will also be issuing a plan to help managers organize their departments for the move.

As anyone who has ever moved a household knows, this isn't a fun process. It's disruptive. It's even upsetting. I've heard it said that, except for death, moving is the most stressful event we face in life. I won't debate that now, but I will admit that moving an operation like ours *will* create its stresses and strains. However, it *is* necessary, and it will mean having a much more comfortable and productive work environment. Even more important, the move will give us room for the future. We are growing, and we will continue to grow. This move is a promise of even better things to come. Thanks for your patience and your cooperation.

→ Tip: Although many of the basic decisions regarding the move have already been made, the speaker leaves the door open for wider participation in the process.

→ Tip: Don't gloss over difficulties, but do keep them in perspective.

MODEL SPEECH 002:
Change in Medical Benefits

Key Use of Speech:	To announce—and justify—changes in this critical and sensitive area: medical benefits.
Style of Speech:	Informal, personal, frank; straight talk.
Audience:	Company employees.
Time:	10 to 12 minutes. [Depends on complexity of charts and other visuals. Leave ample time for questions afterward.]

Fringe. We all know what that is. Decorative trim—a little something extra stitched on to make the principal product more attractive. Fringe is nice, but you can certainly live without it.

➝ Tip: Defining terms, informally and dramatically, is an effective, thought-provoking way to begin a speech.

Now: *fringe benefits.* The main one has always been *medical benefits.* But when is the last time you actually heard someone *dare* to call *medical* benefits *fringe* benefits? Our fathers and mothers—or maybe our grandfathers and grandmothers—wouldn't have been offended by the phrase. It was okay with them. In their day, medical benefits were nice, but they were "something extra." And that was just fine, when a simple trip to the doctor didn't start at three figures and work its way up from there, or a stay in a hospital start the meter running at $1,500 a day.

My friends, these days medical benefits are almost as good a reason to take a job and hold a job as salary is. Where does the main product end and the fringe begin?

Our health plan is important to all of us and to all of our families. When I tell you that we are introducing a new health plan to the company, I know that the first reaction of many of you will be—let's say it—*fear.* Well, unfortunately, that is a *normal* response to the cost realities we face today, when one serious illness may not only threaten us physically, but financially as well. That's why I'm doing something more than pass out a few brochures on our new health plan. I want to walk through it with you, to explain what will be different, what will remain the same, and how it will affect you. And I want to be right here, right now, to answer any questions you may have.

First, let's admit that the current plan has been good for most of us. We chose a doctor, went to him or her, submitted the bill, and—usually—we got paid for all but 20 percent of it. Let me begin by assuring you that the new plan will be good for *all* of us.

But if, for most of us, the old plan wasn't broke, why fix it? Interesting word, *broke*. It about describes where we'd be, in a very few years, if we didn't do something now to control the costs of providing medical benefits. Let me show you something.

[Using charts and other visuals, the speaker illustrates the skyrocketing cost of the company's outgoing health plan and how those costs affect the company's "bottom line."]

Now I understand this much: If "fringe benefits" is a phrase some may find offensive, "bottom line" can sound downright obscene. *You're sacrificing* my *medical benefits to* your *"bottom line"?* I agree, that is an *obscene* proposition.

But let's get these pronouns straightened out. It's not *my* company. It's *our* company. And it's not *my* bottom line. It's *ours*. We're in this together. Sure, each of us has to worry about controlling our own costs, including what it costs to keep or make us well. But, collectively, we all have to control what it costs *our* company to keep or make us well. If we don't control these costs, we face layoffs, and since everyone of us in this room works in this company for a reason, serves a vital purpose, the loss of anyone diminishes this company. Diminish us enough, and we'll have no company. The company will have choked on fringe. And us, no salary, no benefits.

So much for the context of this new medical plan. The reason for it is simple: our survival.

Survival, you'll agree, is good. And the fact is that the new medical plan is good, too. Here's how it works.

The key cost reducer is our changing over to an HMO provider. Oh-oh. Another dirty word. And let's not kid ourselves, a *bad* HMO

→ Tip: Self-interest is a strong motivator. If you can appeal to the self-interest of your audience, you will find yourself in a most persua- sive position.

→ Tip: Anticipate the arguments that run coun- ter to what you propose. Anticipate them and deal with them, disarm them.

→ Tip: The most persua- sive speeches reinforce the idea of team or com- munity or common cause. They transform I versus You into We together.

→ Tip: Concede whatever merit opposing viewpoints might have; then, having made the concession, show how your position or proposition is still superior to that of the opposing side.

can be a nightmare. A bad *doctor* can be a nightmare, too. The solution? Stay away from HMOs? Stay away from doctors? No. The solution is to choose a great HMO, which *is* great because it is staffed by great doctors.

[The speaker, or a representative from the HMO, gives a brief presentation on the medical reputation of the HMO and the credentials of some of its key physicians.]

Now I want to review with you the highlights of the new plan.

[The speaker reviews the highlights, point by point.]

I will answer any questions you may have in just one moment. But, now that I have explained what the new plan will do for each of us individually, I want to show you what it will do for us collectively.

[The speaker uses charts and other visuals to demonstrate graphically the dramatic cost savings of the new health plan.]

→ Tip: Reinforce common cause with the plural possessive pronoun: our.

I admit, this isn't a set of your x-rays that you're looking at, or your EKG or your CAT scan. But it is a picture of *our* health. Now, are there any questions?

OUTLINE

Opening

- Define "fringe"
- Medical benefits no longer just "fringe"

Why a new health plan?

- Defuse audience fear, provide reassurance
- Want to explain the plan
- Virtues of the old plan
- Why change?
- Explanation of the need for change
- Rising costs

• Anticipate and address audience objections

Team-building

• Absolute need to control costs
• Controlling costs benefits all

The new plan

• How it works
• How it reduces costs
• HMO problems
• Solutions to HMO problems
• Highlights of new plan: point of view of the employee
• Highlights of new plan: point of view of the company

Closing

• Conclude with concept of the "health" of the company

———————————

MODEL SPEECH 003:
Change in Retirement Benefits

Key Use of Speech: To announce—and justify—changes in this key employee benefit.

Style of Speech: Informal, personal, frank.

Audience: Company employees.

Time: 8 to 10 minutes. [Leave ample time for questions afterward.]

➡ Tip: Quotations don't always have to be lofty pronouncements from heroes and philosophers. Sometimes the homey and familiar is even more effective.

➡ Tip: In ordinary conversation, we speak from our own experience. Why not do that in a speech as well? Person-to-person communication can be highly effective.

➡ Tip: Humor is always welcome, as long as it is germane to the point you are making.

There is a well-known brokerage firm that uses an advertising slogan I've always liked. It goes something like this: "It's not the money you *make* that counts. It's the money you get to *keep*."

Now, maybe some of you remember the first real paycheck you ever got. I know I do. I tore open that envelope, and I looked at those numbers. A lot of them had little minus signs: minus federal withholding, minus state withholding, minus FICA, and so on. It was a shock.

To tell you the truth, I've never fully recovered from that shock. Each time I break open my pay envelope, it comes right back, sweeping over me. That sinking feeling.

Well, what can you do about it? As old Ben Franklin said, the only sure things in this world are death and taxes.

Now, I guess death is death. But *taxes*? Okay, let's say taxes, too. However, Ben Franklin never said just *how much* tax. *How much* tax is not quite so sure a thing as the fact of taxes.

One way you can save on taxes, of course, is to take less salary. I'm quite open to discussing that. Any takers? [Pauses.] I didn't think so. Fortunately, there is another way to tame the tax bite.

9

As you know, XYZ Corporation has long included in its benefit package a modest retirement pension, which required no contribution on your part. The operative word here, unfortunately, is *modest*.

→ Tip: The speaker does not assume that everyone in his/her audience understands the basic nature of his/her subject. The speaker concisely explains what a 401(k)

Beginning January 1, XYZ Corporation will offer its employees a 401(k) plan in addition to the pension. Now, as many of you undoubtedly already know, a 401(k) plan is contributory; that is, the employee chooses to deposit a portion of his or her income into his or her 401(k) account, *and that amount is not taxed* until it is withdrawn. The catch is that you cannot withdraw the money before age fifty-five without incurring a tax penalty; however, after age fifty-five, the money will be taxed according to whatever income-tax bracket you happen to be in at the time. Assuming that you wait until you're retired before tapping the fund, the bracket will be advantageous to you because you won't be drawing a regular paycheck.

→ Tip: Having provided a picture of the immediate future, the speaker talks about the long-term future.

By offering you a 401(k) plan, then, XYZ Corporation is not only helping you to provide for your retirement, but is also offering you a means of taking at least a measure of control over your tax liability.

And *control* is what this new plan is all about. Not only do you get a significant degree of control over your tax liability, but you also decide how much or how little you want to contribute.

Now, *at this time,* XYZ Corporation will not be making a matching contribution to your 401(k) account; however, our intention is to phase in a contribution program as we phase out the old retirement pension plan. Those who choose not to participate in the 401(k) plan will remain entitled to the pension plan. But, when we finalize the contribution schedule for the 401(k), I believe that the advantages of participating in the 401(k) will be apparent to all of us, and I suspect that the pension will ultimately, well, die of old age.

→ Tip: Whenever you speak of change, it is vitally important to make yourself available interactively, to answer questions your speech may not have addressed or addressed fully.

Friends, XYZ's 401(k) is an exciting change for us all. We have distributed information packets on the plan, but if you have any questions right now, I'll do my best to answer them.

OUTLINE

Opening

- Familiar quotation
- First-person anecdote
- Problem: high taxes

• Humorous solution

The new benefits package

• A real solution to the tax bite
• Official announcement of new plan
• Explanation of new plan
• Advantages of the new plan
• Control and choice as chief advantages

The future

• Immediate
• Long term

Closing

• Enthusiasm for new plan
• Call for questions

MODEL SPEECH 004:
Change to Outsourcing

Key Use of Speech:	To announce, explain, and justify outsourcing of a function formerly performed in house.
Style of Speech:	Informal, personal, with emphasis on team-building.
Audience:	Company employees.
Time:	6 to 7 minutes. [Leave time for questions afterward.]

→ Tip: Pay attention to pronouns. Make your remarks inclusive and team-building with we, us, and our. Speak to individuals and groups directly with you.

We work hard. *All* of us. But, lately, no one has been working harder than the accounting staff. Thanks, folks. You've been doing an incredible job—and hardly a grumble or a grimace out of any of you.

I think I know how you must feel. Like it's time to circle the wagons before the flaming arrows come raining down. Well, as in those good old John Wayne movies, the cavalry is about to arrive—and just in time, too.

As we all know, our accounting department has been faithfully grinding out the payroll every two weeks in addition to performing all of their other financial and accounting duties, which range from paying the vendors' bills that keep us running, to projecting the costs and revenues so that we always know where we are running to.

→ Tip: Be sure that your audience knows the facts needed to understand your message. Provide background. Use numbers sparingly, but for impact.

As we all know, too, XYZ Corporation has grown—overall some 50 percent in the past three years, in fact. But what you probably don't know is that the accounting department has grown by *10* percent during that same period. That's right, in accounting, we've added a single position. Now, you don't have to *be* a CPA to calculate that the gap between the company's growth overall versus the accounting department's near lack of growth equals a lot of work for a few accountants.

It's not fair. And it's not efficient. Our accounting people are so good that payroll problems have not developed. But there is only so much that ten people can do before, sooner or later, the system starts to buckle. But that's not the real issue here. The *real* issue is that payroll is a straightforward, though time-consuming, operation. We have more challenging things for our accounting people to devote their time to, such as developing and refining new, more detailed, and always more accurate analytical and projection procedures. Developing such tools is important to us all.

Of course, it's also pretty important to us all to get a paycheck every couple of weeks.

To give our accounting staff a more manageable work load, to enable them to put their collective talents to the most productive purposes possible, and to keep us all getting paid efficiently and accurately, we have decided to turn our payroll over to a third-party service, WePayU, Inc.

For most of us, this will be a seamless transition—though you may get one or two questions confirming such items as number of withholding exemptions you are claiming and so on. The only major change all of us will be offered is the opportunity to have our checks deposited directly in our bank accounts. Using a third-party service allows us to offer this convenience. But this *is* optional, and for those who prefer to get a good old paper check, WePayU will grind them out.

And don't worry. Pete Smith, from our own accounting department, will serve as our contact person with WePayU. Should you ever have any questions about your payroll status or your check, you can just knock on Pete's door.

For the accounting staff, relief from payroll duty is long overdue. For the company as a whole, going to a third-party provider is a cost-effective way of freeing up a skilled accounting staff for work that is critical to our future. Instead of having to add permanent in-house staff, we are able to reallocate the staff we have.

I hope that you are all as excited as I am about this very positive step. Pete Smith and I invite your questions and comments.

MODEL SPEECH 005:
Departure of Employee

Key Use of Speech: To announce the departure of an employee, to express gratitude to the employee for his or her work, and to reinforce team cohesion.

Style of Speech: Informal, personal, with emphasis on team-building.

Audience: Company employees, including the departing employee.

Time: 5 to 6 minutes. [Leave time for the departing employee to say his/her goodbyes.]

> ➺ Tip: It is a good idea to address the departing employee directly. The audience wants to feel part of the event. They expect you to express their feelings.

> ➺ Tip: Be specific about the departing employee's contributions; however, don't allow the focus to exclude the rest of the team. One objective of this speech is to reassure the team that they can and will get along without the departing employee—valuable as his presence has been.

When you devote a decade of your life and career to a firm, well, no one can accuse you of using their company as a "steppingstone" to something better. So, don't worry, Ed, I won't try to make you feel guilty.

We're a healthy team here at XYZ Corporation—thanks in no small measure to you, by the way—and that means we don't often agree about a lot of things. Lock step is just not our style. But I feel safe in saying that we're unanimous on one thing: Ed Smith has given us ten terrific years, years that saw this company triple its volume of business, years that produced some of the product lines for which we are now best known, including . . . **[list the major products].**

So, Ed, now you're leaving. You've given us so much that I wish I *could* make you feel guilty, because this past decade makes me want another decade just as successful. And it's more than the revenues, Ed. (Well, the money *is* important . . .) But it's more than the money. We've grown accustomed to your ability to spark and nurture new ideas, to your contagious enthusiasm, to your hard-working spirit, and to your incredibly awful jokes, which include some of the worst any

→ Tip: Humor creates strong "insider" bonds.

→ Tip: Acknowledge that you are speaking on behalf of the team.

→ Tip: Include necessary information regarding the transition—what must and will happen after the employee leaves.

of us have ever heard. Ed, now that you're leaving us, it can be told: not a single *one* of your jokes has ever produced an audible laugh. I saw Mary Clark smile at one of them once, but she later told me it was the pepperoni on her lunchtime pizza. Ed, we'll miss those terrible jokes

I want all of you to know that I did all my pleading with Ed in private. He's going to **[name the company and the position]**. It's a major career move for Ed, so we can all understand why he's chosen to make the move. If you'll allow me, then, ladies and gentlemen, to speak on your behalf, all of us at XYZ thank you, Ed, for working with us. We wish you the best of luck.

Now, one last thing. Ed will be with us for another two weeks, preparing for the transition. We expect to have Ed's position filled in six to eight weeks—that's my estimate of how long it will take us to find someone with qualifications comparable to Ed's. In the meantime, after Ed leaves, Sarah James and I will be handling his department. We will try to make the transition to the new person as painless as possible. But we'll need your patience and your help. Even with Ed's leaving, we remain a strong team, and we'll need to call on that strength during these next several weeks.

OUTLINE

Opening

• Humorous remarks to departing employee

Employee's contributions to the firm

• General contributions
• Specific contributions
• Personal contributions
• Expression of affection
• Sharing anecdotes about the employee
Employee's future

• Where he's going
• Why he's going (new opportunity)

Closing: practical matters

- Transition plans and procedures
- Replacement for departing employee
- Appeal to team spirit for cooperation and patience during transition

---

MODEL SPEECH 006:
Downsizing

Key Use of Speech:	To announce and explain a corporate downsizing.
Style of Speech:	Informal straight talk, with emphasis on the positive aspects of the downsizing.
Audience:	Company employees, including those who are being laid off.
Time:	7 to 8 minutes. [Leave time for questions.]

➜ Tip: If at all possible, the employees most directly affected by the downsizing—especially those who are being laid off—should be spoken to individually and in private before any general announcement is made.

Some of what I am about to say to you will not come as a surprise. Those of you most directly affected by the downsizing that will begin after the end of the year have been spoken to individually. As for the rest of us, we've been driven by the rumor mill long enough. It's time for some authoritative information.

In 19XX, we began a program of very rapid expansion to meet a sharply rising market. In recent years, that market has even more sharply contracted. The figures speak for themselves, and they speak *very* loudly. **[Use visuals to illustrate sudden market growth and decline.]** As we can all see, revenues have shrunk and show no signs of rebounding. Now, it's nothing we've done wrong. The shrinkage is a function of the marketplace, not us. It's not our fault. But it is our problem.

➜ Tip: Do not make this speech prematurely. The downsizing program should be discussed with employees only after the action, its scope, and its related policies have been formulated. You don't want to broadcast mis-information or add grist to the rumor mill.

Our problem is that, in this new marketplace, we are overstaffed. If we maintained our present level of staffing, not only would we fail to be competitive, we'd *fail*. Period.

That's where the downsizing program comes in. It's not about greed. It's not about making *more* money. And it's not about punishing anybody. It's about *survival*. Period.

17

Before I continue, let me put this downsizing program in perspective. Business is off almost 30 percent. We are downsizing 6 percent of our people. My point is that our response is very *conservative*—conservative in the sense that we are conserving as many jobs as possible. We are trimming and regulating, not cannibalizing. You cannibalize something that has no future. *We* have a future. Downsizing is one of the necessary means of *realizing* that future.

Of course, that's great for those of us who are still going to be working here. What about the 6 percent who are being . . . let's stop using the cold corporate euphemism. These colleagues aren't being "downsized." They're being laid off.

Face it. Say the words. It's a painful thing. The company is losing—at least for now—valuable human assets. We are all losing valued colleagues; I hope this doesn't mean we will lose friends as well. And for that 6 percent? They, of course, lose jobs.

We *are* investing in severance and outplacement assistance—two strong programs that should ease the transition. And, please remember, this *is* a transition. It's not an end. It's a change. The latest statistics I have tell me that, these days, most folks can expect to change *jobs* eight times in the course of their lives, and change *careers* three or four times. We'll do our best to help all of you, colleagues and friends, make a rapid transition to other jobs.

I want to say just two more things to the people who will be leaving us. First—and I think I speak for everyone who is *not* being laid off—I want to express gratitude, not just for your dedication and for your professionalism under very difficult circumstances, but for consistently showing us such grace and generosity. You have every right to grumble. But I've heard no grumbling. I've heard only kind words and encouraging words. You really are extraordinary professionals and extraordinary people.

But—and here's my second point—it's not all one-sided. Leave here knowing that you are leaving a company with a future. And, let me assure you, *that* is a valuable thing for *you*. Making the transition to another position elsewhere is much easier if you are moving from a going concern rather than to one that is going, or has gone, belly up. All of us—including those of you who are moving on—all of us have a stake in this company's future.

To those who are leaving, you know, as I have told you individually, that you can call on me and on your supervisors for recommen-

→ Tip: Straight talk will be appreciated. Show that you are avoiding corporate euphemisms and are facing reality.

→ Tip: If you can pay tribute to those being laid off, do so.

→ Tip: Again, extract and highlight whatever positive aspects of the situation you can identify.

dations and other kind words to prospective employers. To those of you who are staying on, I know that many of you are concerned about future downsizing. Here's what I know. First, I have no crystal ball. I cannot foretell the future with certainty, and, therefore, I can't make any promises. Second, I *can* tell you that we have no plans at present for additional layoffs. Why? Because we believe that the present action will give us the degree of trim and control we need to adapt not only to the present market, but also to where we see the market going. Third, the action we have taken now will be effective only if all of us who are staying on work to maximize efficiency, to keep operating costs in line, and, above all, to create satisfaction in every single customer we serve.

➡ Tip: End by reinforcing the team's mission.

OUTLINE

Opening

- Address rumors
- Issue authoritative information

Background of downsizing

- Expansion too rapid
- Losses
- Problem: overstaffed for present market conditions
- Motive for downsizing: survival

Downsizing in perspective

- A conservative step
- Not cannibalizing company
- We have a future

Help for those laid off

- Admit step is painful
- Will provide outplacement aid
- Grateful for employees' professionalism

- Not a hopeless situation
- Invitation to call on management for help

Closing

- No plans to lay off more employees
- Team effort, cooperation, efficiency necessary now

———————————————

MODEL SPEECH 007:
Introduction of New Sales Campaign

Key Use of Speech: To announce, explain, and generate excitement about a new sales campaign.

Style of Speech: Informational and motivational.

Audience: Sales and customer service staff.

Time: 7 to 8 minutes.

There's a buzz. I'm hearing it. You're hearing it. The industry is hearing it. Most certainly, our customers are hearing it.

It's about breaking a barrier. The rumors have been flying: a high-resolution, seventeen-inch PC- and MAC-compatible monitor for *under* $400. Incredible!

Well, let me tell you something about rumors. They're 10 percent true and 90 percent false. Except in this case. The buzz is right on target, and the rumors are true. On **[date],** we will be revitalizing our larger-screen monitor line by cutting prices on our intermediate seventeen-inch units.

I don't have to tell you: The price is a breakthrough, and it should really move our customers off the fence and motivate some heavy purchases.

Let me give you a fact. Right now, seventeen-inch monitors account for **[percentage amount]** of our monitor sales. Industry-wide, they account for **[percentage amount].** As you can see, we're just a hair above the industry average. With the new pricing, we expect to capture **[percentage amount]** of the market. Ladies and gentlemen, that means selling **[number]** units by **[target date].**

Now, a great price alone won't achieve these numbers. Here's the plan.

→ Tip: Usually, crystal clarity is the best way to begin a speech. Sometimes, however, a touch of mystery, of suspense, is a valuable "tease" to capture and pique the attention of your audience.

→ Tip: Build and convey excitement by being specific. Let the facts and figures do the loudest talking.

We're beginning with fundamentals. Why do customers chuck the fourteen- or fifteen-inch monitors that come with their computers to buy a seventeen-inch after-market replacement?

[The speaker lists the top reasons, based on market research. The principal reason is the ability to see more of a document on-screen.]

→ Tip: It is no coincidence that the word *campaign* is applied to a series of related battles in a war as often as it is applied to promoting a new product. Just as every military campaign benefits from a stirring battle cry ("Remember the Alamo!"), so an effective sales campaign can draw energy and focus from a concisely stated, compelling, single-sentence "handle" or "selling point."

As you can see, there are a number of reasons for purchasing a seventeen-inch monitor. But our sales campaign won't mess with most of those reasons. We're going to address the *top* reason: buy this monitor, and you'll *see* more; *see* more, and you'll be more *productive*. The campaign, ladies and gentlemen, is simple: We'll begin by selling the benefits the customer says are most important. Then we'll close sales with the benefits the customer may not even know he or she wants.

The cornerstone of this sales campaign is the following selling point: *Get the* big *picture—for a* little *cash*.

We'll push the productivity advantages of the seventeen-inch monitor. Then we'll push the breakthrough price. Behind these two points, we'll sell quality, high-resolution electronics, and EPA Energy Star and low radiation emissions compliance.

→ Tip: Having established the major selling point, the speaker adds the secondary

The new sales campaign will target the following markets and territories. **[Here the speaker lays out the logistics of the sales campaign.]** Hit your major accounts first.

The new sales campaign will support you with advertising in **[list advertising venues],** which will begin running on **[date].**

→ Tip: This speech addresses two related, but distinct, audiences—the sales force and the customer service reps. Here the speaker takes a moment to differentiate between the two and directly address the role of the service reps in this new campaign.

This new campaign will be exciting for you folks in sales, and it will also be exciting for customer service reps. The new campaign will have a major upselling component. We're asking our customer service people to offer information on the seventeen-inch monitors to their customers who call in with product or service questions. No hard sell here, of course. Just information. Believe me, folks, with a seventeen-inch monitor at a breakthrough price to talk about, you won't meet much resistance. Your customers will want to hear about this.

Breakthrough. I've used that word more than once, I know. But that's because I am excited about this *breakthrough* product–price combination. Make no mistake: Our competition will get pretty excited about this, too. It won't be long before many of them will be offering seventeen-inch monitors at or near our price point. Speed, therefore, is key to this new campaign. Let's get in fast. Let's build the excitement fast. Let's close sales fast.

I need to stress that last point. We don't want to be in the position of having used this new campaign to crank up the buzz and build a market only to have our competition harvest after us.

I promise you that production will be in high gear on this monitor. You'll have the merchandise. I promise that advertising will be *very* visible. You'll have the support. Now, move in fast. Give *us* the benefit of our investment.

Folks, please pick up your sales kits on your way out. Line up your sales calls, and get this campaign under way. Now.

OUTLINE

Opening

- "The buzz"
- Build excitement and anticipation with tease
- The new product
- Official announcement of new product launch

Selling points

- Breakthrough price
- Prime market
- Where new product stands in market
- Sales goals

Plan

- Market research data
- Thrust of sales campaign: productivity
- Selling the product's benefits
- Campaign focus slogan
- Detailed plan of campaign
- Logistics of campaign

Implementing the plan

- Approach major accounts first
- Advertising support
- Upselling component of plan

Closing

- "Breakthrough price" theme repeated
- Competition will be heavy
- Need to move fast, close sales fast
- Do it!

MODEL SPEECH 008:
Loss of a Major Customer

Key Use of Speech:	To announce and discuss the loss of a major customer or client, to put the event in perspective, and to avoid panic or loss of morale.
Style of Speech:	Informational (one objective is rumor control) and leadership-asserting.
Audience:	Company employees.
Time:	7 to 8 minutes. [Discussion portion is variable.]

➡ Tip: Tackle rumors head on, but don't scold. Rumors and gossip are a way of life, at home as well as in the workplace. Deal with them by presenting the official and authoritative version of reality.

➡ Tip: In a crisis, nobody wants to listen to a Pollyanna—a person who thinks everything, no matter how terrible, is really pretty good. But don't be a doomsayer, either. Admit the worst, then find and identify the positive and hopeful aspects of the situation.

"It" rhymes with *it,* and it's hit the fan.

At least, that's the rumor. That's what we've all been hearing in the halls. Hearing *or* saying.

"It's really hit the fan now!"

Let me throw a monkey wrench into the rumor mill right now. What you've been hearing is true. XYZ Corporation has pulled its widget contract. At present, XYZ Corporation is no longer our client.

But does that mean "it's" hit the fan? The sky is falling? Heads will roll? People will be on the bread line?

I'm not about to play games with you. Losing XYZ Corporation as a client is not a good thing. XYZ Corporation meant $XXX to us each and every quarter. That's a fact.

But it is also a fact that we are currently doing **[$ amount]** in business each and every quarter. Conclusion: the sky is not falling, and if "it's" hit the fan, well, we all must have ducked at the right time, because we're all here. And we're all going to remain here.

Now is not the time to chop heads, ladies and gentlemen. Losing a

→ Tip: This paragraph
assuages personal
fears—that jobs will be
lost—even while it turns
that fear into something
positive and team-building.

client means we need to find other clients, more business, and that takes all of us, *all* of us, each giving 110 percent. We will recover from this loss, and we will continue to grow.

But that's not the end of my speech.

I said I'm not happy about losing XYZ, and I'm not. But this loss is also an opportunity for us. It's an opportunity to review, and evaluate, to reflect and to think. When something goes wrong, it's a chance to take a look under the hood and see how things work, and how things sometimes fail to work, and how other things might be made to work better. This is an opportunity for us to learn.

Now, here's what happened with XYZ.

[The speaker details the circumstances behind the loss of the client, then offers an analysis of what went wrong. Following this, the speaker throws the meeting open to discussion: How to prevent these problems with other clients and, finally, what strategies might be adopted to get XYZ Corporation back.]

→ Tip: Having put the
crisis in perspective, the
speaker begins to mine
something of positive
value from it.

[After the discussion period, the speaker concludes.] This has been a very useful meeting. I want us to move forward now, without any finger-pointing or grousing. Let's meet again at the end of the week to focus specifically on what we can do to make ourselves attractive to XYZ again. I think we're all agreed that we'd like to get them back. And I believe that, with this team, we can do it, and from what we've learned as a result of this experience, we can and will continue to grow our client base.

MODEL SPEECH 009:
Mergers and Acquisitions

Key Use of Speech:	To announce and celebrate a merger or acquisition.
Style of Speech:	Mergers can be threatening prospects; this speech should be friendly and reassuring in tone.
Audience:	Company employees and (possibly) representatives of the press.
Time	5 to 6 minutes.

→ Tip: Speak the language of business: dollars, dollars earned, and dollars saved.

It gives me great pleasure to announce the completion, today, of the merger of ABC Corporation and XYZ Corporation as the Alphabet Company. This merger is the product of a great deal of hard work by the management and employees of both firms, and it will mean that, united, we can now expect gross revenues of **[$ amount]** this year and an increase in our profit margin of at least **[percentage amount].** By joining our two firms, we have become a truly vertically integrated widget maker, capable of achieving efficiency and offering services on a scale that was simply unthinkable when we operated apart.

So the merger means more productivity and more money. Great! Can't argue with that, right?

Then why are so many of us frightened by the prospect of a merger?

The answer, of course, is as simple as a single very short word: *jobs.*

→ Tip: Be sensitive to the needs and concerns of your audience. Here the speaker recognizes that many in his audience are fearful of losing their jobs in this merger.

Mergers almost always mean that some jobs will be lost, and I would be lying to you if I said that this merger was different. It *is* a revenue-enhancing merger, rather than a merger for efficiency, which means that relatively *few* jobs will be lost. But, make no mistake, some positions *will* be phased out.

Yet just because we will be losing some jobs doesn't mean we want

→ Tip: Having faced the unpleasant truth about the impact the merger will have on jobs, the speaker puts this into perspective: yes, the merger may cost some jobs, but without it, it is possible that no one will have a job. The merger purchases a future for the company.

to lose people. The Alphabet company is investing **[$ amount]** to retrain employees for new positions, and in the case of those for whom no new positions are available, we are investing **[$ amount]** in a generous severance package that emphasizes rapid outplacement.

The sky, then, is not falling on *anyone*. We won't let it.

But without this merger, the sky might have, eventually, fallen on us all. As you are all well aware, the widget industry has become increasingly competitive, and price pressures have increased three-fold over the past five years. By pooling our expertise and resources, we will not only survive in this competitive climate and weather the cost pressures, we will prosper. This merger is about the future, about growing and developing, not retrenching. It is not entirely without pain, but neither is any process of birth. And that is what this merger is: not the end of ABC and XYZ, but the birth of the Alphabet company—newer, brighter, and stronger.

→ Tip: The speaker ends with the future. Note that he does not promise new jobs, but predicts their creation. The focus is on the future—the value of which everyone understands.

I am excited about all that this merger will enable us to do. Ultimately, with the range of new programs that will open up to us, we will *add,* not shed, jobs. It will take a little while, but that's what the future is for. So I hope that you all see our reasons for celebration, and that you will join me in welcoming each other to our new company and our new future together.

MODEL SPEECH 010:
New Major Customer

Key Use of Speech:	To announce the acquisition of a new major customer, and to alert staff to any special needs the customer may have.
Style of Speech:	Informational, congratulatory. Intended to ensure that relevant staff understands the significance of the new customer.
Audience:	Company employees.
5 to 6 minutes.	[Allow additional time for questions.]

→ Tip: When you have something important to announce, it is often best to announce it in a single, simple, declarative sentence. Pause a beat or two after this sentence to let it sink in.

I am delighted to announce that, as of **[date]**, XYZ Corporation has named us as its principal accounting firm.

I know that I don't have to tell you what it means to us to have XYZ as a client. But—well—let me go ahead and tell you what it means to us.

[Speaker discusses the dollar volume of XYZ's business and the approximate revenue the accounting firm can anticipate.]

Equally important is the prestige and credibility this client brings us. *We* know how good we are. *XYZ* knows how good we are. And, because they are such a high-profile client, soon *everyone* will know how good we are.

→ Tip: The speaker purposely delivers a cliché—"I don't have to tell you"—then uses it as a mildly humorous transition to the subject of what the new customer means to the company.

Of course, we have to make sure that we really are *that good*. We *must* deliver.

Now, we have never believed in treating one customer better than another. *All* of our clients are special. All are important. That is how we have built and will continue to build our business: one client at a time. But there is no denying that XYZ is a very big client, and I do want to make all of you aware of its areas of special concern.

29

→ Tip: Don't stop with self-congratulation. Use the speech as an opportunity to outline performance standards and strategies necessary for dealing with the new customer.

→ Tip: Inform company employees of who will be taking primary responsibility for the new customer and who the contact person or persons are.

[The speaker outlines the new client's special interests and areas of particular concern.]

The action plans we develop for this client must reflect these special needs. If that means customizing the features of some of our service, so be it. We want to take a *very* responsive approach to this client.

I have already spoken to the team that will take primary responsibility for the XYZ account. They are **[speaker names the team members],** and the team's liaison with the rest of us is **[name].** Direct all communication concerning XYZ to him.

Well, folks, let's not kid ourselves. Working with XYZ will be a challenge. But let's give ourselves the credit we deserve. This client did not come to us by accident. We have built a reputation, and acquiring XYZ as a client is one consequence of that reputation. Let's congratulate one another, and let's stay on our toes.

MODEL SPEECH 011:
New Plant or Facility

Key Use of Speech: To announce construction of a new plant or other facility.

Style of Speech: Informational and congratulatory. Intended to create excitement and build company pride.

Audience: Company employees.

Time: 4 to 5 minutes. [Allow some additional time for questions.]

"Put up or shut up," high-stakes poker players say. I don't know how many times a week for the past several years I've *talked* about how this company is growing and plans to grow even more. I've talked and talked and talked. The subject is fascinating—*to me.* I could go on talking about growth forever.

→ Tip: It is refreshing to be a little hard on yourself or to poke fun at yourself in order to make your point more emphatically.

But the time has come, at last, to put up or shut up.

Well, Acme Widgets is putting up—in a *very* major way.

On **[date],** ground will be broken at **[place]** for a new, state-of-the-art **[number]**-square-foot widget plant. This plant will include . . . **[The speaker highlights facts about equipment and cutting-edge technology incorporated into the plant.]** We expect to complete construction on **[date]** and to be on line and fully operational by **[date].**

→ Tip: Use relevant numbers and statistics to demonstrate the importance of the new plant or facility. Numbers are always better than vague adjectives, no matter how eloquent or colorful.

Now, the new plant represents an investment of **[$ amount].** A lot of money, all right. But, with the new facility, Acme will boost production by **[number]** units per month, creating additional revenues of **[$ amount].** Locating the plant in **[place]** will also increase the efficiency of our distribution on the West Coast, and that will reduce our costs and increase our margins.

All of this is great for all of us. But perhaps the most important

→ Tip: Make sure that your audience gets your *entire* message: the plant is important to revenue (the figures show this), but it is also evidence of a commitment to the future.

→ Tip: Beware of provoking a too-good-to-be-true reaction. Address any downside issues. Allay fears.

aspect of this new plant is the commitment it represents to the future. Acme is in business for the long term, and it means to build market share and to keep building market share. That means security and advancement for us all.

Now let me show you some pictures. **[Speaker shows slides of architect's renderings of the new plant, exteriors and interiors.]** Whatever the new plant means for added revenue and higher profits, it is also going to be one tremendously beautiful place, a great facility of which we can all be proud.

Maybe some of you are wondering if there is any downside to this new plant? Will jobs be moved from here to there? Will any of us be transferred?

The good news is that no jobs will be lost here, and there will be no mandatory transfers. The even better news is that many of us will be *offered* opportunities at the new facility. Just what those opportunities will be and who will be tapped for them, I don't know at this time. I expect to have further word by **[date].** But I do know that no one will be given any take-it-or-else propositions in connection with the new facility.

Does anyone have any questions?

MODEL SPEECH 012:
Reaction to a Crisis/Emergency

Key Use of Speech:	To establish leadership in time of crisis or emergency.
Style of Speech:	Calm, frank, reassuring, and assertive of leadership.
Audience:	Company employees.
Time:	7 to 8 minutes.

➜ Tip: Starting out with a startling or unexpected statement is a surefire way to capture the attention of your audience.

I am happy. Overjoyed, in fact.

Happy? Overjoyed? Has the fire that swept through our offices yesterday driven me out of my mind?

No. I'm fine. We're all fine. And that's what I'm happy about. This fire could have killed. But it didn't. The building and the things inside of the building, yes, they were damaged or destroyed, and, yes, the company owns those things. But *we* are the company, and *we* are undamaged, healthy, and undiscouraged.

That doesn't mean we aren't facing some problems. Let's begin with what we lost.

[The speaker lists property losses and losses of business records.]

➜ Tip: The most valuable gift a speaker can bestow in times of crisis is a sense of perspective. Put the disaster in perspective, so that the group can take appropriate action and move on.

Now, I won't kid you. This is serious. But not as serious as you might think. Insurance will cover the property loss, and the *really good news* is that we back up our computer data off-site every night, so just about everything that has been entered into our systems is safe and secure. Paper records are another matter, I'm afraid. Once we're up and running in our temporary office space, checking in with customers will be a first order of business. We'll need to assess what customer paperwork we've lost.

→ Tip: After a disaster, people are overwhelmed. Give them focus and direction. Give them a task.

About that temporary space: You're *in* it. We've rented this entire floor, and, as of today, we'll be doing business out of this facility until we can move back into our former space. While there will, of course, be an interruption in our day-to-day business, there will be *zero* interruption in our employment. No layoffs. We are a team, and, at a time like this, we need to function as a team, 100 percent complete.

→ Tip: Emphasize the team. Emphasize continuity.

And we aren't in this alone. We have secured the services of XYZ Disaster Management, a firm that specializes in working with companies to recover quickly and efficiently from losses such as the one we suffered.

Make no mistake. We *will* recover. And we will recover quickly and efficiently.

XYZ will work with each of us to coordinate a complete recovery plan. We are—right now—equipping these temporary offices with phones and computers. As soon as your equipment is installed, I ask each of you to log on to our backup network and recover your files. Then start calling your customers. Please give them this statement. (I will hand out a copy of the statement to each of you.)

[Speaker reads the company's official statement.]

→ Tip: Focus on specific instructions. Tell employees what to communicate to the outside world.

Whatever else you tell your customers, assure them that they will suffer no extended interruption of service. Thank them for their support. Make certain they know that they can reach you any time. Make certain to tell them that you will keep them posted on our recovery—then be sure that you follow through on that promise.

Look, folks, you've heard me grouse and grumble enough over the years to know that I'm not a Pollyanna. I really, really, *really* wish this fire hadn't happened. But it *did* happen, and we can either fall apart because of it, or we can come together as a team that is even tighter and more solid than it was before. Friends, I suggest that is what we do. Let's let this event make us even stronger.

→ Tip: Close with a statement that—convincingly—makes the best of a bad situation.

EXAMPLE SPEECH
Crisis Management: Prevention and Preparation

Speaker: James N. Sullivan,
Vice Chairman of the Board, Chevron Corporation

I want to start by telling each of you how much I personally support the aims of this conference and the efforts of crisis management professionals throughout our industry and especially with my company, Chevron.

And when I say personally, I really mean personally.

Right now, somewhere in the Caribbean is a double-hulled tanker carrying more than a million barrels of crude oil. And on the bow and stern in big white letters is its name, the "James N. Sullivan."

So, if, God forbid, we ever run aground and start coating the beaches with oil, the headlines will scream about the "Sullivan disaster." Or the "Sullivan slick." Or, the one I'm really dreading . . . "Sullivan ruptures."

As if that's not enough to get my attention, there's another tanker out there with my boss' name on it, the "Kenneth T. Derr."

Actually, those of you from Chevron already know this, but most of our tankers carry the name of somebody we wish to honor, and one of our newest ships is named after all our employees, the "Chevron Employee Pride." It's one of the things that makes all of us in the company very committed to safety and incident-free operations.

Commitment is like the difference between bacon and eggs: the chicken may be involved but the pig is definitely committed.

I understand that my task this morning is to tell you something about how crisis management is viewed by senior management.

Well, I am in senior management, but I started 37 years ago as an entry-level refinery process engineer in the chemical industry, and over the years I have lived crisis management.

Back then, we used to say that if you could keep your head while those about you were running around in panic, well then, you obviously didn't understand the situation.

But I did learn the value of keeping your head. I learned, first hand, maybe too many times, what it means to face a 3,000-pound hydrogen-hydrocarbon leak from the business end of a fire hose with the thought "if this thing goes wrong I won't even know about it."

Source: James N. Sullivan, Vice Chairman of the Board, Chevron Corporation. Delivered to the American Petroleum Initiative Crisis Seminar, San Francisco, California, on September 11, 1996. Reprinted by permission of James N. Sullivan and *Vital Speeches of the Day.*

And, believe me, I know a lot of things can go wrong. In the late 70s I was the operations manager of the Richmond Refinery when we had a flash fire that, thankfully, didn't seriously hurt anyone.

But it kept us busy all weekend, and when I had finally gotten home and opened a beer I got a call from our public affairs guy wanting me to come back to the refinery to explain to some TV reporters what happened. It must have been a slow news day. So I did, reluctantly.

Later, when I turned on the set for the 11 o'clock news, there I was explaining that the cloud of black smoke the citizens of Richmond had seen earlier that day really wasn't dangerous, at the same time the camera slowly zoomed in for a closeup of the safety sign behind me that read "Safety First, No Accidents."

So I learned an important lesson that I'll bet all of you have also learned one way or the other, you've got to have a sense of humor.

Or, at the very least, you have to realize that crisis management is always the "Art of the Possible." As an executive, or as anyone in any capacity speaking for the company, you just have to do your best with the circumstances that you're handed.

There will always be news reporters who want to know when your company stopped beating the environment.

By the way, I still believe that the best media policy is to be responsive, never, never say "no comment" to anybody who buys ink by the barrel.

I do have some things to say today, and, I hope you won't mind, but I also have some strong feelings about this subject and I might just get a little emotional. A good title for my comments might be "Five Things I've Always Wanted to Say to a Room Full of Crisis Management Professionals."

And the first thing I want to say is just this, thanks for everything.

Thanks a million. In fact, thanks 10 billion, dollars, that is. Why that number? Because that's how much Chevron's reputation is worth, according to a new book by the Harvard Business Press that is simply called "Reputation."

The book makes a fundamentally important point: in a world of increasing competition, where similar companies are fighting for customers, a good image and a strong reputation is a competitive advantage.

Now, I'm not sure $10 billion is right, might be more or less, but I do know that every company, and especially every oil company, lives in a fish bowl and it can cost us a lot when our brand name is associated with an oil spill, a refinery fire, accusations in a nasty law suit, or a host of other events.

So that's why the first thing I want to say is "thanks."

The second thing I want to say to this group is, I hope your jobs are boring.

The longer we have to go between real crisis situations the happier I'll be. I want you folks to be like the Maytag repairman, under-used and lonely. And nobody calls you for a comment . . . not CNN or *The New York Times* or *The Houston Chronicle*.

And the best way to do that is with prevention and preparation.

I know on organization charts that may not be directly in your bailiwick, it belongs more to line management, to operations people, but I also know that many of the most important things we do don't follow org charts. Like attitudes and behaviors. People who worry about crisis management develop "prevention first" behaviors. I believe these attitudes and behaviors should be everybody's.

A little like the fellow walking down Market Street the other day with a tuba. Every few yards he'd stop and blow one loud note. A police officer stops him and asks, "What are you doing?"

"I'm scaring away the polar bears," he says.

"What are you talking about? There aren't any polar bears in San Francisco," says the officer, and the tuba player answers, "You see! It works."

I don't think it was a tuba player, but I do know that safety at Chevron got a lot better starting over two years ago when we established a goal of having the best safety record among our competitors. In two years we've cut our rate of recordable incidents in half. We did that by making safety-first behaviors and attitudes everybody's business.

So, as I see it, part of your job is putting yourselves out of business, of preventing the crisis in the first place. I want to call up George Jardim and ask him, "What are you doing?" and have him answer, "Nothing, I haven't done any work in months and months." That would be just fine for me.

The third thing I want to say is, downsize your work.

In fact, plan on downsizing, hope for downsizing. When a crisis does comes along, as it will inevitably, I hope you're ready and have the tools and training to take a crisis and downsize it into merely an unfortunate event that Chevron or the industry handled correctly.

The media and industry critics and sometimes even elected officials will want to exaggerate the significance of a mistake. Your job is to get perception back in line with reality: downsize the so-called crisis to a simple description of facts and you've done your jobs.

Do we make mistakes? You bet. Are we villains? No! Only if we let other people depict us as bad guys.

That's why it is important, in crisis management, if we're going to err on one side or the other, let's make it on the side of being too ready or too well-practiced or too responsive.

The view from where I sit is that companies are more and more at risk from public embarrassment and financial loss if we make a mistake and then compound it by not managing the crisis in a responsive, professional and, above all, sensitive manner.

By sensitive I really mean respectful. We have to respect the public's right to know.

Can you imagine government officials or TV reporters or citizens groups complaining that they were given too much information? That's where I'd like to see us err, err in too much respect for the public's right to know.

Most of us here today come out of the technical specialties, I'm an engineer and I've spent a lot of time working in chemical plants and refineries. Most of us know how to attack a problem, how to get the resources lined up in the best possible way to fix something that's broken. That's fine. And we have to do that.

But what makes crisis management so different is that we have to do it on stage. Lots of times we are trying to stop a leak or clean up the spill or whatever, while thousands of people are watching us.

These are people like you and me and we have to respect their legitimate concern about our operations. In effect, they become our immediate customers for crisis management because we've done something which has intruded into their lives.

The fourth thing I want to say is, work like engineers but think like poets.

Never underestimate the emotional side of a crisis.

Again, because we are trained in the analytical side we sometimes misunderstand that there is a symbolic side.

Here's the difference. Suppose there's an oil spill, not from the "James N. Sullivan," thankfully. Suppose there's some waterbirds that die as a result and the beach is fouled.

Now, I have to report this to the media. The analytical side of me wants to put this in perspective and I go on local TV and report proudly that only a few birds died and the beach really isn't as bad as it could have been.

But, I've been trained in the sensitivities of crisis management, and I think to myself, wait a minute, what's the emotional side of this event and what symbolic value does it have.

So, let's do a second take on that interview. I go on local TV and report in serious and human terms that, unfortunately, some birds have died as a result of this incident for which we are using every resource to clean up the oil . . . we're glad the cleanup has not been worse, and we are doing everything we can to limit the damage and restore the area, and we appreciate the feelings of those in the area, and we respect that they're angry toward us.

You see the difference, of course.

Adopting this "symbolic" understanding isn't easy. I know that, I've been there.

Each of us does our best in our jobs and then feels defensive when our best is criticized by the very people that we're trying to help. But that's part of our jobs as well.

I keep thinking of the Navy divers recovering wreckage and bodies from the recent TWA disaster. What they must have gone through, with the heroic and courageous work they were doing while biting their tongues at the criticism and anger that government wasn't moving fast enough.

By the way, I know much of what I'm saying today to you is old hat. You are professionals and there's almost nothing I can say that will be new to you. However, the one thing I can tell you is how senior management, or at least this senior manager, sees your discipline.

And that brings me to the fifth thing I want to say, irritate your bosses.

Get them to understand the risks and rewards of being prepared for crisis management, train them, keep them updated and, probably most important, when something does happen make sure they know about it very, very quickly.

This is a little like the doctor who keeps bugging you about your cholesterol level or to exercise more, he or she is doing it for your own good.

Well, you are the doctors upon whom senior management has to rely for information and judgment about crisis management. It's your responsibility to get your diagnosis and prescription in front of senior management. Bug them a little, maybe even to the point that they become a little irritated with you.

It isn't often that people get fired for trying too hard.

Somewhere I read a story that makes this point.

The King was interviewing drivers for his coach and asked, "How close would you come to the edge of the cliff?" The first driver, wanting to brag about his skill, said "12 inches, your majesty." The second driver, not wanting to be out-done in the skills department, said "6 inches, your majesty." The third driver said, "I'd drive as far away from the cliff's edge as I could, your majesty."

Guess who got the job? The one farthest away.

Well, those are the five things I've always wanted to say to a room full of crisis management professionals.

But I'm not done yet. Now that I think about it, there is a sixth message I'd like to leave you with, crisis management is too important to be left to crisis managers.

You have to find ways to work with many, many different groups that almost never have the same agenda.

Your challenge is to bring out the best in these groups, get them on the side of helping and away from blaming.

I know the media sometimes seems mean and nasty. I know that outside agencies and community groups and other organizations sometimes make our work harder rather than easier. And I know that there is even internal friction from operations groups, or middle management or yes, even from senior management.

I said earlier that organization charts are becoming less important as corporations decentralize and empower employees to face rising marketplace competition.

It's funny to think about it like this, but one of the cutting edges of today's competition has to be the ability to cooperate, within teams, within each company, with other companies, with outside groups, with government, with the media, and the list goes on.

Figure out ways to get everybody helping rather than blaming, and crisis management will improve. In fact, you may help design the corporation of the future, because cooperation is the key to sustainable improvement in a marketplace where every day is a small crisis.

Who knows, maybe tomorrow's Chief Executive Officers will be called Incident Commanders?

In closing, let me say once again, thank you for your work over the years, and thanks for this conference, and thanks for inviting me. Have a good conference.

MODEL SPEECH 013:
Reorganization

Key Use of Speech:	To announce, rationalize, and explain reorganization within a company.
Style of Speech:	Informal and informational, as well as team-building.
Audience:	Company employees.
Time:	4 to 5 minutes.

We all know the famous "Mechanic's Maxim": *If it ain't broke, don't fix it.* Good advice? Sounds like it. But if we actually followed it, we'd still be living in caves.

Now, nothing in this organization is broken. I'm proud of everything we do. But that doesn't mean we can't work even more effectively. But I *am* proud of everything we do, and that means I'm proud of and grateful to everyone on this team. We don't need a change in personnel. We don't need new people, at least not at present, and we certainly would be diminished by the loss of anyone.

The change I am introducing is a change in organization.

Like most companies, we have always had separate sales and customer service departments. So? There must be a reason why most companies do it this way. What can be wrong with this arrangement?

There isn't anything *wrong* with this arrangement. But it's not as *right* as it could be, either. It would be a perfect arrangement—*if* all Sales ever did was solicit orders and fill them, and if all Customer Service did was handle complaints and give out information.

But we don't see Sales that way, do we? For us, Sales is more than a matter of making a particular sale and fulfilling a particular order. It's all about creating ongoing relationships with customers. And that, I would suggest, is also the very heart of Customer Service. It's not

→ Tip: People, like things, are subject to inertia. They resist change. Any speech announcing, rationalizing, and explaining change must address and seek to overcome this natural resistance.

→ Tip: Anticipate the major questions your audience has, ask them yourself, and try to answer them convincingly.

just about handling complaints or giving out routine information. It's about creating customer satisfaction, which requires a longer-term commitment to the customer.

→ Tip: The speaker begins his justification of the reorganization by going straight to the heart of the matter: the company's mission. People are more likely to welcome change and cooperate with it if they feel it is for a truly beneficial purpose and not merely the arbitrary flexing of corporate muscle.

For us, for our mission and goals, Sales and Customer Service are part of a single function: Customer Relations.

After a series of meetings with our senior management, we have decided that we can create customer satisfaction more efficiently, more dependably, and more thoroughly if the structure of our company more accurately reflects our conception of our mission. So, as of **[date],** Sales and Customer Service will be a single, new department: Customer Relations.

Bill Franklin, current head of sales, will be in charge of the new department, and Gail Williams, head of customer service, will be working closely with Bill to supervise both the service rep staff and the sales staff.

Next week, we will have ready for you a complete briefing paper on the organizational change, which will detail mission and responsibilities, as well as new procedures. There will be ample time for all of us to examine this document, and we will meet on **[date]** to discuss and, where necessary, refine and revise the organization.

→ Tip: If at all possible, involve the staff in decisions related to the reorganization. Give them an active role and stake in the change, ask them to invest in it, and it is more likely that the change will meet with acceptance, cooperation, and even enthusiasm.

This is not only a great opportunity for us to approach our customers in a new, refreshing, and—ultimately—more appropriate and effective way, it is also a chance to review and improve and generally tweak our performance. Don't think of it as a shake-up, but as chance to get a fresh grip on what we do, and to take what we do very well now and do it even better.

Please be ready to make time to give next week's briefing paper your full and careful attention. I look forward to meeting with you all again to discuss it.

Awards,
Congratulations

Openings

—*It is a great pleasure to present this year's Achievement Award to a great colleague.*

—*It is my honor to present this year's Achievement Award to someone whose work has meant so much to us for so many years.*

Closings

—*John, no one deserves this award more than you. Congratulations.*

—*On behalf of everyone here at XYZ Corporation, I offer congratulations and thanks.*

MODEL SPEECH 014:
Academic Distinction

Key Use of Speech: To acknowledge employee academic distinction.

Style of Speech: Celebratory, but informal.

Audience: Company employees.

Time: 4 to 5 minutes.

→ Tip: One problem with many congratulatory speeches is that the speaker mistakenly assumes his audience understands the background and significance of the honor. Make certain that your audience understands just why congratulations are in order by providing adequate background explanation.

In **[year],** XYZ Corporation introduced its Employee Development Program. Each year since then, employees who show special promise—and who are willing to make the substantial commitment of effort and time required—have been awarded scholarships to complete advanced degree work in such fields as **[speaker enumerates academic fields].**

The rewards to these employees are obvious: professional enrichment, enhanced satisfaction with their work and with themselves, and the acquisition of a valuable credential. But—and let me go ahead and admit our corporate selfishness—the rewards to XYZ Corporation may be even greater. I don't have to tell you that a company is not about products and cash flow. It's about people. A company *is* its people. And the Employee Development Program is about making our company's people even better qualified, more richly experienced, than they already are. So when I congratulate Pete Williams, Sharon Fowler, and Pat Smith, I'm also congratulating XYZ on the acquisition of some extraordinary employees who have just proven themselves even more extraordinary. And if I congratulate our company, I congratulate us all. We *all* benefit from this program and from the hard work of Pete, Sharon, and Pat.

→ Tip: If possible, draw your audience into the congratulations. Make this a communal occasion.

But we'd better talk a bit about them and what they've done.

45

➤ Tip: In including the group in the congratulations, beware of losing focus on the principal individuals involved.

[The speaker briefly details the academic program each of the employees has pursued.]

All three of this year's graduates have performed near the top of their class. Let's give them a round of applause.

[Speaker waits for applause to end.]

Sharon took an additional step. Her master's thesis, **[title],** has been accepted for publication in **[professional journal].** This is, of course, a great honor for her, but it's also her way of giving back, of sharing what she's learned and studied and thought about.

Sharon, Pete, and Pat, congratulations to you all. We, your XYZ colleagues and friends, are proud of you, and we thank you. Your accomplishments will make ours a stronger, better company, and they bring honor and pride to all of us

➤ Tip: Build team identity by speaking for the group, not just for yourself.

MODEL SPEECH 015:
Civic Achievement Award

Key Use of Speech: To acknowledge and celebrate civic achievement by presenting an award on behalf of your company.

Style of Speech: Straightforward, but ceremonial.

Audience: General audience.

Time: 7 to 8 minutes.

→ Tip: When speaking to a general audience, make certain that you say who you are and whom you represent. Note that the definition of the company here establishes a bond of common interest between the company and the audience.

→ Tip: too many award-presentation speeches are boring because the speaker fails to make the audience fully aware of the significance of the honoree's achievement. Here the speaker takes time to explain the problem facing the city and its symphony orchestra.

My name is Gary Wilson, and I am the president of XYZ Corporation, a multinational producer of **[product]**. We have offices in a dozen cities and five countries. But we are also your neighbors, citizens of this community, and, like you, we are deeply concerned about the quality of life in this city.

Quality of life includes so many things, ranging from matters of life and death—like clean water, clean air, adequate employment, great police and fire departments— to the things that make life—always worth living—even *more* worthwhile, more fulfilling, more pleasurable, richer, and more beautiful.

The loss of a symphony orchestra is not a matter of life and death, it is true, but it is a diminishment of life nevertheless. And this city, ladies and gentlemen, came perilously close last year to losing our symphony orchestra. Even though concerts were well attended, the price of admission did not—and still does not—begin to pay for running a world-class musical organization. There was talk of doubling or even tripling ticket costs, and maybe that would have kept the orchestra alive. But for what? For the pleasure of the relative few who could afford to pay **[$ amount]** for a ticket? High-priced tickets would have excluded many, many concertgoers, including a large number of young people and students. No question that a concert by

47

our orchestra is worth two or three—or ten—times what it now costs to hear. But with admission prices like those, the orchestra would have ceased to exist for a large portion of its audience.

The future of our symphony looked grim at best. Maybe even nonexistent.

That's when Frances Thompson appeared in my office. She proposed a partnership between XYZ Corporation and an organization she had started, called S.O.S.: Save Our Symphony.

I told her that XYZ could probably contribute something, but a full-blown partnership was probably not in the cards.

"We just can't afford . . ."

Frances interrupted me: "I'm not asking for your money," she said. "I'm asking for your help in getting our message to people and companies nationwide. I have a plan for supporting our symphony not just locally, but nationally."

She looked at me with those very penetrating eyes of hers. I could tell that she was more than a passionate music lover—though she *is* that—but that she really did have an idea. Still, you can imagine that I was skeptical. Why would anyone anywhere else pay for *our* symphony? And that is exactly what I asked her.

[The speaker goes on to narrate Frances Thompson's plan, emphasizing its innovative aspects.]

You know, it's one thing to dedicate your time and energy to raising money for a cause you believe in. And it's a wonderful thing to do that. But to create an innovative, imaginative way of expanding the appeal takes not only dedication and hard work, but genius. Frances Thompson is a genius.

She's dedicated and a hard worker—an incredibly hard worker, let me tell you—but she's also a genius. And *that* made our symphony's national fund-raising program a reality.

So while I'm probably supposed to say that XYZ Corporation is presenting its annual Civic Achievement Award to Frances Thompson because she is a great person who is selflessly dedicated to the quality of life in our city, I really want to say that she's getting this because she's a genius.

Working with her, we have raised **[$ amount]** for our symphony orchestra—**[$ amount]** in a city of only **[population]**! How did we get so much from so few? Using Frances's plan, well, we went out of

→ Tip: Adjectives and opinions are important, but facts and figures speak even louder. The speaker uses them effectively here to finalize his company's reasons for presenting the award.

town—*way* out of town: coast to coast and even to three European cities. Now *that's* genius.

So, Frances, please come up here and accept this Civic Achievement Award. You get the award, while we, the citizens of this city, the beneficiaries of all that our symphony orchestra has to offer, get the *reward:* an affordable and, in every sense of the word, world-class symphony orchestra.

OUTLINE

Opening

- Speaker introduces himself and his company
- Speaker establishes common interest with his audience

Background of award

- Definition of quality of life
- Importance of the symphony orchestra
- Problems faced by the symphony
- Danger to the existence of the orchestra
- Background of the honoree's achievement
- The orchestra's crisis

The honoree

- Speaker identifies the honoree
- Summarizes what she set out to do
- Tells how she did it

Evaluation of honoree's contribution/achievement

- Successful outcome of her efforts
- Assessment of her as a "genius"
- Detailed breakdown of the honoree's fund-raising efforts

Closing

- Presentation of award
- Personal thanks to the honoree
- Community gets the *real* award: the symphony orchestra

MODEL SPEECH 016:
Cost-Saving Suggestion

Key Use of Speech:	To acknowledge an employee's cost-saving suggestion and thank him or her for it.
Style of Speech:	Informal, warm, sincere. Intended to encourage department employees to think and to submit suggestions.
Audience:	Employees in a particular department.
Time:	6 to 7 minutes.

➡ Tip: Starting a speech with a quotation or wise saying is a familiar move—maybe too familiar. This speaker adds a new twist to an old ploy by tweaking the old saying about a "penny saved."

Benjamin Franklin was only half right when he said that a penny saved is a penny earned. Actually, a penny saved is more like *two* pennies earned. Why? You don't have to pay taxes on money you *don't* spend, and there's no cost of business tied to money you *don't* spend. But that doesn't mean that each and every cost-saving idea is a good one. After all, it's pretty easy *not* to spend money. What's hard is saving money while still delivering a great product and great service. That, friends, is a real feat.

Let me ask the man who accomplished just that feat to come up here and face you all. Joe Reynolds, three months ago you submitted to me a plan for streamlining customer-service call handling. I *love* getting suggestions from all of you. I can't implement them all, of course, but every single one of them has made me think and rethink some part of what we do. Sometimes, though, an idea comes along that just screams out at you: "Take me! Take me!" Joe's idea was one of those.

➡ Tip: The speaker does not fail to give Joe credit for his innovation—even at his own expense ("a revised plan . . . far better than what I had suggested").

I called Joe in to discuss his plan. I made a few suggestions. He went back to the drawing board, and he returned with a revised plan that was far better than what I had suggested. Here, in a nutshell, is how we'll be streamlining service.

→ Tip: Cost saving is often associated with cheaping out. The speaker, sensitive to what his audience may be thinking, checkmates this perception.

[The speaker explains the plan.]

What will this new system save us? My best guess is **[$ amount]** each quarter. Joe isn't quite as optimistic, but then Joe's the modest type.

How will this impact on the quality of service? Certainly not negatively. The plan does not compromise quality. If anything, it may *enhance* the quality of our customer service by saving time.

Joe, I probably should tell you that I am thrilled to have this cost-saving idea from you. Certainly, it's a great plan, and the cost savings—whatever they will finally be—are real. But I'm not thrilled. Thrilled is something you are when the truly unusual happens—like you win the lottery or you find a vacant spot in the near parking lot. The fact is that I have come to *expect* great ideas from all of you on a pretty regular basis. I'm *almost* spoiled. So, Joe, thanks for doing what's expected from you—and for doing it very, very well. We will all benefit from your idea and the hard work you put in revising and refining it.

→ Tip: How do you hold an audience's attention? One way is to shake them up a bit. Of course, the boss should be "thrilled"; so when he says "I'm not thrilled," it's an attention-grabbing jolt. Once the speaker has secured the ears of his audience, he delivers his message: that he expects innovation and good ideas from everyone.

MODEL SPEECH 017:
Employee Achievement Award

Key Use of Speech:	To accompany the presentation of an achievement award.
Style of Speech:	Sincere but light-hearted.
Audience:	Company employees.
Time:	4 to 5 minutes.

→ Tip: Light, good-natured humor is often welcome in an awards ceremony, as long as it creates or reinforces the bond between the honoree and the group bestowing the honor. The humor should never be sarcastic, nor should it belittle the award in any way.

Mary, you once told me that award ceremonies were "a notch below funerals" and that standing up to receive an award in front of a bunch of people who just finished a rubber-chicken banquet was pretty much the last step before embalming. At least, that's what I recall your saying.

Well, here we are! I hope you'll forgive me, but I have no choice about giving you this award. You see, you've *earned* it, so you've *got* to accept it. And you've got to be polite about it, too!

But I know that you'll be more than polite. Even if praise and recognition from your friends and colleagues makes you squirm, you'll accept it graciously and patiently, because you know it makes *us* feel good, and you are always thinking of the team, of how what you do will benefit the team. In any case, we do promise not to embalm you.

Mary, it would take more than the few minutes I have to list all of your achievements since you joined XYZ Corporation in **[year].** It would take too long even just to hit all the highlights. And then you *would* start to squirm—with modesty—and, well, that would just be *too* painful for us to watch. So I'll just cut to the chase.

Mary, you've been responsible for a major patent that has resulted in **[$ amount]** revenue for us during the past **[number]** years. Now, I'm sure all of us appreciate that, but let me put that another way. The revenue generated by your patent has been responsible for **[number]** jobs here at XYZ.

→ Tip: The one problem all award speakers share is how to avoid a tedious and perfunctory recitation of the honoree's accomplishments. Hit the highlights only, and make it clear that you are doing so.

52

→ Tip: Explain the significance of the honoree's achievement or accomplishments. The most compelling explanation of achievement demonstrates the positive impact the honoree's work has on the lives and well-being of the audience.

→ Tip: The speaker here wisely ends by showing how the award, an acknowledgment of past accomplishment, is also relevant to the future.

Money and jobs are reason enough for giving you the XYZ Excellence Award. But I know that if there's one thing that makes you more uncomfortable than praise, it's the past tense. You don't like to get stuck on what you *have done*. You are focused on what you *will do*. I guess it would be selfish of me if I told you that I hope this award encourages you to maintain that focus. But I *really* want us to maintain our leadership position in this industry, and you and I both know that the way to do that is to continue on the road of innovation. I hope, then, that this award pleases you. I know it pleases all of us to give it to you.

But an award isn't just for the person who receives the plaque. An award is a reminder to all the rest of us, a reminder about the meaning of excellence and, in this case especially, about the rewards of innovation. So, please, Mary, come up here, get your plaque, accept our thanks, and, please, share this award with us. You—me—all of us: let's keep moving forward. This award is our way of saying thanks.

MODEL SPEECH 018:
Exceptional Employee Performance

Key Use of Speech:	To not only acknowledge exceptional performance, but to use it as an instructive example.
Style of Speech:	Upbeat and instructive. This is a team-building speech.
Audience:	Employees in a customer-service department.
Time:	7 to 8 minutes.

➡ Tip: The speaker does not begin by praising the employee, but by narrating the relevant episode. A story is always more interesting than an abstract summary or an expression of opinion.

I want to share with all of you something Jane Cohn did this week. One of her accounts, XYZ Corporation, made a panic call to her. They had made an error setting their general account password and were stymied—stymied big time—by a software roadblock. There was no way they could execute their customers' transactions!

Ladies and gentlemen, customer service does not get any tougher than this!

In the panic of the moment, understandably, XYZ wanted their password problems solved over the phone. Of course, Jane was thinking beyond the crisis, and knew she had to protect her account's security—as well as our own. So Jane's problem was how to stick with the prescribed security protocols without driving the customer nuts. She needed to follow all of the rules scrupulously, making certain that she secured all mandatory confirmations so that she was satisfied she was speaking only with authorized personnel before she could walk them around the roadblocks.

➡ Tip: The speaker provides a clear explanation of a difficult problem.

It's one thing to say that you're going to follow the book—in theory—but quite another to follow it in practice, when you've got a bunch of sweating brokers on a conference call breathing heavily into the receiver. It is perfectly understandable that the customer will put on the pressure for us to bypass the safety rules. And this customer was no exception. However, Jane stayed the course, maintained security, avoided an expensive and time-consuming password change routine, *and* got XYZ back in the money business in as short a time as possible.

Joe Flynn, CEO at XYZ, called me to praise Jane and to thank us all—for *her* good work.

So, thanks, Jane, for satisfying our customer—in spite of himself—and for making all of us look good.

Now, I talked to Jane for quite a while after this episode, because I was very interested in how she managed to keep her focus and preserve security as a top priority. She explained to me that she kept returning to the fact that it was in *XYZ's* interest to *insist* that she follow security protocol. To be sure, she apologized for needing to check for a security breach, but then she went on to explain why she needed to check. She always emphasized that her procedures were of value to XYZ.

Now, Jane observed that the folks at XYZ were rather embarrassed about the snafu and were, therefore, defensive about it. She was careful not to set up an *us* versus *you* situation. Instead, she emphasized that XYZ's internal security, *combined with* our systems, created a formidable shield for the protection of XYZ's customers. She even took the opportunity—in the middle of this crisis—to point out that such interlocking security was actually a terrific selling advantage for XYZ.

Jane, then, didn't merely insist on following security protocol, she *sold* XYZ on the value of security protocol. This is just a great way to deal with customers—during a crisis or not. Jane began by recognizing that she was working with frustrated people—scared people. She was empathetic.

She next refused to take the easy way out by saying that she was "only following procedure." instead, she explained what kind of disaster could occur if XYZ's computers had been breached and we let ourselves be duped into helping a set of hackers. Furthermore, Jane reassured the customer by explaining that she was not accusing anyone at XYZ of wrongdoing. Then—and this is the *really* wonderful part—Jane turned an unpleasant situation into a positive one by explaining how XYZ might use the value of an interlocking security system as a

➡ Tip: Here is objective validation of the speaker's high appraisal of Jane.

➡ Tip: The speaker makes this talk more than a congratulations; he turns it into a lesson in effective customer service.

➡ Tip: The speaker walks his audience through the process, step by step.

➡ Tip: The speaker brings the speech back to its focus on congratulating an employee for exceptional performance.

selling point to maintain current business and acquire new customers.

Jane, you can't do much better than this. We claim to be selling value, and you sure made good on that claim. I, for one, intend to learn from this. Congratulations—and thanks!

OUTLINE

Opening

- Share Jane Cohn's experience with you
- Narrate the event

Significance of the event

- Example of customer service at its most challenging
- Jane thought beyond the crisis
- She knew what to do
- Theory vs. practice

Praise for Jane

- Customer testimonial
- Congratulations and thanks

What we can learn from Jane's actions

- Show how actions are in the interest of the customer
- Explain procedures to customer
- Don't set up an us vs. you situation
- Sell the customer on the value of what you do
- Don't take the easy way out
- Reassure customer

Closing

- Repeat congratulations
- And thanks

MODEL SPEECH 019:
Meeting or Exceeding Production Goals

Key Use of Speech: To congratulate a company team or department on meeting or exceeding a production goal.

Style of Speech: Upbeat, congratulatory, and an expression of gratitude and appreciation.

Audience: Employees in a production department.

Time: 4 to 5 minutes.

➙ Tip: Avoid long, drawn-out quotations at the start of a speech. However, brief, pithy, and—especially— funny quotations can be very effective.

➙ Tip: Gentle self-mockery can be endearing in a speech, especially when a supervisor is addressing subordinates. Irony also works well (Why should I worry? Because I'm way out on a limb!), as long as there is no danger that you will be misunderstood as sarcastic.

I can't remember what witty pessimist it was who said "every silver lining has a cloud," but I can tell you that this is a perfect expression of what I felt, three months ago, when XYZ Corporation ordered ten thousand deluxe widgets from us. *What a sweet order! (Now, how are we possibly going to make this stuff for them by November 15?)*

I've been here for ten years. I don't know how much longer it's going to take before I get it through my thick, thick skull that I do not have to worry about you folks. Sure, turning around ten thousand units in three months is next to impossible. Yes, there's a penalty clause in the contract. True, my—uh—reputation is in a sling.

But *why* should I have even *thought* about worrying?

When I told you about the order, there was no grumbling, no moaning, not even a single instance of head scratching or eye rolling. You got together, drew up a production plan, passed it by me, and then you went to work—nonstop and always, *always,* with maximum quality control, even when the heat was really on.

What a team!

You met a production goal and a deadline that—well, I just don't

➡ Tip: Everyone likes to win. Winning implies beating the competition. The speaker shows his team how they beat the competition.

know of any other outfit that could have done this, and then could have done it without compromising quality.

That in itself is a great accomplishment.

But let me give you an additional view of what you have done. This order, built and delivered on time, means **[$ amount]** in revenue for us.

Now that is one very impressive figure, certainly, but it doesn't tell the whole story. Delivering ten thousand units to XYZ in three months has bought us something that I can't begin to measure accurately in dollars. It has bought us credibility—not only with this customer (and, make no mistake, XYZ is a very important customer), but throughout the industry. We say we're a company that can deliver. Now we've demonstrated that fact—big time. I don't know how much future revenue this will mean for us, but I know that it *will* mean revenue.

➡ Tip: The speaker knows how to up the ante of accomplishment: *You think achieving "A" is impressive? You also achieved "B," which is even more impressive.* The speaker makes his audience aware of the full scope of their achievement.

Making a sale is fine and dandy. I like that. But making *one* sale is nothing compared to making a customer happy. Doing that will bring *multiple* sales. And one happy customer spreads the word, giving us the best advertising we could possibly get: word of mouth. It's better than anything we could pay for. You think you've just made ten thousand deluxe widgets? What you've really made is one satisfied customer, who will produce for us who knows how many more customers. And I know, when those new customers come calling, *you* will deliver—on time and the best. Maybe I'll even stop worrying.

Anyway, folks, congratulations, well done, and thanks!

MODEL SPEECH 020:
Meeting or Exceeding Sales Goals

Key Use of Speech: To congratulate a company team or department on meeting or exceeding a sales goal.

Style of Speech: Congratulatory, but with a strong element of instruction and positive reinforcement.

Audience: Sales staff.

Time: 5 to 6 minutes.

→ Tip: The speaker pauses dramatically here, to let this bombshell explode and the dust settle.

Here's the skinny: We set a goal of **[$ amount]** in sales for this quarter. The quarter ended yesterday. You folks have racked up **[greater $ amount]** in sales. What can I say? Congratulations—and, oh, yeah: thanks!

Now that that's out of the way, let me tell you a little secret. Here it is: I've never cared much about sales.

And, I'm happy to say, I don't think you folks care, either. If you did, you wouldn't have hit **[greater $ amount]** in sales. You might have met our sales goal for the quarter, but you wouldn't have gotten past it.

Making sales is pretty easy, especially if you're lucky enough to have a great product that, like ours, is much in demand. It's no cakewalk, of course, but any competent salesperson can meet his or her goal. That, however, has never been enough for you. You care less about making a sale than about creating a customer.

→ Tip: Riddles and paradoxes—statements that say or seem to say the opposite of what we think is true—almost always rivet the attention. The speaker uses the idea of "not caring" about sales as a more than mildly shocking device to gain attention.

Now *that's* hard work. Nothing hit-and-run about that approach. You get to know a person, you make a commitment to a person, you strive to satisfy that person. You build a genuine business relationship, and because it is a *genuine* business relationship, it is really a very human relationship. This takes real skill, real brains, real commitment, and real heart. It takes everything you've got.

→ Tip: The preceding two paragraphs are a thinly disguised performance analysis. The speaker tells her audience why they have performed well. In order to avoid patronizing or talking down to her audience, the speaker speaks as if she believes the audience is already fully aware of the goals and objectives she mentions. The purpose of this "performance analysis"? Positive reinforcement.

→ Tip: The speaker elaborates on the "performance analysis," explaining why her sales force's accomplishment is so important. She also builds morale by defining sales—as practiced by her sales force—in terms of creativity.

And, with this quarter's sales figures, you've proven that you are ready, willing, and able to give it all. You've made the full commitment, and you've delivered on that commitment.

Well, what does that mean? That you're willing to make sales the hard way?

Partly, that's true. But it doesn't begin to tell the whole story. Creating customers rather than making sales is a way of building business for the long term. You create repeat sales, and you create powerful word-of-mouth advertising. Please don't let that word—create—slip by you. I'm using it on purpose. You know, the folks in design and in production think they've got a monopoly on creativity. Well, I don't want to take anything away from them. If they weren't so creative, our jobs certainly would be a lot harder than they are, and we would not be making the kinds of numbers we saw this quarter. But don't ever sell yourselves short. You also create. You create the conditions that make satisfaction with our product possible, and you create customers.

I've been in sales for **[number]** years, and I *still* think it's fun. Haven't gotten bored with it yet, and, as long as I work with creative people, I don't think I'll ever get bored. People like you are always raising the bar, always coming up with new challenges, always—*creating.*

So, let me thank and congratulate you for creating living, breathing, satisfied customers, for making this quarter a great one, but also for making great quarters not just possible, but likely in the years to come. I'd ask you to keep up the good work, but that would only discourage you. Creative people don't "keep up" anything. They always go after new achievements and set new goals. What I'd better leave you with, then, is a request that you folks just keep on being *you.* Thanks!

MODEL SPEECH 021:
Meeting or Exceeding Other Goals

Key Use of Speech:	To congratulate a company team or department on meeting or exceeding a goal.
Style of Speech:	Congratulatory, with an element of instruction and positive reinforcement.
Audience:	Company or department employees.
Time:	4 to 5 minutes.

➜ Tip: Two pointers about using quotations. First, it is always most effective when the quoted material flows naturally into your own words, as it does here. Second, always make certain that the quotation is directly relevant to your point and makes that point clearer than it would be without the quotation.

I don't usually go around quoting poetry, but something from Robert Browning has always stuck in my mind. I'm sure you know the line—about how your reach should always exceed your grasp, "or what's a heaven for." I think about that whenever we set goals. We want to set realistic goals, but not easy ones. We want to set goals that make us stretch, stretch just beyond our grasp. Such goals are the only objectives worth the effort, I think, and when you reach such goals, well, you know that you have achieved something of value.

[The speaker now gives the background of the goal in question: what it was and why it was set.]

➜ Tip: Be certain that everyone is singing from the same songsheet. Provide all necessary background explanation.

We can all be personally proud, then, of achieving this ambitious goal. But we are also fortunate that this is much more than a *personal* achievement. This is an achievement that benefits all of us, our department, and our firm. Let me take a moment to review what our achievement means to our future together.

→ Tip: An appreciation of motives of self-interest is—let's face it—human nature. The speaker uses an admission of her self-interest to give the speech a strong twist at its conclusion, a twist that lifts these remarks above the ordinary and conventional.

[The speaker details how having achieved the goal benefits the department and company.]

Finally, let me be selfish for a moment. What we have done—what each of you has accomplished—makes *me* look very good. I have to admit: I *like* that. The better I look, the happier I am. But, even more, this achievement feeds my pride—not my pride in myself, but my pride in working with all of you. Reaching goals makes you feel like a winner, and that is certainly a lot of fun. But what makes coming into work every day worthwhile is being proud of what you do and of who you do it with. For that reason—and on behalf of XYZ Corporation—I thank you all. And congratulations.

MODEL SPEECH 022:
Safety Improvement Suggestion

Key Use of Speech:	To acknowledge a safety improvement suggestion and to encourage other such suggestions, as well as a general awareness of safety.
Style of Speech:	Informal congratulations and thanks. Also reinforces safe practices.
Audience:	Company or department employees.
Time:	5 to 6 minutes.

→ Tip: Sometimes it is impossible to avoid clichés. In this case, the idea of the company as a family is central to the speaker's message, but he is also aware that the family analogy is a very badly worn cliché. The speaker begins by lightheartedly admitting this—then goes on to use the analogy anyway.

I don't know about you folks, but whenever I hear somebody in charge talk about the company as "one big family," I have an irresistible impulse to start looking for a new job. Maybe I'm just cynical, but, the way I see it, I *already* have a family. I don't need another one. What I *need* is a job that challenges me and that helps me feed myself—*and* my family, my *real* family.

But I have to tell you that, in some ways, *this* company and *this* department really *are* like a family. It's not because we all seem to like one another. The fact is that people in plenty of families don't like one another. No, if we're like family, it's not because we like one another, but because we look after one another. That's what family members do, and that is what we've always done.

There is genuine concern and caring here. If you ever doubt that, just look at our safety record. This is an achievement that does not come down from management, but comes up from each of us looking after ourselves and the people we work with. Now that is precisely

→ Tip: This speech does not stop with congratulating and thanking the person who made the safety suggestion; it also discusses how the suggestion will be implemented and how it will affect employees.

what Joe Bonner was doing—looking after us all—when he came up with his idea for making our workplace even safer than it is. Joe looked around and saw . . .

[The speaker goes on to describe a safety problem that Joe Bonner identified. Then the speaker continues with a concise summary of the employee's suggestion for addressing the problem.]

Joe's solution is simple and inexpensive, which is certainly a great plus. But even if it weren't so simple and inexpensive, it would be worth doing. It's hard to cheap out when you feel that you're looking out for the family.

We will begin implementing Joe's suggestion . . .

[The speaker outlines when and how the safety suggestion will be implemented.]

→ Tip: The speaker asks for group participation in safety and in ensuring that the safety suggestion will be effectively implemented.

Joe, on behalf of everyone here, thanks. But, ladies and gentlemen, let's not just leave Joe with a pat on the back. We need to get feedback on the new safety measure. This requires *all* of us to observe and participate. And we also need to bear in mind at all times that, brilliant as Joe's suggestion is, it is not a kind of automatic pilot that will take care of all our safety concerns. Stay alert, and keep watching out for yourselves—and for one another.

Celebrations

Openings

——*We come together so often in crisis that it is a distinct pleasure to gather in celebration.*

——*Reach around and pat yourselves on the back. We have good reason to celebrate.*

Closings

——*I want to thank each and every one of you for giving us cause to celebrate.*

——*You are my favorite people to celebrate with. Let's top this quarter's numbers so that we can celebrate again very soon.*

MODEL SPEECH 023:
Citizenship

Key Use of Speech: To celebrate the naturalization of an employee.

Style of Speech: Congratulatory and team-building.

Audience: Company or department employees.

Time: 4 to 5 minutes.

→ Tip: Transformations are powerful events. The speaker expresses the event simply. She lets the transformation from resident alien to citizen speak for itself.

Igor Carnubian joined us here at XYZ Corporation three years ago. When he first walked through our doors, he was a resident alien in the United States—a guest. Just five days ago, he became a citizen. Wow!

We all thought it would be nice to get together and celebrate—and it *is* "nice." But it's so much more. How do you congratulate someone on becoming a citizen of a country such as ours? People have sacrificed everything—including life itself—to create this country. It is blessed in so many ways. It would be easy to congratulate someone, say, on winning the $48 million lottery. That's a lot of money, but it's not so much, either—not when it is compared to being a citizen of a nation that promises and delivers liberty and a fair chance to be whatever you can make yourself.

I guess the best we can do is simply welcome you home, Igor.

You know much better than most of us what America means and what citizenship means, because, unlike most of us, you have had the experience of *not* being an American. You . . .

→ Tip: In any speech of congratulations or celebration, get personal. Show that you know—or have learned something about—the honoree. Share a bit of biography with your audience. The honoree and the audience alike respond to the human and the personal.

[The speaker gives a brief biography of Igor Carnubian, emphasizing how, why, and when he came to the United States.]

Now, there have always been Americans who would like to close the door to any new Americans. It is, of course, understandable to want to keep a good thing to oneself, but, in the case of our country,

➤ Tip: The speaker recognizes that an opposing or dissenting viewpoint exists, that not everyone is happy to greet a new citizen. Unobtrusively, she addresses it by standing the occasion for congratulations on its head. We should not only congratulate Igor, she says, but ourselves. We need citizens like Igor Carnubian.

it is precisely because we do *not* keep it to ourselves that America is *such* a good thing.

Igor thinks he's fortunate to be a citizen. Well, he is. But we are also lucky to have him. A nation is its people, and we need all the hard-working, imaginative, creative people we can get. All of you who have worked with Igor know that he is absolute in his commitment to excellence, and that quality can only make all of us stronger.

So, let's welcome Igor to the land of the free and the home of the brave. Let's congratulate him, too. But let's also congratulate ourselves on having acquired this particular citizen.

MODEL SPEECH 024:
Engagement/Wedding

Key Use of Speech:	To announce and celebrate an employee's engagement.
Style of Speech:	A feel-good speech for a feel-good occasion. Promotes team-building.
Audience:	Company or department employees.
Time:	4 to 5 minutes.

You all know Bill Pickett from Sales, and, lately, a lot of you have gotten to know Jenny Spencer. She's not employed here, but she's been around at lunchtime . . . Well, it's probably no secret that Bill and Jenny are an "item." However, maybe there are still some of you who haven't heard the big news: Bill and Jenny are moving up from *item* status to *engaged* item status.

Now, it just so happens that I know both Bill and Jenny quite well, and I had the singular privilege of having been present when the two of them first met. To tell you the truth, it was a double blind date back in **[year]**.

Blind dates, as you know, can be pretty awful, but, fortunately, *my* date and I hit it off right from the start. We had a great evening.

Bill and Jenny? They were another story altogether. I wish I had the skill and memory to re-create the conversation for you, but I'm afraid you'll have to settle for a bare-bones summary. It went something like this:

Bill, as we all know, is a man of who enjoys the finer things in life. He labored over the selection of a fine French red wine; whereupon Jenny mentioned that the California reds seemed to her more interesting.

Then there was Bill's taste in music: vintage Bebop. Jenny said that any music written before 1965 got on her nerves.

So we talked politics. Bill confessed to be being a card-carrying Republican. Jenny said she always voted Democratic. Straight ticket.

➔ Tip: Depending on the style, size, and atmosphere of your business, the announcement of an engagement or wedding may be made quickly and informally or it may not be made at all. This speech is suited to a small, tightly-knit organization or department, and it is assumed that the speaker is a good friend of Bill Pickett's.

At some point, Bill started raving about his new IBM PC. "What kind of computer do you drive?" he asked Jenny.

"I'm a Macintosh person," she answered.

Bill ordered his usual New York strip, blood red. Jenny got the vegetarian special.

And so it went. My date and I agreed on just about everything—and that, ladies and gentlemen, was our first and last date. Bill and Jenny agreed on almost nothing—and couldn't stop seeing each other from that evening on. And now: *They're getting married!*

What's the point of my little story?

To tell you the truth, I'm not sure. Maybe it suggests that Bill and Jenny are simply out of their minds.

But I don't think so. I think what it means is that here are two people, two *strong* individuals, who have found each another and who will be dedicated to each other and who love and will continue to love each other, but who will always remain delightful *individuals.*

I think my story also means that Bill and Jenny have found in each other something that goes way beyond the superficial level of what we like to drink or listen to, or how we vote, or what we eat. Beneath all that, they've found something of deep love and respect.

Or, as I said, maybe they're just crazy.

Whatever—I know that I speak on behalf of everyone here when I express my joy in this union and my sincere wish that their lives together will be long and happy and wonderful.

> ➤ Tip: In a way, this speech is a "roast." It pokes good-natured fun at Bill Pickett. Just make sure that the fun remains good natured. Here, it's a buildup to the very nice sentiments the speaker has to express.

> ➤ Tip: Beware of taking yourself too seriously. This good-natured sentence adds a touch of comic deflation.

> ➤ Tip: The speaker recognizes his role as spokesman for the group. He concludes by speaking for that group—and making it clear that he is doing so.

OUTLINE

Opening
- Bill Pickett and Jenny Spencer
- Announce engagement

Personal anecdotes
- how they met
- Opposites attract theme
- "Moral" of the story

Closing
- Expression of joy
- Congratulations
- Best wishes for the future

MODEL SPEECH 025:
Opening of New Facility

Key Use of Speech: To inaugurate and celebrate the opening of a new corporate facility.

Style of Speech: Moderately formal and dignified, but also familiar.

Audience: Company employees and (possibly) representatives of the press.

Time: 5 to 6 minutes.

➤ Tip: A touch of wit, a clever turn of phrase, can help deflate pretension and create a friendly bond with the audience.

➤ Tip: the speaker uses a few simple and dramatic facts to demonstrate the intense need for the new facility. Indeed, these remarks suggest that the new facility was not only necessary, but long overdue.

As many of you probably suspect, all corporate CEOs suffer from an Edifice Complex. We like shiny new buildings and state-of-the-art facilities. We have a burning need to spend money on such things. Then we like to hold ceremonies to inaugurate what we build.

Okay. I admit it. I am thrilled to have this new corporate headquarters. But not *just* because I, too, suffer from the Edifice Complex. For **[number]** years, XYZ Corporation has "lived" at **[address],** a facility we purchased when we had fifty employees and did **[$ amount]** in annual business. Today, we have 256 employees and do **[greater $ amount]** each year. Let me put it this way: When Fred Williams, at the southeast corner of the building, sneezes, my hat blows off. And my office is in the northeast corner.

Our magnificent new facility, which we formally open today, has been built to accommodate our present needs and size, but also with an eye toward continued growth. We deserve to be comfortable, to have space for maximum productivity, and, even more important, our *customers* deserve this.

But this new facility is about more than space. XYZ retained the architectural firm of Wright and Sullivan, who worked intensively with all of us to create a design to promote and enable productivity

71

→ Tip: The speaker recognizes that a building is a thing, inanimate. This new facility, however, will help inspire those who work in it to greater and greater levels of achievement.

and efficiency. It is also a design of great aesthetic beauty. And that is important for a variety of reasons. It is important, of course, for our corporate image—something that is difficult to quantify in dollars—and it is important for how we feel every day when we come to work and how our customers and visitors feel when they come to see us. But the beauty of this new facility is also important to our neighbors and our community. XYZ brings great products and services to the world. To our neighborhood and city, we are also proud to bring a beautiful new building.

Whatever else this new headquarters represents for XYZ, it is an expression of our commitment to this company, to its employees, and to its customers, a commitment not just for today, but for the future. It is a beautiful and practical and—thank goodness!—a spacious workplace, but it is also a monument, not to what we were or are, but to what we will yet become.

Before I cut this ribbon, I want to acknowledge and thank, personally and on behalf of everyone who works at XYZ, those who have been instrumental in the planning and creation of our new headquarters.

[The speaker acknowledges several people, briefly explaining each person's role in the conception and completion of the building.]

→ Tip: When listing people whom it is important to acknowledge or thank, try to briefly to say something about the contribution each person has made. This not only honors the people who should be honored, it avoids turning the speech into a mere laundry list of meaningless names.

Now, let me cut this ribbon, and lead you all on a brief tour of the new headquarters of the XYZ Corporation.

Chairperson

Openings

——*Ladies and gentlemen, we have a full agenda, so I ask that we come to order now.*

——*Ladies and gentlemen, welcome to the meeting of the Steering Committee.*

Closings

——*Having concluded our business for the day, I declare this meeting to be adjourned.*

——*Friends, thank you very much for your hard work this past week. It's been both an exhausting and exhilarating experience, and one, I believe, that will have highly rewarding results.*

MODEL SPEECH 026:
Announcement of Program Schedule

Key Use of Speech:	To set the agenda of a meeting or program. It may accompany a printed program.
Style of Speech:	Simple, clear, and straightforward. The objective is to help provide focus.
Audience:	Company or department employees, or other participants in a business meeting or program.
Time:	4 to 5 minutes.

➜ Tip: Prioritize the agenda. Begin with overall goals—the big picture—then start to fill in the details.

➜ Tip: Why present verbally material that is better suited to printed presentation? Programs and agendas, especially if they are lengthy or complex, are best presented on paper. The introductory speech should highlight the printed agenda, not necessarily reproduce it. Remember: it is difficult to memorize a spoken list. If your agenda speech is little more than a list, your audience will tune you out.

It is a pleasure to gather together with all of you for no less a purpose than hammering out our future together. We have, as my mother used to say, our work cut out for us. We need, first, to determine what steps we will take in the coming year to maintain our leadership position in those segments of the market where we presently lead. Second, we need to determine what steps to take to achieve leadership in those areas in which we presently follow others.

Today's meeting will follow the agenda you received a few days ago. We'll begin by reviewing, in detail, this year's performance in our leadership areas. Next, we'll survey performance in what we might call our "followship" categories.

Our marketing manager, Sarah Williams, will review both sets of these figures for us and provide analytical insight.

Next up will be Hank Reynolds, Pete Fontaine, and Ed Doyle, all of whom have strategies to propose to you. That word *propose* is key. Nothing's sacred, and everything's open to debate and discussion. That is the main purpose of this meeting, after all: creative solutions.

Now, after we break for lunch, those "creative solution" sessions will begin. We'll break into groups, according to area of specialization:

[The speaker details these assignments.]

At 3:30 sharp, we'll reconvene as a group here, and the team leaders of the discussion groups will present their reports—each limited to ten minutes.

No discussion of these reports will be permitted today! At 5:30 we'll break, returning at 6:30 for dinner. Then, *tomorrow*, we'll have the free-for-all discussion of the group reports.

Let's get started!

➡ Tip: Sometimes a program or agenda includes necessary ground rules ("No discussion of these reports will be permitted today!"). Make certain all participants understand these rules.

OUTLINE

Opening

• Outline overview of objectives and goals

Detailed agenda

• Review of this year's performance: leadership categories
• Review of this year's performance: "followship" categories
• Proposed strategies
• Creative solution sessions
• Session reports

Closing

• One sentence: "Let's get started!"

MODEL SPEECH 027:
Introduction of Speaker(s)

Key Use of Speech: To introduce a speaker.

Style of Speech: Brief, but clear and complimentary.

Audience: General audience.

Time: 1 to 2 minutes.

→ Tip: A good introduction is brief—not curt or uninformative, but concise. Make certain that all parts of the introduction serve a purpose. The speaker began with a humorous remark, then used the elements of that remark to describe the speaker's subject.

When my son was born, my best friend said to me, "Just remember: You'll spend the first year and a half trying to get him to stand up and say something, and the next eighteen years trying to get him to sit down and shut up."

So much for child psychology!

Well, not quite.

Tonight's featured speaker has devoted herself to the study of those first eighteen years of life, and her object is not to get your child—especially your teenage child—to shut up and sit down, but to stand up, be counted, take responsibility, express himself, and learn, in general, to cooperate and care.

A tall order?

Sometimes. Well, *most* times.

→ Tip: Without exaggeration, build up and highlight the speaker's qualifications. Use facts (degrees, awards, books written, and so forth).

But Dr. June Barnett is up to the assignment. She is Sigmund Freud Professor of Psychology at Southerly University and is the author of the Erik Erikson Prize–winning *How to Talk to Your Teen Without Resorting to Power Tools*. For fifteen years now, Dr. Barnett has been offering her tremendously popular Teen Summit Workshops, and, tonight, she will share with us "The Fifteen Things I *Still* Don't Know About Teenagers."

From what Dr. Barnett does *not* know, we can all learn a lot.

Please welcome Dr. June Barnett.

MODEL SPEECH 028:
Recognition of Distinguished Guest(s)

Key Use of Speech: A featured speaker or master of ceremonies may use this speech to recognize distinguished guests.

Style of Speech: This is usually a portion of a speech, not a speech in itself; the style is respectful, but straightforward; brief, but not terse.

Audience: General audience.

Time: Less than 1 to 2 minutes. [Depends on the number of guests recognized and their significance to the occasion or assembly.]

→ Tip: A good introduction tells who the speaker is (or speakers are) and why they are worth listening to. If you are called on to make an introduction, try to contact beforehand the person you are to introduce. Ask him or her to jot down points to include in your introduction. Above all, make certain that you know how to pronounce the person's name. If necessary, ask the person beforehand, and write out the name phonetically.

Ladies and gentlemen, before I begin this evening, it is my privilege to acknowledge our special guests, Professors Harriet B. Stowe and Lyman W. Beecher. We are honored to have these two Nobel laureates with us tonight. Their contributions to science—Dr. Stowe to molecular biology and Dr. Beecher to DNA research—are profound and represent the level of innovation, knowledge, and insight that, as a society and an industry, we rightly honor. Researchers like these set the benchmark for us all. It doesn't matter that few of us will win a Nobel Prize; we are enriched, and our efforts are enhanced, by the example of our two distinguished guests. Please take a moment to welcome Dr. Harriet B. Stowe and Dr. Lyman W. Beecher to our program tonight.

Commemorations

Openings

——*I welcome you on the occasion of our tenth anniversary.*

——*Twenty-five years ago today, John Smith shook hands with Willim Cain, and our company opened its doors.*

Closings

——*Let's return to our work now, refreshed in vision and determined to make the next ten years even more rewarding than the first ten.*

——*Thank you for celebrating with us.*

MODEL SPEECH 029:
Anniversary of Company

Key Use of Speech: To celebrate an anniversary milestone.

Style of Speech: Commemorative speeches should invite the sharing of an experience. Avoid the pompous or stuffy.

Audience: Company employees and (perhaps) the press and other guests.

Time: 6 to 7 minutes.

→ Tip: The most effective anniversary speeches share experience. Use telling details rather than hollow and abstract adjectives.

So this is the point in the movie when the words appear on the screen: "Twenty-five years later . . ." Here we all are, members of the Save-A-Lot family, a family that's a quarter-century old today. It was my good fortune to be in on the birth of that family, back in 19XX, and it would sure make an exciting story if I could tell you all that our founder, Karl Goldmark, took one of those giant scissors and, with the TV and newspaper reporters crowding around him, snipped the ribbon on the first Save-A-Lot store. There were bands playing, and the mayor was there, and even a delegation from the governor's office . . .

[Speaker pauses two or three beats.]

→ Tip: Audiences love little bits of detail that provide strong images of the past. Be specific.

As I said, it would sure make an exciting story. But the fact is that nothing of the kind happened. Karl, Victor Laemmle, Patty Royal, and I were there. And that was it. No photographers, no news people, no politicians, nobody.

Nobody, that is, until the first customer showed up, about fifteen minutes after we opened our doors.

Karl made a big deal about this guy—a man buying an electric stapler. I still remember the kind of high-pitched grating noise the polyester sleeve of Karl's leisure suit (the height of fashion in 19XX) made as he shot his hand out for a handshake.

> ➤ Tip: Actual dialogue adds a lively, personalizing, and compelling dimension to any speech.

"Sir," Karl said, "do you realize you are my *first* customer."

"How long you been in business?" the guy asked, trying to get his hand back.

"Just opened today!"

"Uh . . ."

And, with that, our first customer went back to the office supply department.

"Look at this," Karl said, nudging my arm, "he's gonna buy something else!"

> ➤ Tip: One of the most effective things to do in an anniversary speech is contrast the humble, even unpromising beginnings of the company with its present level of achievement.

But the fellow returned empty handed, having put the electric stapler back on the shelf.

"Sorry," he said, "but I want to be able to take this thing back if it breaks. Thrif-T, down the street, has been in business for years. You guys—well, here today, gone tomorrow."

And *that* was our first customer.

Fortunately, there were more. And more. We learned fast, but we built the business customer by customer. That's what Karl always said: *Build the business one customer at a time.*

In 19XX, we opened a second store, and, two years later, three more. Today, there are forty-three Save-A-Lot stores in this area, and we plan to open ten more by 19XX.

We're successful, thanks to you, the Sav-A-Lot family, and, of course, to our customers, who appreciate being treated like what they are: the people who make our business possible. I do have one disappointment, however. That first customer never came back for his electric stapler—and I know for a fact that we were selling it for $3.45 less than Thrif-T.

Thrif-T. You remember that chain? It went out of business just about the time we were celebrating our tenth anniversary. Here today . . .

> ➤ Tip: The best anniversary speeches end not by looking backward, but by looking toward the future.

Congratulations, everyone. Congratulations, Karl. Thanks for letting us be our best and for sharing this twenty-five-year adventure with us. We've done great. Now, let's look ahead and do even better!

OUTLINE

Opening

- Where we are now
- Where we were twenty-five years ago
- Day One anecdote

What we learned and how we grew

- Building a business one customer at a time
- Account of growth

Thanks

- To company team
- To customers

Closing

- Congratulations
- Look to the future

MODEL SPEECH 030:
Birthday of Colleague or Employee

Key Use of Speech:	To acknowledge and celebrate the birthday of a colleague.
Style of Speech:	Informal, warm, sincere.
Audience:	Company or department employees—at an office celebration.
Time:	4 to 5 minutes.

➤ Tip: It's fun to mention important world events that occurred on the birthday in question, especially if you can relate the event to the subject of your speech.

October 27, 1962. To you, Ken Watts, that date is significant as the day of your birth. Well, that's understandable. But at least one other event of importance occurred on that day: Soviet premier Nikita Krushchev offered to remove the missiles he had put in Cuba. That ended the Cuban Missile Crisis and prevented World War III. Not exactly a trifle, either.

Now the question I have is this: Your birthday falling on the day the world was saved—coincidence? Or—*drum roll, please*—destiny?

After all, as our firm's chief legal counsel, you've spent the past five years pulling our fat out of the fire or keeping it out of the fire to begin with and, generally, warding off World War III. That's been your job, and you've done it brilliantly and—what's the word I'm looking for?—you've done it *decently.*

➤ Tip: Give everyone a reason to celebrate. Why is this person important to your audience? Your speech should answer that question.

I don't mean that figuratively, but literally. You do your job with great *decency.* It's no secret that, these days, a lot of people just don't like lawyers. But they like and respect you. When you settle an issue, all parties tend to come away, well, if not completely satisfied, at least feeling that they have been treated fairly—*decently.* Yes, Ken, you protect our immediate financial and legal interests, but you also protect our long-term, less tangible interests, our image and good name as a *decent,* caring company.

➞ Tip: Paint a picture of the subject of your speech as a well-rounded human being.

I also have it on good authority that you have a method for getting a hundred extra pages out of a photocopier toner cartridge that everyone else has given up as dead. Yet another accomplishment—and absolutely no surprise to those of us who count you not only as a colleague, but a friend. We know the wide range of your interests, including the wonderful classical music library you've been collecting since you graduated from Lincoln High School in 1976, your passion for your 1964 Triumph Spitfire, which you've been "restoring" (I call it "trying to get it to run") for, well, a number of years now, and, most of all, your dedication to your family, your wife, Cindy, and your sons, Josh and Brad. How you find time to coach both soccer and little league is beyond my comprehension.

What I'm trying to say, Ken, is that a lot of people are happy you were born. Congratulations to you. Congratulations to us. Thanks for everything you do. And, while I'm at it, let me also thank Nikita Krushchev, wherever he may be, for taking his missiles away.

MODEL SPEECH 031:
Employment Anniversary

Key Use of Speech:	To acknowledge the employment anniversary of a colleague or employee.
Style of Speech:	Informal, warm, sincere, grateful, and congratulatory
Audience:	Company or department employees—at an office celebration.
Time:	5 to 6 minutes.

➤ Tip: Draw your audience in by posing a question. The audience does not have actually to answer, but will start thinking.

Do you like statistics? I happen to like statistics. Here's an interesting one I found: According to the U.S. Department of Labor, the average person changes employers seven times during his or her career, and, in fact, changes *careers* three times during his or her working life.

I'm sure that's true. I mean, the *government* says it's true, and that's good enough for me.

So what do we make of Sarah Lane?

➤ Tip: Speeches dealing with anniversary-type occasions are naturally easy to structure. Just use a "before" and "after" approach: "This is what X was like at the beginning, and this is what X is like now. The comparison and contrast will speak for itself.

In 19XX, she graduated with honors from Central University and, that year, came to work for XYZ Corporation as an assistant analyst. Today, twenty-five years later, she's chief of analysis, an executive vice president, and the person we all run to whenever we need to know—well—just about *anything*.

I'd like to say she's an "institution," somebody, quite frankly, we're happy to take for granted. We don't have to worry about her and about what she does. We *depend* on her. But if I put it that way, I make her sound like a fossil. And fossil she is most certainly not.

Sarah is an innovator. I'd say that she has created a state-of-the-art analytical department, but the fact is that *she* created the state of the art itself. She is hailed by this industry as an innovator, someone who is impatient with old ways and restless to find new and better ways to do things.

→ Tip: Another device that grabs and holds an audience is apparent contradiction, paradox, mystery, or riddle. There is a natural desire to reach a solution.

Impatient? Restless?

But she's been here *twenty-five years*!

Well, I think Sarah is about *commitment:* commitment to excellence, commitment to innovation, and commitment to you and me and this company. It's a tribute, quite frankly, to her, of course, but also to all of *us* that *we* have provided an environment in which a restless innovator can feel at home. Provide that environment, and even the most restless people don't *have* to move on. What I'm saying is that we've all had to work hard to keep Sarah all these years. Avoiding complacency and a dedication to the status quo is very hard work indeed. The fact that Sarah is today celebrating twenty-five years here at XYZ suggests that—so far, at least—our work has been successful.

So far.

→ Tip: Most effective commemorative speeches look to the future as well as the past. Here, both the honoree and the company that honors her are seen not as "finished" items, but as works in progress.

Those, Sarah will be the first to tell us all, are the most important words in almost any self-congratulatory phrase. We have to keep moving the bar, setting new goals, reexamining what we do and how we do it, so that we can keep using that phrase accurately: *so far.*

So, Sarah, we want to congratulate you on twenty-five years with us. We want to thank you for each and every one of those years. And we want to tell you that you have done an extraordinary job—so far.

Thank goodness, it's not over yet!

Please come up here, Sarah, and accept a gift from all of us, along with an extended and very loud round of applause.

OUTLINE

Opening

- Statistic: average person changes jobs seven times
- Contrast honoree, Sarah Lane

Story of honoree

- Education
- Came to work for company
- Rose high
- Appraisal of her contribution to the company
- As an innovator

- List of achievements

Her success a tribute to us all

- Company provided environment to make her success possible
- We've avoided complacency

The future

- Keep moving forward, setting new goals
- Reexamine and reevaluate continually

Closing

- Congratulations
- Thanks
- Presentation of gift
- Invitation to applause

———————————

MODEL SPEECH 032:
Historical Building

Key Use of Speech: To commemorate the history of a corporate building.

Style of Speech: Celebratory and reminiscing.

Audience: Company employees.

Time: 3 to 4 minutes.

Today, our headquarters building turns one hundred. In this world of impermanence and change, that in itself is cause for celebration. But we also have another reason to celebrate. Our beautiful old building has been entered onto the National Register of Historical Places. Now the entire nation can share our landmark with us.

XYZ Headquarters is a great building, and all great buildings have great stories behind them.

[The speaker narrates some interesting facts about the building: who built it, who designed it, when it was built, how long it took to build, how big it is, and so on.]

It's no wonder that most of us feel so strongly about this building. But the fact is that it is never a very good idea to get too attached to *things*. We've all read news stories or have seen reports on TV after some disaster—fire, flood, earthquake—in which a family huddles in front of their demolished home.

How must these poor people feel?

Well, usually, they *tell* you.

They feel joy.

"Yes, we lost everything in there, but none of us was hurt, and we're all alive. We can always rebuild."

→ Tip: All too often, commemorative speeches contain little actual information and, instead, are full of high-flown sentiments and empty adjectives. Try sharing a story with your audience.

→ Tip: What gives us pleasure in a good mystery novel? The plot, especially one with plenty of clever and unexpected twists. Consider enlivening a routine commemorative speech with an unexpected turn.

→ Tip: Be careful not to leave the unexpected twist in the "plot" hanging in the air. Tie up your meaning neatly at the end of the speech. Above all things, a commemorative speech should not end ambiguously or trail off into apparent irrelevance. Be careful.

Now, my friends, in bringing this up, I certainly have no buried wish that disaster should befall our headquarters. So, please, hold the psychoanalysis. But I do think it's a good idea for us to remind ourselves that, wonderful as it is, it's not really the building that we love. It's what goes on *inside* the building. It's the passion and commitment and teamwork that this building shelters. It's each other and working with each other. *That's* what we love. As far as the building goes, well, it's just sort of love-by-association. And that, too, is plenty of reason to celebrate.

MODEL SPEECH 033:
Significant Event in the Past

Key Use of Speech:	To commemorate a significant past event.
Style of Speech:	Dignified and informative.
Audience:	Company employees.
Time:	6 to 7 minutes.

→ Tip: We're all too familiar with any number of meaningless commemorations. Make sure that your audience understands the meaning, the significance, and the value of this commemoration.

Each year, on **[date],** we pause from our work to gather together to commemorate the founding of our company. My friends, I don't know of any other company that does this, and when I mention this tradition to some of my colleagues in other companies, well, they either think the tradition is quaint or that we're all pretty corny here.

I don't think there is a lot wrong with being "quaint" or "corny," but, to me, taking these few moments out of our day once a year seems much more important than what those words convey. It gives us a chance to reflect—quietly, but together—on where we've been, where we are, and where we're going. It gives us a chance to define and redefine ourselves and our goals. Finally, it is an opportunity for us to look at ourselves and at our friends and coworkers and to realize what a wonderful thing it is to work together for our mutual benefit.

Now, we can think all these lofty thoughts on this occasion because XYZ Corporation is a *very* special company. The seeds of that special quality were planted at the very beginning of XYZ, and, each year, I tell you a bit about how the company came into existence, who the major players were those **[number]** years ago, and what their vision for this company was. Any of you who have been here for more than a year have heard this story before, of course, but it is a valuable tale for the newcomers to hear and it won't hurt anybody else to hear it again.

➜ Tip: The members of societies bond together, in part, through certain shared traditions and myths. Why not use a commemorative speech to create shared "corporate" myths and traditions? These give members of an organization a sense of pride and identity.

➜ Tip: Change technology, but not ideals. Focus meaning by focusing on a single word or concept—in this case *change.*

[Speaker delivers a brief narrative about the origins of the company.]

To say that there have been a lot of changes in our industry—and, for that matter, in our world—since **[founding year]** is both a cliché and an understatement. Just think for a moment how the technology of producing widgets has evolved in **[number]** years. Back in **[founding year]**, there was no **[the speaker goes on to describe, briefly, the state of technology at the time the company was founded].**

We at XYZ have always been in the vanguard of those changes. Change—change for the better—is good. And we have never had any problem with that. But there are some things we have tried not to change: commitment to excellence, commitment to our customers, and commitment to one another. These were principals that are as much a part of XYZ today as they were when XYZ was founded. We've gone through a lot of equipment modernizations since **[founding year]**, but commitment to excellence, customers, and one another is a piece of equipment we have clung to jealously and will continue to do so.

So, on this day, it is pleasant, fun, and interesting to look back on XYZ as it was in **[founding years]**, to appreciate how we have grown technologically and financially. But it is also, I believe, a profound pleasure to realize that, in important ways, we have refused to "grow," to change. We are still guided by certain principles that cannot be improved on. *That* is our tradition. They have carried us this far, and, if we continue to work according to these principles, they will carry us into the future.

———————————

MODEL SPEECH 034:
Tragedy in the Past

Key Use of Speech: To acknowledge and remember a
                      past tragedy.

Style of Speech: Dignified and compassionate.

Audience: Company employees and others affected
                      by the tragedy.

Time: 6 to 7 minutes.

➡ Tip: It is difficult to put strong emotions into words. Why try? Acknowledge the difficulty, and make it part of your speech. Here the speaker reviews what he could say, implying that words are inadequate to the occasion, but, in the process of pointing this out, giving his audience those words anyway.

We all know why we're here, why I'm speaking with you. I don't need to review the details of that terrible day, one year ago, when I called you all together here to tell you that our executive vice president, our colleague, our friend, Sheila McComb, had been killed in an automobile accident. She's gone. That is a fact. Nothing I can say will change that.

I could talk about how much we miss her. But each of us misses her, and none of us needs to be told *how much* each of us misses her.

It would be fitting and proper for me to talk about some of the things Sheila accomplished and did to grow and improve our company—innovations such as **[the speaker lists Sheila McComb's most important contributions, with minimal elaboration]**. But, in one way or another, most of us fully realize how important these contributions are to us, how they make us more efficient, more profitable, and enable us to give the greatest possible value to our customers. So I'll say no more on this subject.

➡ Tip: The speaker tells his audience what he intends to do.

What you need me to do, I think, is to tell you something you don't already know about Sheila.

Earlier this week, I paid a visit to Frank McComb and his two children, Cindy and Bob. I wanted to see how things were going for them and to tell them that we would be setting aside time today to

→ Tip: Where strong emotions are concerned, a first-person approach is often appropriate. Be careful, however, to avoid becoming so personal that you exclude your audience.

remember Sheila. I have to confess to you that I did not look forward to my visit. If I felt terrible about Sheila, how much worse, how much more devastating must it be for Frank and the kids? I mean, who wants to walk into a home that has suffered such a loss?

I was, first of all, relieved to see that Frank was coping. I've known him as long as I've known Sheila, and, certainly, I could see that something was missing. He didn't have quite the same look in his eye, quite the same energy, but, clearly, he *was* coping, and he was healing.

Then I looked for Cindy and Bob. They weren't in the living room with us.

"Where are the kids?"

"Oh, outside, playing."

→ Tip: A good speaker borrows from a good writer of fiction and uses touches of dialogue as well as vivid images to paint a scene for his audience.

And Frank took me into the kitchen, which has a window onto the backyard. And there they were. Smiling, giggling, running, playing, the two kids and a bunch of their friends.

I have to tell you that a thought crossed my mind, just for an instant: *Don't they remember their mother?*

But no sooner did this occur to me than I smiled and turned to Frank: "They're doing okay, aren't they?"

"Yes," he said, "they're doing okay."

→ Tip: The speaker tells his audience what he was thinking, because he assumes that the audience shares his response to the giggling, playing children.

I share this with you today not to prove the well-worn cliché about time healing all wounds—though, blessedly, that cliché has a lot of truth to it—and not even to reassure you that Frank and his family are all right now and will continue to be all right. I share it with you to suggest that Sheila, who gave our company so many things, gave her girl and boy her love, and her strength, neither of which died with her. She gave her children what they needed to survive, to carry on, to "do okay." Their smiles and giggles and playing with friends doesn't mean that they've forgotten their mother. It means, I think, quite the opposite: that, in the deepest way possible, they hold to their mother's memory as one holds to a precious, enduring gift. In their faces and voices and laughter, I saw and heard Sheila—not a year ago, but just a few days ago. She is still with us.

→ Tip: Tell a good story, then don't be afraid to draw a "moral" from the story.

OUTLINE

Opening

• Death of Sheila McComb

- We miss her
- Her contributions to the company were valuable
- Why her contributions were valuable

Something new about Sheila

- Visit to the family
- Emotionally difficult
- Family is coping
- Surprised that children were playing happily

Closing

- What does this mean?
- Provide comfort and consolation

MODEL SPEECH 035:
Gift/Endowment

Key Use of Speech:	To an important corporate gift to an educational institution.
Style of Speech:	Celebratory, evaluative, and forward-looking.
Audience:	An assembly of university students and officials.
Time:	12 to 15 minutes.

→ Tip: Generally, it is best to avoid well-worn clichés, but, sometimes, a stock phrase is the best expression of an idea. Anticipate and defuse negative reaction to clichés, as this speaker does.

Our nation stands at a crossroads. Faculty members, students, and distinguished guests, I apologize for beginning with such a cliché, but nothing expresses our situation more clearly. The decisions we make in the next few years will determine the quality of our system of higher education, and our system of higher education, to a great degree, will determine our future.

All of us at XYZ Corporation believe this. You see, all of us in management—and 40 percent of us throughout our company—are products of the nation's universities. We rely on you and institutions like yours.

We realize this now, and we realized this back in **[year]**, when XYZ created and endowed the XYZ Challenge Scholarship program.

→ Tip: The speaker doesn't just tell the audience that his company's scholarship program is successful, he shows them. He provides evidence.

[The speaker briefly narrates the history of the program, then mentions some of the prominent and successful graduates who have benefited from the program.]

I could stop here. XYZ has transformed its good intentions into cash for the students of this institution, and those students have excelled. *They've* been given an opportunity, and all of *us* benefit from it: our world has more engineers and scientists, our business has become that much more profitable, and our lives that much better.

I could stop here, then. But this is no time for complacence. Our gift to ABC University notwithstanding, higher education in this country faces grave financial peril. Last year, for the first time in four decades, total state appropriations for public higher education fell below the level of the year before. As our institutions are forced to demand increasingly prohibitive levels of tuition from students, the quality of *undergraduate* education is often increasingly diluted. Most undergraduates, and practically all lower-division courses, have been abandoned to the care of other students—graduate students, to be sure, but still students. Tenure is now the equivalent of insecure, as some scholars, having achieved a guaranteed job for life, settle into light teaching loads and desultory research.

I am being frank with you about this, because the observations I have just made originate not with me, but with Dr. Helen Troy, your university president. Dr. Troy and I discussed these matters a few months ago, when she asked me to speak here today, and I promised her I would address these issues in my speech.

Here goes.

In the face of growing financial pressure and—let's face it, justified—criticism, I can suggest two responses: Dig in, hunker down, resist change. Or: Confront the facts and lead the effort to change.

What has to change?

First, all of us—but especially business—need to invest in higher education. Our nation is as great as its people. Our industries are as great as our people. And never greater. The XYZ endowment is not a charitable enterprise. It is a business investment. It is an investment in our ability to remain competitive. It is survival.

Second, the universities must find ways to be more productive. They must challenge themselves to increase productivity, just as we in industry are always being challenged.

Increasing productivity is a rewarding but painful experience, let me tell you. During the crisis years of the 1970s and 1980s, XYZ Corporation, like so many other companies, was obliged to reevaluate all that we do, to jettison activities that add relatively less value, and to create more efficient ways to serve our customers. Sometimes, we have been forced to "downsize"—which is a weasel word for jettisoning people and not just programs. Does that hurt? Yes. Is it

→ Tip: The speaker has embarked on a risky course. After having praised and celebrated the success of the scholarship program, he launches into a critique of higher education. This can be a powerful strategy, but if the criticism is not fully developed, with solutions suggested, the strategy will backfire, and the speaker may simply seem mean spirited.

→ Tip: Having startled his audience with the sudden turn in his speech from celebration to crisis and criticism, the speaker makes it clear that his sentiments are shared by the education community—namely, the president of this very university. The speaker is, in fact, making good on a promise.

→ Tip: Beware of buzz-words. "Back to basics" is a phrase that can ring pretty hollow if it is not carefully defined. Here the speaker defines it explicitly.

→ Tip: The speaker has drawn an analogy between business and higher education. Now he must make certain that the analogy does not break down. "Customer" is a term unfamiliar to academics. How does it translate into the world of higher education?

→ Tip: The speaker provides evidence to support his assertions.

→ Tip: The speaker draws *positive* conclusions and points out *positive* courses of action.

necessary? Yes. But these are the kinds of decisions that have to be made for the survival of an organization. At XYZ, we understood that we had to get back to basics, refocus on our customers, and dedicate all that we do to serve *them*.

Basics: What are they?

For us, the basics are about quality. Our goal is to create the highest quality possible, then constantly to redefine—upward—what is "possible." Accomplish this, over and over again, and we satisfy our customers. Satisfy our customers, and we continue to succeed. Quality focuses effort.

Productivity, quality, and customer focus, I believe, are just as important to higher education as they are to U.S. industry. Universities need to refocus their missions, accomplish high-priority tasks with less, eliminate lower-priority activities.

Now, let's think about the "customer" of higher education. I'm defining your primary customer as the undergraduate.

What's happened to him and to her?

The undergraduate has been put in the back of the bus. Most large universities have lost sight of this customer. Proportionately little funding goes to the development of teaching programs, teaching personnel, and teaching facilities for undergraduates. Consider: **[the speaker furnishes statistics showing that research and graduate study are funded at significantly higher rates than undergraduate education].**

Any commercial enterprise that treated the bulk of its customers this way would quickly wither and die. Ladies and gentlemen, we need to think about how to increase productivity by redirecting scarce resources to where they will best serve the primary customers of higher education: the undergraduate students.

We at XYZ are thrilled at how extraordinarily well our endowment has been used here at ABC University for undergraduate education. The success of our endowment should stand as a test case and example for other businesses and for other universities. Put resources where they are most needed. If that means rethinking who you are and what you stand for, so be it. Reinvent the institution when it needs reinventing

Universities such as this one make an enormous difference in people's lives. You enable us all to create our futures. Certainly, we at XYZ recognize that your graduates *are* industry. We depend on you. Our whole society depends on quality education, and that begins with achieving and maintaining the kind of focus the XYZ program was created for: a focus on the primary customer of the university, a focus on the undergraduate. We at XYZ are proud and happy to help. We're helping ourselves, after all. Now, let's hope that the XYZ program, celebrating **[number of years]** of quality higher education, inspires other businesses—and other universities—to get back to basics. How basic? Let's start with the three R's: reevaluate, reinvent, and refocus.

OUTLINE

Opening

- Nation at a crossroad
- Decisions we make now determine the future of higher education
- Future of higher education will largely determine our future as a nation

XYZ Corporation's stake in and commitment to higher education

- We need well-educated people
- We have endowed the XYZ Challenge Scholarship
- History of the program
- Its success

We all need to do more

- Good as the scholarship fund is, we all need to do more
- Higher education in grave financial peril
- Quality of undergraduate education diluted
- Problems (list)
- Straight talk—comes from your own university president

What to do

- Confront the facts
- Lead the effort to change

- Business needs to invest in higher education
- Universities must become more productive

Increasing productivity

- Get back to basics
- Refocus on primary "customer:" the undergraduate student
- Concept of quality
- Review main areas of improvement

The "customer"

- How universities fail to serve undergraduate "customer"
- Need to redirect resources

Closing

- Our endowment is an example of such redirection
- We hope it will inspire other businesses to invest . . .
- and other universities to reinvent themselves
- Final review of the "basics": "reevaluate, reinvent, refocus"

———————————————

MODEL SPEECH 036:
Scholarship Program

Key Use of Speech: To inaugurate a scholarship or other endowment program.

Style of Speech: Dignified and idealistic, but with a hard edge of practical business sense.

Audience: Educators and the press.

Time: 12 to 20 minutes.

➤ Tip: The speaker begins conventionally enough by flattering his audience—never a bad idea—however, he concludes the opening paragraph by dropping the bombshell about greed and selfishness.

Ladies and gentlemen, I come before you honored and awed. It isn't every day that one addresses an assembly of such distinguished educators, scientists, scholars, and policymakers. It is an event even more unusual to come before such an august group to own up to an act of absolute, unvarnished greed and selfishness.

We have created a program called the XYZ Tomorrow Scholarship Fund, and we have written to it a check for **[$ amount].** Each year, a committee . . .

[The speaker goes on to explain how scholarship recipients will be selected, how many will be selected, what they will receive, and what will be required of them.]

➤ Tip: The speaker explains the scholarship program. His assertion that his company is acting from selfish and greedy motives is a thread of suspense that holds the attention of his audience.

Now, I want to make it clear that XYZ Scholarship students owe the XYZ Corporation nothing. They must maintain the academic level of excellence that qualified them for the award in the first place, but, beyond this, they are free to pursue whatever course track and career track they choose. They certainly don't have to come to work for us—though we hope that many of them will choose just that as a worthy goal.

But, on behalf of my corporation, I'm trying to confess to an act of selfishness and greed, and I don't believe my confession sounds very convincing.

The fact is that it doesn't matter whether the XYZ Scholarship students come to us or enter government service or become physicians, lawyers, teachers—or even take jobs with our competitors. XYZ Corporation still directly benefits.

→ Tip: The speaker finally explains why he calls his corporation greedy and selfish.

To remain competitive, to become even more profitable, to create higher and higher levels of customer satisfaction—let's face it, *to stay in business*—XYZ Corporation needs a workforce possessed of great skill, great knowledge, and the ability to innovate. Our company devotes **[$ amount]** each year to employee development and training in highly specialized areas. But we don't need specialists. We need extraordinarily well-educated people who possess, in addition, certain special skills. No company, XYZ included, can supply that broad excellence of education through a corporate training program. That is what the nation's institutions of higher learning are for. And that is why we have chosen to invest in them with the XYZ Tomorrow Scholarship Fund.

You buy things you can't make yourself. With our scholarship program, we intend to buy the education we, as a company, cannot make.

Now, I have no idea what percentage of Tomorrow Scholarship graduates will come to work for us. Maybe many, maybe few, maybe none at all. Does this mean that, as a corporate investor in education, XYZ is both greedy *and* dumb?

Not at all.

→ Tip: The speaker places his company's scholarship program in a greater context, as the vanguard of a national movement.

With this scholarship endowment, XYZ joins a growing legion of American businesses that are investing—"selfishly"—in education. And we believe that our action today will prompt many more businesses to join us in making such an investment. Now, we at XYZ don't care whether the research chemist who joins our firm four years form now put herself through college on an XYZ Tomorrow Scholarship or on a WXY Challenge Scholarship. We just care that she comes to us having been prepared by a great education. We at XYZ want to make that possible, and we want to encourage other firms to make that possible as well. All of us—"selfishly"—will benefit.

Before I announce the recipients of the first three XYZ Tomorrow Scholarships, I want to acknowledge the hard work, dedication, judgment, and, yes, genius of our selection committee panel.

→ Tip: Never forget to thank people who deserve thanks. But note how the speaker keeps his audience in suspense by delaying the announcement of the "winners" until the very end of the speech.

[The speaker introduces the distinguished members of the panel, giving the qualifications of each.]

Now, with your permission, I will commence our act of selfishness. I am delighted to present to you the recipients of our first three XYZ Tomorrow Scholarships

[The speaker introduces and congratulates the recipients. He then closes by addressing them.]

→ Tip: The speaker ends by reiterating the theme of the larger benefits of the scholarship program.

We're proud of you, and we're grateful to you. We're proud, because you are the future of our nation and the business of our nation, the success of our nation in a world that becomes increasingly competitive and demanding—as well as rewarding—each day. We're grateful, because the skills and knowledge you acquire will benefit us all, will allow us all to create and to enjoy the ideas, the products, and the services that enhance our lives. Thank you for earning the first three XYZ Tomorrow Scholarships.

OUTLINE

Opening

- Greeting
- "Confession" of corporate greed

The program

- Name of program
- Explanation of program

Benefits of the program

- Development of an educated workforce
- A sound business investment

Announcement of scholarship recipients

- Acknowledge those responsible for the program
- Introduce panel members

- Presentation of scholarships

Closing

- Expression of pride
- Expression of gratitude

MODEL SPEECH 37:
Memorial

Key Use of Speech: This is a speech by a business leader at a civic memorial occasion.

Style of Speech: Reverent, dignified, community-oriented.

Audience: General audience.

Time: 5 to 10 minutes. [Depends on the length of the stories narrated.]

➡ Tip: On an emotionally charged occasion, you may want to let your audience in on the difficulty you have expressing yourself appropriately. The audience will understand, and you will avoid sounding glib.

➡ Tip: The speaker wishes to provide meaningful consolation without intruding on the private emotions of his audience.

Each year, many of us gather at this site . . . I was going to say that we gather here to remember the tragedy of the school fire of **[date]**, a tragedy that hurt this community in ways so profound that only a parent can understand. Two employees at my company, XYZ Industries, lost children in the fire, and four more had children who were seriously injured. Some of you gathered here today also lost a child or suffered through the injury of a child. And, as I look at the representatives of our fine fire department, I am reminded that one firefighter lost his life and ten more were injured.

I was going to begin this way, talking about these losses that, really, are beyond my ability to describe. I was going to begin this way, but, then, were would I have gone from there?

My friends and neighbors, this tragedy needs no more of my words. You know how you feel. You know, you know all too well, what you have lost.

I want to talk about what we did *not* lose that day: 678 children, 23 teachers. Each child saved involved an act of heroism, either by a firefighter, a teacher, or a child. Perhaps you have heard some of these stories.

[The speaker narrates three stories of heroism, including one story involving firefighters, one involving a teacher, and one involving a child.]

→ Tip: The speaker makes it clear that he hopes his words will provide a degree of healing, but he also acknowledges that nothing he says can alter the ultimate reality of the tragedy.

There are many more such stories. I suggest that, on each memorial occasion, we remember at least one of these stories. We won't forget the lives we have lost. We don't need a memorial day for that, for we cannot choose other than to remember. The danger is that, in our grief, we *may* lose sight of the preciousness of what is left to us. So let us remember the acts of courage and calm and dedication and selflessness that preserved these precious lives.

Those are the words I have to offer, and, I think, they are the *best* words I can offer.

Competition

Openings

—*Let's talk about survival and excellence. For us, they are one and the same.*

—*It's a pity our competitors are not here today. I wanted to thank them.*

Closings

—*As we expand into new markets, let us never forget that our customers have many suppliers from which to choose. We must earn their business, one customer at a time.*

—*Thank you for your attention this afternoon. With all of us working together, I know that we will win.*

MODEL SPEECH 038:
Domestic, How to Exceed

Key Use of Speech:	To look within the organization for the competitive edge.
Style of Speech:	Informational and inspirational.
Audience:	Business conference audience.
Time:	10 to 11 minutes.

➡ Tip: Know your audience. The speaker, addressing a business conference, realizes that his audience has heard a number of speeches; therefore, he wastes no time with a preamble, but gets to the substance of his talk immediately.

Good afternoon. I'm here to talk about finding and honing a "competitive edge." Since my company, XYZ Corporation, is the market leader in our industry, I feel justified in speaking from our experience. So I will identify some of the basics that guide us in managing our firm.

What *matters* to us? There are many short-term answers to this question, but there is only one long-term answer that seems to count for anything. It is *people.* People matter. We know that if we get and keep the right people, we will hone and retain our competitive edge.

How do we get and keep the right people?

First, we establish—and we believe in—a core of principles. Second, we devote great effort and energy investing in our workforce. Third, we examine, reexamine, and rework our evaluation and compensation schemes. Let me say a word or two more about this, because one obvious way to get and retain good people is just to pay them a lot of money. Our compensation systems are subjective and flexible. We studiously *avoid* rigid incentive formulas. We want *creativity,* not mindless, so-called "productivity."

➡ Tip: An effective way of stepping your audience through your speech is to ask and answer questions.

What else?

Getting and retaining the right people requires open and free channels of information. Nothing destroys an organization more surely than lack of communication. Communication also makes it easier for top management to encourage people to think big, to take informed risks, and to keep a *creative* eye on cost control.

Communication, encouragement of creativity, encouragement of responsible risk taking, and the fostering of cost control are all part of something we call corporate culture. If we do not have the right team, we get nowhere, and if we to not have a strong, positive corporate culture, we cannot attract and retain the right team. A strong culture begins with the firm's leadership, and the leadership role is made much easier if it is built on strong principles. Here are ours:

1. The customer is all-important.
2. We are a team. We work as a team.
3. Our most valuable assets are our people.

Anchored by these three absolutes, we, as leaders, can afford to be creative and to encourage creativity as well as risk.

So much for broad principles. How about some practical matters? A strong corporate culture, as I have suggested, is essential to attracting and keeping good people—but it doesn't really work like a magnet. We know that we have to be proactive in "attracting" new hires. That's why we invest very heavily in recruiting. We don't relegate recruiting to "human resources," but, instead, put our key people on it.

Time consuming? You bet. Costly? Yes. But not nearly as time consuming or costly as turnover or, worse, having the wrong people in place.

Now, once we make a hire, we continue to make an investment in training and, even more importantly, in mentoring and in continuing education.

We don't stop with education, either. Evaluation is continual, and we have developed what we call a career review process at XYZ Corporation, which is based on months of peer appraisal as well as anonymous evaluation all the way up and down the firm's hierarchy. This, too, is time consuming—but not time wasting.

Just as we have rethought our hiring and training and evaluation processes, so we have reevaluated the traditional separation that has existed between sales functions and support functions—between what used to be called the front office and the back office. That separation doesn't work anymore. We need support and logistics if

→ Tip: The speaker has now developed two main themes: people and corporate culture. He has defined both. Next, he announces a transition from "broad principles" to "practical matters" —from theory to application.

→ Tip: Anticipate your audience's concerns and objections ("Time consuming?. . . Costly?"), then address them. It is a very effective strategy to concede the validity of the objection, but then show how benefits attained outweigh any liabilities.

→ Tip: Note the use of a transitional sentence at the beginning of this paragraph. This signals to the audience a move to a new, but nevertheless related, thought.

we want to stay competitive. It's great to make a sale, but that sale will prove a one-shot dead end if you don't have the ongoing support to back it up. It is no longer just the "front office" that makes or breaks a deal. We need balance between sales and support functions. Some of our best people and some of our best career paths are now in what used to be called the "back office."

While we have torn down the walls separating "front" from "back office," we have tried to tear down walls generally. Internal bureaucracy inhibits the free flow of information. Look, it's the people in the trenches, the people who deal directly with clients and customers, who know *everything* that is going on in our business and in our competitor's business. They know what the clients and customers want. We make it easy for these frontline people to communicate their ideas vertically to management with a minimum of bureaucratic resistance. We work hard at developing our channels of information upward.

While I'm on the subject of communication, let me dare to utter the "M" word. *Meetings*. Meetings get a bum rap. Our knee-jerk response to the notion of a meeting is that it will be, by definition, a waste of time. Well, it is true that big, bureaucratic meetings *are* a waste of time. That's why we encourage the convening of many small, informal meetings. We like our people to take time out several times during the week to brainstorm in groups of three or four—no more than that. The idea that you always have to be hitting the road, pounding the pavement, knocking on doors, "making things happen" is a symptom of a neurotic macho obsession. Its time has come—and gone. It pays to sit down, together, and think once in a while. Thinking generates the kind of "big ideas" that can become a company's bread and butter. Thinking also makes it possible to take *controlled* risks—and that is essential to staying competitive. But, remember, the most effective way of selecting which risks to take, and then controlling them, is to invest in people. It is with people that opportunities begin, that risks may be managed intelligently, and that a company becomes competitive—and stays that way.

OUTLINE

Opening

- Announce subject
- Speaker explains his qualifications to speak on the subject

---

→ Tip: This paragraph begins with another transition, centered on the idea of tearing down walls. Transitions are essential to giving a speech a feeling of sound and persuasive structure.

- Speaks from firsthand experience

Most important competitive factor: people

- How we get and keep the right people
- Our principles
- Investing in our people
- Evaluating and compensating our people
- Communicating with our people
- Encouraging creativity
- Encouraging responsible risk taking
- Encouraging cost control
- Corporate culture

A Strong corporate culture

- What it is
- How we foster it
- Leadership
- Strong principles

Recruiting practices

- Our key people do the recruiting
- We invest much time in recruiting
- Costly, but less costly than making a mistake
- Training
- Mentoring
- Continuing education
- Ongoing evaluation

Rethinking and reorganizing the company

- No distinction between front and back office
- Importance of support and logistical operations
- Reduce internal bureaucracy

Closing

- The value of meetings
- How to produce "big ideas"
- How to encourage controlled risks
- Reiterate importance of investing in people

MODEL SPEECH 039:
Foreign, How to Exceed

Key Use of Speech:	To outline a program for competitiveness in the world marketplace.
Style of Speech:	Frank and frankly prescriptive.
Audience:	Business conference audience.
Time:	12 to 15 minutes.

→ Tip: It is often an effective and simple organizing technique to begin your speech with a question.

How can we compete in the international marketplace?

That is the question I have been asked to answer tonight. Think about this question with me a moment, if you will. The question assumes that we are having difficulty competing, that, somehow, we lack the equipment to compete.

This just isn't true. Our industry has the talent and the will to compete in any market in the world.

So—why the question?

Well, we just aren't as competitive as we could be.

Why not, then?

→ Tip: Don't let yourself be trapped by an assigned topic. If necessary, modify and manipulate the topic— but be certain that you acknowledge that you have modified the assignment, explain how you have modified it, and why.

To answer this question, I need to stand the original question on its head. I need to ask, not how can we compete, but what—all too often—*stops* us from competing.

I've identified four stumbling blocks to international competitiveness in our industry.

First: Our industry is overregulated.

Second: Our industry is subject to crippling litigation.

Third: Our industry is heavily—even punitively—taxed.

Fourth: We are a high-tech industry operating in a nation that has, for too long, neglected education.

Our competitiveness problems aren't economic, then, so much as they are political, social, legal, and attitudinal.

Let's start with regulation. To be sure, some regulation is necessary, but, remember, even necessary regulation comes at a high price. It raises costs to business and consumers and it builds bureaucracies. Do you want to create a competitive economy? Then work with your legislators to keep regulation at the essential minimum.

The *essential minimum*? We're going in the wrong direction. The *Federal Register,* the government's compendium of regulations, was a stout 10,000 pages in 1954. Today, it runs to more than 60,000 pages. And that's 60K pages that any business ignores at great peril. You have to plow through it, understand it, abide by it. And, yes, if there's any time left over, you have to try to make a dollar and a cent. I know I'm hardly alone in bemoaning overregulation. Economist Thomas Hopkins estimates that federal regulations cost American consumers about $400 billion every year. That's about double the annual cost of public education in America, from kindergarten through the twelfth grade. It's one-third more than we spend on defense.

I'm depressed.

Let's move on to the second obstacle, litigation. In **[year],** Americans spent $380 billion on litigation. Of that amount, a mere 15 percent went to clients in the form of settlements of disputes. What happened to the rest? Into the attorneys' pockets. Our nation has a *lot* of attorneys. Take Washington, D.C. In that city, there are more than 15,000 attorneys *in private practice.* That's one for every forty Washingtonians. My friends, we Americans are fighting each other in court while the rest of the world is building VCRs, computers, automobiles, and all the rest.

Now I'm depressed *and* angry.

Better move on to number three: taxation

Taxes are necessary. Period. Now, while the United States is actually not among the most heavily taxed countries, state, local, *and* federal do combine to equal about 40 percent of our gross national product. If we want to be competitive, we must structure taxation to encourage—not punish—investment. This means a relatively low capital gains tax rate. High rates are a sharp *disincentive* to invest in companies, and, in the global marketplace, that is a severe disadvantage.

Finally, there is education—or the lack of it. We need to devote time and energy to educating our workforce. We need to compensate teachers adequately. We need to attract the best and the brightest into

---

→ Tip: Statistics can be powerful weapons in a speech. But use them sparingly and for maximum impact. Don't bombard your listeners with them.

→ Tip: The speaker uses her own mildly humorous reaction to the details of her first point as a transition to her second point.

→ Tip: The speaker interjects her reaction, in effect, on behalf of the audience. She voices the feelings she wants her audience to have.

the teaching profession. We need to keep our children in school longer—not more years, but more days. Students in Japan go to school about 220 days per year. Ours? About 180 days per year. Do we really think our kids can learn as much as Japanese kids in just *80 percent* of the time?

So, my friends, I am afraid I have not answered the question I have been assigned. The best I could do was suggest ways in which we can *fail* to compete in the world marketplace. Take what I've said, turn it 180 degrees, and maybe we can gain—or regain—our edge in this world. Thank you.

➞ Tip: Having modified her speaking assignment, the speaker concludes by explaining how she has actually carried out that assignment.

OUTLINE

Opening

• How can we compete in the international marketplace?
• Redefine question: How do we *fail* to compete?

Competition problems

• Four stumbling blocks
• Industry overregulated
• Industry subject to crippling litigation
• Industry is unfairly taxed
• Our nation neglects education

Closing

• Not answered the question
• Turn my speech 180 degrees
• Remedy the sources of failure

MODEL SPEECH 040:
New Product as a Means to Beat Competition

Key Use of Speech: To stress new product benefits.

Style of Speech: Informational, team-building, and enthusiastic.

Audience: Sales force.

Time: 10 to 30 minutes. [Depends on length of product descriptions.]

➜ Tip: Do what you can to build excitement. Here the speaker makes his audience feel as if they are on the brink of something truly great, truly momentous.

Our friends in the software industry are forever talking about the "Killer App"—the *one* "application," the one item of software so great that everybody, absolutely *everybody,* has got to have it. Well, maybe the Killer App is like hen's teeth or El Dorado. Maybe it just doesn't exist.

Then again—maybe it does.

And maybe, just maybe, we've got it.

This fall, XYZ Corporation will introduce . . .

[The speaker describes the new product.]

In our industry and for our market, this may very well be the fabled Killer App. Here's what it does.

[The speaker describes the product's features.]

➜ Tip: The speaker delivers important information here—building up from "features" to "benefits"—while simultaneously stroking the collective ego of his audience by acknowledging that they are "professionals" who possess the savvy of professionals. Thoughtful flattery of an audience can be very effective. Just be careful not to patronize them.

Ladies and gentlemen, you are professionals. You know that a strong feature set is important in any product, but you also know that there is something even more important. "Features" are crucial, of course, but *benefits* are key. Features are what the product does, but *benefits* are what the consumer believes the product will do *for him or her*. If features are the "steak," benefits are the "sizzle." And we all know how effective selling the sizzle can be.

And what a sizzle we've got to sell! Let me run down this list of terrific product benefits:

[The speaker describes the product's benefits.]

Now, ladies and gentlemen, I'm not going to stand here and tell you that this product is so great that it will sell itself. This *is* a great product, a *revolutionary* product. But precisely because it is so great and so revolutionary, it is up to each of you to take responsibility for learning everything you can about it and then taking that knowledge to the customer. Make no mistake, we're going to support you with an extensive advertising campaign.

[The speaker describes the highlights of the ad campaign.]

Now, a strong ad campaign is a tremendous selling tool, of course, but, with this new product, nothing—absolutely nothing—can take the place of your individually *educating* our customers. Learn about this product. Impart your wisdom.

→ Tip: Thoughtfully used, repetition is an effective means of getting your message across.

This is a classic win–win scenario, my friends. Educate your customers, and they will be grateful to you. Educate your customers, and they will earn you big-time commissions. Educate your customers, and XYZ will enjoy its most successful new product launch ever.

Our goal is to sell **[number]** units in **[time period].** That's **[number]** units for each of you. That's a volume of **[$ amount]** total, or **[$ amount]** per sales person, which means that each of you has the potential of earning **[$ amount]** in commissions by **[date].**

→ Tip: Only after appealing to the self-interest of his audience does the speaker look at the "big picture"—what the goals he has set will mean to the company.

This is a great opportunity for us all—especially when we step back to look at the bigger picture. It's not *just* about commissions. It's about remaining highly competitive in this industry. It's about assuring our market leadership position for a long time to come. It's about taking this market by storm—now —and holding those competitive gains. It's about big commissions today—and even bigger commissions for the long haul. *That* is being competitive. And *that* is the opportunity this new product represents.

Any questions?

[The speaker fields questions.]

I'm proud of our new product, and I'm even prouder of the opportunity to work with all of you to make this the greatest, most successful launch in our history. Let's go!

OUTLINE

Opening

The "Killer App"
Maybe it doesn't exist
Maybe it does
Maybe we've got it!

Introduce new product

Description of new product
The new product's features
Introduce the idea of product's benefits

The benefits

List
Selling the benefits

Sales personnel must take responsibility for learning about the product

Advertising support
Educate the customers

Our sales goals

Number of units
Units per salesperson
Dollar volume
Dollar volume per sales person
Commission potential

Closing: The greater opportunity

Put us in a leadership position
Expression of pride in new product

Dedications

Openings

——*It is with great pride that I welcome you to the dedication of our new facility.*

——*I am deeply honored that you have asked me to speak at the dedication of your beautiful new facility.*

Closings

——*I know that we will make great use of this new and expanded facility.*

——*Thank you all for celebrating the dedication of our new headquarters.*

MODEL SPEECH 041:
Dedication of New Facility

Key Use of Speech: To dedicate a new facility.

Style of Speech: Dignified, informational, and celebratory.

Audience: Beneficiaries of corporate generosity, company employees, public, and press.

Time: 5 to 6 minutes.

→ Tip: The speaker provides some thematic background for the dedication.

Smith Community College has always looked in two directions: ahead and back. It is a forward-looking institution that nevertheless holds to the best of tradition, which includes striving for the highest possible academic excellence and doing whatever is necessary to ensure that Smith students have the greatest educational opportunity possible. This means, among many other things, ensuring the availability of state-of-the-art learning tools.

There is, of course, one learning tool we've all grown accustomed to using: the networked an Internet-connected computer. With this tool, we can create information and share information, offering our best and learning from the best others have to offer.

→ Tip: On behalf of his company, the speaker takes credit for financing the facility that is being dedicated, but, while he takes credit, he also expresses his firm's gratitude at being given the privilege of making a contribution. Note also that the speaker introduces the idea of community (the college and the company are "neighbors." This public-relations strong point is a central theme of the speech.

We at XYZ Industries are very proud that Smith Community College came to us about helping to finance some Internet-ready computers. After we talked to students and teachers here—at this college that is part of *our* neighborhood—we became very excited about the opportunity we were being given. We decided to finance more than a few computers. We decided to help Smith create the facility we are dedicating today: the XYZ Campus Computer Center.

This new, state-of-the-art computer network will allow Smith students to use the Internet not just to meet short-term goals—such as getting that term paper written—but also to become accustomed to living in a community built of knowledge, information, and cooperation.

121

→ Tip: Too often, bene-
factors "throw money at" a
problem, project, or issue.
The speaker makes it
clear that this approach is
not sufficient, and that
XYZ's gift is not so much
about equipment as it is
about people, relation-
ships, and building a
community.

Ladies and gentlemen, let's understand something about this gift XYZ has had the privilege to bestow. It is a very limited gift. Computers will not solve the problems of the world, nor will computers provide the answers to our students' questions. But they can connect people to people in such a way that problems will get solved and questions answered.

The computer facility we are dedicating here today is not just a collection of high-tech copper and silicon. It is a lesson in *connecting*, in communicating, in cooperating, in giving and taking, accepting commitment and making commitment. It is, in short, a lesson in democracy. To "log on" to one of these new computers is to "log on" to society. Yes, my friends, this computer facility will help you write papers more quickly—and they will be better papers, too—but the lessons this system has to teach go much deeper and further.

→ Tip: The speaker
takes time to acknowl-
edge those who helped
make possible the facility
he is dedicating.

While I am speaking about lessons, let me share with you one that I learned in working with Smith on this project. It is both a pleasure and a challenge to work with dedicated people. Dean Cynthia Milhouse was very grateful for XYZ's gift, but she was also demanding and thoroughly knowledgeable about how that gift should be applied. This was true of the faculty members who consulted on this project, **[speaker lists faculty]**. I suppose there are some college administrators and faculty that would be content to sit back and grab the money as it comes. Not Dean Milhouse and her faculty. They worked tirelessly to make this system *Smith's* system, ideally tailored to suit the needs of this institution's students and faculty. Thank you, all, for making our gift to you so much more valuable.

→ Tip: The speaker
takes an inclusive
approach to his subject,
addressing directly the
primary users of the new
facility.

And now, to the students who will benefit from this facility, I suggest that you use it boldly and creatively. I invite you also to take joy in it or, rather, in the new worlds it will open to you.

Ladies and gentlemen, please join me now in officially declaring the XYZ Computer Center operational.

OUTLINE

Opening

- Smith Community College looks two ways
- Tradition
- State of the art, future

Subject of the dedication

• The XYZ Campus Computer Center
• What the new facility will do

Greater significance of the new facility

• A lesson in connecting, communicating, cooperating
• A lesson in democracy

Credit to those who helped create the new facility

• Dedicated people
• College dean
• Faculty members (list)
• Tireless work

Closing

• Direct address to the students (users of the facility)
• Officially open the facility

―――――――――――

MODEL SPEECH 042:
Dedication of Memorial

Key Use of Speech: To dedicate a memorial to the company's founder.

Style of Speech: Dignified and informative, pride and morale building.

Audience: Company employees.

Time: 9 to 10 minutes.

➡ Tip: Beginning with the unexpected is always an effective way to seize and hold the attention of an audience. Arouse curiosity, and your audience will stay with you, waiting for the resolution.

➡ Tip: Do what you can to bring the subject of the memorial to life. Here, the speaker invents some dialogue. Note, also, the humanizing humor: he'd like being told that he's right. Share memories and feelings with the audience.

Tom Smith would not have approved of what we are about to do. Oh, he would have appreciated the gesture: this beautiful memorial sculpture by **[name of artist]**. I mean, it *is* beautiful—magnificent, even—and Tom certainly appreciated beauty. He would have put out his hand to **[name of artist]**, would have shaken her hand, and he would have said, "Well, that's really, *really* nice." And that was very high praise from Tom Smith.

But he still wouldn't have approved.

You see, Tom always looked for the most elegant solution to any problem, and that means he just could not stand redundancy. Now, the fact is that Tom Smith doesn't *need* this wonderful memorial we're dedicating today, because this company, XYZ Industries, *is* his memorial. Yes, he'd say, "I've already got one. Why do I need another?"

He'd be right, you know. So how should we answer him?

Here's what I would say.

"Tom," I'd tell him, "you're right." (Now, I *know* he'd like to hear *that!*) "You're right, but this memorial isn't for you. It's for us. It's for us who knew you and want to make our memories of you even stronger and richer than they are. But, even more, it's for all those

→ Tip: A memorial speech is, in part, an exercise in education: ensuring that your audience understands the significance of the occasion and the memorial.

who will join the company in the years to come, those who never met you, never even saw you. They come to us with a great handicap: your absence. We need to help them, to inspire them as best we can, and that is what this memorial is intended to do."

My friends and colleagues, that's what this memorial statue to Tom Smith is all about. It's not about Tom, but about *us*. Maybe we can stroll by it, pause, reflect, get our minds clear, and look to Tom's example for guidance. That's what a great memorial is for—to help fill the void left by the passing of someone you depend on and look to for leadership.

Before I formally dedicate the Thomas Smith Memorial, I want to acknowledge the work of **[name of artist]**.

→ Tip: The significance of the memorial may go beyond what the speaker personally believes it to be. If possible, approach the subject from more than one perspective.

[The speaker talks briefly about the artist and reads from the artist's own statement about her work.]

I also want to acknowledge the builders of this monument. They include **[the speaker names the firm that erected the memorial]** and they also include the employees of XYZ Industries who contributed freely and generously to the fund that financed this memorial. Folks, this project is *yours*. *You* made it happen. And that is the way it should be, because this memorial is for you—for us, for all of us and for everyone who will come here to work or come here as our guest. Tom, we're sorry, but we just *had* to build this—not for you, but for us.

→ Tip: A good speaker always looks for ways to include his audience.

And now, I dedicate this memorial to the people of XYZ industries.

Farewells

Openings

——*My friends, I knew this day was coming. I tried not to think about it. But I knew it was coming, and it is here.*

——*We are here to celebrate the career of Jane Smith, one of our founding partners, who has given to this company so much of her time, talent, and soul.*

Closings

——*Thank you for being here to say goodbye to me. Not that you'll get rid of me so easily. I plan to come back for frequent visits.*

——*Jane, we all wish you the best of everything, and we thank you, as best we can, for having done so much to make this company of ours a success.*

MODEL SPEECH 043:
Benediction

Key Use of Speech: To be used by a departing employee/executive to wish those he is leaving well.

Style of Speech: Dignified, spiritual, but not sectarian.

Audience: Company employees.

Time: Under 1 minute.

→ Tip: A benediction may be personal, but don't focus on yourself. Emphasize the bond between you and your audience.

It has been a privilege, pleasure, and honor serving with you, and I wish you all continued success as you open new creative paths. You know I will eagerly follow your progress, and even if I cannot share your discoveries firsthand, I shall continue to do so in spirit. God bless you all.

ALTERNATIVE

→ Tip: Benedictions are by definition spiritual pronouncements; however, it is best to avoid sectarian references such as to Jesus, Allah, and so on.

I must leave you now, and I do so with a prayer for your continued success. The work we have done, and the work you continue to do, is important. Its continued development is vital to us all. Never become discouraged. I know that you will prevail. I know that from the personal experience of working with you. Farewell, my good friends.

MODEL SPEECH 044:
Company Moving Out of Town

Key Use of Speech: To bid farewell to nonmoving employees and to others associated with the company.

Style of Speech: Sincere and informative (provides information about why the company is leaving).

Audience: Company employees and other interested parties.

Time: 9 to 10 minutes.

➡ Tip: The speaker begins with the human aspect of the company's departure from town—the loss of personal contact with friends and associates.

➡ Tip: Emotions are difficult to describe. Instead of describing the emotions, talk about the cause of the emotions. Talk about actual events rather than abstract feelings.

Good morning, ladies and gentlemen. As I look out at you this morning, I see a great many friends and colleagues. Some of you will be moving with us to **[new location]**. Many of you will not. I also see the faces of vendors and other associates with whom we have done business in **[name of town]** for **[number of years]**. I hope that we'll still be doing business with you, but it is a sad fact that we won't be shaking one another's hands, person to person, nearly so often.

As I look out at you today, I wonder how many of you remember the emotions you had when you were children and moving day came. Perhaps some of you never moved very far as children. But, perhaps, like me, you had a dad (or a mom) whose business demanded a move or two or more. The emotions of moving day were awfully powerful. Remember? There was the anticipation of excitement, adventure, new people, new scenery, new friends, new experiences, new opportunities at a new school. And there was—just as powerful—the sadness at leaving old scenes, the old school, and, most of all, old friends. You felt this emotion not in your head and not even in your heart, but in your gut.

My friends, moving day for XYZ Corporation is now just two

weeks away. And I'm getting that feeling in my gut—the feeling of a child leaving his home.

It is true that we are excited about this move. It is a very positive and very necessary step for XYZ Corporation.

[The speaker explains the motivation for the move: the business necessities, improved profitability, etc.]

Excited and challenged—but also sad. For **[number of years]**, **[name of town]** has been our home. Let's face it: we will be leaving good friends and good neighbors. We at XYZ have always felt welcome here, and we have tried to give back to the community, to return value to it for the value we have received. We believe that we have left a lasting legacy.

[The speaker discusses some of the company's community-focused programs.]

I want to assure all of you that these programs will continue to receive generous funding from XYZ. Our relationship doesn't have to end just because we are leaving.

To the employees who will not be joining us at **[name of new location]**, we bid farewell and leave you with our thanks. I know that the management team and I are better at what we do for having worked with you, and we modestly hope that your experience at XYZ has advanced your careers and has helped prepare you for whatever else you may pursue. Our outplacement program will remain in place here at **[name of town]** for **[time period]** after we have left. I hope you will take advantage of it freely to help you find continued rewarding employment.

Two weeks from today, my friends, our move will be completed. It sounds hollow or, at least, like an understatement, to say that we'll miss you all. But we *will* miss you all. We hope that you'll stay in touch with us, and any of you here today will find a warm welcome in **[name of new location]**. Visit often. Thank you all, and Godspeed to you.

→ Tip: The speaker takes the opportunity to recount the positive things his company has done for the community—things that will not vanish just because the company is moving.

→ Tip: The speaker acknowledges the employees who will no longer be working for the company. His object is to minimize the impression of abandonment.

MODEL SPEECH 045:
Employee Leaving on Favorable Note

Key Use of Speech:	To express farewell and best wishes to a departing employee.
Style of Speech:	Sincere, informative (provides information about why the employee is leaving), informal.
Audience:	Company or department employees.
Time:	4 to 5 minutes.

➤ Tip: Often, a single word or phrase can focus an entire speech—if it's the right word.

I suppose the word *bittersweet* is overused, but I'm going to use it anyway. *This* is a *bittersweet* occasion.

Here's the bitter part: Sarah Johnson is leaving us.

I don't have to tell you what her ten years here have meant to XYZ Industries. Moving up through the ranks of the Customer Service Department, she has . . .

[The speaker briefly recounts the employee's major contributions to the department.]

Now those contributions help our customers directly and, also directly, add to our bottom line. That's reason enough to feel sad that Sarah is leaving us.

➤ Tip: Incremental structure—going from good to better, bad to worse, big to bigger, etc.—can add a touch of drama to any speech.

But there's more.

Sarah made each day a special pleasure here. She always had a smile and an encouraging word. She was the first person most of us went to for advice. She was a source of—how else can I put it?—*positive energy*. And positive energy is a resource no company can do without.

But I'm overanalyzing what Sarah's presence has meant to us. The

→ Tip: A well-placed question can be an effective way to keep a speech moving. Anticipate the question you audience wants to ask, then ask—and answer—it.

→ Tip: Here's the second part of the "bittersweet" payoff.

point is simple: She likes us, and we like her. And that is what makes us saddest about her leaving.

So why is she leaving?

Well, here's the sweet part.

Sarah is creating her own customer service consulting firm, Sarah Johnson Associates. She will be offering her expertise to a wide variety of firms—including, I'm happy to report, our own.

It takes a lot of guts to start your own company, and it's not for everyone. But, I think we all agree, Sarah's got the "right stuff," and this bold move is great step for her and will be a great benefit to any number of companies who are smart enough to call on her.

Sarah, we'll miss you, but we're proud of you, and we all wish you great success in this exciting enterprise.

EXAMPLE SPEECH

President Clinton's Speech on the Resignation of Warren Christopher

Speaker: Bill Clinton, President of the United States

We are truly about to make a new beginning. Yesterday at the wonderful welcome home that Hillary and Al and Tipper and I had at the White House, we saw a remarkable sight.

Warren Christopher was wearing a T-shirt.

He did have it on underneath his Saville Row suit. Nonetheless, it was there.

This is the same Warren Christopher, I would remind you all, who made *People Magazine*'s best dressed list, the only man ever to eat presidential M&Ms on Air Force One with a knife and fork.

Yesterday, Secretary Christopher gave new meaning to my conviction that we are entering an age of new and remarkable possibility. Today it is with great regret at his departure, but deep gratitude for his service to our administration and to our country that I have accepted Warren Christopher's decision to stand down as secretary of state.

He has left the mark of his hand on history, not in some theoretical, intangible fashion, but in the concrete ways that have made a real difference in the lives of the American people and people around the world.

He has served three previous Democratic administrations as a trade negotiator, a deputy attorney general, a deputy secretary of state, when he brought home our hostages from Iran.

These past four years I have been proud and privileged to have him by my side as secretary of state. Today if the children of the Middle East can imagine a future of cooperation, not conflict, if Bosnia's killing fields are once again playing fields, if the people of Haiti now live in democracy instead of under dictators, in no small measure it is because of Warren Christopher.

The cause of peace and freedom and decency has never had a more tireless or tenacious advocate.

Those of us who have worked with Chris know that his quiet dignity masks a steely determination.

Let me cite just one example. History will record that Bosnia's peace was secured at Dayton. It will also recall that literally until the last minute the outcome was in doubt.

Source: William J. Clinton, President of the United States, announcing the resignation of Warren Christopher, U.S. Secretary of State on November 7, 1996.

134

Our negotiators had their bags packed and were ready to head home without an agreement.

But Chris refused to give up. And the force of will finally convinced the Balkan leaders to give in to the logic of peace.

For all Secretary Christopher's skill at defusing crises, I believe his lasting legacy was built behind the headlines, laying the foundations for our future. Under his leadership, we've taken on new threats, like terrorism, the spread of weapons of mass destruction and environmental degradation.

We are seizing the opportunities to make the 21st century more secure and prosperous for every American: Working toward a Europe that is undivided, democratic and at peace; building a new partnership with a strong and open Russia; meeting the challenges of change in Asia with strength and steadiness; opening more markets abroad and helping American businesses to take advantage of these new opportunities.

Perhaps most important, Warren Christopher's life provides powerful proof that America has a unique responsibility and a unique privilege to lead. He has helped the American people understand that we cannot lead on the cheap. It takes time, energy and resources.

And, as we go forward, I pledge to protect and preserve the resources for our diplomacy that Warren Christopher has put to such good use.

Finally, let me say, as all of you know, I owe Warren Christopher a debt that extends far beyond the broad range of his responsibilities. Few individuals did more to shape my first administration. He chaired our vice presidential search committee. And I'd say he came up with a pretty good recommendation.

The American people have him to thank for my selection of Al Gore and the subsequent development of the most unique partnership in the history of the presidency and the vice presidency. And I think it is clear that the vice president has been the most influential and constructive force ever to occupy the vice presidency's office.

Warren Christopher directed the 1992 transition, in particular in building a Cabinet team that helped to put America on track as we enter the 21st century, one which a scholar of the presidency wrote me and said was the most loyal Cabinet since Thomas Jefferson's first administration.

These past four years, time and again, I have reached out to my friend for his counsel, his judgment, and his support. It is no exaggeration to say that Warren Christopher has literally been America's elder statesman.

It's also no exaggeration today that he retains the energy, the vigor, and the capacity of a person half his age. I thank Secretary Christopher for agreeing to stay on until we select a successor.

I will consult closely with him in that process. In the weeks ahead, I may have a hard time finding him, however. The secretary is continuing to do the vital business of our nation, participating next week in the Cairo conference, traveling to China and throughout Asia, moving on to Europe to work on Bosnia and adapting NATO to the future.

Secretary Christopher already has set a four-year record as America's most traveled diplomat-in-chief.

If you could earn frequent flier miles for government travel, we would owe him at least a round-trip on the space shuttle.

The vice president says that with the travel he's already logged in, he could go to the moon and back and back to the moon again. I want him to travel a few more miles so he will finish on the right planet.

Through dignity, determination, hard work and skill, through an unbelievable powerful combination of his intellect, his integrity, and his good heart Warren Christopher has earned our nation's admiration and a debt that can never be fully repaid.

From the bottom of my heart I thank him for his service to the nation and his unique friendship to the president.

EXAMPLE SPEECH

Resignation as Secretary of State—When a Higher-Level Executive Thanks You Publicly

Speaker: Warren Christopher, Secretary of State

Mr. President, it would just be absolutely impossible for me to express fully my gratitude to you for entrusting this post to me at this extraordinary moment in history. I'm grateful for the unfailing and unstinting support that you have given me in moments of high success and at the difficult times as well. I also want to thank you and Hillary for the many kindnesses that you've extended to Marie and to me and our family. I also want to express appreciation to you, Mr. Vice President, for being here today, as you always have been for me, and want to pay tribute to the remarkable role as the President said that you have played in shaping and carrying out our nation's foreign policy.

Being secretary of state is to take part in history's relay race. It's been a great privilege for me to have an opportunity to run this challenging leg over the last four years. I've done so with the sure sense that we've begun to shape American foreign policy for the 21st century. Mr. President, the world looks to the United States for leadership, and you have responded magnificently.

Thanks to your leadership, America is more secure, more prosperous, and our values are more ascendant than they were when we took office four years ago. No secretary of state could ever have had stronger support than I have had from the President and Vice President, or from my colleagues at the National Security Agency, many of whom I'm proud and pleased are here today. I've also been tremendously honored by an opportunity to work with so many talented members of the State Department, many of whom I see down here today, including the dedicated men and women of the Foreign Service and the Civil Service as well. I'm, of course, also grateful to the American people. It is their values and their aspirations that I have sought to uphold as I've traveled around the world these last four years. I'm convinced that especially at this time of change in the world, this time of challenge and change, the American people expect our nation to maintain a strong and principled

Source: Warren Christopher, Secretary of State, acknowledging President Clinton's remarks about Mr. Christopher's resignation, on November 7, 1996.

global leadership. They can be assured that I will be doing that, maintaining our active engagement, as I travel to the Middle East, Europe, and Asia over the next several weeks before the time of transition actually takes place. I've been very generously blessed by Providence, and I will leave office with a deep sense of gratitude and humility. I also leave with great confidence, Mr. President, that you are laying the foundation for the next American century. Thank you very much.

MODEL SPEECH 046:
Retirement

Key Use of Speech: A retiree says good-bye.

Style of Speech: Personal and sincere.

Audience: Company or department employees.

Time: 5 to 6 minutes.

My friends and colleagues—I am very proud and grateful that I can call you both—thank you for honoring me with this dinner. It means more to me than I can say. Unfortunately, it makes it even harder for me to leave XYZ Industries. Then again, I won't be leaving the planet—or even leaving town, for that matter. You won't get rid of me all that easily. I'll be by from time to time to pester you—**[pause a beat]** much as I've been doing for the past twenty-five years.

➡ Tip: Strike a gracious, warm, and sincere tone. Sly, affectionate humor can certainly be a part of this.

However, it is true that I won't be working with you every day. And that really is hard for me to leave behind—because working with you and with our customers has been a great joy and a challenge that has made me, I believe, the best person I *could* be. That is a real gift you and XYZ have given me.

All of you here are terrific at what you do, and you're wonderful to work with. But I want to remember, in particular, someone who isn't with us anymore. George Williams, president of XYZ, was what fancy folks would call "my mentor." That's just an elaborate way of saying that he was there to give me a well-placed kick in the pants whenever I needed it. (Which was pretty often.) The remarkable thing about George was that he could give you that kick—and make it feel good, make it feel right, make you darn glad you got it! I'm grateful to him. Anyone who knew him feels the same way.

➡ Tip: The speaker creates a community of feeling with his audience by evoking the memory of someone both he and his listeners admire and respect.

I was going to say that George Williams "taught me everything I know," but that wouldn't be *quite* true. George did teach me a lot of

139

things, but what he repeated over and over again was that I should keep my eyes and ears open and learn from *everybody* here, because *everybody* who is here has something valuable to teach. As usual, George was right.

➡ Tip: The speaker expands his tribute from George Williams to just about everybody at XYZ —that is, his audience.

I could spend the next several hours listing what everybody taught me. Here, I'll start: There is Ann Thompson, who taught me more about marketing than I could have learned from a thousand books and from a hundred professors. She's here tonight. And Ed Walters, a great customer service manager, who taught me what creating customer satisfaction really is. There's . . .

Okay, friends, relax. I won't go on with the rest of the list. That would take us into John Smith's retirement. He's almost as old as I am!

Anyway, I've got things to do. I'm not going to bed. I'm not even going fishing. In fact, I'm not really "retiring" at all. I'll be working with Senior Volunteer Service Corps, working with high school students who are interested in pursuing business careers. This is something I am very much looking forward to, and—who knows?—maybe I'll be working with your sons and daughters, corrupting their young minds.

➡ Tip: The speaker's audience will be curious about what the retiree intends to do with the rest of his life. The speaker satisfies that curiosity—and makes a joke at his own expense. Well-placed humor adds a light touch to what might otherwise be a rather melancholy occasion.

I *am* looking forward to this new experience, but, look, I know that, wonderful as it may be, it won't be the same as working with all of you. I will miss you all. I'll keep in touch, and I ask that you do the same. Thanks for everything!

EXAMPLE SPEECH

Reflections on Retirement

**Speaker: Warren Bennis, Distinguished Professor of Business,
Marshall School of Business,
University of Southern California–Los Angeles,
Founding Chairman of the Leadership Institute at USC,
Author of *Organizing Genius* (1997).**

The word "retirement" does not have a very positive connotation. My American Heritage dictionary heartily confirmed why I and others have this notion. It states, "Despite the upbeat books written about retiring and the fact that it is a well-earned time of relaxation from the daily business of work, many people do not find it a particularly pleasant prospect." Perhaps the etymology of the word "retire" may hint at why.

The ultimate source of the word is the old French word "retirer," made up of the prefix "re" meaning back and the verb "tirer" to draw together, meaning to withdraw, to take back. The first English use recorded in 1553 refers to a military force that withdraws and retreats. In regard to the sting in this, we need to look at the source of the word "tirer," meaning to draw out or endure.

This word came from the old French "martir" or in English "martyr" reflecting the fact that martyrs had to endure the torture of being stretched to and beyond the point of dislocating their bones.

That's an interesting background for the word retirement.

Aside from not being entirely happy with the word retirement, I am not completely pleased with the euphemisms for retired people like "senior citizens" or "seasoned citizens" as a friend of mine refers to us.

The second reason for my discomfort, perhaps more importantly is that this is a virgin presentation for me. I have never discussed the issues. I've just begun to think about retirement and have tried to understand my resistance to the topic. I think I had to work that through before I could even really address this subject. I also think it's arrogant of me to talk about a topic that is relatively new to me and relatively new in my thinking.

Source: Warren Bennis, Distinguished Professor of Business, Marshall School of Business, University of Southern California–Los Angeles. Founding Chairman of the Leadership Institute at USC, Los Angeles, California. Author of *Organizing Genius,* 1997. Delivered at the Kickoff Event for the new Andrus School of Gerontology at USC, Los Angeles, California, March 16, 1995. Reprinted by permission of Warren Bennis and *Vital Speeches of the Day.*

When I use the word arrogant, it reminds me very much of when I started my studies of leadership about fifteen years ago. I consulted a lot of people, including an old friend, who still teaches at the Harvard Business School. I told him I wanted to go out and spend the next ten or fifteen years seeing if I could identify the basic characteristics of exemplary, outstanding, excellent leaders to see what they were made up of, what their character was like. My friend sort of scoffed at me and said, "Look, the only thing we can ever say about leadership is that it's like pornography. You can't describe it; you can't define it, but you know it when you see it." He said, "I think it's arrogant of you to think you're going to go out and do that." When he used the word arrogant to describe me, I reminded him of the Harvard University professor's prayer. "Dear Lord, please deliver us from the terrible sin of intellectual arrogance, which for your information means . . ."

And I guess, finally and most personally, having just reached the age of seventy last week, I began thinking, maybe it's denial. Is it the Grateful Dead who have a line in a song which goes, "Denial Ain't Just a River in Egypt"? And I began thinking about that a little bit more. I guess I was jolted out of my denial, when I was attending a conference in Monterey, and somebody came up to me and said, "Didn't you used to be Warren Bennis?" That jolted me.

So anyway, here are some thoughts I'd like to share with you. I picked two basic ideas or notions that I've been thinking about. One of the thoughts was prompted by a question I was asked by a magazine on aging. During the course of the interview, they asked me: "Who were my heroes or whom do I most respect about the whole aging phenomenon?" The people's names I rattled off were the following: Winston Churchill, Bertrand Russell, Clint Eastwood, Mel Torme, Colin Powell, Bill Bradley, Grace Hopper, and Kay Graham. I began thinking. What do they all have in common?

Well think about Churchill, who really didn't get started on his career until he was 66. It was said about Churchill in one of the biographies that he jaywalked his way through life before then. Or Bertrand Russell, who as he got older, took greater risks in writing about philosophy, or Mel Torme, who keeps singing publicly at the age of 70 and keeps cresting, never coasting. All of these people never stop. They keep going on, and I began thinking there were other things they had in common.

First, they never thought about past accomplishments, or they didn't think about retiring. In fact, wouldn't a better word be "transitioning" because we're all in transition and for me, power is the capacity to move from position A to position B, to go on to something else. So these people were always in transition. I don't think they talked about retirement or past accomplishments or "they've done it." They were always redesigning, recomposing and reinventing their own lives.

Think about Colin Powell. He was a Second Lieutenant at the Fulda Gap in Germany, a recent graduate of R.O.T.C. Thirty years later he was the commanding General of the whole American Army, U.S. forces in Germany, and then from there he went to the

National Security Council. Now he's an author, and who knows what he'll be doing next, but you can bet we'll be hearing a lot more about him. Never looking back, never thinking too much about past accomplishments, but always redesigning, recomposing, and reinventing.

The other thing that interests me more about all these people and the successful executives I've known, is that at some point in their lives they stopped trying to prove themselves and began to express themselves. That transition is a very interesting one, one I'm not sure I've accomplished myself. It seems to me there is a profound difference between having to prove yourself vs. using the capacity to express yourself.

Bill Bradley, the Senator from New Jersey, is a good example of that, because it wasn't until he was almost defeated by Christine Todd Whitman in '92 that he began to think about what he was doing in politics. He began to realize that he was beginning to shade his speeches ever so subtly to please his particular audience. It wasn't that he lied or was deceitful. That wasn't it, but he found ways to spin his remarks so that they would please: to seek approval without himself really expressing himself, only trying to prove himself. He said it reminded him of when he played basketball at Princeton where he was a major college star. He said, "Even then, when I was playing for the fans, I wasn't nearly as effective a player as when I was playing to do the best I could for the team."

In his last years with the Knicks, he didn't start. He was on the bench. When he left the Knicks, he said, "Those last two years were like participating in my own death."

Bradley is a very thoughtful man, someone who gave me the inspiration to think about expressing one's self vs. proving one's self.

The second general idea I want to argue is that people who have been successful in their careers and in life, are also successful in all transitions. I think people who have not been very successful in their lives, in their careers, don't adjust well to any transition. And to them and to me, it's simply death on the installment plan. As a matter of fact, it made me think about my studies on outstanding leaders. I realized that all of the five characteristics these 150 leaders manifested in their work would all be true of successful transitions, or if you will, to use a word that I objected to earlier, successful "retirement." I'm just going to give you a brief summary of the five characteristics.

The first is a strong sense of purpose, a passion, a conviction, a sense of wanting to do something important to make a difference. That was true of every single leader. I remember talking with Michael Eisner about his own purposes. He said, "I don't know if I have a purpose, but I have a strong point of view." He said, "Its also interesting for me to watch my staff at meetings every Friday to see which of the people in that group usually win the day. We make major decisions, hundreds of millions of dollars in new projects and new movies. It's always the person with a strong P.O.V. (as he called it, a strong point of view) that wins the day, that wins the argument." He said, "Maybe it's just Hollywood, I don't know, but I'll tell you around here a strong P.O.V. is worth at least 80 I.Q. points."

Or Jack Welch, whenever he takes a new job for G.E. said, "I always want to revolutionize the place."

Again, a strong sense of purpose. Max De Pree, the recently retired chairman of Herman Miller, talked about the vision of the company as a spiritual project. (I'm using some examples from my own research on leaders because I think these characteristics make for effective transitioning in the future.) When Max De Pree used the phrase "spiritual projects," I began recalling that Ernest Becker in his treatise on death talked about the fact that our purposes in life, spiritual projects if you will, are a way in our lifetime of transcending death.

The second thing about these executives is that they are capable of developing and sustaining deep and trusting relationships. They seemed to be constant, caring and authentic with other people. If you just take purposes in life and strong intimate human relationships, I think we have at least two of the major secrets of successful transitioning.

The third characteristic is that every single one of the leaders were purveyors of hope. It was interesting to me that they all had positive illusions about reality. I had been brought up to think that mental health was dependent on perceiving reality. Now I believe these successful leaders had an almost unreal sense of "We can do it"; "I can do it." The first person I actually studied in depth was in Los Angeles. Shortly after I got to know him, he was diagnosed as having an inoperable brain tumor. He was given three years to live. Well he just retired, fifteen years after the diagnosis. Through his incredible sense of optimism and hope, he outlived all the guesses on the median age of people with that condition. As a matter of fact, he wrote a marvelous little essay, a takeoff on McCluhan, called the Median Ain't the Message.

And I must tell you one other story. Richard Wirthlin, who for some years was President Reagan's pollster, would come and visit him every other week. Shortly after the attempted assassination on Reagan's life, his approval ratings were about 90 percent, which is virtually the highest on record. A year later, before we had recovered from the recession in 1982, his poll ratings plummeted to about 30 percent. Now usually when the news was good, Wirthlin told me he had about a dozen White House assistants who wanted to come into the Oval Office and tell President Reagan about the good news. On this occasion, they shoved him solo into that room.

"You tell him, Dick."

So Dick went in and Reagan said, "Well, how was it? How are they? What do the figures look like?"

"Well, they're pretty bad, Mr. President."

"Well, how bad are they?"

"Well, they're as low as they can get."

"So what do you mean?"

"Well, they're about 32 percent."

"Anything lower than that in the second year of the presidency?" Reagan asked.

"I think that's the lowest," Wirthlin replied, kind of ruefully. At that point, Reagan's face brightened up and he smiled. "Dick, Dick, don't worry. I'll just go out there and try to get shot again."

The fourth and next to last point I want to make very briefly is that all these individuals seem to have a balance in their lives between work, power, and family or outside activities. They didn't tie up all of their self-esteem on their position in the organization. I think that's a danger sign. My predecessor at the University of Cincinnati was there for twenty years. During the student riots, when a rock came through a window in the Administration building, it was as if his skin was broken. It was a personal attack on him. Retirement wasn't easy for him because a year or so after he retired, he died.

I got a letter from a friend of mine recently, who had retired from the *Washington Post* which stated that he hadn't heard from me after he had written to me. He said, "If I was still with the *Washington Post,* would you not have responded to my letter?" And then he went on to say, "You know I identified myself so much with that newspaper, so much that I used to think that J.E. (his initials) equaled W.P. (JE =WP) and now I feel shorn of my identity." So I think that balance has to be maintained.

My final point is that although all of these individuals could be reflective, they all had a bias toward action. They all were people who seemed not to hesitate in taking risks, who while not reckless, were able to take action. They love adventure, risk and promise.

As an example, I love to reflect on the autobiography of J. Paul Getty. He once wrote that he had three rules for success in business. One was get up early. The second was work hard, and the third was find oil.

I want to conclude along these lines with a quotation from my favorite management philosopher, the great one, Wayne Gretzky, who said, "You miss 100 percent of the shots you don't take."

And I think that's what I'm talking about when I talk about successful transitioning.

Financial Reports, Meeting About

Opening

——*Ladies and gentlemen, welcome to your company's 45th annual stockholders' meeting.*

——*It is my pleasure and honor to welcome you to our annual stockholders' meeting.*

Closings

——*I trust that you will agree with me that we've had a wonderfully productive year, and that there is every indication that we can look forward to many more.*

——*There is no point in denying that we have had a challenging year. But we have met those challenges, and we are now positioned for growth and profit. Thank you.*

MODEL SPEECH 047:
Financial Report to Executives and Managers

Key Use of Speech:	A CEO reports to her executives and frontline managers.
Style of Speech:	Team-building, showing strong leadership.
Audience:	Company executives and managers.
Time:	10 to 15 minutes. [Depends how much detail is provided.]

Last week you received the quarter's financials. I trust you've had time to study the figures and to think about our performance. I suppose I should apologize for not serving turkey and stuffing at this meeting, since, in many ways, it is a thanksgiving. We've performed well this last quarter, and our numbers show it. I want to thank you all for your hard work and steady leadership.

This statement does not, however, conclude the meeting. We have reason to be thankful—for performance that ranges from great down to good. I've worked with all of you long enough to know that you don't consider the "good" a reason for self-congratulations. You won't be pleased until we're "great" across the board.

Let's look at the trends.

Sales increased **[percentage amount]** in the quarter just ended, and we have every reason to expect similar performance in the current quarter. This is certainly in the "great" range. But there is a "but." While sales have risen, so has cost of sales—by **[percentage amount]** this last quarter. This factor has brought our actual revenue increase down away from the "great" range and toward the "good."

Ladies and gentlemen, we need to work together on a plan to

➥ Tip: When you speak to an audience of experts, be careful to avoid telling them how to interpret data. Instead, guide them by presenting the context in which you want the data viewed.

149

decrease our cost of sales—that is, to sell more efficiently. Here is how I want us to start.

[The speaker outlines an action plan delegating certain managers to study the cost-of-sales situation and report by a certain date.]

Once we have the group's report, we will meet again to discuss it and to formulate a program for reducing the cost of sales.

Now, while we're on the subject of sales, I am concerned that we have been so productive in this area that we will soon find that our current markets have matured. Sales growth will begin to level, despite our best efforts. So I take this quarterly report as a wake-up call in addition to a cause for thanksgiving. We need to accelerate our current efforts to develop new markets. Now, I know that the marketing group is working hard in this direction—but I also know that there is a sense throughout the company that things are going so well, why risk probing new markets? This is an understandable attitude. If it ain't broke, don't fix it. Common sense and understandable. But not the way we should be thinking. Precisely because we are exploiting our current markets so effectively and rapidly, we need to develop new markets. This is no time for complacency. I would like to see increased support for the marketing group. Beginning on **[date]**, the people in this room will meet with the marketing group for informal discussion and brainstorming. We will also set some goals, so that we can be specific about what new markets to develop and how many potential sales we want to add per year.

Folks, these are things this very impressive quarterly report tells me. It is not that we *have* to do better, because we're doing pretty well. But because we're doing so well, we *can* do better, and, I think you'll agree with me, that is something we should plan to do. Based on this report, I am confident that we certainly can.

———————

MODEL SPEECH 048:
Financial Report
to Financial Analysts

Key Use of Speech:	A CEO reports to financial analysts.
Style of Speech:	Frank and positive, with the object of "selling" the viability of the company.
Audience:	Financial analysts.
Time:	10 to 15 minutes. [Depends on level of detail supplied.]

→ Tip: In speaking to financial analysts, expect skepticism. Begin by laying out the situation in "executive summary" fashion. Paint a quick, clear, believable picture.

→ Tip: A good speaker directs his audience by providing ongoing evaluation of the information presented: we have survived, but we will do better than survive in the future.

I don't have to tell an assembly of top financial analysts that **[year]** was a difficult one for many general retailers. We all faced such problems as . . . **[speaker lists the main problems].** As a result, **[number]** retailers reported record *low* earnings for the year and record *high* losses. XYZ Stores fared better than most, I'm pleased to say, with earnings for the year at **[$ amount]**—down, it is true, from the year before, when we earned **[$ amount],** but **[percentage amount]** higher than the average of any of our competitors. XYZ remains the leading general retailer in **[region].**

All in all, we've not only survived a very difficult year, we have maintained our leadership during it. But, ladies and gentlemen, it has never been our policy at XYZ merely to *survive* and *maintain.* We have always embraced development and growth, and I want to assure you that we have acted decisively to put the problems of last year behind us:

[The speaker lists programs started to boost performance in the coming year.]

151

→ Tip: The speaker provides a succinct reason to invest in XYZ.

We are confident that our sustained performance under pressure combined with a spirit of innovation rather than a retreat into a "hunker down" posture makes XYZ Stores a most attractive investment opportunity now and in the future.

But *you* are the professionals, and I will not presume to tell you how to read our financials. I *will,* however, suggest that you read them in light of what I am about to tell you. As you review our financials, you will see that we are planning to invest **[$ amount]** in new facilities for the coming year. We believe that this investment will result in a **[percentage amount]** increase in revenue for the year.

→ Tip: In investment, past and current performance are important, but, remember, investment is all about the future. A financial speech delivered to investment professionals should emphasize future prospects.

That's great. But it isn't the most important investment we will make. While many of our competitors were understandably occupied with digging trenches and making every effort to hold the fort, we have been *thinking*. It is clear that *ideas* are becoming the real engines of growth in the wealth of nations and the wealth of companies. In a time when our competitors are withdrawing funding from new product development, we are increasing ours. We are inaugurating a Special Projects Group, which has as its mandate the accelerated development of new product directions. Let me tell you how this new group will work.

[The speaker discusses the Special Projects Group.]

→ Tip: The speaker sells what is truly innovative about the proposed program.

The unique feature of the Special Projects Group is that it will not be tied to a lockstep calculation of return on investment. We want to give this group the freedom to innovate. We will look at its performance in the long run, of course, but we are determined to give the Special Projects Group the time and space needed to create new products for new markets.

→ Tip: The speaker closes with a big-picture view of the scope of the investment opportunity.

Ladies and gentlemen, I won't insult you by offering you a program that asks your clients to invest in a company that is merely holding its own. We *have* held our own. We are a sound and secure investment, but we are so much more than that. Renewed and sustained growth means investing *now* in knowledge and ideas in the same way we have invested in machines. Investment spurs knowledge. Knowledge spurs investment. XYZ Stores is investing in knowledge and ideas, and we, in turn, are offering your clients the opportunity to invest *with* us—to share the *risk,* to be sure, but also to share the *excitement* and the *rewards*. Real business growth stems from knowledge, from new and better ways of doing things, from ideas that create new products as well as new markets. We are living and working in an Age of Ideas and Innovation, and we at XYZ are determined to lead that age. We invite you to join us.

OUTLINE

Opening

- Difficult year
- Our performance better than that of competitors

Development plans

- We survived, but we want to do more
- Look toward the future
- Investment in new facilities

Special projects group

- What it is
- Accelerated development of new products
- How the group will work
- Freedom to innovate

Closing

- We represent a great investment opportunity
- Invitation to share the risks and rewards

MODEL SPEECH 049:
Financial Report to Stockholders

Key Use of Speech: A CEO reports to stockholders.

Style of Speech: Frank, positive, forward-looking.

Audience: Stockholders at annual meeting.

Time: 10 to 15 minutes. [Depends on how much
                     detail is provided.]

→ Tip: When the news is good, let the good news do the talking. Without preliminaries, the speaker dishes up the opening information.

→ Tip: The key word is highlights. Complex figures are best presented in printed, not spoken form.

→ Tip: Good performance demands explanation just as poor performance does. The impression you want to leave is that the company's success is planned and controlled, not the result of random market conditions or good luck.

Ladies and gentlemen, the financial period ending last October marked three straight years of record income for XYZ Corporation. In **[year]**, XYZ emerged not only as the revenue leader in this industry, but as the leader by any measure of profitability. We have, for the third year in a row, combined higher sales and earnings with, yet again, increased dividends. I am proud to say that this puts XYZ among an elite group of American companies.

Let's hit some of the highlights. Sales rose **[percentage figure]** to **[$ amount]** for the year, and those all-important net earnings did even better, advancing **[percentage figure]** to **[$ amount],** which comes to **[$ amount]** per share.

What accounts for this level of performance?

[Speaker reviews a brief list of success factors, such as better advertising, new store locations, etc.]

Now, I believe it was the British playwright Oscar Wilde who said "Every silver lining has a cloud." Frankly, I've looked hard, and I'm hard-pressed to find the gloom in all this glory. If there *is* one problem we need to confront, it's the specter of complacency. No company, even one as successful as we have been, can afford to sit on its **[pause for a beat]** laurels.

➜ Tip: It is critically important to strike a balance between continuing to grow and innovate, on the one hand, and not, on the other hand, tampering with a good thing. The speaker emphasizes a program of controlled expansion, with monitoring.

➜ Tip: When speaking to investors, it is customary to refer to "the" company as "your" company. The speaker thereby acknowledges the role of the investors as the real owners of the firm.

➜ Tip: Don't forget the folks in the trenches—the employees!

Here's what we have planned for next year. First and foremost is a program of continued, controlled expansion. We will open **[number]** new stores in **[year]**, and we are working toward a target of **[number]** stores nationwide by **[target year]**. I want to emphasize that this will be *controlled* expansion. Performance will be monitored rigorously, and we will maintain flexibility, adjusting our goals upward—or downward—as necessary.

These new stores will be state-of-the-art facilities. Over the past **[number]** years, your company has invested more than **[$ amount]** in new inventory systems, which have resulted in ... **[speaker summarizes bottom-line impact of new inventory systems]**. We are determined to ensure that XYZ remains the leading **[type of chain]** in America.

Now, our balance sheet is very strong, and our financial condition is excellent. Your Board of Directors once again voted a dividend increase—though of a sufficiently conservative amount to assure needed cash for our continued accelerated growth. There's no need to take the money and run. It is obvious that we have a great future, and if we fund growth prudently, our long-term viability and the potential for continued stock appreciation will be greatly enhanced. Not that the December quarterly dividend will be shabby at **[number]** cents per share, an increase of **[percentage amount]** to a rate of **[number]** cents yearly.

We're gratified with the results your company achieved last year, and we're confident in the continued and growing overall strength of your company and its market sector. I know that you will join me in thanking each of our **[number]** employees for their extraordinary contribution to this success. With them, we can all look forward to another successful year for XYZ.

OUTLINE

Opening

- Three years of record income
- We are the leader
- We are in an elite group

Year's highlights

- Sales rose
- Net earnings rose

Why were we so successful?

- Success factors

Problems?

- Only one: danger of complacency

Plans for next year

- Continued expansion
- Expansion target
- Flexibility

Closing

- Regarding dividends
- Gratified with results of the year
- Look forward to another great year
- Thanks to employees

Funerals

Openings

——*This is a sad day, but I would like to spend some small part of it recalling with you the events of a happy life.*

——*It is difficult to believe that Ed Walters will not be in the office tomorrow. He was our rock. We depended on him. He never let us down.*

Closings

——*Ed, goodbye, old friend. We will miss you, and we're sorry you won't be around to see how well we are doing with the company you built.*

——*Let's not be bitter about our loss. Let's think instead about how fortunate we were to have had Mary Wilson with us for so long.*

MODEL SPEECH 050:
Eulogy

Key Use of Speech: To remember the deceased at a funeral or
                     memorial service.

Style of Speech: Sincere, personal.

Audience: Mourners, colleagues of the deceased.

Time: 5 to 6 minutes.

➜ Tip: The sincere eulogy is made most convincing by identifying the specific, rather than general, qualities of the deceased.

It is no secret that Fran Booth was a perfectionist. In fact, she was the only perfectionist I ever really felt comfortable working with. She did not rest until the last detail of a project was completed—not just to her satisfaction, but to the satisfaction of everyone involved. Fran was *always* a perfectionist, but she had the magical power to turn *everyone* else into a perfectionist, too, at least for the length of time it took to see a project through from beginning to end. Fran made us all better than we were.

But this doesn't come as news to any of us.

To me, the real surprise is that she permitted the good Lord to take her from us. I mean, I would have expected her to argue God into making a few modifications first. She wasn't *finished* yet. She wasn't ever *satisfied* with herself. She always saw room for improvement. I'm just surprised she agreed to anything like a compromise—because Fran saw sloppiness, chaos even, in compromise. Certainly, she saw to it that everything our firm produced was the very best we could do, and when we reached that very best, she congratulated us—then raised the bar a notch higher.

➜ Tip: Gentle humor is not out of place in a eulogy, as long as it reflects affectionately and respectfully on the deceased. A eulogy is not supposed to make the mourners feel even worse than they already do.

I apologize for this speech. I apologize to you and to Fran. I *am* making her sound like a neurotic taskmaster.

But, fortunately, we all knew her, and we know that the truly

→ Tip: The speaker amplifies the unique quality of the deceased— that of being a likable perfectionist.

remarkable thing about Fran is that working with her was always a pleasure. She brought out the best in us all without being a taskmaster. None of us ever resented her insistence on doing things right. She got us to work in ways we never thought of working before. And *that* was exciting. It was a gift. It was like being given a gift every time you sat down to work.

Fran was short and slight, and she spoke in a soft voice. She didn't look like the courageous innovator she was. But she *dared* and *dared* repeatedly. Who would dare to try to improve on the design of our top-selling Model XYZ?

→ Tip: The speaker reviews a few of the deceased's specific accomplishments.

Fran dared.

And now the "top" has been redefined. We have a new state of the art.

And here's something even more important: she moved each of *us* to dare as well.

We loved Fran. We'll miss her. We'll miss the sheer excitement of having her around, daring us, daring herself, and daring us to dare ourselves.

She's left us quite a legacy, a legacy of innovation that is the envy of the industry. We won't lose that legacy, but it *will* be that much harder to maintain our leadership position, now that Fran is not there to urge us along.

→ Tip: Addressing the deceased is often appropriate and effective in a eulogy, especially to bid farewell.

We owe Fran a great deal. We can honor her memory by continuing to accept the challenges. We are better at our jobs—and we are just plain *better*—for having known and worked with Fran Booth.

Fran, godspeed. We miss you.

Gifts

Openings

——*Thank you for your gift. It is beautiful, of course, but its true value is that it was you, the people I work with, depend on, and respect so very deeply, who gave it to me.*

——*I am simply overwhelmed by your kindness and generosity.*

Closings

——*The best thing about this gift is that I will think of all of you every time I use it.*

——*Once again, my deepest thanks. I am thrilled with this wonderful gift.*

MODEL SPEECH 51:
Appreciation of Gift Received

Key Use of Speech: A manager thanks his or her staff for a gift.

Style of Speech: Sincere, personal, grateful.

Audience: Department employees.

Time: 1 to 2 minutes.

→ Tip: The difference between a polite thank you and a sincere expression of gratitude is a demonstration that the gift is personally valuable to you, that the giver(s) connected with you personally.

It's easy to go out and buy a gift. But you folks *never* take the easy way—not if there's a better, more creative approach. Now, I talk enough about my book collection to believe that my being a book collector is common knowledge. But you had to do a lot of digging to find out just what I *don't* have in my collection, and then you had to do even more work to track down a first edition of Hawthorne's *Scarlet Letter*. And in such condition! This is a real treasure, and I am very moved by this gift—not just because of the intrinsic value of the gift (though that thrills me, folks!), but because of the thought and caring that went into this gift. You people are the greatest! Thank you for this—and for everything!

MODEL SPEECH 052:
Presentation of Gift

Key Use of Speech: A manager presents a gift to an employee as a token of achievement.

Style of Speech: Sincere, personal, grateful.

Audience: Department employees.

Time: 1 to 2 minutes.

Pete Williams, I'm about to give you something very nice. It's a [identify gift]. I say it's nice, because it's something I would like to have, but can never seem to justify spending the money on. To me, that's the definition of a "nice gift."

But, Pete, this gift is just a symbol, a token of the appreciation all of us in management feel. You've given us all the *real* gift. Because of your hard work and innovative attitude, [the speaker goes on to describe Pete Williams's achievement]. And, nice as what we're giving you is, well, it's not a fair exchange, and it's not meant to be. But whenever you use [gift], I hope that it will remind you of how grateful and proud we all are about having you work with us. Enjoy. And thanks!

→ Tip: The speaker begins with a bit of banter, which is appropriate to the warm relationship between this supervisor and employee. Be careful not to let such banter undercut the significance of the occasion, however. Don't belittle the employee or his accomplishment.

Goals, Corporate

Openings

——*When I started my management career, I made a promise to myself that I would be the one speechmaker who never quoted Yogi Berra. "You got to be very careful if you don't know where you're going," Yogi Berra once said, "because you might not get there." Okay, so I've broken my promise. The point is—we need to talk about goals.*

——*Today, ladies and gentlemen, is a day for understanding where we are as a company, and where we want to be.*

Closings

——*The goals I've set forth are realistic, but they require us to stretch. That's what makes them exciting. That's what makes them worth doing.*

——*The goals we've just discussed will not be easy to accomplish, but I know that, being the team that you are, we will succeed. I look forward to the coming year. Thank you.*

MODEL SPEECH 053:
Plans to Expand
in an Expanding Economy

Key Use of Speech:	A CEO presents a plan for growth in good times.
Style of Speech:	Informal, frank, well-reasoned, inbspiring.
Audience:	Company managers.
Time:	12 to 15 minutes. [Depends on how much detail is given.]

→ Tip: The speaker speaks the language of business: money. Nothing catches the attentlon of business audience faster or more surely.

Our sales for the year advanced **[$ amount increase]** to **[$ amount]**, and net earnings did even better, totaling **[$ amount],** up **[percentage amount]** from **[$ amount]** the year before.

Now this next part of the speech should be the fun part for me. This should be the part where I take the credit for leading this company to one success after another. Okay. I'm not *quite* that bad. I'd be willing to share the credit with every one of you here. You deserve it, of course.

But it's a funny thing. If the situation were 180 degrees different from what it is, if sales were down and earnings down, I wouldn't be so eager to take the credit, would I? I'd probably blame the economy.

The fact is that the nation's economy is healthy, growing, and very friendly to our business, retail sales. So shouldn't I give some of the *credit* for our success to the economy?

→ Tip: The speaker begins to outline a plan for making the most of a healthy economy.

Well, maybe "the economy" doesn't need my praise and congratulations, but, nevertheless, some *part* of our success is a result of the sustained upturn in economic conditions, and I want, as a company, for us to do more than merely *acknowledge* that fact. I want us to take advantage of it.

Our expertise and skill can be leveraged by the economic conditions now prevailing. Ladies and gentlemen, this is the moment to unroll our three-year plan for growth. We are among the top three retailers in *all* of our current markets. Now that we have established a firm base in the Midwest, the time will never be better to expand into two additional major markets: the Northwest and the Southwest.

[The speaker outlines a three-year plan for opening stores in the new regions.]

➛ Tip: An effective speaker anticipates the feelings and thoughts of his audience. Here the speaker addresses the leave-well-enough-alone philosophy.

Folks, we could just lie back and bask in the warmth of this current economy. We're doing—well, we're doing just great! Why not leave "just great" alone?

The answer is twofold. First, the problem with setting records is the expectation that you will continue breaking them again and again. This expectation is *our* expectation—not the public's. For *us*, "status quo" is an unacceptable phrase. For *us*. That's who we are, and how we operate.

But, second, is the knowledge, the certain knowledge, that the great times won't always be great. Right *now*, the economy will help us, push us, to expand. We need to take advantage of this boost now, so that we can take control of new markets. Once we're there, we'll establish stores for good times and not-so- good times. We'll establish ourselves in the strongest possible position now, so that the strength will be there when the economy softens.

➛ Tip: A good leader puts the beliefs of his organization into an effective phrase or slogan.

But our plan for growth involves more than expansion into new markets. We will continue to develop and expand within our current markets as well. We tell people that we're in the retail business. Actually, we're in the preservation-of-time business. Our stores are set up and located to save the customer time. That is a key aspect of the value we add to the customer's each and every purchase. Our dedication to convenience is fanatical. We gladly admit that. And a big part of convenience is location. We need to make it easy to shop. How does the customer define "ease of shopping"? Number one is convenience of location. That means: *I shop at a store near me.*

Here's how we plan to develop and expand within our current markets.

[The speaker lays out this aspect of the expansion program.]

Let's get going *now,* because, while we will surely be stronger, we don't know if the overall economy will be. This is the golden hour for us. And to those who warn that these good times won't last, I wholeheartedly agree. We're *not* building for the good times. We're using the good times to help us build for whatever conditions develop. Control of the market is good in good times, and it is even more important when times turn rough. Let's move!

MODEL SPEECH 054:
Plans to Ride Through Recession

Key Use of Speech: A CEO presents a plan for operating in a poor
                     economy.

Style of Speech: Clear and informative, with an emphasis on
                     leadership.

Audience: Company managers.

Time: 12 to 15 minutes.

→ Tip: The speaker
begins by delivering
straight talk stripped of
bureaucratic euphemism.

Good afternoon. I've asked you to gather with me today to talk about
the goals we need to attain during what is proving to be a prolonged
economic downturn. That's the economists' term for it. You may call
it a "slump." I call it just plain *hard times*.

During times like this it may seem obvious that only one goal really
counts: survival.

Well, that's a fine goal. It's one we share with amoebas and viruses.
I'm not saying it isn't an important goal, but XYZ Industries, I believe,
is at least a few rungs up from the amoeba on the evolutionary ladder.
I propose we do more than survive. I propose that we become *more
effective* in using the terrific resources that we have.

→ Tip: The speaker
asserts leadership by
proposing a proactive
rather than merely
reactive goal.

To accomplish this, I propose two major objectives for our near
future:

1. A move away from diversification and back to doing what we're
best at.
2. The use of outsourcing to enable us to focus on what we do best.

What has been driving us? I believe this can be summed up by two
words: control and dominance. Our strategy has been integration to

170

achieve control and dominance, always expanding, always seeking to extend the scope of the enterprise. We defined our company as, quite simply, *everything*. Bigger was better, and the more stages of production under the corporation's control, the more the corporation could crowd out the competition. We got into every phase of manufacturing, distributing, and even financing widgets.

Then we took this strategy a step further. We diversified, acquired whole new lines of business unrelated to our core products. Our reasoning was that broadening our base afforded protection: if one market declined, another market would expand. Diversification was supposed to average out the bad times while amplifying the good times.

Well, that was the theory.

For decades we grew and we prospered by this strategy, but, slowly and quietly, our competitors began to get a foothold in our traditional markets. Now, with the general economy retreating, we have to move quickly not just to maintain our market share but to regain lost market share.

We're going to do this not by expanding, but by concentrating—by concentrating on the things we do best. Let's face it: the old way of diversification has crumbled because we have had difficulty being "best in the world" at all of the things we attempted. We can't afford that now.

We're going to bring our corporate mission into sharper focus, and that means leveraging more of our talent, more time, and more resources to more singular goals. Our goal is to restructure such that by **[year]**, we will engage only in activities that directly relate to our core business: the design, manufacture, and marketing of great widgets.

We can sum up our near-term strategy in three words: focus, focus, focus.

Creating customer satisfaction through focus, through doing a few things better than anyone else, is the target of this strategy.

To help us hit this target, we will be looking for ways to reduce overhead—and to reduce everything that blurs our central focus. The chief means of accomplishing this will be a new program of outsourcing. We currently employ a dizzying array of specialized personnel, including data processors, accountants, mail clerks, lawyers, janitors, cafeteria workers, security guards, copywriters, nurses, painters. All of these folks do important jobs, but none of them works directly with widgets. We invest tremendous resources in these employees, in the

➔ Tip: Nothing is more persuasive than careful, reasoned analysis of a problem.

➔ Tip: The speaker distinguishes between long-term and short-term goals.

form of salaries, benefits, training, work space, and capital equipment. Outsourcing these kinds of functions would free up management and allow us to focus our talent on widgets and only widgets: our core business.

The outsourcing program will not be developed and carried out painlessly. Managers will have to get used to relinquishing a degree of control. We will lose personnel, and, as a consequence, morale may suffer. People will wonder if *theirs* will be the next function to be outsourced. Well, the fact is that the outsourced functions will not actually disappear. They will just relocate, and many of the jobs will relocate, too. XYZ Corporation will work with our outsourcing partners to help relocate employees whose positions are outsourced.

Finally, I don't want us to view outsourcing as a strictly defensive strategy. We'll lose if we do view it that way. Outsourcing is a positive strategic decision that will enable us to focus on basics in order to meet a hard economy with successful flexibility.

As to those core individuals who remain with XYZ, they will be given greater opportunity and responsibility than ever before. This is good for XYZ, and it's good for individual careers. That opportunity begins *with* the responsibility of holding this company together effectively as we go through a challenging reorganization, repositioning, and rededication.

→ Tip: Having carefully laid the groundwork of analysis of the current crisis, the speaker discusses the outsourcing solution.

OUTLINE

Opening

- Talk about goals
- Economic downturn

Number one goal: survival

- How we will survive
- How we will prosper
- Major objectives for the near future

The past

- Philosophy of control and dominance
- Philosophy of bigger is better

- Diversification strategy
- Situation has changed

New strategy

- Concentration, not diversification
- Focus corporate mission
- Reduce overhead

Outsourcing plans

- Need to relinquish some control
- We will lose personnel
- Outsourcing as a positive step

Closing

- New strategy will give employees greater responsibility
- Will give greater opportunity
- Will provide brighter future

MODEL SPEECH 055:
Plans to Ensure Quality

Key Use of Speech:	A CEO presents a plan for ensuring quality.
Style of Speech:	Frank, well-reasoned
Audience:	Company managers.
Time:	7 to 8 minutes. [Depends on how much detail is given.]

Ladies and gentlemen, we are facing a crisis.

[pause]

I'll let that hang in the air for a moment, because, to look at our annual report and our last quarterly report, you'd never know this statement to be true. Sales are up. Net income is up. What's the problem? Where's the crisis?

As sales have risen, calls to customer service have risen. That's to be expected. But look at *how* they have risen:

[Speaker uses a graph to show that customer service calls outpace sales growth. The graph shows a widening gap between the two.]

This is serious, and, if we allow this gap to continue to grow, we will lose customers because we will fail to satisfy them.

Now, we are not alone. Recent studies have shown that one-quarter to one-third of the time and resources at large companies today are spent *fixing* problems. This is a huge expenditure of resources channeled into *undoing* things instead of *doing* things. Another name for this is *waste*.

In consultation with top management, I have decided to institute here at XYZ Corporation a new quality-control program. It will target three areas:

1. Operations
2. Products, and
3. Customer service.

Quality of operations is one of the keys to profitability. We must lower costs while increasing the efficiency of day-to-day operations. These are *not* mutually exclusive objectives, but, rather, mutually dependent goals. For if we become more efficient, we *will* reduce costs. It costs money to do things wrong.

The second major focus of quality control is on the products themselves. I have appointed a Quality Assurance Committee, which will begin a three-month review of all of our manufacturing quality-control procedures. At the end of the review period, the committee will issue a report and recommendations. Already, however, we have established a goal of **[percentage amount]** decrease in defective product leaving our plants—*and* a **[percentage amount]** *increase* in customer satisfaction as measured by a customer survey program we will introduce next year.

But, in the final analysis, the key to quality control in our industry is how the customer is handled on the telephone, by written communication, or in person. An idea I am asking all managers to communicate, repeatedly, is the belief that customers represent a long-term relationship, not just a transaction. You managers will get corporate support through our renewed commitment to recruiting and developing the highest level of human resources. We intend to stay ahead of the quality-of-service curve by training employees in customer service and by recognizing excellence in customer service with tangible rewards and bonuses. We are bringing customer service out of the back office and putting it up front, where it belongs.

I am confident that together we can close the quality gap and continue to grow at an even more impressive and dramatic rate, one satisfied customer at a time.

OUTLINE

Opening

- Facing a crisis
- Facing a crisis—even though our financial situation is good

The crisis: quality

- Increased calls to customer service
- If trend is unchecked, will lose customers
- Other companies suffer similar problems
- Need to get edge on competition by fixing the problems

New quality-control program

- Operations
- Products
- Customer service

Closing

- Expression of confidence
- We will close the quality gap

Government Regulation

Openings

——*I come to you today to talk about means and ends, about balance, about—sanity.*

——*If you expect me to bash the idea of government regulation today, you'll be disappointed. If you expect me to criticize how that idea is being applied, then you've come to the right place.*

Closings

——*Ladies and gentlemen, we need to get together on this issue, or we'll find that our ability to compete has been chipped away—and the regulators won't have anything to regulate.*

——*My friends, thank you for your attention this afternoon. I hope that you will agree that we have a common cause here, one worth working together to resolve. Thank you.*

MODEL SPEECH 056:
Bureaucratic Overkill

Key Use of Speech: To appeal for common-sense reform of government bureaucracy.

Style of Speech: Level-headed, straight-talking.

Audience: Community organizations, media, general corporate outreach.

Time: 12 to 15 minutes.

I want to talk with you about folklore. Maybe you have some ideas about what "folklore" is: something to do with folk songs, old ballads, childlike paintings by Grandma Moses, Currier and Ives snow scenes, tall tales about Paul Bunyan and the like.

Well, I'm here to tell you that, today, folklore is something different. It's not about tall tales told by an old man whittling on a wrap-around porch. No. The folklore of today is all about bureaucracy.

You hear it all the time.

While our ancestors might have gathered by the fireside to swap stories about hunting a bear in the woods or wrestling with gators in the swamp, many of us congregate around the martini bar, swapping stories about our latest encounter with government red tape. And these are all such long, painful shaggy dog stories, almost always involving some grotesque Catch-22 scenario in which you need A to get B, but can't get A until you obtain C through Z, only to find out that you can't get Z without having B. For example . . .

[The speaker narrates one or two typically astounding "shaggy dog" bureaucracy stories.]

You would think that stories such as these would be so unbeliev-able that speakers who tell them, like me, would have to hook themselves up to a lie detector on top of a stack of Bibles, and they *still* wouldn't be believed. I mean, a story of abduction by UFO-borne alien life forms is more believable than this! Right?

But, no. We have no trouble believing any number of bureaucracy shaggy dog stories, and the shaggier they are, the more credible they seem. Why? Because we've all been there.

Well, I appreciate being believed. But it scares me, too. Because accepting these stories as true without hesitation is just a step ahead of accepting the *inevitability* of an insane and crippling bureaucracy. Once we cease to find such stories unbelievable—incredible—we begin to think that, bad as it is, the bureaucracy is unchangeable.

A lot of us felt that way about, say, the Berlin Wall. It stood for a long time. We hated it, but we accepted it. Finally, though, enough people began to question it and to reject it, and the Berlin Wall fell, and so did the only bureaucratic structure bigger and dumber than our own, the Soviet Union.

But you *have* to start questioning this Berlin Wall of bureaucracy. If you complain about it, but accept it, it will stand, and it will get higher and fatter and bigger.

Maybe some of you remember the early days of the personal computer. The speed of microprocessors was improved so rapidly that development of faster hardware sometimes outstripped the ability of software to cope. You could buy a little program whose function was to *slow down* the microprocessor so that it could handle the older programs. It hobbled the hardware by making it work on nonproductive calculations at the same time that it processed the older program. That is, it made the processor waste time and energy and effort.

Well, the software side of the industry soon caught up—and even overtook—the hardware side of the industry, and we have had no need for such "hobbling" programs for some years now. Nobody uses them. Why would you want to waste your computer's high-speed hardware? That's crazy.

Yet while we have all had the common sense to discard useless computer programs that waste time and effort, and while brave people tore down the Berlin Wall brick by brick, few of us ever think about even questioning the bureaucracy that hobbles our efforts, that causes *every* American business to burn time and energy and cash that would otherwise be invested in improving products, lowering costs, and becoming increasingly competitive in the global market.

"Everybody talks about the weather, but nobody does anything about it."

If I stopped right here, that old saying would be the perfectly appropriate response to this speech. But the bureaucracy is not the weather. *We* built it, *we* support it, and *we can* stop supporting it and start unbuilding it.

How? We are being given the opportunity to take a first step. Congressman John Doe has introduced a bill to reform reporting procedures . . .

[The speaker briefly explains the bill, outlining how it will reduce bureaucracy.]

Make no mistake, this bill is no panacea. It will not bring down the Berlin Wall. It will, however, chip away at the first few bricks in that wall. And that was the beginning of the end of that "permanent" structure. Or, as the Chinese say, "A journey of a thousand miles begins with a single step."

You—we—can take that step, can pry loose that first brick. Here's how.

[The speaker explains what individuals can do to help secure passage of the bill.]

It's up to you. It's up to us. We complain that the government makes it hard, very hard, to take action in our day-to-day business. Now we have an invitation, *presented by the government,* to take action ourselves. Let's do it!

MODEL SPEECH 057:
Environmental Regulation:
The Good and the Ridiculous

Key Use of Speech:	To talk about the need for moderation, intelligence, and balance in formulating and applying government regulation.
Style of Speech:	Informal, personal, frank.
Audience:	Community organizations, media, general corporate outreach.
Time:	10 to 12 minutes.

→ Tip: A crystal-clear statement of subject at the outset is a key to successful speaking. Here the statement has been honed to a single word: Balance. The word will be repeated at strategic points throughout the speech.

Balance. That's what I want to talk about today—keeping environmental issues and economic issues in perspective. Environmentalists and government regulators want to save the planet. That is a laudable goal. But it is one that will take more than environmentalists and government regulators. It will take balance, a balance between the allocation of resources and preserving the environment. If we can achieve that, we will, indeed, save the planet.

Now, I'm in the chemical business, and, let's face it, the chemical business has a bad rep as far as the environment goes. Let's talk about that rep: If you listen to the environmentalists and the regulators, you'd believe we were in the business of pollution.

Well, let me tell you what business we're *really* in:

→ Tip: The language of business is dollars. Dollars speak loudly. Use dollars—and other numbers—sparingly but prominently. They make for powerful persuasion.

[The speaker briefly describes the business, emphasizing the range of useful and essential products produced and the dollars invested in the local economy, number of jobs, dollars invested in local salaries.]

Now, those are big numbers. Here are some more:

[Speaker describes company's environmental initiatives, with strong emphasis on dollar amounts spent and on percentage of revenue devoted to environmental protection. Speaker describes key innovative waste-treatment and recycling projects.]

→ Tip: A speech that redefines the familiar and expected in new and unexpected ways is always compelling. Here the motive for environmental responsibility is redefined from the expected—government regulation—to the unexpected: the profit motive.

The fact is this: We're making good progress cleaning up the environment. **[Speaker cites supporting statistics.]** Yes, of course, we need to accomplish more. Well, we will. We're not standing still.

But it's not the EPA or any other government regulator that's pushing us along. The incentive for reducing waste is the bottom line on a balance sheet, not the top line on an EPA list.

Friends, waste costs money. It hurts when you make it, and it hurts when you have to get rid of it. The incentive? Don't make waste in the first place. That's just good business sense.

Good business policy makes good environmental policy, not the other way around.

→ Tip: Look for opportunities to turn a phrase. Pithy statements are what your listeners will retain longest.

The chemical industry provides some of this country's highest-paying jobs, and that increases our standard of living. Moreover, chemicals—our product—raise the standard of living, providing life-saving drugs, increasing the productivity of farms, extending the longevity of houses with special paints, and on and on.

Is manufacturing chemicals safe? If by "safe" you mean without risk, the answer is no. The notion of a zero-risk society, which some environmental and regulatory extremists demand, is unreasonable. There is no reward without risk. Risks are inherent in life. Every day we assess and judge risk, then take action accordingly.

But let us suppose that zero risk were possible to achieve. What does zero risk mean? The Food and Drug Administration, a very conservative federal agency, says that a risk of one-in-a-million equals zero. But the environmental regulators of the EPA want even *less* of a risk. The result: crippling regulation that reduces the quality of life, and, with a reduced quality of life, risks actually increase: more people will die because chemicals are not available to fight disease, and fewer people will have jobs, because the cost of producing chemical products—or other "risky" products—will become prohibitive. With people out of work, what kinds of risks does our society face?

→ Tip: If you want to change people's minds, you have to do more than tell them what to think. Present the evidence, clearly and concisely. Guide your audience toward the conclusion you want them to reach. Don't force them toward it.

Blind regulation is out of balance. It puts our environment out of balance—and at risk.

Remember, ladies and gentleman, the so-called *natural* environment is not our only pressing problem. The quality of human life, the quality of civilization, the day-to-day economics of survival and prosperity—these, too, are problems in our "environment." Focusing on a single aspect of the environment puts the other aspects at risk.

Environmental risks should be assessed by the proper use of scientific data, not emotion. We also need to place common-sense faith in the basic motives of business: a healthy environment is good for business—including the chemical business—and business-generated dollars are good for the environment. A poor nation has precious little to spend on preserving and protecting the natural environment. But, just as it is bad business to devote disproportionate funds and energy to a single phase of a process or element in a system, so it is bad environmental policy to devote funding and regulation to a narrow slice of the environment, putting at risk everything else, including the very economic engine that makes it possible even to think about defending nature and our health.

OUTLINE

Opening

- Balance
- Keeping environmental and economic issues in perspective
- Balance allocation of resources with preservation of environment
- With balance, we will "save the planet"

Chemical industry has bad rep

- People think we're in the pollution business
- Correct this misconception
- Facts
- We make progress on the environmental front
- We will do even better in the future

Not the regulators that drive us to improve the environment

- Incentive is our bottom line
- Environmental protection is good business

Chemical industry provides many good things

Good jobs
Enhanced standard of living
Life-saving drugs
Increased farm productivity

Is chemical industry safe?

Yes
Yes, but not zero risk
Zero risk costs too much—for everyone

Closing

Blind regulation is out of balance
Threatens quality of life
Risks should be assessed through scientific data, not emotion

MODEL SPEECH 058:
Market Price, Regulation

Key Use of Speech:	An appeal for qualified support of government regulation of pricing.
Style of Speech:	Vigorous, but soundly reasoned.
Audience:	Industry leaders at a convention.
Time:	6 to 7 minutes.

➤ Tip: The speaker begins by defining right and wrong in a special way, thereby providing the context for the rest of her remarks.

People in our industry are accustomed to a certain amount of arrogance. Most of us are pretty aggressive, and we make some bold claims now and again. So I don't feel that I have to ask your forgiveness when I lecture you about right and wrong.

Here comes the lecture.

Some things—a *few* things—are right, and some things—a *few* things—are wrong, but, mostly, we live in a world of gray, where most right things have a little bit of wrong in them, and in many wrongs you can find a bit of right.

That's my lecture on right and wrong.

Now I'll talk to you about what I've been asked to comment on: the new bill before Congress to regulate prices in our industry.

➤ Tip: The speaker states the popular view.

I'd like to stand up here and tell you that this bill is wrong, because government regulation of our industry is wrong. We're capitalists, after all, and this is a free-market economy!

I'd like to say this, because it would make me very popular with all of you, and, I must confess, I really do like to be liked.

➤ Tip: After stating the popular view, the speaker dramatically but straightforwardly springs on the audience her unpopular view.

But I can't say this. The fact is that this bill does contain a certain amount of *wrong,* but it is—mostly—*right,* and we should support it.

In principle, I'm in favor of a 100 percent free market. I think we all are—in principle. In practice, however, the market is never free. We are constrained by . . .

186

[The speaker goes on to outline the constraints on the market, the pressures under which the industry works.]

The greatest pressure of all is what our customers demand. *Pressure*? Isn't customer demand a *driver,* not a *pressure*? Isn't customer demand what it's all about?

Absolutely. But what happens when the *customers* demand government regulation? If they demanded features A, B, and C on one of our products, we would endeavor to give them to them. Well, our customers are demanding government regulation of market prices as a product feature. How should we respond?

We could mount an expensive and extensive media campaign to change their minds. But I'd rather spend my company's media money on directly productive advertising, not political campaigning.

We could simply fight the legislation, without regard to our customers. Now, what would happen if we pursued that line of action? We'd meet with customer resistance in the form of demands for even tighter and more constraining government price regulation. Worse, such a defiant and high-handed stance would betray the relationship each of us has with our customers. We would create a climate of resentment and distrust that would erect barriers to sales and would disrupt ongoing relationships. Prices in such a climate, I guarantee you, would descend well *below* any cap the government put on them.

In principle, I don't like this new bill. In practice, I believe that our industry will ultimately benefit from it. It is something that, for better or worse, our customers want, and it is something we can live with. I recommend that our association support it.

➔ Tip: A convincing speech examines the alternatives, then shows how they all fall short.

➔ Tip: The speaker makes her conclusion unmistakable and unambiguous.

MODEL SPEECH 059:
Product Safety Regulation

Key Use of Speech:	To explain how to implement government-mandated product-safety regulations.
Style of Speech:	Clear and unambiguous, conveying the company's full support of product safety regulations.
Audience:	Customer service department; Company employees.
Time:	12 to 15 minutes.

➔ Tip: Succinctly and directly, the speaker states his company's policy on safety.

XYZ Corporation has always regarded product safety as a key aspect of our corporate mission. First and foremost, a corporation is a group of human beings—of husbands, wives, fathers, mothers—and, as such, we want to protect those we serve as well as those we love. We freely and enthusiastically support the government regulations that apply to the safety of our products. Product safety is good business—and it's good *human* business.

I want, then, to speak to you about what those of us in customer service can do to enhance product safety.

➔ Tip: Having established the importance of safety, the speaker states his subject: how we can promote safety.

Coordinating and transmitting product safety information is one of the most important of all our customer service functions. When you communicate safety information, you must ensure that you do so accurately and authoritatively, taking into account all possible liability issues. This means that you must avoid issuing *opinions* regarding the safety of a procedure or product. Whatever information you convey must be founded on verifiable research and must be part and parcel of a company-wide policy as stated in the latest edition of the Company Manual.

Most customer inquiries about product safety can be answered directly from the literature available to you on your terminals. Here is the procedure:

➡ Tip: Procedures are most often best outlined step by numbered step.

1. Listen to the customer's question. Be certain that you understand it.

2. Look up the appropriate response.

3. Read this to the customer.

4. Ask the customer: "Does this answer your question?"

5. Once you have confirmed that your response does address the customer's question, obtain the customer's address or fax number. Tell the customer that you would like to send a printed version of your response, so that the customer will have this on record.

➡ Tip: The speaker recognizes that there might be conflict of values here—between the value of self-reliance and the need for absolutely accurate information. He addresses this conflict and explains how to resolve it.

Now, I realize that all of us here in customer service pride ourselves on our self-reliance. We do not want to shift a customer from one department to another in order to get an answer to a question, and we do not like to call in the cavalry when we're unsure of something. However, where product safety is concerned, we must ensure that we are giving absolutely accurate information. If a question goes beyond the scope of the Company Manual, you should consult the appropriate in-house experts. Explain to the customer that you are doing this, and arrange a time for a callback.

It is always a good idea to back up any safety information you issue on the telephone with a written response in the form of a letter or a fax. Such a response promotes greater clarity than a phone conversation alone. The written response may also be fuller and more complete than the phone response. You have more time to research an issue, if necessary, to ensure that the response given is, in every way, correct.

Whether you respond by phone or in writing, all safety issues must be taken seriously. None should be dismissed as silly or inconsequential. Nor should you ever adopt a defensive tone, either in your voice or in your writing. Instead, make it clear that you, as a representative of XYZ Corporation, are eager to cooperate with the customer to promote the safe and efficient use of the company's product.

→ Tip: The speaker shifts to a different subject, press releases, and recognizes that he is now speaking only to a portion of his audience. He makes this shift clear with a transitional sentence.

Some of you have the added responsibility of preparing safety-related press releases and industry memoranda.

First, be certain that you have all relevant documentation from the various departments involved in the product in question.

Second, approach press releases and memoranda as efforts at public service education. Secondarily, these also function as public relations and publicity *opportunities*. This means that, in explaining the safe use of your product, you should promote the inherent safety of the product as a product *feature*. Do not under any circumstances distort or disguise important safety information, but, in showing how to use the product safely, you should approach the task not so much as an effort to point out potential hazards, but as a demonstration that the product is so well made that it *can* be used effectively and safely.

→ Tip: The speaker makes another transition, to another customer service safety responsibility.

There is another side to our corporately and government-mandated product safety responsibilities. Just as we must communicate effectively, clearly, and honestly with our customers, so we must act as the eyes and ears of the company. Many times, we in customer service are the first to learn of issues of concern to customers and to the public alike, including issues related to safety. All such issues should be reported to the appropriate departments in the form of memos that make the following crystal clear:

1. The subject of the memo

2. The source of information in the memo

3. The context of the memo. You should explain how the issue in question was raised. For example, perhaps a customer called about another issue and mentioned the safety-related one, or perhaps a customer was injured. Provide the context.

4. Include mention of any related calls, and provide an accurate report of the volume of such calls.

→ Tip: The speaker recognizes another possible conflict—between Customer Service and Public Relations "turf"; but he resolves it.

Now, it is certainly not up to us in Customer Service to tell Public Relations how to treat a particular safety-related issue. However, we should attempt to present—and represent—to Public Relations the *customer's* point of view on issues of safety.

Ladies and gentlemen, I want to repeat that XYZ Corporation supports and promotes product safety. We believe in the current government regulations regarding safety, but we would design safety into each of our products with or without a government mandate to do so. An important part of our job as customer service representatives is to help our customers take advantage of the inherent safety features of our products. Approach the task positively; for safety is a great product benefit.

OUTLINE

Opening

Product safety is key aspect of corporate mission
Support government safety regulations
Safety is good business
Safety is our human decency and responsibility

What customer service can do to promote product safety

Coordinate and transmit product safety information
Be accurate and authoritative
Use approved literature to answer customer questions

Self-reliance of customer service reps

We may be reluctant to call in other help
Must ensure that we are giving the best information
Use in-house experts

Back up verbal information with written response

Written response has greater clarity
Written response is fuller, more complete
Written response is more likely to be absolutely correct

All safety issues must be taken seriously

Dismiss none
Don't be defensive

- Attitude: eagerness to cooperate and help

Preparing safety-related press releases and industry memoranda
- Gather all relevant documentation
- Approach task as public service, education

Act as the eyes and ears of the company
- Listen to customers' safety issues
- Report them to appropriate departments
- Memo procedure

Closing
- Reiterate company's support of product safety
- Safety: a design priority, irrespective of government regulation
- Safety education is important part of Customer Service function

---

MODEL SPEECH 060:
Work-site Safety Regulation

Key Use of Speech:	To explain work-site safety regulations to employees.
Style of Speech:	Clear and unambiguous, conveying the company's full support of safety regulations.
Audience:	Company employees.
Time:	10 to 12 minutes. [Depends on how many new regulations require review.]

➤ Tip: The speaker makes everyone's responsibilities clear.

Earlier this week, you all received XYZ Corporation's revised *Employee Safety Manual*. A great deal of thought and experience—some of it hard and painful experience—has gone into creating the original manual and this revision. You are *required* to read the manual, but I also *ask* you to read the manual. I don't want to get hurt here, and I don't want anyone else to get hurt. Take the time necessary to read and understand the manual.

➤ Tip: Definition of basic terms can be a very effective tool in any speech.

The management of your company very willingly takes on the responsibility of making this a safe place to work. But, ultimately, safety is up to each of us. It's *our* business. We owe it to ourselves and to one another to practice safety.

Before we review the *new* safety regulations, let's pause a moment to think about what safety means.

Accidents cost American industry . . .

➤ Tip: Statistics used sparingly are an effective means of communication.

[The speaker recites a *few* relevant statistics.]

In **[year],** accidents cost XYZ Corporation **[$ amount].**
In and of themselves, these are impressive—frightening—numbers.

193

→ Tip: The speaker puts statistics in perspective, pointing out that the human costs are the issues of greatest importance here.

But it's what behind the numbers that is most terrifying: pain, injury, disability, shattered lives, the pain suffered by loved ones, and even death. These are the *human* costs of accidents. And this is one set of costs each of us can *easily* reduce.

Now, here are the new regulations you should be aware of:

[The speaker reviews new safety regulations.]

Folks, let's work together to make this the safest year in XYZ's history.

Graduation

Openings

——*I am deeply honored that you have asked me to say a few words on this, one of the great days in your lives.*

——*Graduates, I'm sure I'm not the first to congratulate you, but let me be the first to welcome you to the start of a new phase of your education.*

Closings

——*I am proud that you have asked me to speak on this occasion, and I hope that some of my words will prove useful to you. Congratulations, and I look forward to seeing how you will improve the world.*

——*Be proud, and be pleased. But don't let yourselves ever become complacent. This is a beginning, not an ending.*

MODEL SPEECH 061:
Academic Graduation

Key Use of Speech: To a high school graduation class.

Style of Speech: Friendly and inspiring.

Audience: Graduates, teachers, parents.

Time: 10 to 12 minutes.

→ Tip: Usually, the best way to begin a commencement address is with congratulations to the graduates—and to those who supported them.

Let's begin where we should begin: with all of you. To the teachers and administrators, to the parents, the students, and all members of the Class of **[year],** congratulations and well done!

I am deeply honored that you have asked me to speak to you on your day. I've been around for a good many years, so I suppose that it is my duty to issue some advice. Well, here goes.

I remember what I was thinking and feeling when I graduated from high school. I was relieved, first and foremost, that I had actually made it. But part of me realized that this was only the first big milestone in my life. I was going on to college to study **[subject],** and I was certainly eager to get started. But I was also scared. It's a big world, I knew, and had I learned enough to start fitting into it.

→ Tip: Commencement addresses often require the speaker to pass on wisdom to the graduates. This speaker does so while avoiding pretentiousness.

Maybe some of you are feeling the same things. Let me tell you what I learned about those feelings. First of all, you should feel relieved, and you should feel proud. This diploma you are about to receive means something: you have persevered and succeeded in the first big, public challenge of your lives. A lot of people don't. More than 20 percent of American youngsters give up and drop out.

And if you're also scared, well, I'm not going to say that you *should* be, but *I* was, and I suspect that most of my classmates were, too. After all, you're not finished with your education. In fact, hard and demand-

→ Tip: The speaker en-
deavors to put the
graduates' experience
and achievement in
helpful perspective.

→ Tip: A big part of
passing on experience is
telling your audience
what to expect in the
world beyond high school.

→ Tip: The speaker
defines graduation as a
beginning rather than an
ending.

ing as high school is, it just provides you with your first set of learning tools. The purpose of these tools is to learn more. You've begun to learn how to learn. (And *that,* by the way, is a lot!) Whether you are going off to college, on to work, or into the military, the people you'll meet and work with care less about the facts you happen to know than they do about how much more you can learn and how quickly and efficiently you can learn it.

And now here's the hard part. These people will care about how and how fast you learn, but they won't be of much help in *teaching* you. That's a big difference between high school and college, let alone the world of work. You are expected to learn on your own, using the equipment you've acquired in high school. You won't have the helpful, coaxing, encouraging, and firm hand of a teacher pushing you along. You have to learn, for the most part, on your own, and if you stop learning, the world will pass you by very, very fast.

Let me tell you that one thing that has kept me going—kept me learning—all these years is a fear of living out my life eating the dust of those who have raced ahead of me.

Everything changes. In fact, you'll be a part of that change. But you have to stay ahead of change, or it will control and dominate you. You will never know enough, of course, but if you let that discourage you, well, you'll just be eating dust.

The great thing is that never knowing enough probably won't discourage you at all. I have found my ignorance exciting. It is a kind of vacuum that wants to be filled. I'm never bored. I'm too ignorant to be bored. I don't think you'll be, either. You can't afford to be, because, right now, having just completed four rigorous high school years, you don't know enough to get you through the five years, let alone twenty, thirty, forty, fifty, and beyond.

You *do* know enough to learn more, however. You've earned the tools.

Why do you need to know so much?

In part, it's because you have so many choices to make. There are many, many routes you can take from this high school, and, after that, you'll find the road branches even more.

That's the part that's really exciting—and frightening, too, because the consequences of making the wrong choices are almost always fewer and fewer choices available. Keep your eyes and minds and hearts open, because all the choices won't come at once, and they

→ Tip: The speaker returns to the most emotionally urgent and compelling topic: fear.

→ Tip: If possible, deliver a surprise in your speech. Here the speaker praises failure.

won't come with big, bright labels on them, either. Stay alert, stay informed, and you'll discover what you *need* to be. But don't be afraid to explore—or to change your mind. These days, you can expect to change jobs ten times in your working life and change careers probably four times. Do be aware, though, that you will be held *accountable* for the choices you make. As long as you do a particular job, you are responsible for doing it well, for giving it your best.

Now, let's linger a moment on this subject of fear.

Are you afraid of failing?

Well, don't be. I can tell you from experience, you *will* fail. Everybody fails. It's expected. It is okay to fail. It's just not okay to quit. Failure is an opportunity to learn. It ceases to be an opportunity only if you give up.

Congratulations to you all, and I wish you the best of luck in the years ahead.

OUTLINE

Opening
- Congratulations
- Honored to speak to you
- Issue some advice

What I felt when I graduated
- Relief
- I made it!
- Also scared
- Maybe you feel the same way
- I'll tell you what I learned about these feelings

Not finished with your education
- You've acquired the tools to learn more
- Now expected to learn on your own, using the tools you've acquired
- Stop learning and the world will pass you by

Everything changes
- Stay ahead of change or it will control you
- You will never know enough
- At least you'll never be bored

You have choices to make
- Exciting, but frightening
- Making the wrong choices narrows the range of your subsequent choices
- Stay alert and informed

Fear
- Afraid of failing?
- Everybody fails
- It's okay to fail, but not okay to quit
- Failure is a learning opportunity

Conclusion
- Repeat congratulations

MODEL SPEECH 062:
Employee Training Program

Key Use of Speech: To employees who have completed a corporate training program.

Style of Speech: Friendly and inspiring.

Audience: Graduates and possibly their families.

Time: 5 to 7 minutes.

At XYZ Corporation, we value all of our employees. We do this not just because we're all pretty decent human beings (we *are* that!), but also because our staff is the most valuable asset we have. We're only as good as our people. XYZ *is* its people.

But there are certain employees we at XYZ value in a very special way. Those who have enrolled in, survived, and graduated from our Employee Training Program have shown profound commitment not only to XYZ, but to themselves. They've demonstrated a will to excel.

Commitment. Let's think about that word. Most of us think we know what it means. It's a synonym for sticking with something or someone, isn't it?

Well, no.

Perseverance is a part of commitment, to be sure, but it's only a part. Commitment also requires a dedication to the work ethic and a willingness and ability to solve problems creatively. Finally, it requires focus. It does take a certain amount of character just to stick with something, but true commitment requires these other qualities as well.

Graduates of our training program prove they are committed, and that makes them precious indeed. They contribute to this company above and beyond any job description or any employment contract.

201

→ Tip: The speaker is sensitive to her audience and purposely redirects her speech from "they" to "you."

They. Let me stop using that pronoun. Because I'm talking about *you,* you who have completed the XYZ Employee Training Program, you who are about to step into positions of highest responsibility in our organization.

To *you,* I say thanks, on behalf of everyone who works at or invests in or is served by XYZ. *You* are the reason this company is the most respected widget developer in the world.

→ Tip: Since her audience includes graduates as well as guests, the speaker ensures that all members of the audience are equally well informed.

For our guests here who may not be aware of the truly comprehensive and rigorous nature of the program these trainees have emerged from, let me describe it.

[The speaker outlines the program.]

This is a total-immersion program, as complete and as demanding as we can make it. To excel in it is an achievement in which you should take great pride.

Graduates, I congratulate you, and I thank you. I look forward to working with you and to seeing the results of your skill in piloting this firm to greater and greater achievements.

EXAMPLE SPEECH

The Ultimate Knowledge-Based Product—You: Developing Qualities to Drive Your Own Career

Speaker: Dominic Tarantino,
Former Chairman, Price Waterhouse World Firm

I thought about my remarks for today, I tried to recall what I heard from the commencement speaker at my USF graduation. Even though that was only 41 years ago, I can't remember a word that was said, or even who the speaker was. It is very humbling to realize my remarks could leave the same indelible impression on each of you!

I asked for advice from my daughter, a recent graduate of the University's College of Arts and Sciences, and my wife, who is an USF Alum by her graduation from Lone Mountain college. They replied in unison: There is a first time for everything, Dad. Why not try to be brief and funny!

Armed with all of this encouragement, my theme this afternoon is focused on you—The Ultimate Knowledge-Based Product.

To be called a product at this moment of tremendous personal achievement may seem strange or even demeaning to you. I can appreciate this reaction. After all, you are prepared to conquer the business world and improve society with your array of finely honed and individually tailored skills and a moral and spiritual grounding that is the core of a USF education. This foundation served me well and will do the same for each of you!

My intention with the knowledge-based product theme is not only to strike a chord with your memory bands, but to describe the business world as I see it and what it will take to achieve your dreams.

Perhaps you've been on those high-technology virtual reality rides at Disney World or the movie studio theme parks. You sit still while a totally artificial world races by, drawing you in, making you forget where you are, and making the unreal seem real. If so, you were going through the best possible preparation for your business future.

You are headed for a thrilling but risky ride! You could find yourself speeding down steep hills, around hairpin turns, or into dark tunnels. You could climb to great heights.

Source: Dominic Tarantino, former Chairman, Price Waterhouse World Firm. Commencement address, McLaren Business School, University of San Francisco, San Francisco, California, June 1995. Reprinted by permission of Dominic Tarantino and *Vital Speeches of the Day.*

When the ride is over, you could discover that you really didn't go anywhere, or worse, that you went backwards. If you want to control this ride instead of letting it control you, you have to get in the driver's seat.

And what will put you in the driver's seat? Technology? No. Information? No. You've got to be able to access and use both, but they're not enough any more. Welcome to the Knowledge Age, where those who have the best rides will be those who continually acquire, apply, share, and create knowledge.

The most sophisticated technology does nothing but process, manipulate, and distribute information. It cannot produce knowledge. Knowledge comes the old-fashioned way—from working old-fashioned human brainpower, which has yet to be replaced by any series of electronic impulses. Knowledge helps us create, control, and stay one step ahead of technology. Knowledge is what we get by evaluating the vast quantities of information technology feeds us, eliminating the junk, rearranging the rest, and adding something a little extra—creativity, judgment, experience, and thought.

So, I'm up here telling you to think? Big deal. Well, there are a lot of people out there who started believing that they didn't need to think. They had this wonderful technology which enabled them to generate piles of information and stick it in charts and reports and circulate it all over their companies or sell it to clients. And you know where many of those people are now? They're a silicon chip. They're a software program. They're an unemployment statistic. If all you do is produce and process information, technology is going to overtake you.

I recently read a fascinating article that says the future will belong to those who can combine brainpower, technology, and information to create knowledge-based products. A knowledge-based product is one which—to quote—"filters and interprets information to enable the user to act more effectively." If you want a piece of the future, you—yes, you—have to become a knowledge-based product.

You have to be a self-contained, self-motivating, totally unique, continually improving package of technology, information, and brainpower that makes your users more effective, whether they be employers, colleagues, customers, or clients.

Let's look at the key characteristics of the business world you are about to enter. And then let's talk about how you mold yourself into a knowledge-based product that will succeed in that world.

One characteristic is nonstop innovation. Innovation used to be the way to stay on top. Now it's the only way to stay alive. And you have to keep on innovating, because no product is unique or state-of-the-art for very long. Imitations start springing up like mushrooms, and then some other product comes along that makes yours obsolete. Just think for a moment about the changes you have seen in how your favorite music is recorded and distributed.

What's more, in a world where the miraculous is commonplace, winning the serious game of "Can you top this?" has become increasingly difficult. The story is told about the Chairman of a big European electronics company who came back from a trade fair looking miserable. Had the company's competitors displayed better computers? No. The problem was that their computers and everyone else's computers were pretty much the same. All high quality. All reliable. All indestructible. And without labels, no one could tell them apart. How can any business stand out in this type of market?

One way is by adding brainpower to technology and information to come up with a knowledge-based product. Here's an example. I travel a lot. I stay in a lot of hotels. Usually can't tell one from another! But one chain has developed a knowledge-based product that sets it apart. It's created a worldwide database of guest preferences and requests. Let's say I request hypoallergenic pillows. The next time I check into a hotel room in that chain anywhere in the world, there will be hypoallergenic pillows on the bed. The random requests that guests make to concierges, housekeeping, or restaurants normally vanish into thin air and become useless. Instead, this hotel chain is capturing and filtering this information to help its guests act more effectively.

Of course, the hotel chain's knowledge-based product will be unique for only so long. Success will breed imitators, and the originator will once more be faced with the need to innovate.

Another characteristic of the current business world—the marketplace rules. Many times a day you will hear the terms "customer focused" and "market driven." They're not jargon. They're reality. Gone are the days of captive markets, when customers bought your product, or did without because you were the only game in town. These days companies must produce quality goods and services the marketplace wants at a price the marketplace is willing to pay. If they don't, someone else somewhere in the world will. Just ask the U.S. automobile and apparel industries about that. And while you're at it, ask them about another characteristic of the current business world—Competition—intense, unending competition. Think of it as the last two minutes of an NBA playoff game. That intense. That focused. An exaggeration, perhaps, but you do have to be lean, fast, and flexible. No frills. No excesses. Everything and everyone in the company must contribute directly to getting a top-quality product or service that the marketplace wants to the marketplace as quickly as possible, at the best possible price. And the competition doesn't stop there. Quick, effective follow-up is equally important. If you don't repair or replace a product quickly if it breaks, or if callers are left hanging endlessly on your "instant" help line, you've got a problem.

Yet another characteristic—a new kind of business organization. There is a lot of jargon here. Call it the horizontal, virtual, hollow, or porous corporation. Call it the flat or inverted pyramid. Whatever—the new business organization is built for action. Competition made it essential. Technology made it possible. Technology has revolutionized production processes. It has eliminated numerous administrative, technical, and management functions. It has maximized mobility and minimized distances. It has reduced the office to a laptop and a cellular phone.

The new business organization has fewer layers between the production floor and the executive suite. There are fewer people in those layers, particularly as you move towards the top. The only managers left are those whose functions contribute directly to the bottom line. And people at every level have more responsibility and authority. They are multitalented and multifunctional, and they work in teams with customers scattered around the country, or around the world. They can expect less of the time-honored upward mobility, but far more lateral and geographic mobility, and far more excitement.

The current business world is also characterized by change—constant, ceaseless, sudden. Business restructuring is far from over. Many companies didn't get it quite right the first time. So they will keep trying until they get it right. And it will probably be right for only so long. Then external forces will require them to change again. Innovation spells change. Market focus spells change. Competition spells change. And finally, you can add one more attribute of the current business world—globalization. Take all the characteristics I've mentioned today, and globalize them. Now that really spells change. Get ready to travel the globe, either physically or through cyberspace. And get ready to relate to colleagues and customers functioning in environments at different stages of change.

If you're good at change, then you're one step closer to making yourself a knowledge-based product. Knowledge-based products should be able to adjust to changing circumstances fluidly, and effortlessly.

For example, there's a fabric that automatically "knows" when to change its temperature. A ski jacket made of the fabric will get warmer as the air around it gets colder. You have to be like that fabric, but you have to do even better. The fabric can only react to change after it happens, and it has just one response. You should be able to anticipate change, shape it to your advantage if possible, and have a range of responses based on what the situation requires and what you want. And you should always regard change as an opportunity.

Say you lose a position with a large company. Do you really want to go to a similar position at another large company? Maybe this is an opportunity to change your work style—go into business for yourself. Maybe this is the chance to do what you've always wanted to do and move to Alaska. Remember what that great philosopher, Yogi Berra said:

"When you come to a fork in the road—take it."

By now you might be asking: What do you have to do to become a knowledge-based product?

First, think of yourself as a product—a self-contained, portable package that combines information and technology with brainpower. Your employer is your customer. And your association with that customer lasts only as long as the terms of sale are acceptable to both sides.

Second, take full responsibility for product development. No one is going to do it for you. Learn, learn, learn, and keep on learning. Regard every position or work assignment as an opportunity to absorb technology, information, and skills that will improve you as a product.

Also, learn as much as you can from the people around you. Look at them as knowledge-based products that can help you act more effectively. Use them.

Third—be market-driven. No matter how great a product you are, you're not going to sell unless someone wants to buy you. Try to make yourself saleable in multiple markets. Also, define the term "market" broadly. The company you work for shouldn't be your only market. You should also regard individuals and groups within the company as potential markets. If you can sell yourself to them as a product that makes them more effective, you're automatically selling yourself to the company. This is especially true in the current team-oriented business environment.

Fourth, customize. Absorbing technology and information won't make you fully competitive in the marketplace. You have to offer something the market wants that it can't get anywhere else. Do you have superior analytical capabilities? Are you a good idea person? Are you a great communicator? Are you a super salesperson? Are you a natural teacher? Then continually hone these talents and acquire whatever additional training or skills are necessary to "customize" your product for the market or markets you want to serve.

Fifth, innovate. Let's say you've turned yourself into a really competitive product. Your customers think you're the greatest. Don't get complacent! Success breeds imitation. Imitation may be flattering, but in this case it can eat your lunch. Obsolescence is a constant threat. You must innovate! Dedicate a part of your brainpower to research and development for yourself. Please remember that it's the skills—not the titles—you acquire that will really count.

If you get one message from me today, it should be that nothing can replace the human qualities. Brainpower is obviously one. But there are other human qualities you must include in your "product mix" if you want a truly challenging and meaningful career.

One is respect. You will deserve respect for the unique qualities and skills you bring to the marketplace. You owe similar respect to all your colleagues, at every level. They also have something valuable to contribute, or they wouldn't be there. Respect is essential to the teamwork that is now the way to go in most companies. It's the foundation for a mutual commitment of the team members to each other and to their collective success.

Humility is considered much more of an asset than it used to be. Ask a few CEOs who thought they knew it all, and got replaced by other CEOs humble enough to listen to customers—and the employees who serve those customers. Humility is not being imbued with an inflated sense of your own importance. Rather, it is recognizing that you can learn something from just about anyone. Humility is critical to success.

But so is pride. Pride is not the opposite of humility. Arrogance is the opposite of humility. Pride is a commitment to your own excellence, and the excellence of those who work with you. And it's celebrating that excellence when it's achieved. By all means take time out to celebrate your achievements, just as you are celebrating your very significant achievement today.

And be sure to continually sharpen three closely-linked senses—sense of compassion, sense of balance, and sense of humor. Compassion is best expressed as the ability to walk a mile in someone else's shoes—an awareness of the needs, sensitivities, and aspirations of all those who count on you, and a willingness to act on that awareness. It also means an acceptance of human limitations, including your own.

Sometimes on the job you have to stretch people's limitations. A sense of balance means being able to tell when that's necessary, and when it isn't. You push to the limit when you're up against a deadline on a major proposal, not when you're trying to make Federal Express with a report no one's going to read for two weeks anyway. Believe it or not, there are many people who take the same crisis-oriented approach to both situations. They exhaust themselves and those around them mentally, physically, and emotionally, for no good reason.

And speaking of knowing what is and isn't important, you can still marry your job if you want to. You can camp out in your office on weekends. But most companies these days will tell you to "get a life." They've learned that their best performers are the people whose existence is not confined within the walls of their offices. They are nourished by ties to family and friends, and by outside interests.

Humor springs from compassion and balance. It means knowing when you and the people around you need a good laugh—like when everything that can go wrong has gone wrong and nothing you do is going to make a difference. If everyone has done the best job possible, self-flagellation won't help. And it's highly unlikely that the world will end. Realizing that requires not taking yourself too seriously.

Finally, the most powerful products are building blocks rather than stand-alones. Make it a point to transfer your knowledge and skills to others. Inspire them by your example and guidance. In other words, branch out and help other people become knowledge-based products.

Make no mistake. Many of the twists and turns and traps in today's business world aren't imaginary. They are real. But you can avoid these hazards and have an exhilarating, challenging, and rewarding ride.

Happily, each of you has a head start on a successful journey. Just build on what you have learned from the devoted Jesuit and lay faculty. It was a solid foundation for me, and it will be for each of you, as well. What I learned here so many years ago has been my reliable partner, always there ready to help wherever my travels have taken me. There is nothing like a Jesuit education—a USF education! You find a strong bond among the graduates of the Jesuit Universities, as I have over and over again.

Just cultivate what you have learned here on The Hilltop, along with the qualities I've talked about today. The ability to think, innovate, and create. The ability to add something to the ongoing flow of knowledge. The ability to motivate and inspire others, and to help them enrich their skills and their lives. If you fully develop these qualities, you will drive your own career. You will never be obsolete. You will be the ultimate knowledge-based product, and your life's journey will lead to an enjoyable and rewarding future.

History of Company

Openings

—*There is nothing I enjoy more than telling people about our company.*

—*I have a remarkable story to tell you. I believe you will enjoy it.*

Closings

—*So this is what we do, who we are, and how we got that way. I thank you for your attention.*

—*The story of XYZ Incorporated is, I think you'll agree, an exciting one. I hope that, like me, you look forward to the next chapter.*

MODEL SPEECH 063:
Products and Services

Key Use of Speech: To recount and celebrate the history of the
                      company.

Style of Speech: Storytelling, familiar, and inspiring.

Audience: Employees and friends of the company.

Time: 12 to 15 minutes.

→ Tip: The speaker avoids a solemn opening, but his opening nevertheless clearly sets out his subject and provides a good reason for making the speech.

→ Tip: History, especially when it is delivered in the form of a speech, is always enlivened by a personal and anecdotal approach.

They say that if you don't know where you've been, you won't know where you're going, and, as Yogi Berra once memorably remarked, "You got to be very careful if you don't know where you're going, because you might not get there." So we're gathered here today to celebrate nearly a century of Greenwood Stores history. Some of you already know this story, and many of you have heard parts of it. But, like any good story, it's worth repeating.

Our founder, George Greenwood, borrowed $20 from his sister to move from Pine Bluff, Illinois, to Chicago, where, in 1898, he believed opportunity was to be found. He took a job as a clerk in a dry goods store and studied at a business college at night. Times were tough, and, at one point, he had only a nickel to his name. With it, he bought a two-cent newspaper and threw the other three cents into the Chicago River for good luck. The gesture paid off—after a while.

Through careful habits of spending—or, I should say, saving—Mr. Greenwood amassed part of the $5,000 he needed to buy the small dry goods store in which he was a clerk. He borrowed $2,000 from his father, and then took the plunge.

In 1900, Chicago had no shortage of dry goods stores. What could make Mr. Greenwood's store stand out from the crowd?

At first, it was small things: Mr. Greenwood's manner was enthusiastic and energetic. He made it clear to each and every customer

213

→ Tip: This anecdote not only paints the company founder as a man who was both shrewd and affable, it establishes the idea of building a business one customer at a time, as the speaker points out in the next paragraph.

who walked into his shop that he was determined to deliver satisfaction. When a phone order would come in, Mr. Greenwood always answered the call personally, then repeated the customer's order so the delivery boy could hear it. Now, Mr. Greenwood did not end the conversation. He kept talking to the customer, passing the time of day—and, often, the delivery boy would arrive at the customer's door *before* the telephone conversation had ended.

After ten years of building his business one customer at a time— the very principle we continue to observe today—Mr. Greenwood purchased one of the busiest dry goods stores in the city. Mr. Greenwood understood that this was both a big risk and a big opportunity. He made the most of it, installing dazzling displays and beautifully merchandised windows. This was in brilliant contrast to the other small dry goods stores of the day. *Now* he had a business that stood out, boldly, from the rest.

Mr. Greenwood also began manufacturing certain items himself, including **[the speaker lists the first products].** These in-store brands were of the highest quality, and, because they were manufactured exclusively for the Greenwood's store, they could be sold at lower prices than comparable merchandise elsewhere. By 1920, George Greenwood had twenty stores in Chicago.

→ Tip: The speaker tracks the history of his company's growth by indicating the growth in the number of stores the company boasted as the years went by.

Over the years, new products and services were introduced. **[The speaker highlights the most important products and services.]**

The public responded very well to the combination of great products from many manufacturers, a high-quality, inexpensive in-store line, and—always—top-notch customer service: the same friendly and efficient service Mr. Greenwood gave each customer when he opened his first store. By 1929, there were 200 Greenwood Stores in and around Chicago.

Then, in 1933, came Chicago's World's Fair—the Century of Progress. Mr. Greenwood opened three stores on the fairgrounds, and he used them as experimental test beds to try out innovative fixture design, new lighting techniques, and an unprecedented use of colors. What he learned he applied to every new store he opened. The World's Fair also brought Greenwood Stores *national* recognition, and the company began to expand rapidly outside of Chicago.

By the 1950s, Greenwood Stores, grown to some 500 units nationwide now, made another major change. The stores began a transition

→ Tip: Another milestone: the move toward self-service.

from total clerk service to self-service. This meant investing in larger stores; they had to be about twice the usual size to make room for aisles. And it meant retraining thousands of employees. For "self-service" by no means meant *no* service. Clerks were always there to help. The objective was to create quicker, easier customer service—*better* service, not less service.

While the stores underwent evolution and revolution, so did the Greenwood distribution network. In the 1960s, Greenwood Stores was in the forefront of computerized inventory systems. Today, we're the industry leader in fast, cost-efficient distribution through our six full-line distribution centers nationwide.

In 1975, George Greenwood passed away, and Mr. Greenwood's son, George Greenwood II, became president and CEO. Under his direction and that of *his* son, George Greenwood III, we have continued to grow, always retaining leadership in the industry. This year, we will open our 2,000th store. That's *two thousand* stores, each of which looks a world apart from the first dry goods establishment Mr. Greenwood purchased at the beginning of the century, yet each of which is animated by the founder's spirit of efficiency, courtesy, and a total commitment to customer satisfaction. That's two thousand stores continuing to build our business one customer at a time.

OUTLINE

Opening

- Know where you've been so that you'll know where you are going
- Celebrate a century of Greenwood Stores history

The founder, George Greenwood

- Humble beginnings
- Saved and borrowed to purchase first store

How did he make the store a success?

- His personality: enthusiastic
- Dedication to customer satisfaction
- Delivery boy anecdote

Growth

- Bought one of the business stores in the city
- Used excellent merchandising techniques
- Made the store stand out boldly from the rest
- Began manufacturing house brands
- Continually introduced new products and services
- Always delivered great customer service

Innovations

- Experimented with new store formats
- Applied the lessons of innovation to new stores
- Through World's Fair, achieved national recognition
- Began to expand nationally

Pioneered self-service concept

- Quicker
- More efficient
- Better customer service, not less

Innovated distribution network

- Computerized the network
- Became industry leader in distribution technology

Closing

- Founder died, son and then grandson continued business
- Growth phenomenal
- Now 2,000 stores
- Continue to adhere to founder's principles

MODEL SPEECH 064:
People and Labor Relations

Key Use of Speech: To explain the history of the company in terms of employee relations.

Style of Speech: Tells a story, familiar, friendly.

Audience: Employees and friends of the company.

Time: 10 to 12 minutes.

There are many ways to tell the story of a company. We could talk about growth, about the introduction of new products and services, about swelling profits, about overcoming hard times. But when all is said and done, a company is people, and the most dramatic story of any great company is a story about people.

➤ Tip: With a few deft strokes, the speaker paints the background of his subject.

When XYZ Corporation began operations in the 1950s, relations between labor and management were pretty simple. Labor had almost no stake in the company and was supposed to do what management told it to do. When this didn't work out, labor called a strike. In short, the story of labor and management was a tale of intimidation, conflict, and opposition.

Put this way, the scenario sounds pretty crazy. But that's the way it was, and few people questioned it back then.

Frank Miller, founder of XYZ, *did* question it. In 1959, he introduced what he called a "Workplace of Choice" program, in which the relationship between management and labor would become a genuine *working* relationship. Frank introduced a policy and a corporate culture of open communication and teamwork. This was not just because he was a nice guy—though, in fact, Frank *was* a pretty nice guy. No, it was because Frank realized that working as a *team* was the most effective way of doing business. Why, he asked, should

217

→ Tip: Having painted the background, the speaker can now show how his company stands out in contrast to it.

→ Tip: The speaker proceeds chronologically, using innovations in labor relations as milestones in the company's history.

→ Tip: The speaker develops the team concept.

→ Tip: This is an example of incremental dramatic structure. The speaker builds to a high point, then raises the ante even further. See the next sentence.

the company pay labor *not* to think and *not* to contribute? Frank wanted to give everyone a stake in the company, reasoning that this was a far more effective motivator and driver of excellence than, say, the fear of losing your job—which, really, was the chief motivator prevailing in American industry at the time.

Under Frank's guidance, XYZ developed many ways for people to be heard, to be informed, and to be involved. He instituted an "Open Door Policy," which is still a key feature of this company, and which invites and encourages employees at all levels to ask questions and raise and resolve issues.

In the 1950s and 1960s, that "open door" was quite literally an *open door*. You had a question, you made an appointment with the manager concerned, and you walked in. Today, we have developed our corporate-wide electronic mail system, which allows anyone in the company to communicate—unannounced—with *anyone* else.

Another leap forward came in 1964, when XYZ initiated its Open Forums program, in which senior managers, each and every quarter, directly update everyone on what's happening in the company. This isn't a one-way meeting, however; it's an open forum, and everyone is invited to ask questions and raise issues and share ideas.

By 1970, we took another step by rejecting the old system of manager evaluation and replacing it with "360–degree" assessments. These incorporate comments from the employee, his or her peers, his or her supervisors, and his or her clients and customers.

Corporations of the 1950s were hierarchical places and, usually, highly bureaucratized. Over the years, XYZ has been tearing down walls and creating multifunctional teams to accomplish given goals, plan and execute given projects, address given problems. Not only are these teams multifunctional, they are intra-organizational as well, cutting across any and all departments as necessary. The only "turf" around here is the ground on which are headquarters is built.

As a result of the open, team approach, XYZ had grown into an industry leader by the early 1970s.

But we still weren't satisfied with the way we as a corporation related to and made use of our people. Like many companies born in the 1950s, XYZ began as a rather culturally and ethnically homogeneous organization. We didn't talk much about culture or values or perspectives, because, we assumed, we pretty much shared these things in common. There was no *need* to talk about them. By the

1970s, however, XYZ management came to realize that the workforce here—and throughout the country—had become far more diverse. In 1975, we instituted a Multicultural Awareness Program. Its immediate aims were:

→ Tip: The speaker is careful to define, with a list of attributes, just what the Multicultural Awareness Program is.

- To foster respect and trust among all of us
- To promote greater openness in all of our communications and dealings
- To promote teamwork across cultural and ethnic boundaries
- To ensure equal opportunity and fair treatment for everyone in the corporation.

One very visible outgrowth of this program was a recognition of the special needs of two-worker families, and, in 1985, XYZ opened its Employee Day-care Facility as part of an ongoing program to support the professional and personal needs of our people.

Again, why have we done all this?

→ Tip: The speaker shows how high human and ethical values can coexist with business efficiency and other business goals.

Well, I like to think it's because we're all pretty wonderful human beings. But it is also true that good *human* policies are usually good *business* policies as well. We want to attract, develop, and retain the best people, and that means we must treat one another with humanity and respect. We also want the company to develop, and, in a multicultural marketplace, that means developing as a multicultural company.

The history of XYZ has been a history of team development and of diversity recognition. This has been a history of growth—not just in dollars and cents, but in consciousness. And that has made us not only better people, I think, but also better *business* people, better equipped to meet the needs of our clients and customers, better equipped to compete against others who also want to meet those needs.

Holiday Celebrations

Openings

——*How pleased I am to celebrate this holiday with you all!*

——*I am honored that you have asked me to say a few words on this important day we share.*

Closings

——*Thanks for listening to me, and I wish you the very best at this happy time!*

——*Once again, thank you for honoring me by allowing me to share this important time with you.*

MODEL SPEECH 065:
New Year's Day

Key Use of Speech: To celebrate the New Year.

Style of Speech: Familiar and friendly.

Audience: Employees and friends of the company.

Time: 4 to 6 minutes. [Depends on the level of detail.]

→ Tip: New Year's is a natural time for reflection on the year gone by.

We've come to the end of another great year, a year in which our sales increased **[percentage amount]** and a year in which we opened a new facility in **[location].** It is a year that saw the addition of three new people here in the main office, **[the speaker names and identifies the new people].** It is a year that saw the launch of a new program, **[speaker names and briefly discusses the program].**

We have plenty to celebrate.

But we have even more to look forward to. This last year has been one of beginnings: new successes, a new facility, new people, a new program. In this *new* year we can look forward to all that will unfold from these beginnings, and we can also look forward to what else we may begin, projects such as **[the speaker outlines a few plans for the future].**

→ Tip: The speaker points out that New Year's is not just about looking back, it's about looking ahead, too. And he does just that.

What's great about New Year's is that it looks backward and forward, and we are truly blessed to have so much good to look back on and so much excitement to anticipate. Let's learn from this past year—which taught us the value of teamwork—and let's apply that to the new year. With that approach, we can only do better and better.

I wish you all a very happy and prosperous New Year.

MODEL SPEECH 066:
Memorial Day

Key Use of Speech:	To commemorate Memorial Day.
Style of Speech:	Friendly, but serious.
Audience:	Civic group.
Time:	5 to 6 minutes.

For most of us, Memorial Day is about getting out for a day in the park, perhaps, or taking advantage of any of a number of Memorial Day sales. We forget that Memorial Day is really a very solemn holiday, a time intended to be dedicated to those American soldiers, sailors, air force personnel, and others who gave their lives in service to our nation.

Indeed, the holiday was born out of the most desperate and dismal and destructive struggle this nation ever endured, the Civil War. Originally called Decoration Day, Memorial Day was a time for honoring those who died, as the saying went, fighting brother against brother. The custom of decorating—with flowers and other tokens of affection and respect—the graves of the war dead actually began even before the Civil War ended. In the South, the town of Columbus, Mississippi, claims to have originated the formal observance of a Decoration Day, to honor the Union as well as the Confederate dead, in 1866. In the North, during that same year, Waterloo, New York, held the first Northern Decoration Day ceremonies. Then, in 1868, former general John A. Logan, who was commander in chief of the Grand Army of the Republic, a Civil War veterans' organization, issued a general order designating May 30, 1868, "for the purpose of strewing with flowers or otherwise decorating the graves of comrades who died in defense of their country during the late rebellion." In 1971, the federal government moved the holiday to the last Monday in May.

➡ Tip: Like Veterans' Day, Memorial Day is a poorly understood holiday. The speaker takes this opportunity to present a capsule history of the holiday.

→ Tip: After explaining the solemn significance of Memorial Day, the speaker takes an unexpected turn.

So, now you know what the holiday was supposed to mean. I've chosen the tense of my verb carefully: *was*. I'm sure that any number of Memorial Day speakers across the nation today are self-righteously and sternly scolding their listeners for having lost the spirit of the day.

But I'm not so inclined.

Instead, I suggest that we celebrate our "thoughtlessness" on this day. I suggest that we celebrate the fact that we can dedicate this day of mourning to playing with our kids in the park or spending a few mad hours in search of bargains. I suggest we celebrate the fact that very, very few of us even have the *need* to decorate the grave of a loved one who fell in war.

If we celebrate these things, we do more honor than we know to all those who have made the supreme sacrifice in battle. For the very fact that we do *not* have to mourn on this day, that we *can* play in freedom with our children, that we *can* treat ourselves to the material fruits of democracy—all these things do the very greatest honor to those who have fought and died to preserve our freedom, our many freedoms, and our way of life.

→ Tip: A speech that prompts an audience to think about something in a new way is almost always successful and interesting.

My friends, I think it is fitting and proper that we enjoy this day and look on it as a carefree occasion in the very heart of this beautiful spring season. Spring is the season of hope and renewal, after all, and it is for hope and renewal that so many brave young men and women have given their lives. They don't ask that we mourn them. We honor them by gratefully partaking of all that their sacrifice has made possible. Let's *enjoy* this Memorial Day, which they have given us.

MODEL SPEECH 067:
Fourth of July

Key Use of Speech:	To commemorate Fourth of July.
Style of Speech:	Friendly and celebratory.
Audience:	Civic group.
Time:	5 to 6 minutes.

→ Tip: Sometimes you need to prepare your audience to accept something you're about to say.

I take the time to listen to a speaker because I expect to hear something new. Hearing the same old thing over and over again is a waste of time. I'm afraid many of you feel the same way. I say I'm *afraid* because what I am about to say is nothing new. In fact, it falls into that category of pronouncement known as the "BGO": the blinding glimpse of the obvious.

Oh well, here goes anyway: *The Fourth of July is the most American of all our holidays.*

Well, thank *you,* Paul Revere!

→ Tip: A very effective device in any speech is taking the obvious and showing it in a new light. Everyone enjoys a revelation now and then.

But before you all start throwing firecrackers at me to chase me down off this platform, I ask you to think for a few moments about that all-too-obvious statement I just made.

Why is the Fourth of July so American?

Obviously, the holiday celebrates our nation's birthday. How could it be anything other than American?

But, you know, that whole birthday thing, the fact that the holiday commemorates the signing of the Declaration of Independence—this is only a *definition.* It's not the *meaning* of the Fourth of July. The definition has to do with words, while the *meaning* has to do with how we feel.

How we *feel* on the Fourth of July is what makes this day so American.

→ Tip: A good speaker speaks from personal experience, but broadens his experience so that it has universal meaning.

How *do* we feel?

Well, I can only speak from my own experience. For me, the Fourth of July is all about being a kid—summer vacation in full swing, no school in sight—running free in the hot sun, swimming, eating hot dogs, having a picnic, free, and carefree. It really *is* a birthday *party.* It's fun. It's pleasure. Can you imagine the so-called former Soviet Union celebrating their May Day the way we celebrate the Fourth of July? I can't. That was an official celebration, full of tanks and missiles and uniforms and speeches—speeches much longer than mine! I doubt anyone had fun. I'm sure there were patriotic emotions associated with that day, but joy? I doubt it.

No, it's the *feelings* this warm, sunny summer holiday creates in us all that make the Fourth of July so American.

They are the feelings of people who are free—freer than any other people on earth have ever been. It's not a holiday about words, but about feelings, about really wonderful *feelings.*

So where do we go from here?

→ Tip: The speaker's strategy is to show how this holiday's significance begins with the individual.

My suggestion is that you get me to shut up and stop *moralizing* about the Fourth of July and start *enjoying* it instead. Be carefree on this holiday. *Feel* it instead of *think* about it. Then try to carry those feelings over into the next day and the next and the next. On those other days, while continuing to feel those Fourth of July feelings, think every once in a while about what we all need to do to keep the Fourth of July what it is. Think about working hard at what you do to make it the best. Think about working hard at building your relationships to make them stronger and deeper—relationships with your kids, your spouse, your family, your colleagues, your friends, your customers. These very basic things are what give our free and glorious nation the strength to continue to be free and glorious.

For now, though, for today, just breathe this summer breeze and soak up the summer sun, and feel the way we're all meant to feel on the Fourth of July.

MODEL SPEECH 068:
Veterans' Day

Key Use of Speech:	To commemorate Veterans' Day.
Style of Speech:	Informative.
Audience:	Civic group.
Time:	7 to 8 minutes.

→ Tip: The speaker recognizes that observance of this holiday has faded. He takes the opportunity to give a brief history of Veterans' Day, since it is likely that many in his audience are unaware of this background.

Veterans' Day: With each passing year, it seems to me that fewer and fewer people celebrate it. My grandparents still called it Armistice Day, the day set aside in the United States, Great Britain, and France to commemorate the end of World War I on November 11, 1918—the eleventh hour of the eleventh day of the eleventh month. Then, after World War II, it was recognized as a day of tribute to the veterans and the dead of that war as well. After this came the Korean War, and Veterans' Day was designated to honor all U.S. servicemen and women in all U.S. wars.

But something's happened to this day of remembrance. It's gradually being forgotten. In town after town, year after year, the Veterans' Day parade becomes a thing of the past.

Why is this happening?

→ Tip: Returning to the "disappearance" of Veterans' Day, the speaker makes this the motivating topic of his speech. Asking a question is a natural driver for any speech. Your audience will want to hear the answer—if the question's a good one.

Well, for one thing, we have been blessed with several years of peace, and, when we're not immediately threatened, we all too easily forget the men and women who risked—and in some cases lost—their lives to win for us this peace. But I also think that Veterans' Day has faded because it's not a holiday so much as a day of remembrance. We don't get a day off of work. It's just—well, it's just another day.

A couple of weeks back, I was trying to think of what I might say on this occasion to show how this day really *is* special. I was *trying* to think—and then, I must confess, my mind wandered to thinking

→ Tip: Personal anec-
dotes can be very
powerful attention-
holders in a speech.
Just be sure that you
are able to make clear
the relevance of the
anecdote to the point or
points you are making.
Nothing falls flatter than
an irrelevant anecdote.

about all the *bills* I have to pay by November 11: utilities, tutoring for my kids, a couple of car payments, mortgage payment, credit cards, food, food, and more food, doctors. I know that these kinds of problems are hardly unique to me or new to any of you. They're called the "high cost of living."

Well, there it was. The high cost of living. And I was thinking about *it* instead of thinking about this speech.

You know, the United States is an expensive place to live.

[The speaker pauses a beat.]

Until you start looking elsewhere.

[Pauses half a beat.]

I mean, how much did it "cost" to live in what used to be called the Soviet Union? What do you have to "pay," each and every day, to live in, say, Iraq? My grandparents fled Nazi Germany. What did that cost them? And, more to the point, what did it cost those who did not or could not flee?

The cost of living *is* very high here, too—higher than most of us ever realize. Some have paid with their lives. Many more have paid with backbreaking work and heartbreaking sacrifice. Some of us are fortunate enough merely to pay with some portion of what is in our wallets. But just look at the rest of the world! Look down the corridors of history, too. What you quickly discover is that life here is a real bargain—the greatest bargain ever.

→ Tip: The speaker
smoothly transitions
from his anecdote about
the high cost of living to
the real costs of living.
This leads him to the
subject of sacrifice and
thanks, which is what
Veterans' Day is all
about, then to a reflec-
tion on the personal
debts we owe to our-
selves and our nation.

Our freedom, of course, did not and does not come free of charge. It continues to require material sacrifice and also vigilance—not just vigilance against threats from the outside, but, more important, from within, especially from within ourselves. We must fight our own cynicism, our own short-sightedness, our own selfishness, and, above all, our own intolerance.

The great bargain we enjoy cannot be taken for granted as something permanent. It must be maintained, and maintained at some cost and effort. On this day of remembrance and honor, we must all realize the necessity for universal patriotism.

Now what do I mean by that?

→ Tip: The speaker
introduces a new
concept: "universal
patriotism." Then he
defines it.

It's got nothing to do about waving a flag and marching in a parade, but it's got everything to do with honoring—in our hearts, in our minds, and in our actions—what our country means, what our country stands for.

We pay for everything in our lives, but in a world of truly exorbitant costs and dubious deals, the United States, our country, is one value that is always at an all-time and unprecedented high. And that is because of the legion of veterans who have paid the high prices—sometimes the *highest* price—to secure this bargain for us. Let's set aside a few minutes, at least, in this otherwise rather ordinary day to thank them.

OUTLINE

Opening

- Veterans' Day: the vanishing holiday
- Background of Veterans' Day

Why is it being forgotten?

- We're at peace
- We forget easily
- Not a day-off-of-work holiday

High cost of living

- Anecdote lead-in
- True meaning of a "high cost of living"
- The things we love about America were paid for with lives
- Life here is a real bargain

Freedom

- What it requires of us
- Need for vigilance
- Need to resist cynicism
- Never take freedom for granted

Concept of "universal patriotism"

- What it means
- Honoring the nation in our hearts

Closing

- The United States: a "great value"
- Let's set aside a few minutes to thank those who made our freedom possible

MODEL SPEECH 069:
Thanksgiving

Key Use of Speech: To celebrate Thanksgiving Day.

Style of Speech: Warm, reflective speech by manager.

Audience: Company employees.

Time: 2 to 3 minutes.

→ Tip: The speaker twists this traditional holiday just a bit to use it as a platform for giving thanks to her staff.

You don't need me to tell you what tomorrow is. It's Thanksgiving—and the start of a long weekend, during which we can refresh ourselves, enjoy our families, and, yes, give thanks for all that we have.

I'd like to send you off on this holiday with a thanksgiving of my own. *You've* done the giving all year, and now I want to thank *you*.

We've accomplished a great deal this year, **[the speaker lists some key achievements].** I am thankful to each and every one of you for making these achievements possible, and I am thankful not just for the end results, but for the process of getting to them. It is a pleasure working with this team.

→ Tip: The speaker is careful not to thank her staff for their accomplishments alone, but also for being who they are.

Thanksgiving is about family, and I don't want to intrude on that. Like many of you, I will be spending some much-needed, much-valued time with the ones I love. But, next to my family, I am most thankful for having the privilege—the personal and creative privilege—of working with all of you.

So, happy Thanksgiving! I hope you enjoy it as much as I know I will.

MODEL SPEECH 070:
Christmas and Chanukah

Key Use of Speech:	To kick off Christmas/Chanukah season.
Style of Speech:	Warm, sincere.
Audience:	Company employees.
Time:	3 or 4 minutes.

→ Tip: We all like to think that the holiday season is magically joyous, but sometimes circumstances make it a trying time. The speaker acknowledges that this has been a rough year for the company. She does not try to manufacture false optimism.

Let's face it, folks. This year has been a bear. We have taken a beating. **[The speaker recaps the difficulties the company endured during the year.]** And it's not over. We still have to get through . . . **[The speaker outlines upcoming problems].** This means that next year is likely to be a bear as well.

Happy Holidays?

Well, yes. I hope so. They should be. Christmas and Chanukah are about joy and family, and, for these reasons, I believe this holiday season has come to us just in the nick of time. We're pressured, all of us, and what we need is just what these joyful holidays provide: a sense of perspective.

Christmas and Chanukah remind us of what is really most important to each of us: the human connections, our families, and our loved ones.

→ Tip: The speaker uses the occasion to assert leadership by calling for the maintenance of perspective on the difficult situation at work.

I won't kid you. We're facing some tough times. But we've also come through some tough times. The trick is not to get overwhelmed by the difficulties that we have encountered and will yet encounter. All businesses face such problems. We *will* come through this. Let this holiday season help you keep your perspective on it. That is my Christmas and Chanukah wish for us all.

So let this holiday season refresh you and recharge you and renew your spirits. Together, we will meet all the challenges. I haven't the slightest doubt of that.

Informal Events

Openings

——*Welcome to our company picnic. The stated purpose of this event is to build team spirit. The real purpose is to eat massive quantities of great food.*

——*How pleased I am to see you all here. Allow me a moment, please, to share with you why I believe this annual event is so valuable for us all.*

Closings

——*I'm shutting my mouth now, so that we can all start having a really good time together.*

——*Thanks for coming here, for sharing your family time with all of us.*

MODEL SPEECH 071:
Company Picnic/Sports Event

Key Use of Speech: At a company picnic or sporting event

Style of Speech: Friendly, informal, team-building.

Audience: Company employees.

Time: 1 to 2 minutes.

→ Tip: Fun "pop" statistics are a fresh way of getting your audience involved with what you have to say.

We sleep away almost a third of our lives, and of the two-thirds left, we use up another third at work. So is it such a good idea to spend a part of the third that's left to *us* with the people from that working third?

That is a good question, and I hope you won't all leap to answer it in a way that will embarrass me!

The reason we hold this annual company **[picnic, sporting event, etc.]** is to improve that working third of our lives by providing an opportunity to get to know one another and one another's families. This event, I believe, lets us see one another as more than "one-third people." We are entire, whole, rounded individuals, and the better we can appreciate one another as such, the more effectively we can operate as a team.

That said, I also happen to think this is a lot of fun—and, besides, the food's on the company! Let's play and let's eat!

MODEL SPEECH 072:
Holiday Season

Key Use of Speech:	At a company holiday office party.
Style of Speech:	Friendly, informal, team-building.
Audience:	Company employees, some clients, vendors, etc.
Time:	2 to 3 minutes.

→ Tip: The speaker balances business news with "human interest" news. He and his company clearly view employees as people, not cogs in a machine.

This season is about family and friends and joyful reflection. I hope nobody objects to my thinking of you as a kind of *working* family, and, certainly, we have many of our friends here today. Finally, we have ample reason for joyful reflection. This has been a standout year for XYZ Corporation, in terms of sales and in terms of establishing some great new client and vendor relationships. **[The speaker acknowledges the new clients and vendors, who are present at the party.]**

It has also been a great year for Joe and Kathy Smith, who have a new daughter, Stephanie, and for John and Carlo Abelson, whose son Pete just finished medical school.

Back to our "working" family, three new folks, **[the speaker names them],** have joined us this year and have already proven to be marvelous additions to the staff. Welcome to your first XYZ holiday party!

Now, if I may, let's raise whatever it is we're drinking, and toast: To all our families! To one another! To another great year!

→ Tip: A toast is never out of place—provided everyone has a drink in hand.

Introductions

Openings

——*Being asked to introduce our next guest is a profound honor.*

——*It is my great pleasure to introduce our next speaker, who will share her marketing insights with us.*

Closings

——*Please join me in welcoming John Smith to the podium.*

——*Ladies and gentleman, I give you our next chairman, John Smith!*

MODEL SPEECH 073:
New Employee

Key Use of Speech:	To introduce a new employee.
Style of Speech:	Informational; intended both to acquaint current employees with the new person and to make the new employee feel welcome.
Audience:	Company employees.
Time:	5 to 6 minutes. [Exclusive of the new employee's own remarks.]

→ Tip: The direct route is not always the best. This speech starts a bit indirectly and takes an opportunity for some self-directed humor.

Now that we've been in business for more than five years, I started thinking it was high time to crack some of those business textbooks I was supposed to be studying in college. One of the items I found is something many of you have been saying to me for years now: Sales and marketing aren't the same thing, and sales people shouldn't be expected to do marketing, too.

Well, you can't blame me for ignoring your advice for so long. After all, you folks in sales have been doing one hell of a marketing job, and, I thought, if it ain't broke—well, why fix it?

The fact is that we have *all* been doing such a good job at a lot of things that we've grown, and we've grown well beyond the point where we can expect our salespeople to keep handling marketing as well. Now that we have grown, if we want to *keep* growing, we need

→ Tip: Take time out for team-building and pats on the company's collective back.

somebody who can devote herself full-time to identifying new and changing markets and advising us on how we can serve those markets.

Some of you have already met that "someone." She is Mary Smith, and she comes to us from XYZ Corporation, where she was associate marketing director. Mary was part of the team that created . . . **[Here the speaker mentions one or two well-known marketing projects**

239

→ Tip: Be specific about the highlights of the new employee's background. Instead of heaping her with vague adjectives, list some real, concrete, and specific accomplishments.

→ Tip: Nitty-gritty time. Be clear and succinct about the new hire's responsibilities and how she fits into the current structure of the company.

→ Tip: Let people know where the new hire will be located and how to reach her.

in which the new employee played a role in her previous position.]

In addition to her work at XYZ, Mary has . . . [The speaker hits the highlights of Mary's résumé.]

Let people know where the new hire will be located and how to reach her.

We are incredibly lucky to have Mary on board.

I'm going to ask her to say a few words in a moment, but I want to outline for you what her responsibilities will be, to whom she will report, and how her work will complement the revised mission of Sales.

[The speaker lays out the new employee's responsibilities and her position within the structure of the company. Since Sales is the department most directly impacted by the addition of this new marketing person, the speaker pays particular attention to how she will interact with Sales.]

Mary's office will be on the second floor, next to Joe Bailey's office. Her extension is 123, and she'll be on the e-mail within the next day or two.

Folks, please join me in welcoming Mary Smith to Acme Widget!

[After applause, the speaker invites Mary to say a few words.]

MODEL SPEECH 074:
New Executive Manager

Key Use of Speech:	To introduce a new manager to those he or she will supervise.
Style of Speech:	Informal, providing clear information and generating excitement about the new manager.
Audience:	Company employees.
Time:	3 to 4 minutes. [Exclusive of the new manager's own remarks.]

→ Tip: Put the intro-
duction in the context of
ongoing events.

The last time we met, I had some unwelcome news: the announcement that Dan Johnson, your manager, was leaving. I promised, though, that, while Dan was a tough act to follow, we would find a great manager. So now I come to you with very good news: we *have* found that great manager, and we've hired him.

Pete Reynolds has been in the widget industry for X years. He comes to us from the XYZ Corporation, where he was . . .

→ Tip: Give the new
manager the buildup he
deserves; but avoid
vague adjectives.
Focus on specific
achievements.

[The speaker goes on to hit the highlights of the new manager's background. It is most effective to begin with the most recent experience, then work back. If the new manager's experience is extensive, don't deliver a tedious laundry list, just the highlights.]

I don't have to tell you that XYZ is a fine company, and it was Pete who helped make XYZ one of the industry's leaders. He was instrumental in . . . **[The speaker lists one or two major projects the new employee was involved in.]** What can I say? XYZ's loss is very much our gain.

241

➤ Tip: Put the staff in a receptive frame of mind. Invite them to be impressed with their new manager.

So, now you know that your department's new manager is super experienced. But experience is not all that it takes to be a great manager. Leadership is about being a great person, with sound judgment, quick insight, and a willingness to listen. These qualities are apparent after you've spent three or four minutes talking to Pete. That's one reason I hired him. Let me get out of the way, then, and ask Pete Reynolds to talk with you. He's his own best introduction.

Please join me in welcoming Pete aboard!

Legislative Affairs

Openings

——*Madam Chairman, members of the committee, I am very pleased that you have invited me to address you today.*

——*Mr. Chairman, members of the committee, you have asked me to speak with you about deregulation in the widget industry.*

Closings

——*I am pleased to have been given this opportunity to make the views of our company known to you.*

——*Mr. Chairman, members of the committee, I thank you for your time and attention and for the privilege of speaking to you.*

MODEL SPEECH 075:
Testimony Before Investigation Committee

Key Use of Speech:	A formal presentation of testimony.
Style of Speech:	Clear and cooperative.
Audience:	Legislators, attorneys, members of the public.
Time:	15 to 30 minutes. [Depends on the level of detail. Question time is variable.]

→ Tip: Testimony requires absolute clarity. The speaker states her name, position, and the subject of her testimony. She also expresses a desire to be helpful.

Mr. Chairman and members of the committee, my name is Sarah Johnson, and I am responsible for the XYZ Corporate Child Care Program. I want to thank you for the opportunity to appear before you today to describe what we at XYZ have been doing to help make child care available where our employees live. I hope that my testimony will aid you in your investigation of the status of child care among American corporations.

→ Tip: The speaker shows how her company is exemplary in the area of corporate child care.

XYZ has long been recognized for addressing our employees' personal and family issues and for providing them with benefits that better enable them to come to work and be productive. We were among the first American companies to offer employees paid vacation plans and retirement benefits during the 1930s, and we began offering medical benefits shortly after World War II. More recently, we have developed a set of what we call Worklife Programs, and the National Association of Working Mothers has recognized the child care aspect of our program as being of special benefit to working mothers.

Why has XYZ made such an investment in child care and other aspects of "Worklife"?

By the end of the 1970s, we recognized that a highly significant demographic phenomenon was taking place in this country, and that more women were not only entering the workforce, but staying there. We realized that we would have to address the new realities of child care for both two-income families and single-parent families.

Part of the answer, we found, was creating flexible working hours. For many two-income, two-parent families, this alone may substitute for corporate child care or, at least, supplement it.

But we didn't stop there. In 1980, we created what I believe was the first national child care referral service, which was designed to help employees identify dependable and affordable sources of child care.

By the end of the 1980s, it was becoming clear that XYZ needed to do even more—more for our employees to enable them to be at their most effective in the workplace. We created a **[$ amount]** special fund for child care assistance and, a year later, expanded the program to address issues of elder care as well. Funding was made directly to agencies within the communities where our employees live and work. Within five years, we had funded **[number]** projects, including **[speaker lists several projects]**.

With regard specifically to child care, XYZ has developed a rigorous set of criteria child care providers must meet in order to qualify for funding. These criteria were prepared in cooperation with **[speaker lists agencies that helped develop the criteria]**. XYZ has made these criteria available to the public in the interest of improving child care standards nationally. The standards we develop include, among other things:

[The speaker lists the major child care criteria.]

Now, in some communities where XYZ is based, the child care infrastructure simply didn't exist. There were, in short, no agencies, businesses, or individuals to fund. We have made, in these cases, efforts to increase the supply of child care, including . . .

[The speaker lists these programs.]

The most recent new direction XYZ is exploring is partnership with other concerned corporations to create community-wide child care centers, centers aimed at serving not just our company, but the community. To date, we have joined with . . .

→ Tip: The speaker provides the historical background from which her company's current child care program developed. Use such background to enhance your audience's understanding and appreciation of the current state of affairs.

[The speaker explains the company's pilot partnership.]

We are still in the early stages of this cooperative joint venture in corporate child care, but we already have enough evidence to believe that, in many communities, such partnerships will prove the most effective means of creating the child care infrastructure this nation so sorely needs.

Ladies and gentlemen of the committee, I am pleased that you are discussing a number of government initiatives to help industry create this infrastructure. We at XYZ welcome this assistance. But we also believe that the responsibility is primarily that of the private sector, and that our example, as well as the experience of a growing number of other companies, will soon educate American industry generally to the fact that child care is a great investment—and not only for women employees. A large percentage of our employees—and of all American workers—male or female, face challenges in balancing work and personal responsibilities. If industry can assist workers in coping with these challenges, our workforce will become increasingly productive. Such programs, then, are sound corporate investments and sound investments in the nation's future.

I greatly appreciate this opportunity to testify, and I am, of course, available for the committee's questions.

> ➤ Tip: Having established her company's leadership in the area of child care, the speaker is now sufficiently "qualified" to offer far-reaching opinions on the subject.

OUTLINE

Opening

- Speaker identifies self
- Announces purpose
- Announces subject

Company's reputation

- Among the first to offer paid vacation
- Medical benefits
- "Worklife Programs"

Why company has made an investment in child care

- Recognized change in workforce demographics

- Address new realities
- Need to create flexible work hours
- First national child care referral service
- By the 1980s, wanted to do even more
- Special fund for child care assistance

The child care program

- Developed criteria for providers
- Criteria available to the public
- Efforts to increase supply of child care

Most recent new directions in policy

- Partnership with other companies
- Effective

Closing

- Responsibility for child care primarily in private sector
- A great business investment
- Investment in nation's future

MODEL SPEECH 076:
Testimony in Support of a Bill

Key Use of Speech: A formal presentation of testimony.

Style of Speech: Clear and cooperative.

Audience: Legislators, attorneys, members of the public.

Time: 12 to 30 minutes. [Depends on the level of detail. Question time is variable.]

→ Tip: The speaker establishes the scope of his testimony, which (he asserts) reaches beyond the fate of his own company.

→ Tip: Provide the minimum historical background necessary for the audience to understand the current situation and to appreciate plans for the future.

Mr. Chairman, Members of the Commerce Committee, on behalf of XYZ Airways, I appreciate the opportunity to offer this testimony to present my company's views on issues that are critical not only to the future of XYZ Airways, but to the U.S. airline industry.

As you know, XYZ Airways is primarily a short-haul carrier, with routes along the East Coast, in the Northeast and Mid-Atlantic regions. The skies over this region are highly congested, and the costs of weather-related and other delays are often very high. In addition, the region has some of the highest landing fees in the country. **[The speaker gives a few examples.]** For years now, XYZ has struggled under the burden of these high costs and has endured staggering losses and several rounds of downsizing. Our new management team has a plan to reinvigorate this airline by growing rather than shrinking. Our goal is to see XYZ Airways grow into a major international airline. We need to do this if we are to survive—and continue serving our shorter-haul passengers with competitive fares and convenient flights.

The key to unlocking the growth potential of this airline is a truly competitive cost structure, which will enable XYZ Airways to compete both with the other major carriers and with the low-cost, low-fare carriers that have now spread their service throughout the East Coast and the Mid-Atlantic. We have just reached a tentative agreement with the various unions that represent our labor force, which will enable us to begin to put into place a highly competitive cost structure; however, a key component of this tentative agreement is the creation of a separate, lower-cost airline within XYZ Airways, which will specifically serve, in a highly competitive manner, our current short-haul markets, while our other airline develops the international markets.

What we need from this committee, ladies and gentlemen, is the authorization to license and create the new airline.

For XYZ Airways, the benefits of such authorization are starkly obvious: survival.

For the nation, the benefits include continued competitive service to the most densely populated, heavily traveled region of our country. If XYZ Airways is forced to raise its fares, the average price of a ticket from **[city]** to **[city]** will rise **[percentage amount]** to **[$ amount]** within **[time frame]**. If we drop out of this market, we estimate that the ticket for that same ride will jump **[percentage amount]** to **[$ amount]**.

Furthermore, XYZ Airways has spent **[$ amount]** to buy **[quantity]** take-off and landing slots at **[name of airport 1]** and **[name of airport 2]**. We have also invested hundreds of millions of dollars to develop facilities at these airports. Indeed, at **[name of airport 1]**, XYZ Airways is responsible for paying full debt service on **[$ amount]** bond issue to build the new terminal. At **[name of airport 2]**, we have effectively funded **[$ amount]** in improvements.

I should point out as well that XYZ Airways' investment in these two airports also fulfills congressional objectives because it helps sustain service to small and medium-sized communities, which would otherwise not have nonstop service to high-density airports. We also provide single-carrier connecting service between numerous other small communities where nonstop service is simply not feasible.

If we are not given the authorization to create the new airline, however, all that we have been trying to build, including our long-standing commitment to providing nonstop service to smaller communities, will be put in jeopardy.

Ladies and gentlemen, allow me to point out that the government and the people will *lose* nothing by this authorization. XYZ Airways is assuming all of the risks involved. Moreover, the initial authorization period is limited to **[years]**, which means that this committee can,

→ Tip: The speaker's strategy is to maintain a twin focus—on the problems of his company and on the public that his company serves.

→ Tip: Be aware of the thin line that separates threats from the real consequences of an action. Make no threats.

→ Tip: Having built a strong case in favor of the authorization, the speaker now shows that there is little or no downside to the authorization. It is a win–win scenario.

→ Tip: These are consequences—not threats.

within a reasonable amount of time, review and revise its decision.

On the other hand, the people and the government have much to lose if we are not granted this authorization. First to go will be competitive pricing over many short-haul routes. Second will be the loss of jobs at XYZ Airways as we are forced to downsize yet again. Third is the likelihood that we will be forced to curtail or eliminate a number of short-haul routes, thereby depriving many communities of convenient, competitive service. Fourth is the impact on two important airports of reduced fees from us. Fifth—and this is indeed the worst case—fifth is the eventual dissolution of this airline.

Ladies and gentlemen, thank you for hearing me. I am, of course, available to answer any questions the committee may have.

OUTLINE

Opening

- Appreciation of opportunity to testify

Description of XYZ Airways

- Challenges airline faces
- Congestion
- High landing fees
- Losses
    New management team's goal for company: survive and continue
    to serve

Key to unlocking growth potential

- Competitive cost structure
- Creation of a separate lower-cost subsidiary for short-haul runs
- Authorization needed

Benefits of authorization

- Benefits for the airline
- Benefits for the nation
- XYZ's contribution to consumers

- XYZ's contribution to economy

Consequences of failure to grant authorization

- Jeopardize short routes, service to small cities
- People have nothing to risk but much to lose

Closing

- Thanks for hearing my case
- Call for questions

Media

Openings

——*Ladies and gentlemen, I have a brief statement to make concerning the recent controversy, and then I will take questions.*

——*It is a pleasure to be here. I always enjoy sharing my views with you.*

Closings

——*This concludes my statement. I will now take questions.*

——*Thank you for your attention. I will now try to answer any questions you may have.*

MODEL SPEECH 077:
Interview, Print

Key Use of Speech:	A model interview.
Style of Speech:	Clear, with an emphasis on concise statements suitable for quotation.
Audience:	The interviewer—and the readers of the publication.
Time:	10 to 12 minutes.

INTERVIEWER: Your name is Joseph Wisniewski?

➤ Tip: For print interviews, spell out difficult names. Identify yourself concisely and clearly.

INTERVIEWEE: Yes. That's spelled W-i-s-n-i-e-w-s-k-y. I am executive vice president of XYZ Corporation, and I am in charge of the XYZ Corporate Child Care Program.

INTERVIEWER: How long have you been in charge of the program?

➤ Tip: Tell the interviewer a *little more* than he has asked you for. The additional information should, however, be closely related to the interviewer's question.

INTERVIEWEE: For three years. I began in **[year]**. The program has been in operation for eight years. It began in **[year]**.

INTERVIEWER: Tell me about the program. What is its purpose?

➤ Tip: The speaker provides enough historical background to enhance appreciation of the current program, but he is careful to answer the question and not to get bogged down in the background.

INTERVIEWEE: Well, we at XYZ have long been recognized for addressing our employees' personal and family issues and for providing them with benefits that better enable them to come to work and be productive. We were among the first American companies to offer employees paid vacation plans and retirement benefits during the 1930s, and we began offering medical benefits shortly after World War II. More recently, we have developed a set of what we call

Worklife Programs, and the National Association of Working Mothers has recognized the child care aspect of our program as being of special benefit to working mothers. Through a variety of means, XYZ ensures that first-quality child care is conveniently available to our employees.

INTERVIEWER: Child care is pretty expensive and has a lot of liability costs attached to it. Why has XYZ made such an investment in it?

➡ Tip: Avoid short, clipped answers. Answer to the point, but answer fully. Give the impression of the richness of the subject.

INTERVIEWEE: By the end of the 1970s, we recognized that a highly significant demographic phenomenon was taking place in this country, and that more women were not only entering the workforce, but were staying there. We realized that we would have to address the new realities of child care for both two-income families and single-parent families. In part, we invested in child care because we are decent, caring people—many of us with families and children of our own. But child care is also a very sound business investment. It ensures that *all* of our employees can work to their maximum level of productivity.

INTERVIEWER: Just how is that?

INTERVIEWEE: First of all, having adequate, dependable day-care near the workplace greatly reduces absenteeism. Second—and even more important—is the fact that you cannot perform at your best if you are worried about your kids. The availability of child care also allows us to diversify our workforce.

INTERVIEWER: How's that? By allowing more women to work?

➡ Tip: Try not to simply contradict the interviewer. Yield whatever ground you can, then go on to make your expanded or corrected point.

INTERVIEWEE: In part, yes. But, these days, child care is not only about working mothers. It's about single-parent families. It's about working, two-income families.

INTERVIEWER: Not all corporations can afford to support child care. What does a parent do in these situations?

INTERVIEWEE: While I agree that many companies are in no

position to finance stand-alone child care programs or even to make grants to community child care programs, most companies can address some aspect of the child care issue. For example, they may try flextime—flexible working hours. For many two-income, two-parent families, this alone may substitute for corporate child care or, at least, supplement it. We at XYZ have had a flextime program since **[year]**. A longer-term, more ambitious solution is the development of cooperative partnerships with other companies in a community.

➤ Tip: Avoid a simple yes or no. Incorporate the question into your answer.

INTERVIEWER: You mean banding together to finance child care?

INTERVIEWEE: Yes, banding together to finance child care facilities. These benefit all businesses in a community.

INTERVIEWER: How would you characterize the present state of child care in this country?

➤ Tip: You may be quoted out of context. Try to create a number of quotable, stand-alone phrases.

INTERVIEWEE: In a word, improving. In a few more words, improving, but with a long way yet to go. However, business and industry have been increasingly realizing that child care is a great investment. It increases productivity. It decreases absenteeism. It increases employee loyalty and morale. It builds better companies—and it builds better communities, so it extends beyond the workforce to customers. It's an idea whose time has come, and we at XYZ are proud to be at the forefront of what we believe is a movement to corporately financed child care in this country.

MODEL SPEECH 078:
Interview, TV or Radio

Key Use of Speech: A model interview.

Style of Speech: Clear, with an emphasis on concise statements suitable for quotation.

Audience: The interviewer—and the audience.

Time: 5 to 6 minutes.

→ Tip: If you have a difficult name, be prepared to pronounce it phonetically.

INTERVIEWER: We're speaking with Joseph—Joe, you're going to have to help me with your name.

INTERVIEWEE: It's pronounced Wiz-nev-sky, but "Joe" will do just fine.

INTERVIEWER: Now, you created a child care program at XYZ Corporation?

→ Tip: If the interviewer gets something wrong, don't tell him he's wrong. Instead, smoothly supply the correct information. Never dwell on the error; if you do, you run the risk that the error, not the correct material, will be quoted out of context.

INTERVIEWER: I am executive an vice president at XYZ, and I have been directing the XYZ Corporate Child Care Program for some three years now. But the program actually began **[number]** years ago in **[year],** and has been evolving and growing ever since.

INTERVIEWER: Tell us something about this program.

INTERVIEWEE: Well, we at XYZ have long been recognized for addressing our employees' personal and family issues and for providing them with benefits that better enable them to come to work and be productive day after day. Most recently, we have developed what we call the Worklife Programs, which the National Association of

→ Tip: The interviewee doesn't disagree with the interviewer's positive appraisal, but he does add to it.

Working Mothers has recognized as being of special benefit to working mothers. The child care aspect of the Worklife Programs ensures that first-quality, safe, dependable, and educationally stimulating child care is conveniently available to our employees.

INTERVIEWER: Who pays for it?

INTERVIEWEE: This is a subsidized program. We share the costs with our employees who participate.

INTERVIEWER: Well, XYZ sounds like a big-hearted company to be footing even part of that bill.

INTERVIEWEE: We *are* big-hearted, but child care is also a very sound business investment. It ensures that *all* of our employees can work to their maximum level of productivity.

INTERVIEWER: How?

INTERVIEWEE: Well, just think about how hard it is to put in a 100 percent day at work if you're worrying about your children's welfare.

INTERVIEWER: I see.

→ Tip: "I see" is the interviewer's signal to the interviewee to keep going.

INTERVIEWEE: There's also the aspect of diversity. This program helps us to diversify our workforce.

INTERVIEWER: By allowing more women to work?

INTERVIEWEE: In part, yes. But, these days, child care is not only about working mothers. It's about single-parent families. It's about working, two-income families.

INTERVIEWER: We've got about fifteen seconds left. What would you like to say to wrap this program up for our viewers (listeners)?

→ Tip: In a broadcast interview, be prepared to make an overall, quotable summary.

INTERVIEWEE: I'd urge everyone out there to start working with their employers to create child care solutions nationwide. This is not something you do just for yourself and your family. It's something that will strengthen America and certainly strengthen American business.

MODEL SPEECH 079:
News Conference

Key Use of Speech: A statement for a news conference.

Style of Speech: Clear and quotable out of context.

Audience: Press and public.

Time: 3 to 4 minutes for statement; question period variable.

➡ Tip: A news conference should begin with a clear and unmistakable statement of the conference's topic. The speaker should also introduce herself.

Ladies and gentlemen, my name is Sarah Johnson, executive responsible for XYZ's Corporate Child Care Program, and it is my pleasure to announce the official opening of our new child care program in **[name of community]**.

XYZ has long been recognized for addressing our employees' personal and family issues and for providing them with benefits that better enable them to come to work and be productive. During the 1930s, we were among the first American companies to offer employees paid vacation plans and retirement benefits. After World War II, we began offering medical benefits. More recently, we have developed what we call Worklife Programs, and the new XYZ Corporate Community Child Care Center is an outgrowth of these programs.

➡ Tip: Structure the news conference statement as succinctly as possible. Make it quotable.

The new facility is state-of-the-art.

[The speaker describes the main features of the facility.]

➡ Tip: Make the transitions from topic to topic very clear.

While the XYZ Corporate Community Child Care Center is intended primarily for the children of XYZ employees, we do anticipate the availability of additional spaces, and the facility will be open to the community on a first come, first served basis.

If I may, I will now briefly discuss the background of the new facility. By the end of the 1970s, the management of XYZ Corporation had come to recognize that a highly significant demographic shift was taking place in this country, and that more women were not only entering the workforce, but staying there. XYZ realized that it would have to address the new realities of child care for these two-income families and child care for single-parent families. The new XYZ Corporate Community Child Care Center is the latest in a long line of our innovative corporate solutions, providing effective, safe, dependable child care.

I will now open the conference to questions.

➤ Tip: The statement ends, and the news conference is opened to questions.

Motivating Employees

Openings

——*We have an opportunity, one that can enhance all of our professional lives. Let me tell you about it.*

——*The topic for today: survival. Yours. Mine. Ours.*

Closings

——*We now have a choice: to act, or to be acted upon. To seize opportunity, or to be seized by forces we cannot control.*

——*Thank you for your attention. I know that we can act as a team, and, as a team, I also know that we cannot be defeated.*

MODEL SPEECH 080:
Call to Action

Key Use of Speech: To call for action when faced with poor
                       financial news.

Style of Speech: Clear, frank, inspiring.

Audience: Company employees.

Time: 5 to 6 minutes.

➤ Tip: If you want to motivate action, begin with a sharp, succinct, nonsugar-coated description of the current situation.

Here's the situation: Subscription renewal is off 15 percent this year, compared to last year. Over a five-year period, subscriptions have declined a total of 34 percent. Ladies and gentlemen, let's start thinking about the choices this news compels us to make.

Here are those choices, as I see them. We can ignore this latest subscription renewal report and simply let subscription levels settle wherever they will. The drawback of this approach is that we have no way of knowing just where the drift will stop. If subscriptions fall below sustainable levels, we will have to raise subscription prices, and that, inevitably, will prompt more subscribers to decline renewal. If our numbers dwindle sufficiently, our only choice will be to cease publication.

Here's the next choice: We can take the report to heart, worry about it, make ourselves generally miserable, and devote the balance of our careers to talking about the Good Old Days.

And now, the final choice: Take the report seriously, discuss it, think about what the decline in subscription renewals is telling us, and formulate strategies for reversing the trend. It is this choice I want to prepare us for.

➤ Tip: The speaker makes clear the action he wants, including the purpose of the action.

I ask that each of you think about what our newsletter offers and what it fails to offer. I ask that each of you ponder strategies for

265

increasing subscriptions and for retaining those who are currently subscribers. Let's think about these issues individually, then come together at our next meeting, on **[date]**, to create an effective program for turning this situation around.

Our goal is to produce an action plan.

→ Tip: An effective leader helps to solve the problems he raises.

I have some suggestions to get us started. We need to assess the roster of special features we offer, with the object of broadening our traditional areas of appeal in the following ways: **[the speaker lists the ways].**

We need to reevaluate the price of subscriptions. I believe we might find a graduated schedule of subscriptions, divided in this way: **[the speaker explains a gradation plan]**. We might also consider adopting different subscription durations, with attractive pricing on the long end.

We need to look at our publicity efforts. Should we redirect them? If so, how? And our advertising: Are there more effective venues for us?

Finally, we must take a hard, objective look at our image in the professional community. One of the greatest features of our publication is that no two issues are alike—and no two staffers think alike. We are founded on diversity. So I do not expect universal agreement on what we should do to reverse the present trend. What I do expect is that we will find answers and that we will unite to keep this newsletter rolling off the presses.

→ Tip: The speaker ends on a positive note.

It is all too easy to let figures such as these erode our morale. But do consider this: We retain a substantial core of loyal subscribers. Thirty percent of our subscribers have been subscribers for more than five years. Obviously, we are publishing something of enduring value. We need to enlarge our subscriber base while retaining the loyal subscribers. Let's pool our diverse resources, then, to rethink this newsletter. Let's retain and strengthen what's great about it, let's shed what isn't working, and let's formulate a roster of fresh, new features to attract new subscribers.

I am very eager to hear what you will come up with on **[date]**.

OUTLINE

Opening

- Crisis: subscription renewal down
- Start thinking about our choices

The choices

- Ignore the problem
- Consequences of this approach
- Make ourselves miserable
- Final choice: formulate strategies to regain subscribers

Evaluate product

- Call for strategies
- Call for help in turning situation around

Speaker's suggestions

- Assess the features we offer
- Reevaluate price
- Assess publicity efforts
- Assess our image

Closing

- Don't lose heart
- Our strength is a core of loyal subscribers
- Retain what is great, shed what isn't working, formulate new features to attract additional subscribers
- Eager to hear suggestions

The Qualities of Success: Leadership, Diversity, Community Service, and Career Development

Speaker: Richard Lidstad, Vice President for Human Resources, Minnesota Mining and Manufacturing Company

Good evening. It's a real pleasure for me to be with you tonight to take part in these festivities honoring students who have completed the requirements for the Emerging Leadership Program. I want to applaud all of you who have accomplished this feat.

I was asked to talk to you today, because I have always felt a strong, personal link to the University of Minnesota. My bachelor of science in business degree was from the University, more years ago than I'd like to remember. My relationship with the University has been strengthened over the last few years, partly because I have been a part of the Executive Mentoring Program for MBA students. I'll talk a little more about that later.

Before I begin my remarks, I want to issue two caveats. First, unlike many people today, I have spent my entire business career at one company, 3M. So anything I say is colored by my experiences there.

Second, you need to know that I don't consider myself an intellectual. I don't know everything.

That's not all bad, however, since President Dwight Eisenhower once said, "An intellectual is a man who takes more words than necessary to tell more than he knows."

With that in mind, I'll try to keep these remarks short.

I'm going to spend the next few minutes talking about the criteria that are emphasized in the Emerging Leadership Program: Leadership, Diversity, Community Service and Career Development. I think these qualities are right on, since they are all important qualities for anyone who wants to succeed in modern business.

Let's talk about leadership first. This is the single most important criterion for those of you who aspire to a management position . . . and it's almost as important for those of you who don't.

That's because a lot of teaming is going on now in corporate America. And these teams

---

Source: Richard Lidstad, Vice President for Human Resources, Minnesota Mining and Manufacturing Company. Delivered to the Carlson School of Management, Minneapolis, Minnesota, May 11, 1995. Reprinted with permission of Richard Lidstad and *Vital Speeches of the Day.*

are not hierarchical. Leadership is passed around, so the ability to get the most out of people is a critical skill for everyone.

The traditional method of management—command and control—is dead. (Well, perhaps still kicking and screaming in a few quarters.) Now we are looking for managers who can act as teachers . . . as coaches . . . as cheerleaders. Businesses need people who are visionary and who know how to reward those who work for them.

I hope you'll excuse a sports analogy here. The old hierarchical corporation looked and acted like a football team. In football, there is narrow specialization of function. Each man plays only one position, and they all look to the quarterback or the coach for the next play. And when the play is executed, each person has a carefully defined job to execute.

The new way to look at business is more like a hockey team. There is rapid, continuous action . . . and everyone must pass, shoot and play defense, even though each player may have a primary role.

Teamwork is the most critical element in hockey, since individuals play multiple and often interchangeable roles. Success depends on how well those roles are blended.

It's also true that when the puck drops, nobody knows for sure what's going to happen . . . and yet, a skilled and well coached team gets amazing synergy from these interactions.

The change from traditional top down management to this new leadership model is difficult to learn for many of us from the old school. It's tough for us to grasp this new style, which instead of stressing command, stresses interpersonal skills . . . like listening, questioning and getting along with others. This change is good, however, and very necessary.

Not too long ago, we went through an issues prioritization exercise in Human Resources at 3M. Guess what? The Number One issue globally is the identification, assessment and development of leaders. And as you know, leaders can come from any background.

That leads me right to the next criterion: diversity. Learning to work with others, who may be different from yourself, is a critical part of being a good leader. Recently, I read that the old model saw America as a melting pot, with all the various races, religions and cultures merging into each other, until they represented a whole. Ideally, it visualized an "homogenized" America, sort of like Velveeta Cheese.

The new model is more like a salad bowl. The dressing binds the ingredients together, but they remain separate while enhancing and enriching each other. Each individual keeps his or her own identity and unique attributes, while working together toward a common goal.

If you accept this concept of diversity, that means you respect people with different backgrounds and different points of view. It doesn't mean you just tolerate people who aren't like yourself, it means you embrace them and their cultures. You see how their viewpoint can be valuable to the team.

In the end, respect is what diversity is all about. When we first started talking about diversity at 3M about 20 years ago, I realized that my first lesson in diversity actually occurred right after I started work at 3M more than 15 years earlier.

You're much too young to remember but, in the '50s and '60s, business people dressed very formally. The concept of casual business attire, which some still say is an oxymoron, was in the very distant future. Men . . . and I stress men . . . wore white shirts, navy blue suits, narrow ties and a hat. We had short hair cuts, and we were clean shaven.

So I was very surprised, during my orientation in the laboratory where I worked, to see a guy who was wearing a sport shirt and Hush Puppies and sporting a scraggly beard. That man turned out to be one of our top inventors. He had 13 patents. People had so much respect for what he had accomplished that they had learned to ignore the way he dressed. He could wear anything he wanted to wear, and he still got respect . . . because of his contributions.

And that's the way it should be. One should get credit for what one does, not be judged by the way they look or speak or think.

You can take that little story of mine and transfer it to the whole issue of diversity. Remember, you don't just have to look at obvious differences like race, age or gender. Look at the family traditions people celebrate . . . look at the differences in culture that make up the various individual backgrounds.

One way to learn more about diversity is to work with some of the key charitable organizations here in the Twin Cities. You'll find a lot of diversity at the Red Cross, United Way, Salvation Army and Goodwill. And you'll learn that it is because of their broad outlook . . . their diversity . . . that these organizations succeed.

Obviously, that brings me to the third criterion for your program: community service. My own experience tells me that nothing I have done in my career has been more valuable to me than my experience as a volunteer. I love the work I do for the United Way, for example.

It's extra work and it takes time I don't have, but it is extremely rewarding. It helps me understand where 3M fits into the community at large, and it frequently takes me out of my comfort zone, so I learn new things.

Earlier I mentioned that I mentor four MBA students at the Carlson School of Business. I thoroughly enjoy my relationship with these students. I get as much, if not more, from them as they get from me.

Sometimes I can bring what I learn from them back to 3M and apply a fresh perspective to my work. And when you've reached my mature age (in the Human Resources field, we call it chronologically gifted), bringing a fresh, new perspective to the job isn't easy. The relationship I have with these students helps to make this possible.

If I have any regrets about my community service, it's that I didn't really get active in it until about five years ago. Once you leave school, you'll be busy building your careers and perhaps your families as well, but you need to take time to give something back to your community, too.

And you're sure to find that community service helps you develop skills that will make you more valuable on the job. I'm talking about skills like leadership and finding a balance in your lives. Of course, there is another obvious advantage to community service. It enhances your network of friends and business associates. But the real payoff of volunteerism is very personal . . . you feel good about your contributions.

The last criterion I'm going to discuss is career development. And the first thing I'm going to tell you is that when you plan your career and set your personal goals, I want you to be very selfish. This is one area that definitely needs to be "me colored."

The first thing you have to ask yourself is "What do I really like to do?" Involve your emotions in this decision, and don't feel guilty if you find out you don't want to be CEO of a company. Of course, if you want to be a trapeze artist or a rock star, you probably shouldn't be attending the Carlson School of Business. But, let's assume you want to go into business: The question is, which spot is the right one for you?

Whatever makes you happy is where you should concentrate your efforts, because that is what you will be the best at. You have to please yourself before you can please anyone else.

Only when you follow your own instincts will you be happily successful. Intellectually, you may think you should strive to be CEO. But if that isn't what makes you happy, you'll probably fail to achieve your goal.

British journalist Katharine Whitehorn said, "The best career advice given to the young is, 'Find out what you like doing best and get someone to pay you for doing it.' "

I can only echo those remarks.

When I came to 3M in 1958, I came because I was offered a good job, not a career. I was there several years before I gave much thought to what I wanted to do with the rest of my life.

As a matter of fact, I didn't even have my college degree when I joined 3M, although I worked to remedy that rather quickly . . . thanks to the evening and summer sessions offered at the University of Minnesota.

I've been pretty successful at 3M, because I followed my instincts about what was fun and interesting to do. For example, I once turned down a quality manager's position to become a technical instructor. I did it, because I love to teach . . . and I'm pretty good at it, too.

So the management position waited a few years, but guess what? I wound up managing a technical education center, plus a lot more.

There are too many students today who, in trying to crack the puzzle of career success, do all the right things, like going to the right school, studying the right things and getting the right grades. To some extent, every student in this room is doing that.

I want you to promise yourself that, after tonight, you'll spend a little more time being selfish. Because if there isn't some "me" in the equation, you won't be successful.

The other thing you have to do to succeed in meeting your career goals is to be prepared for a lifetime of learning. Good organizations have to continue to grow to meet new challenges. Some of you may think that your education is finished once you get your degree (or degrees), and that's wrong . . . even if your degree is from a good school like the University of Minnesota.

Over the last decade, life-long learning has received renewed emphasis at 3M and, from what I've heard from my HR colleagues in other companies, that's true almost everywhere. We encourage all 3Mers—our top executives, scientists, marketers, manufacturing employees and clerical people—to continuously improve their capabilities every year.

After all, how can a corporation like 3M get better every year, unless its people do? 3M is its people . . . and that's true of every other company as well.

This learning can involve formal training; participation in teams or task forces or new assignments. Companies today cannot be competitive in the global marketplace, unless all their people renew their old skills and develop new ones.

You need to be willing to leave your comfort zone. As Alvin Toffler said, "The illiterate of the future are not those who cannot read or write, but those who cannot learn, unlearn and relearn."

That's a real challenge, but it's one you will face again and again in your careers. Learning is what will keep your mind young, even when you are as old as I am!

I've shared my thoughts with you on leadership, diversity, community service and career planning, and I hope you found them helpful. I hope some of what I've said may make your travels down your career path a little easier.

I'd like to congratulate the University of Minnesota and the Carlson School for sponsoring this program, because it is so contemporary and forward looking.

And, once again, I want to congratulate tonight's honored guests. And I want to wish all the students here the kind of career I've had . . . one that is happy, personally fulfilling and satisfying in every way.

Thank you again for inviting me. And thank you for listening.

MODEL SPEECH 081:
Challenges to Meet

Key Use of Speech: A speech outlining challenges to be met.

Style of Speech: Clarifying and inspiring.

Audience: Company employees.

Time: 5 to 6 minutes.

➤ Tip: "Challenges" is too often used as an abstract word. This speaker spells out the challenges in very specific terms.

Here's the bad news: Subscription renewal is off 15 percent this year, compared to last year. Over a five-year period, subscriptions have declined a total of 34 percent. We are faced with increasing competition from television and from such newsletters as **[speaker names several]**.

That news bad enough for you?

Well, here's the good news: Thirty percent of our subscribers have been subscribers for five years or longer. This is an unprecedented rate of long-term loyalty in our market segment. *Unprecedented.*

The challenges we are facing are both clear and difficult:

Number one—We must reverse the decline in subscription renewal.

Number two—We must *add* subscribers. We must attract new readers.

And number three—We must not betray the loyalty of our core subscribers.

What this means, ladies and gentlemen, is that we need to analyze the situation carefully in order to determine what we can reshape, what we can jettison, and what we must retain. In some cases, these objectives are going to be mutually exclusive, and we will have to find alternative courses.

There is yet another challenge: We must act quickly. We cannot long endure erosion in our subscriber base.

273

→ Tip: Having spelled out the challenges, the speaker spells out the basic methods by which he intends to meet them successfully.

Since we are facing *challenges,* I feel that it is necessary for me to issue some *challenges* of my own. I am creating the following working groups.

Working Group Number One will consist of **[speaker assigns members of this group].** This working group will formulate ten strategies for increasing subscription renewal.

Working Group Two, **[speaker assigns members],** will formulate ten strategies for attracting new subscribers.

Working Group Three, consisting of **[speaker assigns members],** will formulate a list of newsletter features that are indispensable and must not be changed. These are the features that hold our loyal core.

Now I want these three groups to work independently and *only* on their assigned problem. On **[date],** we will meet for reports of the working groups. Beginning at that time, we will try to mesh the results of the three groups' work.

Here's one more challenge: I *expect* conflict. We will have to resolve that conflict to produce a viable action plan that will ensure that our newsletter not only survives, but has a genuine future—that is, a future of growth and development and profitability.

→ Tip: The speaker acknowledges the difficulty of the challenges, but also the desirability and necessity of meeting them successfully.

These are difficult challenges, but the alternative, while not more difficult, is a lot more painful. The alternative is to shrink, shrivel, and eventually die. Even if we can maintain our core subscribers, we cannot continue to attract advertising in a context of steady decline. The one thing that's easy about these challenges is that we have no real choice—if we want to continue as a living enterprise. We *have* to face these challenges and face them successfully.

Let's get started!

Integrated Health Care: The Patient Is Waiting

Speaker: Lodewijk J.R. de Vink,
President and Chief Operating Officer, Warner-Lambert Company

I must confess as I take the gavel, I am less conscious of its honor than its obligation. I place great importance on PhRMA, and its potential as a unifying force for the pharmaceutical industry. I say this not so much as a compliment but as a challenge: because I believe in the year ahead that PhRMA's resources and resolve will be put to the test as never before. Unity, if not uniformity, is vital.

It may be a cliche—but sometimes cliches contain a kernel of truth. A window of opportunity has now opened for us—a world of opportunity. My challenge as Chairman of PhRMA—and our goal as an industry—is to take advantage of this moment at the same time we meet the monumental challenges of the marketplace.

And I am confident we can. PhRMA as an organization has never been better prepared. Our sharpened focus, our retooled staff, the degree of Board-member involvement—each will be key to the challenges we face: changing the way America views our industry, encouraging FDA reform, growing international markets, and dealing with government as both a customer and a regulator in this budget-conscious era. PhRMA's vision is a strong future, and its mission is advocacy. For these, the organization is ready.

The opportunities don't change the fact that we meet at a moment of maximum uncertainty for our industry. Such a statement may sound strange to anyone who observed—to anyone who endured the health care debate. Now, with that debate in political remission, a lay person might assume that the war is over, the winds of change have calmed, and our industry should get on with business as usual.

But we know there is no business as usual.

For the moment, the recent period of health care reform may be behind us. But in the world we deal with every day, the fulcrum of change is not a hearing room on Capitol Hill, not a War Room at 1600 Pennsylvania Avenue, or indeed any political power base anywhere in Washington. The catalyst for change is economic. Throughout the world, governments closely watch markets as the lines blur between public and private health care.

The market is driving change—farther, faster than anyone thought possible.

Source: Lodewijk J.R. de Vink, President and Chief Operating Officer, Warner-Lambert Company. Delivered to Annual Meeting of Pharmaceutical Research and Manufacturers of America (PhRMA), Washington, D.C., March 22, 1995. Reprinted by permission of Lodewijk J.R. de Vink and *Vital Speeches of the Day*.

As a result, our industry environment in 1995 is not at all what it was in 1992 or 1993. The changes we see are so dramatic, so comprehensive and so constant that we no longer plan in years, but in weeks and months.

At the same time, government is government around the globe. It can be a positive force in our future, or it can be a burden. As partners, we must work with governments to break the old paradigms and approach public policy with a common goal: Better and more cost-effective therapies for the public health.

When it comes to the market or to public policy, the old assumptions no longer hold. Let's take research—the heart of what we do. As an industry, we will commit approximately 15 billion dollars to research during the twelve months that I am chairman of PhRMA. As a percentage of sales, this is head and shoulders above any other global or domestic industry, double the highly admired computer industry, four times the aerospace industry, and nearly five times the telecommunications industry.

But given the new arithmetic of research, and the shifting sands of government policies around the world, the pharmaceutical industry can project the glow of health when in fact our condition is far more serious. It is a little like the light from a dying star, far across the galaxy. To the observer, the light burns bright, but at the source, at that very moment, the star is dead, a dark cinder suspended in space.

Can our industry, an industry that has manufactured so many miracles in the past, sustain research at its current levels? This is perhaps our greatest challenge, a challenge that goes to our very core.

In the past, we have triumphed over the "targets of opportunity," but the diseases we have yet to conquer will be more stubborn foes. From heart disease and cancer to AIDS and Alzheimer's, the diseases we battle today contain mysteries that will push our capabilities to the limit.

We see any number of troublesome signs in the marketplace.

Life-cycles are shortening: It was 10 years from Inderal to Lopressor, six years from Tagamet to Zantac, four years from Prozac to Zoloft, and now one year from Recombinate to Kogenate. We can see, in the future, the distance from King-of-the-Hill to challengers will be measured in months, not years.

Add to that the fact that R&D costs escalate as the number of NDA approvals stays flat, as generics are making it more difficult to "feed" R&D with established products.

Then look at governments. In Europe, we face reference prices and direct government price controls. In Japan, it is automatic price reductions. Here in the U.S., look at Waxman-Hatch; OBRA-90; mandated rebates, discounts, and formularies; user fees; and greater tax burdens under OBRA-93: almost one-third of the profitability of the industry effectively taken away since 1990. At some point, we pass the "point of no return."

Each is an alarm bell for anyone in this industry or in the public policy domain who believes we can sustain our historic level of R&D from now to the year 2000 and beyond.

As we look to the future we need a vision we all can share—a vision of a vibrant, productive industry: innovating, advancing frontiers, biotechnology, outcomes metrics, and hope.

But to get to that future, we need to challenge ourselves, to change our mindset.

Add to the competitive challenges we face, the power of public perception, and the way it shapes our industry.

Suppose we were to open today's newspaper or turn on the television to a steady stream of health advisories and alerts, houses under quarantine, schools shut down, cities in epidemic. Imagine living in a world where:

A group of 20 diseases claimed nearly 1000 lives a day.

Where certain diseases killed one in five victims, and consigned others to years in institutional care.

What sort of nightmare vision is this? Some sort of modern-day plague? Not at all. What I am describing is our world without the last generation of medicines and other therapies: A simple projection of the trends of 1960 carried forward to today. Tuberculosis, rheumatic fever, advanced-stage Hodgkins disease: A generation ago, these were killer diseases. That's a world we all lived in, and lived through. Today, they're either nonexistent or easily treated. Our world has been made significantly safer by the discoveries we have made and the drugs we have developed.

And still, to the public we are nameless and faceless. At best, we are invisible. At worst, we are an object of anger.

How do we respond? We marshall our numbers. How many of us have not cited the fact that pharmaceutical costs amount to only seven percent of the total price tag for health care in this country?

Quite frankly, I believe the world would be served better in terms of the cost of health care—better in terms of the quality of health—if overall costs were lower and more were spent on innovative medicines. Compare the United States to almost any industrialized democracy. You will find those countries spend a smaller percentage of GDP on health care, and at the same time, a larger piece of the pie on pharmaceuticals.

Nevertheless, we have made the magic number "7" something of a mantra when any of us testifies before the Congress or takes our case to the Administration or to the individual states.

Now, of course it is true. But that is not what the public sees. For the public in the U.S., prescription medicines account for a full 40 percent of their out-of-pocket health care costs. That is a reality that fuels their frustration. Even in those countries where drug coverage is available through public programs, this industry is not readily viewed as a positive force in health care.

There is a reason for the passion people feel, a reason that is evident if we recognize that what we do is bound up with the most emotional, personal, even primal of human desires. The fact is: What we make, makes people well. Our discoveries cure disease. Our discoveries relieve pain. Our discoveries restore the will to live, not just health, but hope.

As an industry, we bear a great deal of the blame for the public anger aimed our way, because we have done a great deal to insulate ourselves from the human factors I'm talking about. To too many people, our industry is like a tall building with no windows. Important, imposing, even inspiring, but also mysterious, secretive, frightening.

We need to end the arm's-length relationship with the people who put their health in our hands. We need to open ourselves up, take people inside.

We need to implement the vision Shelly Gilgore articulated this morning.

Let me share with you something I wish every patient could see, something that gets to the heart of what I mean. It is a bulletin board outside a research office in a Parke-Davis building in Ann Arbor, Michigan. On it, along with the meeting announcements and company bulletins, is a note, posted there by a researcher. On that smaller slip of paper are four simple words—four words that contain a world of meaning:

"The patient is waiting."

For that researcher, for all of us, it is a reminder that behind the Rubik's Cube of clinical challenges are real people. Human beings in urgent need.

Not long ago, a letter came to my office from a woman, Theresa P., whose mother was one of the first patients to be put on Cognex. Now, like any medicine that is first in its class, Cognex has its limitations. It can cause adverse reactions; not all patients can tolerate it. Not all improve. Sometimes at this stage of our knowledge, all we can hope in combating Alzheimer's is to slow the cruel pace of this progressive disease.

Before Cognex, what was happening to Theresa's mother is all-too-painful, and all-too-familiar. As the disease progressed, she could not dress or feed herself. She forgot faces and names. One by one, her memories of neighbors, friends, and family flickered out. One day, even her daughter became a stranger.

At first, Cognex appeared to have no effect. Then, one afternoon as Theresa was talking with the visiting nurse, she laughed. At that moment, her mother's face showed a glimmer of recognition. For the first time in a long time, her mother spoke.

"Theresa?" she said. "When did you get back?"

Now, you can tell Theresa the cost of Cognex.

Can anyone tell Theresa: What is it worth?

Unless we understand that distinction, we will never begin to know how people see our industry.

To me, stories like these point the way forward through all of the chaos and all of the change. We are suggesting today that this industry put the patient at the center of our enterprise. That we build a system, a true system of integrated health care that addresses an individual's needs in living a healthy and productive life. A system that is applicable around the world.

Where do we start? As an industry, we have got to do more than say take two aspirin and call me in the morning, even if it's two prescription-strength substitutes.

Together, we must embrace a vision in keeping with the great legacy of innovation we share. A vision that challenges us to make the discoveries that help people live longer, healthier, more productive lives—at the same time we make those medicines and therapies more affordable.

Innovation of the kind I'm talking about begins with integration: with an end to the old approach to health care, the old, piece-meal practice that carved health care into a succession of parts rather than a whole. That has been true in terms of the delivery of health care, and, in recent years as we have begun to focus on cost, it has been true there as well. We squeeze prescription costs to save money, only to find the patient hospitalized later at greater expense. Like building an automobile piece by piece, it should come as no surprise that the price of the parts is greater than the whole.

Eighteen short months ago, we may have been under the illusion that cheaper was better. But we now know, managed care is no panacea.

As critical as cost undoubtedly is, quality of care must be our priority.

We know what we don't want: cookbook medicine and pocketbook protocols.

But we also know that managed care is here to stay. It has arrived in the U.S. It is emerging in Europe. Capitation, formularies, quality measurements: these are the new fixed points in the delivery of health-care. And it is up to us to incorporate them into our own methods and measures of doing business. But they are not the key, the key is quality.

Now, it should come as no surprise—given the nature of the work we do—that we have unleashed an enormous amount of experimentation.

Horizontal—some add therapeutic categories. Vertical—others purchase PBMs or move toward comprehensive disease management. Still others pursue not vertical integration, but virtual integration: alliances rather than acquisitions.

Yet all this experimentation leads to the same place: We seek to integrate from product to service, to create an integrated system that will provide innovative new products, manage information to make the best use of knowledge, monitor drug use, offer feedback to the physician, to the pharmacist, and to the patient.

The examples I've offered by no means exhaust the options open to us. There is no formulary to follow as we adapt to the market, as we evolve new approaches to the twin goals of quality care and reduced cost. But there are several suggestions that seem to be imperative to the kind of integrated care I'm talking about.

First, to get closer to the patient, we must transform our relationship with the physician and the pharmacist. Pharmaceuticals ought to be integral to the practice of medicine at every phase. The way we do that is to expand beyond the business of selling a pill, and begin exploiting our knowledge about disease.

Again, I'm talking about a change in mindset: from a focus on what has been up to now a disease system, to a health system. A change from what Joe Califano, the former HEW Secretary, calls "sick care" to "health care."

To see what I mean, consider the continuum of care: prevent, diagnose, treat, and cure. A health focus will take medicines and other therapies back along that chain, toward the preventive measures that preserve health.

If we move in that direction, I believe we will see the emergence of a more sophisticated accounting of the "cost" of drugs. Not the one-dimensional price of a pill, but the impact it has on reducing hospital stays, speeding recovery, eliminating surgeries, and improving quality of life.

We have always proclaimed that medicines can do these things, we must develop systems that document the measurable difference we make.

Second, we must tap the talent of our research capabilities. We possess a knowledge base we have not even begun to leverage, a knowledge bank of human capital more valuable to us than any patent we possess. And it is critical to the kind of information industry our companies must become.

Third, we need to realize that as advanced as we are in terms of clinical capability, we are decades behind the curve in the Information Revolution. We're still scrawling on the physician's chart in the day of the data base. In health care, integration demands information.

Partners in Change

Now, we should be ready to acknowledge that some of our ideas are anything but new. Take the mechanics of the market model, for instance. There is a provincial tradition in the Chinese village: The physician is responsible for the health care of all, and every person in the village contributes to the doctor's salary, until they get sick. At that point, they stop paying. So the doctor has a direct incentive to help the sick get well.

Whether the Chinese have a word for this, I don't know. But surely, the concept is the same in any language and any place.

Up to this point, I have focused on the market forces compelling change within our industry. But pharmaceutical companies are just one part of the picture. Integration implies a lowering of the high walls that have traditionally divided the health care kingdom into separate fiefdoms, often acting as if the others simply do not exist.

Here, in many ways, we confront the most stubborn mindset of all: overcoming the old paradigm to become partners in change.

We have got to invite physicians to become partners in change. Doctors are facing the same competitive pressures that we are. While resistance to change remains, reality is setting in. Physicians are, slowly but surely, learning to live with managed care, just as managed care itself adapts to the physician-patient relationship. Very few physicians maintain strict fee-for-service practice these days, most have made their peace with the HMOs and PPOs that account for an increasing share of health care. Some doctors are even forming their own.

In addition to physicians, we have got to invite pharmacists to become partners in change. Yes, pharmacists too, face stark new economic realities, and a challenging new competitive climate. The days of pharmacies as "filling stations," counting pills into bottles—those days are over. If pharmacists wish to survive, they're going to have to have to fill a role for patients, not simply fill prescriptions.

We, the pharmaceutical industry, cannot resolve the economics of pharmacies. But their professional future and ours are linked.

Neighborhood pharmacists may not be the most efficient distributors of prescription drugs. But they are situated where "the action is": with the patient and the physician. If they emphasize their professional role, rather than their role as a distributor; if they focus on patient counseling, compliance, and monitoring outcomes; then pharmacists can be truly indispensable.

But change is by no means confined to the private sector alone. I want to focus for a moment on another key player in the pharmaceutical industry, and a critical partner in change: the government. Because as far-reaching as the forces of the marketplace may be, there is still a role only public policy can play.

PhRMA's mission is advocacy, and, as advocates, several clear challenges lie before us.

First, given the demographic pressures of a graying society, Medicare cannot continue with its costs unchecked. As bad as double-digit growth is today, the peak costs have yet to come. That's something our nation doesn't want to know, but demography is destiny. Managed care is coming to Medicare.

Second, the innovations I've spoken of today will not of themselves take care of the uninsured and the disadvantaged. Recognizing budget realities, we must continue to support a drug benefit for targeted senior citizen populations. Until we do, we remain in the political cross-hairs of a potent, and, if targeted appropriately, deserving, political constituency.

Third, politically speaking, Rome may not be burning, but Nashville, Sacramento, Harrisburg, Austin, and Oklahoma City are. As governors across the country put out budget fires, our customers in government look to us for savings.

Fourth, government policy must evolve in parallel with new market realities. Common sense tells us that the government entities involved in our industry cannot be the only institutions immune to change.

Consider the FDA, for example. For all our complaints, if the FDA did not exist, I believe we would have to invent it. We need government to referee the claims companies might be tempted to make about their products and their results. The FDA helps separate solid evidence from the snake oil.

But when government refuses to part with policies that reflect the old paradigm—policies that build walls that actually impede the emergence of integrated care—the result can be catastrophic as well as costly.

Just as we in the industry must evolve new approaches, government policy must make room for the innovations that serve the patient and make economic sense at the same time. That is what FDA reform is all about.

Fifth and finally, tax policy influences the competitiveness of all industries, ours included. Certain governments understand that tax incentives attract investment. Japan, for instance, offers generous R&D credits. Other countries maintain policies that provide tax-deferrals, special rates, certain and stable R&D incentives. Their policies are a magnet for competitive industries.

Tax increases, on the other hand, put domestic industry at a competitive disadvantage. Here, sad to say, America is the only country that penalizes companies that conduct R&D in the U.S. by not allowing them to take full advantage of the R&D deduction. And in the only U.S. jurisdiction where tax-deferral is available, Congress is making noises about reversing its policy. As an industry, we must send a signal that you cannot raise revenue by destroying jobs.

The key is forging a partnership in change: Not a tug-of-war for total control between industry and government, but a cooperative effort to evolve a system that allows the efficiencies and effectiveness integrated care can bring.

The Patient Is Waiting

The challenges I've laid out today will demand all of our expertise and energy—as individual companies, to be sure—but also as members of a common industry.

And as an industry, we have much to contribute, much to bring to the evolving system of integrated health care that is our goal. We should not be defensive, we must not be defiant. But above all, we simply cannot delay.

Because for all the complexity of our challenge, for all of the chaos we must clear away, we must see always the eloquent urgency of that small sign:

"The patient is waiting."

Thank you for your attention.

MODEL SPEECH 082:
Collaboration and Cooperation Between Departments

Key Use of Speech: To build teamwork.

Style of Speech: Instructional and inspiring.

Audience: Company employees.

Time: 8 to 10 minutes.

→ Tip: The speaker clearly states her subject, but then raises a "problem" issue. This kind of opening is very effective at capturing listeners' attention.

I want to speak to you today about promises, about *making* promises and about *keeping* promises. Specifically, I am going to talk about the promises we make to our customers and what we must do to keep them. Now, the problem with the sentence I just spoke is the word *we*. Who are "we"?

We are people with a *common* purpose: to make and keep this company successful. But *we* are also *different* departments with *different* responsibilities, and, too often, those differences conflict. Where we should have cooperation and collaboration, we sometimes have conflict.

Today, I want to zero in on a recent problem we experienced with the new Super Widget. A *problem*? But the Super Widget was a runaway success! Customers were tearing down walls and trampling one another to get it! Where's the problem?

→ Tip: The speaker makes it clear that she is about to use a recent event to illustrate her point.

It was just this: demand for the Super Widget exceeded supply, and while customers were very happy with the product, many, who could not get it when they wanted it, were angry with us. We made a lot of sales, but who knows how many customers we lost. Fortunately, the problem was ultimately solved, and I want to talk about how it was solved.

First, I am happy to report that Production has done an incredible

283

job of getting Super Widgets off the line, and we are now meeting customer demand well. But there was a period of crisis. Here's what happened.

We launched Super Widget. Demand had been underforecast, and customers began screaming for a product that simply did not exist. Now, Customer Service was soon overwhelmed with complaints, and Marketing responded by asking Customer Service to "come up with excuses" in order to protect the wonderful sales figures.

Make no mistake, too much demand is a lot better than no demand. But the danger is that sales exceeding projections can be hypnotic: "Just tell them to drop off the orders, and we will ship when we get around to it" becomes a kind of trance phrase, a mantra. But this bonanza is an illusion. Beneath the rising sales numbers, customer frustration starts building, and company credibility erodes.

Customer Service reported the complaints to Marketing, telling them that "We must do something. Incoming order entry lines are jammed, Production is losing ground, even on overtime, lateness is accumulating, and distributors are running out of product." Marketing replied that we had "just hit a home run." But Service just heard the screaming: from customers and from distributors. Customer Service asked for a moratorium on the sales campaign.

You can imagine how well Marketing liked *that* suggestion. Momentum had built, all the marketing dollars were committed, and those same distributors were expecting the campaign. Now this is where Customer Service started reasoning. Karen Willington, head of Service, explained that, while we didn't want to risk losing momentum, the risks to our reputation were getting much too high. Karen reasoned that those distributors, who do indeed want the campaign, also assumed that we could deliver product. Ultimately, they and those frustrated customers will not create sales numbers, but will generate hugely negative PR.

"We've got to take the heat off now and slow this thing down before we do any serious damage," Karen said.

Understandably, Marketing replied that stopping the campaign was impossible and that it was the job of Service to handle complaints, to take the heat.

At this, Karen shifted to another point of view, pointing out that the new business we were showing was nothing more than an illusion.

"We don't have new business, because we have no product to ship."

→ Tip: A few colorful quotations or half-quotations make the story more vivid.

Ultimately, Karen's arguments were persuasive. Service and Marketing collaborated on a *positive* strategy that bought time without sacrificing too much momentum. They decided to continue to support customers in regions already supplied, and to tell customers in new regions that the market does love the product, which has proven very successful—so successful that demand has *temporarily* outstripped supply. Until **[date],** we are halting distribution east of **[region].** In the meantime, our production operations are running flat out, and we are searching for alternative manufacturing sites to expand our capacity. We expect to meet all demand by **[date].**

Together, Service and Marketing presented this strategy to top management as something positive: customer accountability. Management bought it, and a case of conflicting interests between departments became an instance of productive collaboration. Our company came out a winner and, ultimately, so did our customers.

→ Tip: The speaker draws a clear "moral" from this story.

MODEL SPEECH 083:
Employee Commitment

Key Use of Speech: To define and create employee commitment.

Style of Speech: Instructional and inspiring.

Audience: Company or department employees.

Time: 10 to 15 minutes.

➡ Tip: Defining a deceptively familiar term is an effective speech opener, especially if you imply that the audience does not really know the meaning of the word in question.

➡ Tip: One of the best ways to bring an abstract concept down to earth is to apply it to a familiar procedure, process, or task.

"Commitment" is a word we hear so often that, for many of us, it has almost ceased to have meaning. For too many of us, "commitment" is simply the same as sticking with something—whether we like it or not. Well, perseverance is certainly an important part of commitment, but there is more.

There is caring. There is a desire to excel. There is a desire to satisfy the customer. There is a willingness to work a bit harder to care, to excel, and to satisfy. And, finally, there is the willingness and ability to solve problems creatively.

All of these are fine and noble goals, but just how do they work?

Let's apply this concept of commitment to something we all do every day: answer the phone.

Like *us,* when *we* pick up the phone to call a business with a question or a problem, most of our customers dial *us* with dread. They fear that they are about to waste valuable time and emotional energy in a frustrating process of being handed off from one department or individual to another.

Is this just customer paranoia?

Hardly.

The fact is that customers are *routinely* given an unwanted tour of a company's many departments before they finally reach someone who can actually help them—if they ever do reach that person.

→ Tip: Bring in supporting facts or research to bolster what otherwise might be taken as personal feelings and beliefs.

→ Tip: The speaker introduces a new set of interesting concepts, then explores them with his audience.

→ Tip: Use sound dramatic structure, beginning with the simplest or easiest problem and progressing to the most challenging.

We know from research that it is almost impossible to create customer satisfaction *after* a customer has been transferred to three or four different individuals or departments.

How can commitment kill this destructive routine?

When you pick up the phone, think of yourself as *committed* to the call and the caller. *Once you pick up that phone, you* own *the call.* It's *yours.* You *must* handle it. You *must* take responsibility for it. You are committed to it, and you *own* the call until one of three conditions is met:

The caller's question is answered.

The caller's issue is resolved.

Or you manage to "sell" the call to someone else who *can* answer he customer's question or resolve the issue.

Now, "selling" a call is absolutely not the same as "transferring" a call. Selling requires commitment, whereas merely transferring requires nothing at all. If you accept the commitment to the call, you are pledged to help the customer.

If you are lucky, the call you answer will be an easy one—or, at least, one for which you have a good, useful answer.

Answer the phone by assuring your customer that you *can* and *will* help. A customer calls to order Item A. You respond, "I can help you with that."

That was simple enough, but what do you do when a caller tells you that he ordered three dozen Model 123 widgets on March 5 and wants to know if he can change the order to two dozen Model 345's and *still* get delivery by March 15? While it is true that, based on your experience, you believe that it *is* possible that the modified shipment will arrive on time, you don't want to commit the folks in Production or in Shipping to a promise they *may not* be able to keep.

Should you hand off the caller to somebody in Production or Shipping?

Not if you believe that you own the call. Not if you are *committed* to this customer.

Instead, you reply "I can easily get that answer for you." And then you tell the customer what you need to do: "I need to check in with our Production Department and with our Shipping Department. I can do that right now. It should take about two to three minutes. May I put you on hold for that long? Or would you like me to get the information and call you back?"

This is commitment to customer satisfaction. You began by telling the customer that you *can* and *will* obtain the needed information. Then you told him what this will involve and how long it will take—how much of the *customer's* time it will take. Finally, you give the customer a choice. If you cannot give the customer a choice, at least ask his *permission* before you put him on hold.

→ Tip: Many good speeches alternate narrative or illustration with analysis or explanation.

Ladies and gentlemen, even if obtaining the requested information involves nothing more than looking up a computer file on your terminal screen—something that takes a few seconds—keep your caller informed by "sharing" your computer screen with him. Tell him what you see. If it takes a few moments for the requested information to appear, tell him that: "I'm typing in your name and order number. The computer is processing it. This should take just another second . . . There. Here we go. Your order is up on my screen."

True commitment to the customer caller requires you to behave a bit like a radio disc jockey. Never create "dead air"—silence. Remember, like the radio listener, your listener cannot see what you are doing and cannot see the expression on your face. Dead air over the radio airwaves means that listeners will start reaching for the dial. Dead air on a customer call creates anxiety and doubt in the caller, who may think that you have forgotten about him and are attending to another caller. It works against customer satisfaction. Avoid it by telling the customer what you are doing.

Does this sound like hard work? It *is*—though creating customer satisfaction is also *gratifying* work. But, so far, this has been *pretty* easy. What happens when someone calls with a problem you have no idea how to handle?

→ Tip: The speaker ups the ante and announces the most difficult challenge.

You're still committed. You still own the call.

You have two choices, then: either attempt to obtain the answer or information yourself or "sell" the call to somebody who has the answer or information. The choice you do *not* have is to send the *caller* off packing on an expedition to find the answer. *You* must do the legwork for him. This may mean putting the caller on hold for a length of time, or it may mean promising to call the customer back. In both cases, you must find either the answer or the appropriate person to supply the answer.

Whatever you do, avoid handling the tough call as if it were a hot potato, something to be tossed to someone else as soon as possible. This call, tough as it is, is a *valuable* item because it represents contact with a customer—and *any* contact with a customer is valuable. The customer, after all, is the source of our income.

When you sell the tough call, do so with care born of commitment. First secure permission to place the caller on hold while you first identify and then brief the colleague to whom you intend to sell the call. (If you think that it will take some time to track down the colleague, arrange to return the caller's call, setting a specific time for the return call.) Next, brief the colleague concisely but thoroughly. The caller should *not* be put in a position of having to tell *his* story over again. Ideally, the customer should never have to repeat that issue again to anyone within the company.

If the colleague tells you that he cannot help this customer, ask him for advice on whom else you might consult. Do *not* shatter the aura of commitment by whining to the customer that So-and-so was no help and that you have to contact somebody else. Instead, inform the customer that John Doe referred you to another staff member and that you need another minute or two to contact him.

And so it goes. Stick with the call and the caller until you can answer his question.

Is this time consuming?

You bet.

But what better way is there for us to spend our time than in creating customer satisfaction? This is what I mean by commitment.

OUTLINE

Opening

• Subject is "commitment"

What "commitment" really means

• Caring
• Desire to excel
• Desire to create customer satisfaction
• Willingness to work
• Solve problems creatively

Apply commitment to how we answer the phone

- Customers' fears
- Customers' frustrations
- Transferring customer from department to department kills customer satisfaction

What can commitment do?

- Call ownership concept
- How it works
- Call ownership is commitment to customer satisfaction
- "Sharing" computer screen with the caller
- Hard work, but worth it

What if you can't handle a problem?

- Obtain the answer or "sell" the call
- How to "sell" a call

Closing

- Stick with the caller
- Time consuming, but creates a satisfied customer

MODEL SPEECH 084:
Customer Service Importance

Key Use of Speech: To define good customer service.

Style of Speech: Instructional and inspiring.

Audience: Company or department employees.

Time: 12 to 15 minutes.

Customer service—there was a time when those two words, spoken in business circles, produced little reaction beyond a yawn. Customer service was a back-office operation. It was something a company did because it had to. It was not expected to generate revenue, and it was certainly not a place where careers were made.

There *was* a time when this was true.

➡ Tip: "Before and after" or "then and now" contrasts can be effective speech openers.

Today, *the* hot-button topic in business is none other than customer service. And the more high tech the industry and its product, the hotter that hot button is. In many high tech industries, including our own, most of the major players can offer their customers essentially the same high level of technology. What differentiates value, as the customer sees it, is price and customer service. Customer service has become a major product feature.

Beginning on **[date],** WXY Industries will launch a new ad campaign highlighting customer service.

[The speaker goes on to highlight the main features of the ad campaign.]

➡ Tip: The speaker makes the company's strategy and purposes clear so that everyone can work together toward a common goal.

So let me make this clear: we are promoting customer service. Now it is up to each of us to *deliver* all the customer service our ads will promise.

291

→ Tip: For conveying the desired message, anecdotes, real-life stories, are almost always more effective than abstract lectures.

I could spend the next—oh—several hours trying to detail standards for outstanding customer service. But relax. Instead, I would like to tell you a story. This comes to me from Ted Reynolds, director of Customer Service, who recently honored one of his staff for delivering a great example of top-level customer service.

One of service rep Jane Cohn's accounts, XYZ Corporation, made a panic call to her. Someone there had made an error setting their general account password and they were suddenly stymied by a software roadblock. This was an urgent problem: There was no way these folks could execute their customers' transactions!

So now there was a hyperventilating caller on the other end of Jane's phone. What XYZ wanted was their password problems solved *now,* over the phone.

→ Tip: Know your audience. The speaker shows that he is aware that his audience, presumably customer service professionals, understand the seriousness of Jane's problem; however, having acknowledged his audience's savvy, the speaker goes on to explain the dilemma anyway. Do not take the understanding for granted.

I see by the expression on some of your faces that you fully understand the seriousness of this situation. Jane did, too. She was thinking beyond the crisis. She knew that she had to protect her account's security—as well as our own. So now Jane was faced with the problem of adhering to prescribed security protocols without driving the customer out the nearest window. Jane knew that she had to secure all the mandatory confirmations so that she could be satisfied that she was speaking only with authorized personnel before she could walk them around the roadblocks

It's one thing to *say* that you're going to go by the book— in theory—but quite another always to go by the book in practice, when you've got a bunch of brokers on a conference call breathing hard into the receiver. They poured the pressure on Jane to by-pass the security rules.

"You know us, Jane! Just walk us through. It's *our* system! Bend the rules—just this once. We're in trouble!"

Or words to that effect.

→ Tip: The speaker doesn't know exactly what the customer said, but he interpolates a bit of dialogue anyway, to make the situation more immediate and vivid.

But Jane knew what she *had* to do. The security protocol requires her presence during the password by-pass procedure. She dropped everything else and got into her car. Once she was on site, you can be sure the faces she met were not warm and cheery. Jane apologized for needing to check for a security breach, but then she went on to explain why she needed to check.

"I emphasized to them that these procedures were of value to XYZ. They were the part of the security package the company had bought and paid for."

Jane understood that a big part of customer service is continually selling the *value* of *everything* the company does for the customer. She was also sensitive to the situation and observed that, in addition to being anxious and even angry, the people at XYZ were also embarrassed about the snafu they had brought upon themselves. So Jane followed another golden rule of great customer service: don't turn a crisis into an *us* versus *you* situation. Instead of dwelling on the customer's error, she emphasized that XYZ's internal security, *combined with* our systems, actually created a formidable shield for the protection of XYZ's customers. She pointed out that things weren't "going wrong" at all, but, on the contrary, the system was working the way it was supposed, protecting everyone involved.

In all of this uproar, Jane never took the easy way out by telling the customer that she was "only following procedure." Instead, she *explained* what kind of disaster could occur if XYZ's computers had been breached and we all let ourselves be duped into helping a gang of hackers. Then, once the system was up and running again, Jane took the opportunity to turn a disaster into positive contact with the customer. She pointed out XYZ might want to feature the value of an interlocking security system as a positive selling point in their advertising and promotional literature.

➡ Tip: At strategic points in the speech, summarize and underscore the principal issues and their meaning.

This, then, is customer service: rapid response, level-headed response, a high regard for the interests of the customer and of our company, the know-how to fix problems, and a talent for making customers feel good—and feel satisfied—even when things go awry.

This episode taught me a lot about customer service, and I hope that it was also instructive to you. It is this level of intelligence and commitment that we intend to sell as an important feature in each and every product we design.

Thank you for your attention.

OUTLINE

Opening

- Customer service used to be a back-office operation
- Today it is the "hot-button" topic in business
- Customers buy customer service

Launch a new ad campaign highlighting customer service

• Each of us must deliver what the ads promise
• Anecdote: example of top-level service
• Difference between theory and practice
• Customer service rep knew her job
• Never took the easy way out

What customer service is

• Rapid response
• Level-headed response
• Know-how
• Creation of customer satisfaction

Closing

• This example teaches us about customer service
• An important product feature
• Thank you for listening

———————————

MODEL SPEECH 085:
Decision-Making Skills

Key Use of Speech: To suggest ways of honing decision-making skills.

Style of Speech: Instructional and helpful.

Audience: Company or department employees.

Time: 20 to 30 minutes. [Depends on the length of the exercises.]

➡ Tip: Most questions will engage your audience's attention, but questions calling for an exercise of imagination do so most effectively.

Can you imagine what it would be like if, with every step you took, you went off balance, were propelled forward, and came perilously close to falling down?

A terrifying prospect?

Some horrible symptom of a dread disease?

The result of a terrible automobile accident?

No.

➡ Tip: The skillful speaker will have fun with this series of questions and will build them up dramatically. Your audience will want to hear the answer.

What I have described is walking, and we do it every day. If we seriously stopped to think about it the way I described it—well, I suspect there would be a lot of us taking to all fours.

Like walking, decision making is something we do every day. However, it can become a frightening, intimidating, and seemingly strange process if we begin to doubt our native ability to make decisions. And make no mistake about it: you *do* have native, natural decision-making ability. If you didn't, you would not be working here. We are a *very* demanding employer.

So I would like to begin by suggesting some ways that we can all use to get in touch with our native, natural decision-making ability.

Start simply by thinking about some decisions you made in the past—simple, direct decisions: an automobile purchase, perhaps, or

→ Tip: Try giving your audience a concrete, specific assignment. Avoid abstraction wherever possible.

a personal computer. What went into your decision? Make a list. Write it down. Your list should include a minimum of ten factors.

After you have written your list, put it away for two or three days. Then take it out. Look at each of those factors, one by one, and, one by one, evaluate them. What made you think about this or that factor? Why was this or that factor important? How did you decide on this particular set of factors? Then how did you put them all together to reach your decision?

I believe that what you will find is that your decision was much more complex than you ever realized. You probably put a lot more into it than you were aware of—just as your mind and muscles put a lot more into walking than (thank goodness!) you are aware of.

I have a few more basic decision-making exercises to tell you about.

[The speaker describes several more exercises.]

If you try these exercises—devote a little time to them—I believe that you will discover that the most natural decision-making processes involve what I call "trees" and "balance."

Let me show you a picture of a decision tree.

→ Tip: Use visual aids only if they will help you make your point more clearly. Don't use them as window dressing.

[The speaker uses slides or other graphics to show logic or decision tree diagrams.]

What these diagrams illustrate is that most decisions can be broken down into yes, no, and if–then blocks. For most of the decisions we habitually and routinely make every day, there is no need to go through a formal decision-tree process. But for complex decisions with high stakes—regarding, say, the welfare of the company—decision trees can be very helpful. A good rule is to take decisions that seem to involve overwhelming or overwhelmingly complex factors and break them down into their elements. Arrange the elements on a decision tree.

[The speaker goes through two or three decision-tree examples.]

A second decision-making process is weighing. We do this all the time, comparing two or more alternatives and judging their "weight"—that is, their relative value. Here's an example of how you can apply weighing to a complex decision.

[The speaker gives and discusses his example.]

➔ Tip: Let your audience know what you would like them to "take away" from your speech.

I hope these exercises will help you to make decisions more effectively, by tapping into your own, very real, very capable decision-making capacity. Before I close, I want to say a word or two about *living with* the decisions you make.

There are two unpleasant realities about decision making. First: not every decision you make will be a good decision. Second: even good decisions may turn out disappointingly or downright disastrously. When either of these outcomes occurs, you have at least three choices:

You can walk away from the consequences and try to forget the whole bloody thing. Few of us have the ability to do this.

You can brood miserably about the decision for days, weeks, months, decades. All too many of us *are* capable of doing this.

➔ Tip: Don't be afraid of addressing negative results and adverse consequences.

Or you can examine the decision and its outcome, and you can endeavor to learn from what happened. Very few of us have the presence of mind, when that certain substance hits the fan, to do this. And that is a pity—because failure is a great teacher, and failure is final only if we fail to learn from it.

Learning to live with your decisions does not mean running away from them or brooding about them, but learning from them. As much as you can learn from your successes, you can almost always learn even more from your failures. Learning to value both success and failure will make living with any decision much easier.

MODEL SPEECH 086:
Determination and Perseverance

Key Use of Speech:	To promote intelligent perseverance.
Style of Speech:	Instructional and inspiring.
Audience:	Company or department employees.
Time:	8 to 10 minutes.

→ Tip: Everyone is fascinated by anecdotes about the famous. Starting with one is a good way to capture the attention of your audience.

By 1879, when he invented the first practical incandescent electric lamp, Thomas Alva Edison was already a living legend—a folk hero, really—called the "Wizard of Menlo Park." People expected him to create technological miracles—at will and one right after another. Newspaper reporters did not wait for him to invent the electric light; they came to his workshops periodically to interview him as he was working on the project. They seemed to take it as a personal disappointment when, week after week, they would inquire about the progress of the invention, only to be told that the Wizard had not yet succeeded.

At one point, Edison told a reporter that he had tried some 1,600 substances as filaments for the lamp. All had failed.

"You must be very disappointed at all that wasted effort," the reporter observed.

"Wasted?" Edison replied. "Not at all. Now I know 1,600 substances that will *not* work as a filament for my lamp."

I certainly am not the first to tell this story, which is often held up as a dramatic "good old American" example of perseverance and determination. Edison, after all, also famously remarked that genius was 1 percent inspiration and 99 percent perspiration.

Well, who could have been more successful than Edison? Obviously, he was right. Determination and perseverance are of paramount importance.

➡ Tip: Surprise—here, questioning an obvious truism—is a very arresting device in any speech. The audience is now set up in expectation of a revelation.

Or *are* they?

Who could have been more successful than Edison?

Maybe the answer is **[pause a beat]:** *Edison.*

Here is America's greatest inventor, the holder of some three thousand patents. He grew wealthy from his inventions—but not nearly on the scale, say, of a Bill Gates or, for that matter, not on the scale of his contemporary, Alexander Graham Bell, the inventor of the telephone. While Edison certainly lived well enough and worked harder than any of his many employees, much of what he invented was invented one or two steps ahead of bill collectors and creditors. With three thousand patents, he was surely productive—but most of the patents were for commercially unfeasible projects, the products of his determined, persevering, trial-and-error approach to projects and problems.

➡ Tip: The speaker reveals a surprising fact about Edison. The audience should be truly focused on the speech as a result.

The fact is that, if Tom Edison were hired by a modern R&D department, he'd soon be canned—fired. What contemporary company can afford all that determination and perseverance, let alone the 99 percent perspiration?

My friends, I'm here to preach perseverance and determination—but perseverance and determination tempered by intelligence and an appreciation of reality. It's not that we must know when to call it quits, but when to approach a problem from a new direction or, if necessary, redefine the problem or even find a new problem to approach.

➡ Tip: Here is the statement of the speaker's principal subject.

Determination and perseverance are important qualities. You should approach any project and any problem armed with them. They are abstract, multisyllabic ways of simply, boldly saying "I can" and "I will."

But determination and perseverance should never *chain* you to a project or a problem after it has proven itself unproductive. No. These two admirable qualities should function to keep you wedded to the faith you have in yourself and in your abilities and, ultimately, in your judgment—one function of which is to know when it is time to move on, to try other approaches, to explore other possibilities.

Remain determined to use your skills and talents and to stand by them. Persevere in the exercise of your native and trained abilities. But don't become irrationally attached to any particular project or problem.

With due apologies to Thomas A. Edison, I thank you for your attention.

MODEL SPEECH 087:
Education

Key Use of Speech:	To encourage employees to take advantage of corporate educational development programs.
Style of Speech:	Instructional and inspiring.
Audience:	Company or department employees.
Time:	10 to 12 minutes. [Depends how much time is devoted to outlining the specific programs.]

→ Tip: Beginning with a personal anecdote can be an effective opener, especially if the "personal" situation is really universal—something just about everyone can identify with.

I have a young son—age ten—who likes me to help him with his homework. "Help" isn't really the word for it. He likes me to *do* his homework, if he can get me to. I used to fall for it. My *helping* him would imperceptibly become transformed into my *doing* the work. But now I've wised up. When too much of the burden of the work starts to fall on my head, I just say, "John, I already finished fifth grade. *You* haven't. *You* work these problems."

And, yes, I *have* graduated—all the way through graduate school, in fact. All of us here have graduated from some academic program or other. We have the diplomas to prove it.

Nevertheless, the world is rapidly changing. Technology, information, and geopolitics are all causing rapid shifts in how we do business. Getting a diploma gives you enough knowledge for the next two years at best. After that, you'd better be learning a lot more.

Of course, most of us do learn a lot more—on the job and randomly, "in life." But XYZ Industries has developed a series of educational-assistance and employee development programs to make this learning more formal, more focused, and more effective.

You will find in your mailboxes a pamphlet relating the details of our programs. Let me just hit the highlights here.

[The speaker outlines the highlights of the educational programs offered.]

These programs certainly can benefit you individually, but they are also essential to our collective success, which depends on the high quality of our workforce. That's why XYZ invests in assisting you. And it *really* is an investment: an investment in people; an investment in the future. As W.H. Pillsbury once said: "The businessman is coming to realize that education is to business what fertilizer is to farming." And believe me—as a businessman who's committed to education and as someone who grew up on a farm in **[location]**, I know darn well there's a connection between the two!

Ladies and gentlemen, the word "employee" is derived from the Latin word *implicare,* which means "to engage." Now, to me, that means not only to employ, but to stimulate, to win over or attract, to draw into, to involve. That's what we try to do with *all* our employees: to attract them, to stimulate them, to involve them. This includes junior-level people as well as top-level managers.

Managers aren't "supposed to" need any more development. At least, that's the conventional thinking. But we—the managers—discover every day that we are not always fully prepared to deal with today's changing business environment. Often, we also need ongoing training not just to keep up, but to stay ahead of the curve. Many of our in-house learning programs include top-level executives, along with middle-level and first-line managers, whom the company has identified as having high potential.

Make no mistake: we all need ongoing learning. We can't depend on a few top executives. Nobody can just give orders anymore. Teams and flattened organization are creating an entirely new set of behavior patterns, attitudes, and methods of communication. Everyone, at every level, needs to understand such things as international competition, organizational versatility, and how to structure international teams and alliances. Indeed, we expect to devote more and more of our resources to employee development.

The main focus of our educational programs is to give us all a foundation of knowledge upon which to build an awareness of global and other key issues. Our programs put the emphasis on the learner rather than the teacher. Ideally, these programs will spark interest, stimulating those of us who take advantage of the programs to

→ Tip: A touch of humor at the right moment keeps the speech from becoming preachy.

→ Tip: Get your audience to think about the key words in your speech.

→ Tip: Don't talk down to your audience. Here the speaker is careful to include "managers" in the group that should take advantage of the employee development program.

continue the ongoing process of learning on our own. For the company, I believe these programs are essential. For each of us, individually, they can be the start of any number of exciting journeys.

EXAMPLE SPEECH

Working in Interesting Times

Speaker: Thomas W. White,
President, GTE Telephone Operations

Have you ever heard the phrase, "May you live in interesting times." Within the past month, I've read two different articles that used that very phrase to describe life in the '90s.

One said the phrase is an Irish blessing, and the other said it's a Chinese curse.

I don't know the true origin. I doubt that anyone does. What's important is that we do live in interesting times, and whether it's a blessing or a curse depends on your individual point of view.

More to the point for all of us here today, we work in interesting—and dynamic— times.

Everything in our business has turned upside down, and we can expect it to keep on turning, especially in light of the telecom bill.

Typically, when people like us get together to talk about changes in our industry, we spend our time examining new technology applications, and what they mean for our customers.

That's the purpose of meetings such as this Forum. And, for the most part, that's what's on the agenda this week.

For my presentation today, however, I'd like to look at how the blitzkrieg of change has affected employees.

How have the survivors of downsizing responded to unrelenting change? What should companies do to help them? And how can we create mutual benefits for both employees and the company?

In other words, after you reengineer the organization, how do you reengineer the psychology that makes it work?

I have picked this topic for discussion because I view workforce concerns as one of the most critical issues facing our industry today.

If we're going to succeed, we need motivated, knowledgeable employees. And, that means that we need to understand what's happening to them and—let's face it—ourselves.

Source: Thomas W. White, President, GTE Telephone Operations. Delivered to the 1996 Western Communications Forum, Dallas, Texas, on February 19, 1996. Reprinted by permission of Thomas W. White and *Vital Speeches of the Day.*

Today, I'm going to focus on three aspects of the employee issue:

First—the overall mood of America today and how it affects the workforce;
Second—the need for a new attitude in the workplace; and
Third—the need for better balance between our work and personal lives.

I guess you could say that America has fallen into a bad mood. We live in difficult times.

Bad news is everywhere—shouted at us on television, splashed across newspapers and the topic of practically every cocktail party conversation. We are stuck on the negative.

I don't know about your experience, but I overhear a lot of conversations in the cafeteria about how tough it is out there. It's become a badge of courage among workers to be tired, grumpy and overworked.

In some ways, it makes sense. We are asking employees to do more with less. We are asking employees to adjust and readjust and readjust again. And, we aren't promising them a whole lot in return for their efforts.

It takes courage and resolve to keep up today. Many of our people are tired, frustrated and scared.

But, looking at life as a glass half empty—or, even worse, as a glass with a chronic leak—is not making it easier for anyone.

As president of GTE Telephone Operations, I'm dealing daily with downsizing, culture shifts and workforce insecurity.

I've spent quite a bit of time thinking about these issues—how I feel about them organizationally—and how I feel about them personally.

In the process of this introspection, I've been fortunate to spend time with some experts who have helped me—and who I believe can help all of us.

First, I'd like to share some ideas I've learned from a rather unassuming young man from Case Western Reserve University who is making a name for himself in organizational development circles. His thoughts are simultaneously revolutionary out there-thinking and plain old common sense.

His name is Dr. David Cooperrider and his concept is called "appreciative inquiry."

Appreciative inquiry focuses us on the positive aspects of our lives and leverages them to correct the negative. It's the opposite of "problem-solving."

Let me give you a real example.

Dr. Cooperrider conducted a study in which two separate groups of people tried to improve their bowling skills. Both were videotaped as they bowled.

For the first group, the instructor pointed out their weaknesses and concentrated on helping the team work through them.

In the second group, the instructor pointed out strengths, helped the team analyze what made them strong and offered suggestions on how to apply that strength to other aspects of the game.

So, what do you suppose happened?

If you're like I was when I first heard the story, you're probably saying, "Oh, I know. The first group got worse and the second group got better."

Well, that's not the case. The first group improved. The traditional approach to problem solving does work.

The second group also improved—but, much more quickly and to a much greater degree.

Dr. Cooperrider believes—and has proven—that you can use this approach in business. Appreciative inquiry can get you much better results than seeking out and solving problems.

That's an interesting concept for me—and I imagine for most of you—because telephone companies are among the best problem-solvers in the world.

We trouble-shoot everything. We concentrate enormous resources on correcting problems that have relatively minor impact on our overall service performance. We don't tolerate imperfection.

This has led to some excellent results. But, Dr. Cooperrider suggests that, when used continually and over a long period of time, this approach can lead to a negative culture.

If you combine a negative culture with all the challenges we face today, it could be easy to convince ourselves that we have too many problems to overcome—to slip into a paralyzing sense of hopelessness.

And, yet if we flip the coin, we have so much to be excited about.

We are in the most dynamic, and the most influential business of our times.

We ought to be excited, motivated and energized.

We can be . . . if we just turn ourselves around and start looking at our jobs—and ourselves—differently . . . if we kill negative self-talk and celebrate our successes.

If we dissect what we do right and apply the lessons to what we do wrong, we can solve our problems and re-energize the organization at the same time.

Test yourself: When you get survey results that tell you that 94 percent of your customers are satisfied, what do you do?

Do you conduct additional research to find out what makes those 94 out of 100 people so happy—or do you send your entire research department out to gather as many negative stories as you can from the miserable 6 percent?

In the long run, what is likely to be more useful: Demoralizing a successful workforce by concentrating on their failures or helping them over their last few hurdles by building a bridge with their successes?

Don't get me wrong. I'm not advocating mindless happy talk. Appreciative inquiry is a complex science designed to make things better. We can't ignore problems—we just need to approach them from another side.

We need to turn our curses into blessings.

Try this exercise the next time you assemble a team to address a sticky issue. Don't start the meeting by assaulting everyone with the problem.

Instead, before you get going, ask everyone in the room to think about—or, better yet, to discuss among themselves—a time when they felt most energized, productive, and useful. As the conversation progresses you can literally watch the energy build in the room.

Now, ask your team to apply the same approaches that made them successful before to the problem at hand. Instead of throwing out a daunting and depressing assignment, you've provided them with a new opportunity to shine.

Your people know they can succeed because you've just reminded them they've done it before. Your people want to succeed because you've just reminded them how good they felt when they did it before.

Try it. I have. And, it works.

Now, let's talk a little more about attitude.

Webster defines attitude as "a mental position."

Successful companies—and employees—take the position that change is positive and challenge is good.

They accept the environment in which they find themselves instead of wishing for the "good old days." They know that change creates opportunities to win if—and only if—we're willing to look for new ways to operate instead of letting the challenges overwhelm us.

Tomorrow's winners share similar characteristics:

They're positive and they believe in themselves;

They listen because they understand that most good ideas build from others' thoughts;

They're committed and don't easily give up;

They take accountability for results;

They take charge of their own attitude because they know that it comes from within their own minds and their own hearts; and

Finally, winners have balance.

That's the last point I'd like to discuss.

Back when the economy was less global, when technological change was more orderly and when customers were less demanding, companies were in charge. The degree of control varied depending upon the business and, in telecommunications, it was significant.

Well, that's not the case anymore. The marketplace is in control—and it often feels as though no one's at the helm. Now, we answer to the customer.

Now, the marketplace tells us when and where to deploy technology.

Now, the competition helps define how many people we can employ, how much we can afford to pay them and how much equipment we can provide them to do their jobs.

As I said, we live in interesting times.

In the past decade alone, 3 million white collar jobs were eliminated in the United States and some say that up to 80 percent of middle management jobs could be eliminated in the coming years.

The people who remain are faced with doing more with what seems like less. There's not much that companies can do to reverse that trend.

And yet, employees who are used to employers that call the shots are befuddled, confused—and, quite often, angry.

Well, I have a potential solution to that one. This one's not quite as "easy" as the appreciative inquiry approach, but it does make as much sense.

It's simple. As individuals, we each need to take control. To stop being victims. To get ourselves back in balance.

Many of us have responded to the feeling of spinning out of control by putting all of our energies into work. We spend too many hours on the job and we spend all our time off the job worrying about work.

Now, imagine your world and each of your employees' worlds as a triangle. One point is work. One is family. And, one is self.

When we put all our weight in one corner of our triangle, that weight just keeps us spinning and spinning and spinning. And, if we do it for too long, when we stop spinning, we're finding ourselves burned out.

I believe that we need to redistribute our energy to each corner of the triad. By focusing equally on our work, our non-work selves and the ones we love, we balance ourselves out. And, by personally deciding how much energy we expend on the three facets of ourselves, we regain the control that we felt has been lost.

The result is more confidence, less stress and, quite frankly, more receptivity to an appreciative approach to life.

This is not easy to do. When you are terrified of losing your job, it takes incredible courage to stand up and say, "Stop!" when the demands become too great.

And yet, I've found that employees who set the proper parameters on their own time and who have a life outside of work are actually more productive. They're more creative, sharper and, quite frankly, a whole lot more fun to be around.

But, employees can't easily do this by themselves. Companies need to make it OK for them to take back control of their own lives.

For example, we can:

Offer flextime, compressed work weeks, jobsharing and telecommuting options so that employees can tailor jobs to specific lifestyle preferences and obligations;

We can provide training to help employees understand themselves and their needs;

We can offer exercise facilities and wellness programs so that workers can build positive mental health through improved physical health;

We can increase workplace efficiency by eliminating duties that suck up employee time without producing positive results;

We can share "how-to" literature to help employees deal with their own balance issues;

We can be more sensitive to the work demands we place on our employees—and on ourselves;

And we can watch what behaviors we reward to make sure that we're not subconsciously asking employees to live unbalanced lives.

To reinforce the importance of balance, and to provide some helpful hints that we all can apply, I would like to refer to the book, *Walking the Tightrope* by Dr. Tom Barrett.

Dr. Barrett is a family counselor and therapist from the Washington, D.C., area who has spent much of his career working with members of congress.

Talk about a group that's out of control and out of balance!

In his book, he asks the question, "If you found that you only had one week more to live, what would you do?"

Your answer to the question identifies what is most important to you. Then, if you ask yourself how much time you spend today on the activity you identified, you get a real glimpse into how much balance—or unbalance—you have in your life.

I guarantee that if you were to take more time to do those things that are most important, you would be happier, healthier and feel more in control.

That's just one exercise Dr. Barrett prescribes. He also recommends that:

We should share our spotlight with the others—family and co-workers—who help us succeed;

We should take time to listen to the concerns and issues that affect the other people around us;

And, we should stop asking our families and our co-workers to "hold their breath" just a little longer until we get past our current crunch and can devote more time to them.

Each of these actions requires a conscious choice. But, each lifts us out of the victim role and puts us back in control.

I consider the issues that I raised today as critical. And yet, I don't generally believe that business people do a very good job of addressing them.

We need to help our employees take that control because a better outlook on life in general, a more positive attitude in the workplace and better work/family balance all lead to happier and more productive employees, which in turn leads to a more successful company.

By success, I mean a company with financial and market strength as well as a work environment where personal relationships and teamwork can flourish, where employees have a positive self-image and a positive company image . . . where accomplishments are celebrated and where employees are respected for their contributions to the organization.

Achieving that in these interesting times might appear to be a challenge, but with the right outlook and attitude, it's not. Let's look at the opportunities we have as not a curse, but a blessing.

I hope that I have been able to provide you with some food for thought toward that end.

Let me say what I mean another way and leave you with this thought:

Life is not a problem to be solved, but rather a gift to be enjoyed.

You've been a great audience, thank you!

MODEL SPEECH 088:
Ethics

Key Use of Speech:	A statement and definition of the company's values.
Style of Speech:	Informative and sincere.
Audience:	Company employees.
Time:	10 to 12 minutes.

I always look forward to speaking with all of you at this quarterly meeting. It's an opportunity to touch base on the fundamentals of our business, and, ladies and gentleman, there's nothing more fundamental than ethics and values.

→ Tip: Speeches about values can be deadly dull or priggish. The speaker avoids this by making a brief statement on the importance of values (they're fundamental) and then defining key values. The speaker avoids abstraction and preachiness.

Whenever I think about fundamental values, I think about small-town America. Now, I realize that our nation is far more diverse than what most of us think of when we think of small towns. Nevertheless, the small town remains a cherished place of the American heart, if not always of actual American demographics, and most of the values we associate with small-town America still flourish in each of us, no matter where we live or where we were raised.

What are some of those values?

Each of us could probably prepare a long list, but I'll zero in on a half dozen that I see as the most fundamental of all.

→ Tip: The speaker acknowledges that he has no monopoly on knowing what values are the most important.

The first is the family. Today, families come in many configurations, but the underlying *value* of family is, I believe, absolute. For it is within the family that children learn values as diverse as love, responsibility, communication, and respect for authority, as well as a spiritual reverence. Within the family, children also learn about living up to their potential and doing the right thing, as well as doing things right. I have always thought of XYZ Corporation as a family working together for each of us individually and for the common good. Family values—that nearly worn-out phrase—are *our* corporate values.

The second great value, for me, is independence. Our country is built on this value, and our company has always followed what it thought was the best path, rather than the path of expediency, of least resistance, or simply what others were doing. We are independent, and we cherish independence. We also encourage employees to think independently and not to jump on any bandwagons.

The third value of particular importance to our company is integrity. We strive to be scrupulously fair and honest in all of our dealings: with customers, with vendors, and with each other. Integrity shapes every one of our products. We do not believe in offering loss leaders or in cutting corners.

Now we come to the fourth value: self-determination. Each of us has the right to determine his or her own destiny. Our own ability and hard work determine our output and our success. No one of us can afford to be complacent.

Next, the fifth fundamental value: loyalty. At XYZ, we believe in and are loyal to our customers. We also believe in and are loyal to our employees. Those of us in management expect the same loyalty in return. For loyalty to and belief in our company empowers us to fight for what we believe in.

There is a sixth value I wish to propose to you today: compassion. Americans have always been noted for lending a helping hand and for looking out for the less fortunate. Likewise, at XYZ, we believe in "doing well by doing good." We care about our customers and about those who work with us. We also care about our communities, as evidenced by the incredible range of community activities most of us engage in. We are a company of volunteers.

[The speaker gives a few examples of community participation.]

XYZ and everyone associated with it make a difference—a very large difference—in the communities we serve.

Ladies and gentlemen, I believe that XYZ Corporation is a value-based company in every sense of the word. Our company is founded on the values of the family, independence, integrity, self-determination, loyalty, and compassion, and it is our mission, both individually and collectively, to preserve those values. Not only do they have great intrinsic worth, they are intimately linked to our reputation— and that is one of the greatest things we have going for us. Repeat-

➜ Tip: A final paragraph reinforces the importance of maintaining and upholding values.

edly, we are named in "most admired company" lists—and not just because of our balance sheet. Please remember that every employee represents our company. Remain alert, and cherish the values of our company.

As we look into the future, our challenge is to continue to embody the values that have built our company.

———————————————

MODEL SPEECH 089:
Excellence

Key Use of Speech:	To define and inspire excellence, with emphasis on research and development.
Style of Speech:	Informative and sincere.
Audience:	R&D personnel.
Time:	10 to 12 minutes.

I am always delighted to speak with our R&D staff. Today, I'd like us to step back for a moment or two and look at what we do from the point of view of excellence as an objective. Key to achieving excellence in the R&D function are a clear vision, a sense of mission, stability of direction and constancy of purpose. Now, I know that you folks in R&D have lofty goals and have always responded to a clear vision and a sense of mission; however, it is our job in management to ensure that the organization has a vision, a mission, values, and operating principles so carefully stated that they give strong guidance even under the most dynamic market conditions. Without this leadership, excellence will remain an elusive goal, no matter how dedicated all of you are.

Another issue at the heart of excellence is closeness to customers. Achieving excellence requires allegiance to customers even more than allegiance to function. We can't just be satisfied with functioning well as an R&D department. We can only be satisfied when the customer is totally satisfied. This means bringing R&D together with manufacturing and business management into small, highly focused, and very nimble teams that respond quickly and appropriately to customer requirements.

Perhaps the most powerful driver of customer satisfaction is the pervasive application of quality principles. We define quality in terms

> → Tip: The speaker outlines the difficult essentials of defining excellence in the context of this particular company.

> → Tip: The speaker uses the concept of excellence as a motive for a number of actions and qualities, including interdepartmental

313

of customer satisfaction. We are in the midst of a quality revolution in American business, and, because of its vital link to customer satisfaction, quality must ultimately be defined by the customer, both domestic and global. Quality includes the features the customer wants, the timeliness the customer wants, and a price the customer is willing to pay.

Now here's the *really* tricky part. While cooperating and coordinating with other departments, and while focusing on the customer, R&D needs to maintain and even to enhance its particular functional excellence. We do this by encouraging you to cultivate your sense of professional community. We believe that R&D should have a large measure of influence over its destiny, as well as that of the company. Part of this sense of professional community depends on enhancing the synergy between personal goals and company needs. Fortunately, most of our R&D staff *personally* delights in creating exciting new products, so this synergy is relatively easy to achieve.

→ Tip: The speaker both expands and focuses the definition of excellence by showing how it is related to other qualities.

Excellence and diversity also go hand-in-hand in building an outstanding R&D organization. I'm proud that our R&D department is broadly diverse. I'm also proud of the level of technical supervision in this department, which has not been developed at the expense of excellent people skills and business savvy.

While we're talking about people and excellence, let me reinforce my encouragement of self-development. Our object at XYZ is to offer an exciting and rewarding future to everyone, and we recognize that this requires a wider range of education and training available as part of your employment.

All of these factors are essential contributors to excellence. But there is one more set of ingredients. We must ensure that all employees have challenging work, that they are well matched to their work, and that they have needed support and needed information. In other words, we must ensure that all employees are used to the very limit of their personal capabilities—and then we must provide the means to help those personal capabilities grow every day. In return for your commitment to excellence and your willingness *routinely* to push the envelope of your personal capabilities, senior management at XYZ promises that we, too, will keep the faith and strive for excellence, always providing you with new challenges—and new rewards!

MODEL SPEECH 090:
Goal Attainment

Key Use of Speech:	To define current goals and to inspire employees to achieve them.
Style of Speech:	Informative and inspirational.
Audience:	Production department employees.
Time:	5 to 8 minutes.

→ Tip: Want to communicate a no-nonsense, roll-up-your-sleeves attitude? Begin the speech without preliminaries. Dive in.

Please make a note of the following three goals. During this quarter, I am asking Production to achieve:

1. **[Quantity]** units out the door
2. **[Percentage amount]** reduction in rejected units
3. **[Time frame]** turnaround in retooling for production of the new models.

Believe me, folks, I recognize that these are not easy goals to achieve, but I am confident that you *can* achieve them. For our part, corporate management will give you maximum support.

[The speaker outlines the support program.]

For your part, what achieving these goals will require is focus. Department managers must determine how much overtime will be required to make all three goals, and I expect cooperation from the production staff in contributing the necessary overtime.

Time management will also be critical. I suggest that managers allocate *more* time to quality assurance in order to reduce rejected units. This investment in additional time will, I am confident, result

315

→ Tip: The order of the speaker's specific instructions and recommendations follows the order of the goals set forth at the opening of the speech. A well-structured speech sets up expectations, then fulfills them.

in an overall time savings. Remanufacturing rejected units costs more time than manufacturing good units to begin with. Don't let the raw production numbers tempt you into shorting the inspection process and the other quality-assurance functions.

Time and project management will also be critical in the retooling operation, which must be effectively coordinated with ongoing production. Teamwork will be paramount in achieving this goal.

Focus, teamwork, time management, and a willingness to invest time in order to save time: these are the keys to achieving the challenging goals I've established.

There is one other factor. Please note that these are not *my* goals. They are *our* goals. Lay claim to them, because you very definitely have a big stake in them. We need to get product into the marketplace in order to exploit the *narrow* lead we have on our competition. The firm that gets a toehold into this market first will win the lion's share of the market in the long haul. Achieving all three production goals is very important to us all as a company. Our current leadership position and our ultimate viability as a competitor depend on what you achieve in the next three months. I know that I can count on you. We all count on you.

MODEL SPEECH 091:
Goal Setting

Key Use of Speech: To choose and define goals.

Style of Speech: Informative and helpful.

Audience: Company employees.

Time: 6 to 7 minutes.

➤ Tip: You can never go far wrong quoting Yogi Berra.

Yogi Berra, the Yankee who told us it wasn't over until it was over, also cautioned that "You got to be very careful if you don't know where you're going, because you might not get there."

How do we know where we're going?

The most effective way is to get into the habit of setting goals—or, more accurately, setting goals and determining objectives to get you to those goals.

As with any planning process, this requires an investment of time; however, the investment at the front end will save you time and effort later on. You'll be less likely to spin your wheels or to chase down blind alleys, only to have to double back again.

➤ Tip: The speaker emphasizes process rather than abstract generalizations.

In most tasks, we're accustomed to *building,* to moving from relatively small step to the next small step until we have put together the larger whole. Setting goals works just the opposite way. Begin with the big picture: the major things you wish to accomplish. These are your goals.

Don't settle for the first goal you establish. Try to establish several alternatives, then analyze them:

First: Is this goal worth achieving?

Let's pause a minute to discuss this first point in terms of our company's overall mission, which you should use as your ultimate yardstick in determining whether a goal is worth achieving.

[The speaker reviews the company's mission.]

→ Tip: The speaker takes a walk-you-through approach to the process of setting goals.

Second: What benefit will be derived from achieving this goal?
Third: What liabilities does achieving this goal create?
Fourth: What will this goal cost in time and other resources?
Fifth: Is this goal achievable?

Once you have selected a prime candidate for a goal, work backward through the steps necessary to achieve that goal. These steps are called objectives. They are the building blocks that make up the goal.

List the objectives, then analyze them in terms of the time, effort, and resources each objective requires. You may discover one or more objectives that seem unfeasible. If this is the case, you will probably have to revise your goal.

After you have set your goal and determined your objectives, you will find that you have created a kind of road map to get you from where you are to where you want to be.

→ Tip: The speaker uses the idea of a road map as an illustrative figure of speech, then goes on to develop the analogy in the next paragraph. Figures of speech should not simply decorate your speech. They should serve to make your points more vividly and clearly.

Now, it is one thing to have a map and quite another actually to travel the road. Objectives and goals are points on which we focus our energy and resources. They are targets. The aim they require is commitment and an ability to husband energy and to organize resources.

Setting goals provides a kind of feedback loop. We have direction, and we can measure the distances we have traveled and have yet to travel. While achieving goals gives a great sense of satisfaction, even failing to achieve a goal is useful. With a goal firmly established, we can measure how wide we are of the mark and make the necessary corrections to hit it next time.

→ Tip: The speaker addresses the feelings she perceives her audience has.

Goals are also a bit frightening or, at least, intimidating. Once you set a goal, you make yourself accountable—and that frightens some people. But business is all about accountability, and it is also about avoiding drift. Setting good goals introduces accountability and, hit or miss, combats drift. Personally, I'd rather fall short of a goal than drift directionless. *That* is truly frightening, and not just intimidating.

Setting goals requires a mental, emotional, and even a physical commitment. It also requires confronting problems and facing obstacles. And, make no mistake, setting goals consumes time. Yet, I am confident that you will find such commitment, confrontation, and time well invested. If you don't know where you're going, you might just never get there.

MODEL SPEECH 092:
Imagination and Creativity

Key Use of Speech: To encourage the exercise of imagination.

Style of Speech: Informative, helpful, encouraging.

Audience: Company employees.

Time: 10 to 12 minutes.

➜ Tip: If your topic is imagination, why not begin imaginatively?

Those of you who are fans of TV's *Seinfeld* sitcom may remember the episode in which Jerry Seinfeld and his friend George Costanza sit down to develop a pilot for a TV comedy series and end up scripting "a show about nothing." Well, the playwright Samuel Beckett actually beat them to this by about forty years with his *Waiting for Godot.* What's that play about? Two tramps waiting for a mysterious guy named Godot who never arrives. **[pause]** End of play.

Now Beckett got the Nobel Prize. Why? Maybe because he managed to describe life so well—or, at least, what all too many of us do in life: sit, shoot the breeze, hold meetings, conduct studies, hire consultants, and, basically, wait. Wait for the Big Idea and the Ultimate Product, what software developers call the "Killer App"— the one application the world absolutely cannot do without. Problem is that the Big Idea is usually like Godot. It never arrives. End of play.

➜ Tip: Obviously, imagination is difficult to define, and the speaker acknowledges this by quoting a humorously convoluted definition.

Here at XYZ, we cannot afford to *wait* for a Big Idea, which may or may not come to us. We have to *create* Big Ideas. This requires imagination. What is imagination? Author George M. Prince provided a provocative definition in his 1970 book, *The Practice of Creativity,* calling it "an arbitrary harmony, an expected astonishment, a habitual revelation, a familiar surprise, a generous selfishness, an unexpected certainty, a formable stubbornness, a vital triviality, a disciplined freedom, an intoxicating steadiness, a repeated initiation, a difficult delight, a predictable gamble, an ephemeral solidity, a unifying difference, a demanding satisfier, a miraculous expectation, an accustomed amazement."

Well, I guess *that* clears this matter up!

Really, all we need to know is that imagination is something you gotta have. But what do you do if you ain't got it?

I could say: You *get* it. But, in fact, you *do* have it. You *got* it. You've just gotta get *to* it.

Maybe you don't believe me. Maybe you believe that you simply do not have imagination.

Well, you *are* earning a living from XYZ Corporation. You have managed to survive so far. You have gotten at least some of the things you want. All of this proves that you have the capacity for creative, effective, imagination. There are few old sayings older than "Necessity is the mother of invention." But that old saying describes how most of us exercise creative imagination. We come up with inventive solutions to problems whenever we absolutely have to. And that is probably every day. Most of the time, we don't even think about it.

This doesn't mean that you can't *start* thinking about it— that is start thinking about how to use your imagination in a more focused, practically creative way. You *can* learn to access more of the creativity you already have, and to turn it on when you need it.

Perhaps the easiest and most enjoyable way of accessing creative imagination is through brainstorming. This is a creativity technique that got its start back in the 1930s with Alex Osborne of the advertising agency Batten, Barton, Durstine, and Osborne. Osborne developed an unstructured imaginative process in which stern judgment—your boss bellowing *"Are you out of your mind? It will never work!"*—is suspended and deferred while a group of brainstormers focuses exclusively on generating a *quantity* of ideas.

Many of you have probably brainstormed in the past. The classic setup puts half a dozen to a dozen people in a room and encourages a freewheeling and purposely fast-paced stream of ideas—some generated independently, some triggered by an idea that came before. The key is that neither comment nor criticism is permitted. The only objective of brainstorming is to grind out as many ideas as possible— the wilder and more unworkable the better. Somebody is delegated to take careful written notes, and, some time after the brainstorming

Tip: Now the speaker cuts to the heart of the matter.

Tip: The promise of being shown how to make the most of a faculty you didn't even know you had is exciting and will rivet the attention of any audience.

Tip: The speaker transitions from the abstract topic of imagination to a very concrete way of harnessing imagination: brainstorming.

session, the brainstormers review the notes and only *then* begin judging, debating, analyzing, *and* filtering and rejecting the ideas.

You may find various variations on the basic brainstorming technique helpful. For example, there is "reverse brainstorming," in which the group lists all the possible weaknesses of a new idea. Then, after listing these, they address each weakness in order to eliminate or improve it. Or you might try "buzz groups," small subgroups who brainstorm for very brief, very intensive periods, then reconvene as a larger group and exchange ideas. There's also "trigger response," in which a group of eight to twelve people defines the problem they will work on, then must agree on the solution desired. Once these agreements are reached, the group generates as many ideas as possible to achieve that solution.

Now brainstorming works best in groups, but you can also work alone. Give *yourself* permission to list wild ideas while suspending judgment on them. Don't censor or self-criticize. You might jot the ideas down, though many solo brainstormers find it easier to use a tape recorder. But before you begin, set a time limit of a half-hour, and set a timer to signal the expiration.

Strangely enough, one of the secrets of brainstorming—of successfully tapping into your imagination to find new ideas or solutions to problems—is not to look *too* hard. Perhaps you've had the experience of going out on a clear night to see how many stars you can find—even the dimmest. Well, you'll never find the dimmest stars if you actually look for them. The dimmest stars are most visible to your eye in your *peripheral* vision—where you are hardly looking at all. You have more "rods" (black-and-white optical receptors) than "cones" (color receptors) at the periphery. Now while the rods don't "see" as clearly as the cones, they are more sensitive to dim light. Something like this is true of solo brainstorming. Don't *try* too hard. State the problem or issue, and then let yourself go. Free associate. Don't evaluate. Let yourself flounder and stumble rather than consciously search.

Brainstorming is just one set of ways to tap into your imagination. In and of itself, brainstorming is a very simple process. What many find difficult, however, is, in a business setting, letting themselves go. In business, we're trained to be productive—to produce some *thing*—and wild ideas (many of us believe) are not solid accomplishments. We feel as if we are wasting time. We feel as if we are unproductive.

→ Tip: The speaker recognizes and addresses what is most likely a special concern of his audience.

The fact is that most ideas will *not* result in a profit-making product. But it is also true that all profit-making products start with ideas. We need them. Consider the imagination phase the "fuzzy front end" of creativity. It's hard to define. It may even make you a bit uncomfortable. But imagination is essential—and you never have to apologize for it.

OUTLINE

Opening

• "Waiting for Godot"

Meaning of the Godot anecdote

• What too many of us do: sit passively and wait for ideas to come
• At our company, we can't afford to wait
• We create ideas

Imagination

• What is it?
• Do you have it?

How to use your imagination constructively and productively

• Brainstorming
• How to brainstorm
• Variations on the brainstorming technique
• Brainstorming solo

Secrets of better brainstorming

• Don't look too hard
• Free association

Inhibitions

• What they are
• Why business people are inhibited
• Overcoming inhibition of creativity

Closing

• The importance of the "fuzzy front end"

MODEL SPEECH 093:
Increase Productivity

Key Use of Speech: To increase personal productivity.

Style of Speech: Informative, helpful, encouraging.

Audience: Company employees.

Time: 12 to 14 minutes.

XYZ Industries is not the kind of place where you have bosses breathing down the necks of their staff or cracking the whip and bellowing for more "productivity." Here we pride ourselves on being self-starters, and if anyone is dissatisfied with the level of productivity generated, it is each of us ourselves. We self-starters are our own harshest critics. It seems that no matter how hard we work, most of the time we feel that we just don't get enough accomplished.

➤ Tip: The speaker defines productivity very specifically, in terms of time management.

I think it is a mistake to talk about productivity in the abstract. It certainly doesn't help to tell yourself to "work harder." No, increasing personal productivity is a matter of working on the little things in your life to make them more convenient and efficient. It's about time management.

Let's begin at the best place to begin: the beginning. Begin by asking yourself: "Am I efficient?" Answer this question by making a private list. Divide the page in half. In the left-hand column, write tasks you ordinarily perform during a typical day. In the right-hand column, assess how well you do them. For example, in the left-hand column you write: "Finishing projects on time," and in the right-hand column: "I usually only finish the projects I'm interested in first, then get around to the others." That's an honest start. Now keep going. You'll end up with a snapshot of your level of efficiency.

➤ Tip: The speaker leaps into practical advice.

Since, in essence, productivity is a matter of time management, work toward getting a handle on your time. Keeping time sheets or using a computer program that tracks the hours you spend on specific tasks is a concrete method of managing your time and gauging your productivity. You may discover, for example, that you've spent eight hours on a relatively trivial project that should have been done in no time, and yet, in that same month, you spent only three hours on a project that is critical both to your career and to the company. Einstein told us that time is relative. Who are we to argue with Einstein? But that eight hours spent on trivial tasks is still five hours more than you spent on the really important work. Don't just record your time, *track* it. Look for the important patterns by studying time sheets from several months.

Now let's talk about "free time."

If the concept of "free time" makes you laugh because you're constantly bringing home work, you're either just extremely busy or not being productive enough during regular working hours. Is there something *wrong* with you? Do you have colleagues who seem always to get their work done on time and at work rather than at home? What is it about their work habits that makes this possible? Do they get to work early? Do they take work home with them? Do they take shorter lunch breaks? Make a list of what you feel gives them the advantage. Study the list. Is there something you should be doing differently?

One thing you may do differently is to plan out your day. Start the morning by making a schedule of what you have to accomplish before leaving the office that day. Write down how long you think it should take to complete each individual task. Don't cheat! As you go through the day, mark down the start and stop times for each task. How did you do? Did some tasks take longer than expected? This is a sign that there may be a better way to get the task done. You just haven't thought of it yet. You can take a high-tech approach to this exercise by using your contact manager PC or Mac program. Set start and stop points for each task. You can set the alarm on your program to sound when it's time to start wrapping things up. Be sure to record how you well you keep to your original schedule as you go through each task. Be sure to keep a record of all of your starts and stops. This will help you diagnose problem areas.

Now, we've been talking about managing time at the office. But who said travel time has to be "down time?" If you commute to work

→ Tip: In a speech that consists mainly of lists, transitional sentences announcing a shift to a new topic are of particular importance.

→ Tip: The first sentence of the next paragraph begins by indicating a shift to another new topic.

on the bus or subway, bring something work-related to read. Create a "traveling folder" in which you keep all the papers you're working on at the moment. This way, they stay in one place and are easily accessible, ready for you to grab for the commute to and from the office. You might also use the morning commute to plan your day. If you manage to grab a seat on the subway, bus, or train, open up your planner (you do have a planner, don't you?) and jot down what you need to get done today. You might also use your evening commute to take stock of what needs to be done the next day.

Now for those of you who drive to work, don't try to read while you're driving. However, you can still use driving time for more than just driving. If a great idea comes to you while you're driving, don't let it pass. As soon as you can stop—at a traffic light, say—jot down a note or two. Most auto parts and accessories stores sell paper pads that can be mounted on your dash. It is even a better idea to invest in a small hand-held Dictaphone-type microchip recorder. Speak your ideas into one of these.

While we're on the subject of the commute, give some thought to whether or not you're really taking the shortest route to work. Plan it carefully, taking into account traffic as well as distance. For a variety of good reasons, you might also consider car pooling. Now this won't save commuting time, but it may buy work time, including early-morning discussions with your colleagues and coworkers. You know, if nothing else, car-pool conversation gets out of the way a lot of the small talk that often adds to first-thing-in-the-morning office inertia.

→ Tip: The next paragraph begins with a major shift in topic.

Speaking of colleagues, you might start thinking of ways to coax others—not just yourself—to greater personal productivity. Begin by communicating your expectations clearly. For example: "I'm going to need that report by 4 P.M. tomorrow. If we don't have it ready by then we risk losing this account. If you have any questions or concerns, please talk to me while we can still do something about them. Thanks."

In addition to open, clear communication, remember to plan the work, and work the plan. Sit down with those you work with and plan for the month, the week, or even just the day ahead. Be certain that you're all agreed on which projects have priority, what the deadlines are, and just how the tasks should be executed.

Just as you hold yourself accountable, don't be afraid to hold others accountable as well. While you shouldn't point fingers, browbeat, or terrorize, you don't have to be overly eager to express understanding and to accept excuses. React honestly and helpfully if you receive work that is just not up to par. Remember, though, address the issues of the work, *not* the personality of the worker. Separate the person from the problem. Then attack the problem, not the person.

Don't be reluctant to criticize constructively, but don't just criticize, either. Suggest solutions. As a manager or colleague, it is your responsibility to offer *constructive* solutions to the problems you detect.

Remember that information is the single most valuable driver of productivity. Get people to feel closer to what you are doing by empowering them with information: distribute copies of important memos and other documents. Keep them "in the loop," even if the memos are only FYI.

Folks, these are all small things—small, real, concrete things. You can do them, and they will add up. Their sum will be greater than the parts. You *will* be more productive, and, almost even better, you will *feel* more productive.

OUTLINE

Opening

- At this company, we pride ourselves on our initiative
- Sometimes we don't feel we get enough accomplished
- Productivity = time management

Are you efficient?

- List your typical day's activities
- Evaluate list

Getting a handle on your use of time

- Keep time sheets
- Use a computer time-tracking program
- Evaluate your productivity

Study your colleagues

- What do they do right?
- Analyze their work habits
- Learn from them

Create schedules

- Advantages
- How to
- Diagnose problem areas

Use travel time productively

- How to
- Plan your day
- Evaluate next day
- Using drive time
- Plan shortest route

Getting greater productivity from others

- Communicate your expectations
- Plan the work, work the plan
- Enforce accountability
- Criticize constructively
- Provide appropriate information

Closing

- Small steps result in enhanced productivity

MODEL SPEECH 094:
Leadership

Key Use of Speech:	To define leadership.
Style of Speech:	Informative, helpful, inspiring.
Audience:	Company managers.
Time:	6 to 8 minutes.

As managers, you are the leaders at XYZ Corporation. I want to speak with you, in practical, down-to-earth terms, about what leadership means.

If you are looking for a nutshell definition of what a manger is expected to do in our organization, it is that he or she is not expected to *do* anything, but, rather, to ensure that whatever needs to *be* done *gets* done.

Is a manager a leader or a boss?

Truly effective managers are leaders, not bosses. Bosses bark out orders, whereas leaders give direction—not just "directions," but *direction.* Bosses, naturally, are always right, whereas leaders are willing to admit that others may have good ideas. Bosses bully, but leaders motivate. Bosses intimidate, whereas leaders educate. The boss is a driver, the leader a coach. The boss stands upon the principle of authority, the leader on good will. The boss inspires fear, the leader enthusiasm. Whereas the boss commands "go," the leader says, "let's go."

That's all well and good—inspiring people, leading rather than bossing. But management is not only about inspiration. Effective management is about controlling time, money, and people. "Administrative management" is what we call the time and money part of the job. It includes budgets, policies, and procedures. The people part includes hiring, training, coaching, setting goals, motivating, counseling, and, when necessary, terminating.

→ Tip: Begin any complex definition with the most general statement you can make, then drill downward to specifics.

→ Tip: Comparison and contrast of attributes is an effective means of definition.

328

➡ Tip: Wherever possible, quantify your definitions.

➡ Tip: The speaker has prepared his audience for fairly repetitive material by referring to it as a "menu."

➡ Tip: Wring all you can out of the words you use. Here "leading" is not just an abstraction; it is shown in physical terms—leading from the front rather than pushing from behind.

Now, as a manager, you will be evaluated chiefly—almost exclusively—on the basis of how well your people do. An effective leader, therefore, devotes most of his or her time to developing and improving staff members. Spend at least three-quarters of your time working the "people" side of the management job and only about a quarter of your time on "administrative management." If you spend more time than that on administration, you may be managing, but you are not *leading*.

Now let's talk about leadership *style*. There's more than one right way to lead. You might pick and choose your favored methods from the following menu:

You may lead through example. This means working harder than anyone else in the office and knowing more about the product line than anyone else. Leading by example is incredibly hard work. It's also one of the most consistently successful leadership styles.

You may lead through encouragement. Since the early days of scientific psychology, tests and studies have repeatedly shown that people respond more favorably to positive rather than negative reinforcement. They learn faster, and they comply more willingly and readily. Learn to take genuine and generous pleasure in the accomplishments of your staff. Always have something positive to say. Stimulate and inspire.

You may lead through teaching. This requires a high level of technical expertise and a tireless willingness to share your knowledge. You need to cultivate within yourself a passion for solving problems.

You may lead through motivation, through tirelessly encouraging individual staff members to improve themselves, to work harder, and to work smarter. This style of leadership requires frequent and crystal-clear goal setting. Make rewards visible, tangible, and available. Cultivate top people. Groom them for promotion.

I've removed one highly popular leadership style from the menu I just offered. Many, many managers try to lead through intimidation. This isn't really *leading* at all. It's pushing. You lead from the front, not the rear.

An effective leader creates loyalty. This is a quality that cannot be bought or bullied. Loyalty must be earned, and managers who earn it generally do the following:

They treat people fairly.

They are always accessible.

They *listen* well.

They recognize achievement.

They praise achievement.

They reward achievement.

They themselves are loyal. When appropriate, an effective manager stands up for his staff, defending them to senior management and, when necessary, to customers.

They are helpful and expedite important matters with other areas of the company.

They ensure that credit is given where credit is due.

They are dependably knowledgeable.

They are great coaches, mentors, teachers.

They have and they communicate a clear sense of purpose.

This is the last leadership point I will leave you with: an effective leader has and communicates a clear sense of purpose. When all is said and done, this is the single most important aspect of leadership. On this, all the rest depends.

OUTLINE

Opening

• What leadership means

Leadership defined

• Leadership ensures that what needs to be done gets done
• Be a leader, not a boss
• Leader vs. boss

Effective management

• What it is about
• Administrative management
• People management

Leadership styles

• Example
• Encouragement

- Teaching
- Motivation
- Intimidation

Loyalty

- How to earn loyalty
- Treat people fairly
- Be accessible
- Listen
- Recognize achievement
- Praise achievement
- Reward achievement

Closing

- Effective leaders communicate a clear sense of purpose

———————————

MODEL SPEECH 095:
Mission of Company

Key Use of Speech: To define the company's mission.

Style of Speech: Informative and inspiring.

Audience: Company employees.

Time: 5 to 10 minutes. [Depends on the level of detail given in departmental assignments.]

→ Tip: The speaker differentiates between what the company does and what its mission is.

We make widgets.

That's what we *do* at XYZ Widget, but what we *do* is not one and the same with our mission.

The mission of XYZ Widget goes beyond making widgets. Stated succinctly, our mission is *to make high-value widgets, to innovate in the widget industry, to be responsive to the widget needs of our customers, and to develop creative partnerships with retailers and distributors in order to gain a greater share of the widget market.*

This overall mission requires a commitment from each department.

[The speaker then lists the company's major department, assigning to each of them a relevant portion of the mission.]

→ Tip: Everything the company does should somehow flow from the statement of mission.

I hope, ladies and gentlemen, that you will measure your activities, allocation of resources, and assignment of priorities against the yardstick of this statement of mission. Let us allow the mission to focus our efforts intensively so that we can more effectively create customer satisfaction and, having ensured customer satisfaction, continue to grow in an orderly fashion, always directing our growth in conformity with our mission.

MODEL SPEECH 096:
Optimism Is Contagious

Key Use of Speech: To encourage positive thinking.

Style of Speech: Inspiring, but believable.

Audience: Company or department managers.

Time: 5 to 7 minutes.

On July 2, 1862, the Union Army was about to lose the Battle of Gettysburg. With the loss of Gettysburg, very likely, would come an end not only to the Civil War, but to the United States as a single nation. The Northern United States would have a slave-holding neighbor on its Southern border.

All the Confederates had to do was take the high ground, and the Union forces wouldn't have had a prayer.

The end of the Union's line of troops—its flank, its most vulnerable point—was occupied by a badly weakened regiment from Maine, whose colonel, Joshua Chamberlain, had been a professor of rhetoric at Bowdoin College. The rebels charged repeatedly, but, somehow, Chamberlain and his men held firm.

Finally, there came a massive charge. Chamberlain's regiment, exhausted, was also out of ammunition. The proper thing to do was to surrender.

But Chamberlain knew that to surrender the flank would mean losing the battle and, quite probably, the war. In a desperate, depressing, no-win situation, Chamberlain, trained as a teacher and not as a military commander, chose the road of optimism.

➤ Tip: A rousing story can be a most effective way to begin a speech. Entertain as well as inform your audience.

He ordered his men to attack, to charge—using bayonets, if they had no ammunition.

The Confederates, shocked, retreated, then surrendered. The tide

333

→ Tip: Don't let the anecdote dangle in mid-air. Draw the significance or the moral of the story.

→ Tip: Your audience will be skeptical about the power of optimism. Begin by pointing out that they at least have nothing to lose by being optimistic.

→ Tip: Temper optimism with realism.

→ Tip: Another anecdote provides a concrete example of realistic optimism.

of Gettysburg turned, and, on the next day, the Union won a victory that effectively sealed the doom of the Confederacy and the resurrection of the Union.

By all reports, Chamberlain was a soft-spoken, scholarly man. He did not lead by terrorizing his troops, but by inspiring them with confidence and optimism. His optimism outlasted his ammunition and, in the end, was far more effective. Deeply felt, that optimism was contagious.

Most contagions, of course, are not so positive. Gloom, doubt, and defeatism are, if anything, even more contagious than optimism. If we allow these feelings to dominate us, we will create defeat. Now it is true that, just because we are driven by optimism, it doesn't necessarily follow that victory will be ours. However, it is far more likely that a defeatist attitude will spread and will bring disaster than it is that an optimistic attitude will create *anything* negative. With defeatism, then, we have everything to lose, whereas with optimism, we have nothing to lose and, perhaps, much to gain.

To be sure, both defeatism and optimism are only feelings. But feelings are fuel. They do not *determine,* but they do *drive* our success—or our failure.

So how do we "spread" optimism?

The answer is most definitely *not* to deny the reality of setbacks, challenges, problems, and disasters. However, we must embrace and broadcast a faith in our ability to cope with and even profit from setbacks, challenges, problems, and disasters.

When Thomas Alva Edison was laboring away at inventing the electric light, he told a newspaper reporter that he had tested some 1,600 substances as potential filaments for his lamp, all of which had failed.

"You must be very disappointed at the waste of time and labor," the reporter remarked.

"Not at all. Nothing was wasted," Edison replied. "Now I know of 1,600 things that will *not* work."

Edison had found a positive—and true—way of looking at his experience. This drove him, of course, to ultimate success.

Our task, as managers, is to help our employees look at their experience as positive. Is a customer calling to complain about a problem with a widget? Look at this as an *opportunity* to satisfy this customer by making that problem right. Cultivate this attitude in yourselves, and it *will* be broadcast to your staff.

MODEL SPEECH 097:
Procrastination Avoidance

Key Use of Speech: To help employees get things done.

Style of Speech: Informative, helpful.

Audience: Company or department employees.

Time: 8 to 10 minutes.

➡ Tip: Get a handle on a slippery subject by presenting a key word for definition and contemplation.

Inertia, any high school physics teacher will tell you, is the property of a body by virtue of which it opposes any agency that attempts to put it in motion or, if it is moving, to change the magnitude or direction of its velocity. In other words, inertia opposes action or change.

Physical objects have no monopoly on inertia. It is also a property of human beings. Many, many of us have trouble starting projects that need to be started. Call this procrastination, if you like, but it's inertia all the same.

➡ Tip: The speaker is careful to develop the analogy between physical and mental inertia.

As with physical inertia, mental inertia often requires the application of an outside force to get moving: A client screams; a boss threatens; your kids clamor for food, clothing, shelter, and a college education. These are all highly effective outside forces.

But you cannot always depend on the timely application of outside forces. Besides, if you're kicked hard enough, well, you'll bruise.

The better answer to procrastination is to formulate ways in which you yourself can overcome inertia and break free of the procrastination pattern. Now, this does not mean simply telling yourself to "work harder" or to "get going." Procrastination has little or nothing to do with laziness. It's about structure—or, rather, lack of it. Without structure and direction, it is very difficult to get things started—and, conversely, very easy to find excuses to put things off.

➡ Tip: It is important to define your topic as you want to define it. Here, the speaker is careful to distance procrastination from laziness.

Your most powerful weapon in the war against procrastination,

335

→ Tip: Provide practical advice for overcoming problems.

then, is creating a schedule. Do you have trouble keeping to a schedule? Well, maybe that is because you don't *create* a daily or weekly or monthly schedule. The fact is that making and keeping schedules is vital to getting ahead and staying ahead in business.

Let's start with the most basic schedule for the typical workday. Plan what you're going to do for the day at the *beginning* of each day. Plan what you're going to accomplish during the week at the *beginning* of the week. Here's how to get started: Take out a piece of paper and write down the projects you are working on. Number them in priority order, starting with the most critical projects and working your way down. Now, take out your calendar—or fire up your desktop computer calendar program—and begin plugging in time slots for the most important projects at the *beginning* of the week. If you prefer, divide the time for each project each day, but always give proportionately more time to the critical tasks.

Next, set firm deadlines. Remember when you were in college and you knew you were going to be tested on a chunk of material—but you didn't know when? I bet you cracked those books right away!

Sure.

The truth is that only when a firm date for the exam was set did you start to study. Let's face it, given a choice, we wander down the path of least resistance. With a firm deadline and a little discipline, however, you'd be surprised at all that you can accomplish. Set personal deadlines, write them down, and plan your work to meet them.

→ Tip: Speak for your audience. Ask the questions you believe they want answered.

Procrastination begins at the start of the day. Well, you say, you're just not a morning person? You simply *can't* get your work going at 9 A.M. sharp?

Then try getting into the office just a little earlier, say 8:45. By the time you've had you're first cup of coffee, checked your e-mail, and shot the breeze with everyone, you're ready to go—and, wonder of wonders, it's 9:00, or just a bit past the hour.

Now, when you plan your schedule, do be realistic. Don't expect to produce in a half hour an hour-long presentation on a subject you don't know much about. And don't schedule for yourself more time to work on something you really enjoy, but that you know you could complete in a matter of minutes. Schedule according to needs, not desires.

Intelligent, thoughtful scheduling provides the framework you need to help you climb out of the pit called procrastination. I urge you to try it.

OUTLINE

Opening

- Inertia defined
- Physical inertia and mental/emotional inertia
- Inertia = procrastination

Solutions to procrastination

- Procrastination is not laziness
- Need structure
- Create a schedule

Schedule basics

- Plan the workday
- Plan the workweek
- How to
- Set firm deadlines
- Get to work a little earlier
- Be realistic in your objectives

Closing

- Scheduling is key to ending procrastination

MODEL SPEECH 098:
Public Image Improvement

Key Use of Speech: To suggest ways in which employees can help improve a company's image.

Style of Speech: Informative, helpful, persuasive.

Audience: Company employees.

Time: 10 to 15 minutes. [Depends on the number and detail of the speaker's action directives.]

→ Tip: Get your audience to start thinking about your topic. Prepare them to look at it from several different angles.

"Corporate image." That's a phrase that tends to provoke at least a couple of reactions. The first is cynicism. "Corporate image" is manufactured, created, made up, or simply bought. And that last item brings up the second reaction: Creating a corporate image is expensive, requiring the work of expert consultants.

I'm not going to tell you that these two responses are wrong. A corporate image *can* be phony, and it *can* be bought at great expense.

I will assure you, however, that this is not how XYZ Corporation has earned its image.

Earned is the operative word here. But let's back up a step and take a look at just what our image is.

→ Tip: The speaker is careful to strip "corporate image" of its negative connotations—at least in the case of his company.

XYZ has long been perceived as an honest producer of a high-quality products. That's the good news. Unfortunately, there is another aspect to this traditional image. We are also seen as a rather old-fashioned firm, whose products, while of a high quality, may not always represent the state of the art. Also, while customers believe our service to be courteous and caring, they see it as slow and, likewise, old-fashioned.

We want to *earn* a new image, while saving the best of the old.

How do we *earn* it?

➝ Tip: The speaker
clearly states the issues
at hand and the goals
relating to them.

Each of us has to do this, every day.

Let's begin with Customer Service. Each service rep should deliver friendly, but prompt information and help. *Sell* the "service advantage" to our customers by offering them a bit more than they asked for. Use expressions such as "state of the art" to describe not only our products, but our service. . . .

[The speaker continues to specify ways in which service reps can upgrade the company's image. The speaker then goes through other departments, such as sales, design, manufacturing, and so on, giving recommendations to each.]

➝ Tip: The effective
speaker is like the effective manager: he or she
doesn't merely point out
problems, but also sug-
gests solutions.

➝ Tip: The speaker
concludes by empowe-
ring the individuals in
his company, showing
them how they can
make a difference.

At XYZ, each of us is responsible for building and improving our corporate image. We have created—and will continue to create and upgrade—that image one satisfied customer at a time. It is up to each of us, with each all-important customer contact that we make, to build and rebuild and revitalize our image. No consultants or public relations hired gun can do this job more thoroughly and effectively than each of us can, working product by product and person by person. Our customers don't deal with a company. They deal with us. People. You—we—*are* the company. And *we* are the company's image.

MODEL SPEECH 099:
Quality Improvement

Key Use of Speech:	To set quality improvement as a goal.
Style of Speech:	Informative, helpful, inspiring.
Audience:	Company employees.
Time:	8 to 10 minutes. [Depends on the number of specific recommendations the speaker makes.]

→ Tip: One important function of the opening portion of a speech is the establishment of a relationship between the speaker and the audience. Here, the speaker strives to create a relationship of equality, mutual self-interest, and mutual responsibility.

You will find distributed in your e-mail a report of our most recent customer survey project. In many companies, a report like this would be for the eyes of top management only. But that's not the way we work at XYZ. We believe this report and the information in it is of crucial interest to all of us, not just a few men and women "at the top." We believe that the more information we share, the better off we all are. We believe this because this is *our* company—yours and mine. *Our* welfare, *our* future is on the line.

The report contains a great deal of interesting information. I want to alert you to one piece of data in particular.

→ Tip: Effective speeches can be built around shared data—in this case, a report that the speaker as well as his audience are familiar with.

The number one concern our customers have is not price and not technology, but *quality.*

Now that is important to know.

Also important is the overall rating they gave our products for quality: 7 out of a possible 10.

Not bad, 7 out of 10—but, I submit to you, not acceptable when our customers are telling us that *quality* is what matters to them most.

Ladies and gentlemen, we are conducting another survey beginning on **[date].** By that time, I want to see us up at 9 out of 10, and by the next survey after that, on **[date],** at 10 out of 10.

Why do we need to achieve this?

→ Tip: Make the stakes crystal clear.

Because our customers tell us we need to. And *that* is reason enough. It is ample reason. If we fail to satisfy our customers, our customers will find a supplier who *will* satisfy them

How can we attain this improvement?

You tell me. This is, after all, your company as much as mine. On [date], we will meet to discuss ideas for quality improvement. I expect each of you to come to that meeting with ideas and with a willingness to comment on the ideas of others.

In the meantime, I have some recommendations.

[The speaker presents his quality-improvement recommendations.]

→ Tip: The speaker suggests solutions; she does not just point out problems.

Excellence of quality is worth pursuing for its own sake, of course. We all have an instinct for craftsmanship, I believe. However, we also all have a major stake in this company, and, ladies and gentlemen, we cannot afford for this company to come in second best. Our customers won't let us survive as second best.

MODEL SPEECH 100:
Risk Taking

Key Use of Speech: To encourage controlled risk taking.

Style of Speech: Informative and authoritative.

Audience: Company managers.

Time: 10 to 12 minutes. [Depends on the nature of the guidelines discussed.]

➜ Tip: Basic comparison and contrast gives your audience something to revolve in their minds.

This building rests on a foundation. It's stable. It isn't going anywhere. It's rock solid. We work in this building, but this building is *not* our business.

Our business is built on a foundation, but it does not rest there. It is inherently *un*stable—that is, in constant motion, fluid, changing.

There is almost zero risk that this building will collapse. But, in business, we never get anywhere near zero risk. Risk is how we make our money. We are rewarded for risk—and, make no mistake, the risks are very real.

➜ Tip: Crucial terms like "risk" can be dangerous; make certain that you define the term precisely: what it is and what it is not.

If we play it safe—and by "safe" I mean try to remain as motionless as possible—we eliminate a lot of risk, but we ensure failure. Without risk there is no reward. But taking risks—profitably—does not mean gambling, either. The risks we take must be calculated and controlled.

On **[date],** those of us in this room will begin a series of meetings to evaluate and revise our current guidelines on acceptable risk. We will, in particular, look at the following factors:

[The speaker reviews the elements of risk decision.]

I am not going to stand here and advise you to "think boldly" or to "take bigger risks." I *am* suggesting, however, that you should leave

342

behind any lingering notions of zero risk, and that you be prepared to think dynamically in order to produce more elastic risk-decision guidelines than what we have now.

The reality is that the consequences of missed opportunities, even if they were missed in the name of avoiding risk, are often far more serious than controlled, analyzed risk. The greatest degree of stability and stasis, after all, is death.

→ Tip: For many, risk is a frightening proposition. The speaker shows that, given the choice between taking controlled risks and doing nothing, only the path of risk has the potential for survival.

I know that it is all well and good for me to preach to you the gospel of risk when it is your jobs—ultimately—that are on the line. Well, I am prepared to take a risk on each and every one of you. This company will support reasonable risk. The senior management of this company is grown up enough to accept losses—especially if we learn something from them. However, the losses we suffer from failing to take reasonable risks—that is, the losses resulting from inaction—are without any redeeming value. We learn nothing from them. We do not grow.

Growth is risk. Failure to grow is, in our business, ultimately failure to exist. If we want to continue to live as a company, then, we have no choice but to takes risks, and if we're going to take risks, we need to agree on reasonable and flexible guidelines for measuring risk against reward. This is what our company is all about.

MODEL SPEECH 101:
Safety

Key Use of Speech: To encourage workplace safety.

Style of Speech: Informative and authoritative.

Audience: Company or department employees.

Time: 5 to 6 minutes.

→ Tip: Beginning with a familiar, common experience can be very effective, prompting your audience to identify with your message.

A week ago, I boarded a plane to fly back from our meeting in **[place]**. You know the routine as you're about ready to taxi our onto the field. There's a monotonous spiel about how to use your seat belt and about the oxygen masks and the whole nine yards. I happened to observe my fellow passengers during the safety presentation. Clearly, nobody was listening. People were reading magazines or looking out the window.

→ Tip: Always interpret your anecdotes for the audience. Point them in the direction you want them to go.

Now, we've all witnessed this little tableau a hundred times. But, for the first time, I gave it a bit of thought, and my first thought was *How impolite!* Here were these nice flight attendants giving a speech and a demonstration, just trying to do their jobs, and everyone was blatantly and purposely ignoring them. I mean, that's got to be demoralizing after a while.

Then I thought some more.

Impolite?

Crazy is a better word.

We were being told how to save our lives, and nobody really cared! Then we took off, flew, landed, and all survived.

→ Tip: The speaker recognizes an obstacle—that most people find the subject of safety dull. He negotiates the obstacle by recognizing and admitting it.

Let's face it: safety is boring. Obviously, it's vitally important. But there's something about the subject that just turns us off and puts us into a trance or a coma or some zombie-like state.

You may remember how the subject of safety was addressed in

344

high school driver's ed: with graphic films and slides showing bloody accidents, mangled metal, and mangled passengers. It was a scare-'em-straight gross out.

Well, I could show you pictures of the consequences of failing to observe basic safety rules. But I won't insult you with those.

I could also tell you what you already know: that you owe it to your families to stay healthy, whole, and alive, and you owe it to your coworkers to help them stay healthy, whole, and alive.

➤ Tip: The speaker introduces the topics of physical injury and responsibility without belaboring them— and he uses them to build to a third consequence of failing to work safely:

So I'll approach the topic of safety this way. From **[year]** to **[year]**, accidents costs this firm **[$ amount]**. That's the equivalent of an average **[percentage amount]** raise for everyone in this room. It's the equivalent of a **[percentage amount]** increase in sales. It's a huge amount of money—that we don't have any more.

If you're not excited about safety just because it saves lives, then be excited about it because it is cost-saving and profit-protecting. All of you have a stake in the financial well-being of this company, and safety, in addition to hard work, is a good way to protect that stake and to see it grow. Safety is good business.

➤ Tip: Want a fresh approach to a tired topic? Hit your audience in the pocketbook.

Safety is good business. So I urge you to study the new safety manuals, which you will find in your mailboxes by the end of the day. Make time to study them *this week,* and let us gather again at **[time]** on **[date]** to hit the highlights and to discuss anything that is either unclear or that you believe could be improved. Let's make more money—and, okay, save a limb or a life in the process.

MODEL SPEECH 102:
Teamwork

Key Use of Speech:	To encourage and inspire cooperation and teamwork.
Style of Speech:	Informative, authoritative, supportive.
Audience:	Company employees.
Time:	10 to 12 minutes.

I have a true story to share with you.

On **[date]**, Pete Williams, in Customer Service, received a— well, I was going to say a "frantic call" from a customer. But just about all the calls that come to Pete are frantic, because he is the tech support point man. So let's just say that Pete took a *routinely* frantic call from a customer whose XYZ Computer System had just **[speaker describes problem]**.

Pete is "the tech guy." It's his *job* to fix these things. He talked the customer through the troubleshooting procedure, then instructed him to reboot, and . . . *nothing*.

The problem was still there.

Pete stuck with it and went through the standard procedures, step by step. Nothing worked.

At this point, standard procedure calls for us to schedule an on-site visit. But Pete's customer needed immediate action. He had thousands of dollars of production hung up on software—*our* software—that just wasn't working.

"Look," the customer said, "you're not going to be able to get someone out here until *tomorrow*. My problem is *today*."

Now, there is nothing in this customer's contract that calls for same-day service, and Pete knew this. He also knew that a customer was hurting.

"Mary, let me do some consulting here, and see if I can get you up and running before the end of the day. In the meantime, I'll schedule a call for tomorrow."

[The speaker then narrates how the technician assembled a team to troubleshoot the customer's problem.]

None of the half-dozen people Pete got on the case had direct contact with this customer. Contractually and professionally, they didn't owe her anything. But Pete had no trouble getting them to interrupt the work they had at hand to focus, as a team, on this customer's problem.

Why?

Because, like a great team, they share the same values—with service to the customer number one among those values. For his part, Pete knew when it was time to call for help, and the rest of the folks responded as a team. Within two hours, working together, they had solved the customer's problem and had gotten her up and running again.

How much did this instance of teamwork cost our company? In terms of combined salary for two hours, **[$ amount].** How much did the action net us? In direct revenue, absolutely nothing. In terms of customer satisfaction, the revenue is impossible to calculate—but is nevertheless very real: we've earned this customer's continued business and, doubtless, this episode of efficient teamwork will result in great word of mouth. How much new business will that bring? Who knows.

What I do know is that teamwork works, and it is our surest means of creating consistent customer satisfaction. I congratulate Pete Williams and **[the speaker names the other members of the "team"]** on a job very well done.

→ Tip: This going-the-extra-mile anecdote is made more vivid by the addition of a few lines of dialogue.

→ Tip: Whenever it is possible to define a concept by a truly representative example, do so. It is almost always more effective than an abstract definition.

→ Tip: Going the extra mile is the right thing to do, certainly, but convince your skeptical audience of this by showing that it is also very good business.

Policies

Openings

—— *"Company policy" can be a big, stupid, unyielding thing. Or it can be a vehicle that enables a business to run from day to day. The difference is largely a matter of understanding and execution. Let's talk about policy.*

——*Ladies and gentlemen, as managers you need to ensure that you are fully familiar with our company policy on affirmative action. Please give me a few minutes of your attention.*

Closings

——*Never hide behind "company policy." Know it, and use it—but exercise imagination and common sense. Let's make policy work for us. Let's not work for policy.*

——*Thank you for your attention to these important matters of company policy concerning affirmative action. Please consult with me whenever you feel that you need interpretation of the policy in a particular case.*

MODEL SPEECH 103:
Affirmative Action and EEO

Key Use of Speech: To explain the firm's equal employment
                       opportunity policies.

Style of Speech: Informative, authoritative, and positive.

Audience: Company managers with authority to hire.

Time: 10 to 15 minutes. [Depends on the level of
                       detail used in explaining the specifics of the
                       company's policies.]

→ Tip: Don't talk about the law and other regulations unless you know the facts absolutely. Confirm your facts before speaking.

Let's start with the law. Federal and state laws forbid employers from making hiring decisions based in any way on marital status, sexual orientation, age, ethnic background, national origin, race, religious beliefs, absence of religious beliefs, gender, or disabilities. The law allows certain exceptions in cases where a bona fide occupational qualification (what legal types like to call a BFOQ) can be demonstrated. In very few situations, here at XYZ Industries, the BFOQ exception applies: for example, our delivery drivers must be able to lift eighty pounds—a BFOQ that precludes persons with certain disabilities. For the most part, however, our hiring and promotion practices *must* be governed by the basic federal and state statutes.

The bottom line: It is illegal for any of us to discriminate in hiring.

→ Tip: The speaker starts with the law as a benchmark requirement, then shows how his company goes beyond those basic requirements. He transforms a legal issue into a moral one—and also a business one.

But I want to set the law aside for a few moments—because even if that weren't a law, nondiscrimination would be our company policy. We treat our customers fairly. We treat our vendors fairly. And we treat each other fairly. Law or no law, it's what is right—right for the individual employee and right for us as a company. Our customer base is diverse in every way—age, race, gender, and so on—so it stands to reason that we can better serve that customer base, and can more effectively compete in the marketplace, if we are staffed diversely.

→ Tip: It is easy to theorize about moral issues, but often more difficult to apply them. The speaker understands this and addresses it.

It feels good to do the right thing, of course, but it is not always easy to decide *which* right thing to do. There are instances where affirmative action may conflict with nondiscrimination. Let me make our policy clear on affirmative action:

[The speaker explains the company's policy on affirmative action.]

If you stay within these affirmative action guidelines, you should be able to avoid conflicts in hiring as well as in promotion. While we absolutely shun the notion of racial, ethnic, or gender hiring and promotion quotas, we, as a company, embrace the principle of hiring a diverse workforce. Quite apart from its moral status, this is a sound business policy, and it is with that positive attitude that I hope you will make your hiring and promotion decisions.

MODEL SPEECH 104:
Employee Development

Key Use of Speech:	To explain the firm's policy on employee development.
Style of Speech:	Informative and authoritative.
Audience:	Company employees.
Time:	10 to 15 minutes.

➡ Tip: The unexpected request or plea is an arresting way to begin a speech.

I come before you this afternoon with a request that you exploit us. That's right. Wring out every last thing you are entitled to as an XYZ corporate employee.

Now, in addition to your salary, what you're entitled to includes discount passes to Funworld Amusement Park and some other very nice perks.

Hooray!

It also includes the XYZ Employee Development Program.

➡ Tip: The speaker builds to the really important employee benefit— the subject of his speech.

Ladies and gentlemen, this is a program offering some of the best business-relevant courses available anywhere, and offering them to you at no cost—beyond the time and effort you put into them.

Available courses include . . .

[The speaker lists the courses, highlighting a few along the way.]

➡ Tip: The speaker outlines the scope of the program.

And don't feel limited by this list. Sarah Young, our director of Employee Development, is prepared to listen to your proposals for business-relevant courses that are not on this list. This is truly a remarkable opportunity.

Hey, aren't the discount Funworld tickets generosity enough? Why does XYZ want to finance your education, too? Is there a catch?

→ Tip: The speaker plays on his audience's skepticism. After all, there is no free lunch . . .

→ Tip: The speaker expresses the "catch" in purposely crass terms. This holds the attention of the audience—and allows him to build to his next point: the win–win nature of the program.

XYZ finances your education to make *you* more valuable to XYZ. We want to get even more out of you than we do now. We want you to be more productive, more imaginative, more knowledgeable. XYZ wants to invest in you in order to make XYZ a more profitable company.

Fortunately, the "catch" is just part of what is clearly a win–win proposition. Take advantage of the Development Program, and you will acquire expensive training at no cost to yourselves. Emerge from the program, and you will add to the value of XYZ Industries.

If you want to find out more about the programs available . . .

[The speaker tells his audience how to get more information.]

I hope you'll exploit us so that we can better exploit you and, together, become a stronger, smarter company.

MODEL SPEECH 105:
Employee Empowerment

Key Use of Speech: To define "employee empowerment" and how
                      it works.

Style of Speech: Informative, authoritative, and team-building.

Audience: Company employees.

Time: 6 to 7 minutes.

→ Tip: The speaker be-
gins by attacking the
traditional and outworn
definition of "employee
empowerment." Her
object is to set up a
contrast, to show how
her company is different

Employee empowerment. Not too long ago, this phrase meant one
of two things: a note in the rusty-hinged suggestion box next to the
water cooler, or a strike. There was very little middle ground.
Employees were either docile, meek, and did what they were told,
or they were defiant and defined themselves in opposition to
management.

At XYZ, we don't work that way. We don't work that way, because
"that way" doesn't work.

We invest heavily in our employees. Our payroll is **[$ amount]**,
which is **[percentage amount]** of our operating costs. These are
impressive numbers, and this company would not survive, let alone
prosper, if this money were *spent* rather than *invested*. It's the difference between making a purchase and making an investment. A
purchase may or may not appreciate. It may even depreciate. An
investment, however, if it's a wise one, increases in value.

→ Tip: Enliven ordinary
phrases by twisting them
a bit. Transform them
into quotable formulas.

All of you are tremendously valuable members of this enterprise.
The value of this enterprise will grow in proportion to the value you
add to it. This means doing your day-to-day jobs very well, of course,
but it also means taking on greater levels of responsibility.

The XYZ Employee Empowerment program consists of . . .

[The speaker outlines the program, explaining the opportunities it offers for employee participation in planning and creating projects, etc.]

The rewards of the empowerment program are threefold. First, by supporting your contributions to this enterprise *at every level,* XYZ gives each employee multiple opportunities to excel and to *demonstrate* excellence. This means that we are eager to promote from within. Your career is on a fast track here, if you choose to put it there. And this is great for you.

Secondly, XYZ benefits by getting a fuller investment value from its employees. The corporation *exploits* you—and I mean that in the nicest way possible!

Finally, though, employee empowerment benefits all of us. We are, after all, in this together. There is no division between management and labor. We're *all* management *and* labor. Our success as a company can only benefit us all. You are invited to claim a bigger stake in that success by participating in employee empowerment. Become more active in determining the direction of the company. Become more involved. This is *your* company.

MODEL SPEECH 106:
Environmental Protection

Key Use of Speech: To define the company's environmental policy.

Style of Speech: Informative and authoritative.

Audience: Community group

Time: 10 to 12 minutes.

➨ Tip: The speaker enlivens what might otherwise be a routine rundown of environmental legislation by identifying his company's growth with the progress of the legislation.

XYZ Industries grew up during a historical period of burgeoning environmental consciousness and conscience. The year we were founded, 1962, the great environmental writer Rachel Carson published her *Silent Spring,* a fictional account of a world in which the cumulative effects of environmental neglect manifest themselves through cataclysmic impacts on ecosystems and, ultimately of course, on people. *Silent Spring* heightened the general public's awareness of environmental issues and certainly helped to shape our emphasis on environmental responsibility as we established our first chemical processing plant here in **[location].** The year that we opened the plant, 1963, the first federal Clean Air Act was passed, followed in 1965 by the Solid Waste Disposal Act, the Water Quality Act, the Motor Vehicle Air Pollution Control Act, and the Air Quality Act in 1967.

This first round of legislation focused on specific media—air, water, and land. The next decade brought broader measures. In 1970, the National Environmental Policy Act and the Occupational Safety and Health Act were passed, the Environmental Protection Agency (EPA) was created, and the first Earth Day demonstrations were held. Two years later, the Clean Water Act was passed, followed in 1973 by the Endangered Species Act. The Safe Drinking Water Act came along in 1974, followed by the Toxic Substances Control Act and the Resource Conservation and Recovery Act in 1976. In 1978, Congress passed the Endangered American Wilderness Act. The year 1980 saw enactment of the Comprehensive Environmental Response, Compensation and Liability Act, better known as the "Superfund." Superfund was amended in 1986 and expanded to provide for public reporting of releases under the Emergency Planning and Community Right-to-Know title, and, along with the twentieth anniversary of Earth Day in 1990, Congress celebrated by passing amendments to the Clean Air Act—considered the most expensive piece of environmental legislation that has ever been conceived.

Where was XYZ during all of this?

We were growing into the most successful chemical processing plant in this region—*and* we were not only obeying the new laws, we were doing better than what their guidelines mandated. For example . . .

[The speaker highlights areas in which XYZ Industries performed better than required by law.]

→ Tip: After impressing his audience with the wide range of environmental legislation, the speaker shows how it has been the policy of his firm not only to meet, but to exceed legislative mandates

Of *course,* we support environmental protection. We live here, and we work here, and our customers—the people who make our business possible—live and work here. During the last twenty years in the United States, the air has become cleaner, more water is fishable, swimmable, and drinkable, and a huge quantity of potentially hazardous materials has been reduced or managed.

XYZ supports this, upholds this, and, as I say, often exceeds the requirements of federal and state legislation.

→ Tip: Having established a firm position on the environment, the speaker now turns his attention to problems with environmental regulation.

But all of this comes at a cost. The cost to the American public since 1970 of addressing environmental concerns in this way has been about $1.4 trillion in taxes *and higher prices* for products and services—including ours. **[Percentage amount]** of every dollar you spend on an XYZ product goes to cover expenses associated with protecting the environment.

This is, I think you'll agree, an excellent investment, at least *in theory. In practice,* the added costs could, however, be a better value. The fact is that we at XYZ believe that the costs of environmental protection have become *too* high. That does not mean that environmental protection should not receive ample funding and investment. But, as with any other good thing we desire, we should not be willing to pay *any* price for it. Technology is such these days that we can measure incredibly small quantities of chemicals. Because we can

→ Tip: Audiences want you to come down 100 percent for or against an issue. Of course, this is not always possible. Be sure to define your position with great care —especially if it is more complex than a matter of black and white.

→ Tip: When dealing in controversial areas, lean heavily on quantifiable, dollars-and-cents facts.

measure the infinitesimal, regulators have begun to demand that we regulate to these same infinitesimally low levels. Ten years ago, we measured and reported pollutant emissions at the parts-per-million level. Think about that. That's like being able to pick out and isolate any one-minute interval over a two-year period! Amazing? Yes. But, today, we regularly measure emissions at the parts-per-*billion* level— the equivalent of picking out one second in *thirty-two* years. Legislators and others are now discussing controlling emissions of certain chemicals, including some we at XYZ produce, at the parts-per-*quadrillion* level. Moreover, we make extreme assumptions about the potential harmfulness of chemical substances. For example, we assume that one molecule of an agent will cause cancer in humans if it causes cancer in rats —and these are rats force-fed huge quantities of the substance in question.

Neither the public nor legislators and regulators seems to understand the concept of reasonable risk. The media often hypes stories about environmental risks. Bombarded by scare stories, the public is no longer able to distinguish between real and imagined risks.

We at XYZ observe environmental policies that keep the risks very, very low. But the risks cannot be eliminated totally. Nothing in this world can be manufactured without some degree of risk; indeed, nothing in this world can be accomplished without risk. Life is risk. Risk management costs time, people, technology, money—all costs that are passed on to the consumer. Consider that, in **[year]**, XYZ Industries spent about 40 percent of its **[$ amount]** capital budget on environmental expenditures. Yet a study in which we participated (along with **[speaker names several companies and government agencies]**) in **[year]** indicated that equivalent levels of environmental protection could be achieved for about 25 percent of the cost mandated by regulation—if we were allowed to invest in cost-effective alternatives.

The XYZ policy on the environment is simple: we love, respect, and cherish it; however, we intend to keep working with legislators and regulators to bring environmental regulation in line not merely with the realities of the marketplace, but with the realities of life in a civilization. We want our industry to work together with government to achieve mutually understood scientific objectives, with costs very much in mind. If we are successful in this, we may not only help to moderate the trend in regulation that is imposing increasingly destructive costs on our company and on our industry as a whole, but actually make protection of the environment more efficient, effective, and thorough. Thank you.

OUTLINE

Opening

- XYZ Industries grew in a period of growing environmental legislation

History of environmental legislation

- Chronology of major acts: 1960s
- Major acts: 1970s
- Major acts: 1980s

Where was XYZ during this?

- We were supporting the laws
- We were doing even more than the laws mandated

XYZ Supports environmental protection

- Why
- The cost of environmental regulation
- An excellent investment—in principle
- In practice, we could, as a nation, invest more wisely in environmental protection
- Costs too high
- Why

Concept of reasonable risk

- Media hypes environmental issues
- Public is misled
- Risks cannot be eliminated totall
- Reevaluating risks will lower costs, allowing even more efficient environmental protection

Closing: XYZ's environmental policy

- Bring environmental regulation in line with reality
- Make environmental protection efficient, effective, thorough

EXAMPLE SPEECH

Standing at the Edge of History:
Sustainable Development and the Chemical Industry

Speaker: Earnest W. Deavenport, Jr.,
Chairman and CEO, Eastman Chemical Company

Thank you, and good afternoon, ladies and gentlemen. Let me set the stage for my talk today with a phrase coined by the American economist, Barbara Ward, nearly 25 years ago.

She was concerned that the biosphere of our inheritance and the technosphere of our creation were out of balance, and that the door of the future was opening onto a crisis unlike any other we had ever experienced.

As a result, she said, we were standing at "the hinge of history."

The actions we take now in support of the concept of sustainable development—at this "hinge of history"—have the potential to generate change on a global scale for the benefit or detriment—of all life on earth.

As nations around the world come together to more fully focus on the economic, environmental, and social legacy our generation leaves on this earth for future generations, I believe, now more than ever, that good environmental policy hinges on good business policy.

If history has taught us anything, it is that environmental performance and economic performance work best when they work together. The record shows that our industry can do more good for the world economy, more good for the global environment, and more good for the social welfare of people everywhere if it is allowed to fully utilize its scientific principles, its ability to prioritize risks, and its ability to make value judgments based on objective cost-benefit analysis.

Simply put, the key to sustainable development is cost effective risk management, and that is what I want to talk about today.

But first, let me explain the principle of cost-effective risk management.

The role of risk and how to manage risk are the focal points in the current struggle to reform and remake the environmental regulatory framework in the United States.

The U.S. chemical industry championed the use of risk management and its key

Source: Earnest W. Deavenport, Jr., Chairman and CEO, Eastman Chemical Company. Delivered to the Fourth Forum of the World Chemical Industries, Paris, France, April 25, 1996. Reprinted by permission of Earnest W. Deavenport, Jr. and *Vital Speeches of the Day.*

elements of risk assessment, risk prioritization, cost-benefit analysis, and peer review of scientific data as a way of improving the U.S. environment and increasing its standard of living through a strong economy.

We view the principle of risk management as a common sense process for allocating scarce financial, human, and natural resources to activities that can provide the most benefit at the least cost to society.

We are also firm in our belief that we have a moral obligation to future generations to protect and use our limited resources wisely. Without such an obligation, the goal of sustainable development cannot be achieved. Although we today cannot define the needs of tomorrow's generations, we can work together to make certain that future generations are not limited in their choices when it comes their time to forge their own destiny.

Choices leading to a healthy environment and social equity will be theirs for the making if our generation will commit to the principle of cost effective risk management and obligate itself to a strong world economy.

And we are making great progress.

For more than 25 years now, industries worldwide have been going through a generational change in attitude toward the environment. Environmental ethics are now an integral part of our business strategies, and we have developed cleaner, energy- efficient processes that manufacture products that are healthier, safer, and more environmentally responsible.

In the U.S., we have now reached the point with this shift in attitude that leading-edge environmental technology no longer resides with government, but resides now with the business community.

Out of this change is emerging a new and modern environmental model.

This new model is replacing the old U.S. "command and control" model because society is recognizing that industry, with its advance technologies, can provide a cleaner environment at a lower cost than government can provide.

Unlike the command and control model, this new model is based on the fact that, when individual consumers are provided with truthful and accurate information in an open and free marketplace, they will make an educated and moral choice that will simultaneously lead to economic prosperity, environmental improvement, and social equity.

This emerging model is also based on the principles of risk management that, when applied in a free market, lead to an improved environment and an ever increasing standard of living.

Studies show that as a nation becomes more economically efficient through industrial specialization and open trade, per capita income increases. And as personal income increases, environmental quality and social well-being improve.

According to the World Bank, an annual per capita income of $5,000 is the threshold at which a society will choose to make environmental improvements, and usually does.

Perhaps you have witnessed, as I have, examples that bear this out.

Back in the mid-60's, I visited Tokyo for the very first time. It was a lot bigger, a lot more crowded, and a whole lot more polluted than I ever expected.

Today, thirty years later, Tokyo is still a big, crowded city, but it has one remarkable difference. Of all the major world cities I occasionally visit, Tokyo is now my favorite because it is so environmentally clean.

The major reason for Tokyo's environmental transformation, I believe, is an increase in Japan's per capita income.

Back in the mid-60s, Japan's per capita income was in the neighborhood of $6,000 a year, just above the World Bank threshold. Today it is over $21,000.

I recently made a world tour as a guest of *Time Magazine* that included visits to Havana, Moscow, Hanoi, Bangalore, India and several other hot spots. On that tour I witnessed first hand that environmental quality hinges on a sound economy.

I saw these once great cities in decline, their nations' economic potential being squandered, their local environment being slowly and methodically stripped of its natural resources, and their populations subjected to abject poverty. All because their governments are still waiting to recognize the power of the free market and the potential of cost effective risk management.

That tour confirmed for me, more than anything in my life, that when too much responsibility is shifted to government, individual freedom to make a responsible choice in a free market is reduced at the expense of the environment.

When the OECD Environmental Ministers met here in Paris just two months ago, there was concern that the rapid globalization now taking place throughout the world might have a detrimental effect on the world environment.

Those of us on the front lines of this globalization effort find comfort in the knowledge that our industry, with its development and transfer of clean technologies, is doing more to improve the environment by establishing economic stability and peace than ever before in industrial history.

The chemical industries in 40 countries have voluntarily developed long-term plans to integrate environmental performance with economic activity through a worldwide initiative we call Responsible Care.

Recycling, waste minimization, and product stewardship have now become an integral part of our business code of conduct because these responsible environmental activities make good economic and social sense.

In a just published report to President Clinton, the President's Council on Sustainable Development officially acknowledges the vital role that economic growth plays in the progress toward environmental quality.

It is comforting to know that the President's council recognizes the role of a strong economy in achieving sustainable development.

However, the reality is that our industry, as a major player in the world economy, is threatened by a series of existing and potential international conventions that limit our ability to contribute to a strong global economy, thereby rolling back sustainable development.

Under the current concept of sustainable development, there is a broadbased drive to stagnate industry in order to control consumption. This approach to improving the environment by impairing industrial activity is misguided and will eventually do the environment more harm than good.

Supposedly, exceptions would be made for environmental technology. But this centralized form of decision-making can have perverse and contradicting results.

Here is a case in point. The President's Council on Sustainable Development proposes, as a pilot project, to create a new form of development called eco-industrial parks. This new form of development follows a system of design in which one facility's waste becomes another facility's feedstock. If this concept of development is believed to be workable in our local villages, is it not reasonable to believe that such a development system should work in our global village as well?

If so, why are international conventions, such as the Basel Convention, driven to stop open trade between developed and developing nations in such valuable materials as scrap metals?

Conventions like these virtually eliminate the power of choice in a free market and impede sustainable development by retarding the progress of increasing per capita income.

In a recent speech at Harvard University, U.S. Secretary of State, Warren Christopher, announced the unprecedented move to fully integrate U.S. environmental goals into international diplomacy. This further intrusion by government could be a detriment to the advancement of sustainable development by diminishing the power of the free market and open trade.

If the concept of sustainable development is to become a reality, we must work together to build an international regulatory system that encourages industry to voluntarily change its behavior.

Instead, we are forced to react to prescriptive international conventions that stifle innovation, institutionalize misinformation, and perpetuate command and control.

The best way to save our planet is to save the people on it from poor sanitation, dirty drinking water, and from using "age old" farming techniques that deplete the land, hasten deforestation, and promote soil erosion.

I call upon environmentalists everywhere, who really want to improve the global environment, to join me and my industrial colleagues in eradicating poverty, improving literacy rates, and elevating educational standards.

These are life-long, sustaining fundamentals that provide for a wider bottom-up, rather than a narrow top-down, participation in risk management. Only through full participation will the goal of sustainable development be achieved.

Indira Ghandi said, "A nation's strength ultimately consists in what it can do on its own, and not in what it can borrow from others."

Strong national economies based on the principle of cost effective risk management is the key.

Governments can play an important role by demanding truth in advertising and by assuring that quality and relevant information is available for making individual moral choices.

In closing, risk management must be considered by national and local governments, as well as by international organizations, as a vehicle emphasizing the role of a strong economy in achieving the goal of sustainable development.

The message for all of us here today is that we should not merely settle for those actions that promise an easy path to the future.

It would be far easier for us all to simply accept the current economic, environmental, and social situation for what it is, and continue to travel along a path in which the promise of sustainable development will always be just beyond our reach.

A giant of our time, Charles de Gaulle, once said that France was never its true self except when it has engaged in a great enterprise. I believe that the same is true of companies and individuals. I believe it's certainly true of the concerned and dedicated men and women of the chemical industry worldwide.

Our great enterprise is a healthy environment for our small planet.

If we pursue the right course at this hinge of history—a course of cost effective risk management—I have no doubt that the door of the future will open onto great promise and opportunity for generations to come.

MODEL SPEECH 107:
Foreign Manufacturing Facility

Key Use of Speech: To define some policies for establishing foreign facilities.

Style of Speech: Informative and authoritative.

Audience: Company employees.

Time: 10 to 15 minutes.

→ Tip: Too often, policy seems to be set in a vacuum. The speaker makes it clear that, in this case, policy is based on actual experience.

As you all know, XYZ Corporation recently established a manufacturing plant in **[country].** I am happy to report that the plant is up and running—but it *was* quite an experience getting it to that point. I want to share with you some of the lessons we learned in setting up this plant. These lessons, I believe, can profitably be integrated into an overall statement of policy guidelines to govern the creation of additional plants in other countries.

→ Tip: Impose order on apparently random observations by numbering them.

The first lesson we learned is that communication is of paramount importance in establishing a new plant in a foreign country; however, lesson number two is that you can't get to the communications issues until you have solved the business issues. And lesson number three is that you can't solve the business issues until you have formed a solid understanding of the local market, culture, and business environment. In **[country],** for example, many people are accustomed to arriving at work around 10 in the morning. Now it's not that **[citizens of country]** are lazy, it's just that this is the way a work day has always been defined. We had to adapt to it, extending the working hours on the back end of the day.

The fourth lesson we learned is that most of the public relations and promotions techniques that work well in the U.S. actually work surprisingly well in **[country].** A direct mail campaign announcing

366

our presence was quite successful—but you need to know that you'd better send your material registered mail and in a plain brown envelope. Any attractive mailing tends to get "lost" in the [country] postal system. Fortunately, registered mail is cheap in [country] and payable in the local currency.

Lesson number five: While we need to learn as much as we can about the countries in which we do business, we should not abandon trust in our professional instincts and knowledge. We were repeatedly advised that news conferences would never work to promote our products in [country]. We held them anyway, and they generated a great deal of interest.

On to lesson six: A "back to basics" approach is essential to success. In countries such as [country], people have little or no knowledge of our brands and company. We needed to take time up front to develop detailed business and marketing plans to support the production of the new plant. We did market research early, but we could have done it even earlier. We thought through positioning, which proved key to early success. At this point, we're concentrating on one or two simple messages, which we repeat—over and over again.

[The speaker briefly outlines how the company positioned its products in the new country.]

Repetition is vitally important. Once we were up and running, we never missed an opportunity to picture our products *and* our logo.

This brings me to a seventh lesson: Pay unremitting attention to details. We continually reviewed the responsibilities and competencies of all our employees, especially the local people, and we learned very quickly the importance of reviewing, personally, all translations. These were reviewed and cross-checked before anything in print was made public.

Now, at last, the eighth lesson: communications. Even today, there are a mere [number] international phone lines going into [country]. We learned that we had to plan our calling and faxing carefully—and allow plenty of time for redialing. Postal service was neither reliable nor secure; for anything of even remote importance, we learned to rely on private overnight courier services.

But problems like these pale beside the age-old problems of the

→ Tip: The speaker is careful not to let his speech become a mere list. He transitions carefully to the issue of communication, which was mentioned at the beginning of the speech, and then builds up to the issue of language—obviously a key aspect of communication.

language barrier. Each conversation in a foreign country takes place on two levels. You are thinking and speaking in English, but your colleagues probably have to do the translation in their heads before they can comprehend and respond. Many employees and customers, of course, speak no English at all. Worse, to be polite, many people *pretend* to understand, not wanting to interrupt the flow of the conversation for clarification. We learned to state things as simply as possible and to be crystal clear in our communications. Whenever possible, we communicated in writing.

Let's continue on to a ninth lesson. We found that we needed to build in a generous margin of extra time to accomplish each activity. In general, we found that it was necessary to add **[percentage amount]** to the schedules we would make here at home. A tenth lesson: Keep pushing—but be tolerant. You *will* win out in the end.

OUTLINE

Opening

- Recently established plant in **[foreign country]**
- Up and running
- We learned lessons from this experience

Lessons 1–3

1. Communication is paramount
2. Can't communicate before solving basic business issues
3. Can't address business issues without understanding local culture and customs

Lesson 4: Public relations and promotion

- Direct mail worked well
- Must use registered mail

Lesson 5: Trust professional instincts and know-how

Lesson 6: Back to basics approach is essential

- Develop detailed business and marketing plans
- Think through positioning
- Employ repetition in positioning campaign

Lesson 7: Pay attention to details

- Frequently review responsibilities of employees
- Provide excellent translations

Lesson 8: Communications

- Work around phone problems in **[foreign country]**
- Plan your calls and faxes
- Use private courier services

Language barrier is most formidable problem

- The problems
- Communicate in writing whenever possible

Lesson 9: Allow extra time

- How much extra?

Conclusion

- The tenth lesson is tolerance and perseverance
- You will win out in the end

MODEL SPEECH 108:
Free Speech

Key Use of Speech:	To define corporate policy on free speech.
Style of Speech:	Informative and authoritative.
Audience:	Company employees.
Time:	5 to 6 minutes.

→ Tip: Taking an arbitrarily authoritarian approach to this issue will almost certainly fail. The speaker takes pains to acknowledge the importance of free speech—then to define its practical limits.

Our biggest investment at XYZ Corporation is in people: in you and in me. We invest in high-quality people, intelligent people, creative people, free-thinking people. Lock-step robots are not a good investment. We need to encourage and nurture creativity, not discourage it.

In our business, freedom of expression is an important aspect of creativity, and free speech is a right we all cherish as Americans. However, we must also face certain realities about our highly competitive, technologically innovative industry. Speech, if it is *too* free, can damage our company and cripple our competitiveness.

There are two areas in which, as XYZ employees, we have the responsibility of monitoring and, if necessary, self-censoring our speech.

The first area is in technology itself. We are not doing pure science here at XYZ. We are doing science for profit, and the knowledge we create here is proprietary. As a result, we cannot freely share with our colleagues at other companies—and, often, in other departments of *this* company—what we discover here. Corporate policy is unmistakably clear on this, and we all sign, as a condition of our employment, a detailed agreement to protect trade secrets.

[The speaker reviews highlights of the standard agreement.]

→ Tip: Define and explain policy—don't just set it. If employees appreciate the logic of a policy, they will be more eager to comply with it.

The second area in which we must agree to curtail free expression is in the area of personal opinion about the value of the technology we produce. By their nature, certain of our products are controversial. None of us must participate in this controversy without explicit authorization from management. XYZ Corporation invests many thousands of dollars annually in educating the public about our products. If we take it upon ourselves to speak individually about them, we are perceived as the voice of the company, and this may well lead to public confusion and to dilution and distortion of our image. It is vitally important that we present a unified front to the public. Accordingly, each of us is required to clear with management all public statements relating to our products.

Within the confines of our offices—and except for certain interdepartmental restrictions on technical information—XYZ encourages us all to engage in free, lively dialogue, including issues of controversy, ethics, and value. Let's keep such issues within the XYZ family, debate and discuss them, and agree on authoritative public statements of policy.

→ Tip: Don't apologize for stringent rules. State them. Stand by them.

I am obliged to remind everyone in this room that compliance with XYZ's policies on trade secrets and on refraining from unauthorized evaluative comments is a condition of employment. Violating this condition of employment is grounds for discipline, including dismissal.

But, even more important, violation of these regulations can have disastrous effects on our business and our continued ability to compete in this most exciting, challenging, and, yes, demanding industry.

MODEL SPEECH 109:
Growth

Key Use of Speech: To define corporate policy on growth.

Style of Speech: Informative and authoritative.

Audience: Company employees.

Time: 10 to 15 minutes. [Depends on detail of
                      guidelines discussed.]

→ Tip: State something clearly, and it will probably be believed and accepted.

Biological organisms have a simple policy on growth. They get bigger, reach maturity, stay the same size, thrive for a time, and then they die. Fortunately for us, as a company, we can adopt a more flexible growth policy. In a nutshell, it is this: As market conditions permit, we intend to grow—with the objective of maintaining control of our current markets and entering into selected new markets. We will not engage in growth for its own sake. Market conditions drive our decisions to grow.

Let's talk about "market conditions."

[The speaker sets out his company's guidelines for growth, laying out the market numbers that trigger growth.]

I want to stress that these are guidelines, not absolutes. Other intangibles may influence and modify our decision to grow in certain markets. For example . . .

[The speaker elaborates on these other factors.]

I began by saying that we enjoy an advantage over biological organisms in that we can regulate our growth. This includes "ungrow-

→ Tip: The problem with policy statements is that they are often inflexible and then, like political campaign promises, prove impossible to keep. Build in flexibility to policy statements. Make them fit for the real world.

ing," if necessary—downsizing in certain areas, if conditions seem to warrant this. I tell you this because I do not want managers operating under a false understanding of growth as an absolute policy mandate. The absolute policy mandate is that we should assume the size and volume necessary to compete effectively and, ultimately, to maintain current markets while expanding into key new markets. When this isn't possible or profitable, we refrain from growth. If necessary, well, we even shrink. Our policy is plastic rather than iron. Our policy allows for change. Growth is the kind of change that is most exciting and most fun, but we shall grow only when growth is warranted, and always with the principle of flexibility in mind.

MODEL SPEECH 110:
Labor Contracts

Key Use of Speech:	To define corporate policy on work-for-hire contracts.
Style of Speech:	Informative and authoritative.
Audience:	Company managers.
Time:	8 to 10 minutes.

→ Tip: The good news/ bad news approach, though hardly a new idea, is a highly effective way of opening a speech. Everyone will listen intently for the other shoe to drop.

I come to you bearing good news and pain-in-the-neck news. The good news is that our year-old policy encouraging the use of contract, work-for-hire, and temporary labor for such operations as **[speaker lists several task areas]** has saved this company **[$ amount]** in overhead during fiscal **[year]**. This is better than *good* news, actually. It's exciting news, since this figure betters by **[percentage amount]** our target projection.

Now the other side of the coin.

While the overall quality of our products and services has not suffered as a result of the increased use of contract labor, we have had problems in the following areas:

- some turnaround delays
- Social Security and benefits worries
- potential security worries.

To address these issues, we have introduced a number of new policies governing contract labor.

First, we have created a contract labor evaluation form, which all managers are required to complete within ninety days of concluding a work-for-hire agreement. This evaluation form . . .

374

→ Tip: The speaker is telling his audience that they will have to do more work—fill out more forms; however, explaining the *need* for this extra work should help secure willing compliance.

[The speaker describes the form, with emphasis on the areas evaluated.]

The evaluations are to be filed with Human Resources, and are to be updated every **[time interval].** In this way, all managers will be able to track the performance of individual vendors in a systematic and at least more or less objective way.

Second, all work-for-hire contracts must specify starting and completion dates for projects and, if necessary, starting and completion dates for various phases of more complex projects. The new agreement guidelines, which will be issued on **[date],** contain guidelines for creating late penalties. Our object is to ensure that our outside labor contracts become time-is-of-the-essence agreements. We need to get a firm handle on the problem of scheduling. It is true that whenever you go out of house for labor, you relinquish a large measure of control; but timeliness is one area we cannot afford to let slip.

Third, in order to prevent problems with Social Security contributions and other benefits issues, each contract worker must complete a work-for-hire questionnaire, which is designed to serve as prima facie evidence that the worker is *not* being employed in the manner of a regular employee, but is, indeed, an outside vendor. These questionnaires . . .

[The speaker briefly summarizes the content of the questionnaires.]

→ Tip: When you have step-by-step information to convey, a systematic, numbered approach is a highly effective mode of presentation.

Fourth, all work-for-hire contracts will now contain strong language concerning such security issues as **[speaker lists these issues].** We have not had any security problems with outside contractors to date, but we must be proactive in this area and close the barn door *before* any of our horses run out.

Many of us have long-term, good-faith relationships with our vendors, and we are understandably reluctant to introduce new elements into our agreements, but, as a company, we just cannot afford the liabilities that inadequate agreements expose us to. Your work-for-hire vendors will understand that, I believe, and accept it.

MODEL SPEECH 111:
Outsourcing

Key Use of Speech: To define corporate policy on outsourcing.

Style of Speech: Informative and authoritative.

Audience: Company managers.

Time: 5 to 10 minutes.

➤ Tip: When delivering vital operational information, take a no-frills approach. Note that the speaker is careful to include in the very first paragraph reassurance about the absence of layoffs.

Next quarter, XYZ Corporation will introduce the first phase of our new outsourcing policy. The following functions will be outsourced: **[speaker lists the functions].** No layoffs are called for in these areas; instead, managers will reallocate their in-house staff to other duties.

Our objective in this first phase of outsourcing is to reduce overhead and increase efficiency. Outsourcing gives us the flexibility to add and delete resources as necessary in response to demand. It makes us a more efficient, flexible, and competitive organization.

Outsourcing does come at a cost, however. We as managers must be sensitive to the anxieties and uncertainties outsourcing may create in some of our in-house staff. Some staff members may fear for their jobs. Others may be reluctant to relinquish control over certain functions. Still others may have difficulty creating effective relationships with outside sources.

➤ Tip: Balance the negative and the positive clearly, then suggest ways of addressing the negative issues.

We must be supportive and instructive.

Emphasize to your staff that outsourcing is a positive step and will enable them to redirect their efforts to critically important areas. Emphasize that no layoffs are mandated—although, in subsequent phases of the outsourcing program, some positions may be eliminated through attrition. Emphasize the importance of closely managing the out-of-house personnel, and suggest to your staff that the outsourcing program represents a challenge of additional management responsibility for the employees who must work with the outside people.

While all outsourcing contracts will be issued by the divisional office, individual managers will be responsible for negotiating rates, terms, and schedules within prescribed guidelines. Outsourcing assets will become additional items on your operating budgets.

It is our firm policy that all outside vendors agree to certain universal provisions governing out-of-house, contract labor. These provisions include . . .

[The speaker outlines common provisions.]

Managers must not make or imply any agreements or terms that conflict in any way with company policy as stated in these common provisions.

Ladies and gentlemen, I want to conclude by making it clear that, for XYZ, outsourcing is a positive step. It is most certainly *not* a way of saying that senior management is dissatisfied with the way we have been handling things in-house. It is, rather, an acknowledgment that certain functions can be performed more cost-effectively and, often, more efficiently out of house, leaving us all more time to devote to the functions we perform best and for which our customers come to us. Outsourcing is a way for us to sharpen our focus, become more profitable, and, on an individual level, create for each of us careers that are increasingly satisfying.

→ Tip: Don't get lost in the details, however necessary those details are. End on a positive note.

MODEL SPEECH 112:
Promotion

Key Use of Speech: To define corporate policy on promotion.

Style of Speech: Informative and authoritative; motivational.

Audience: Company managers.

Time: 10 to 15 minutes.

→ Tip: The speaker begins by putting the topic in the context of the corporate good.

XYZ Corporation has a reputation for giving its staff room and opportunity for growth. We don't like the idea of dead-end jobs, and we believe that it is in everyone's interest to recognize ability and to reward it. Promotion not only ensures that XYZ will have the leaders it needs, it also fosters a more cohesive, loyal, team-working organization.

I want to speak with you about three aspects of promotion. First: I want us all to be clear on XYZ's promotion policies with regard to equal opportunity and affirmative action. Second: I want to discuss promotion as a motivator of performance. Third: I want to make clear how managers benefit from promoting appropriate employees.

First: equal opportunity and affirmative action.

→ Tip: When you have relatively few main points to convey—no more than three or four, say—it is an effective strategy to preview them in an opening paragraph. Tell your audience what you are going to say—then say it.

[The speaker sets forth the official company policy in these areas.]

Now, the second area I want to discuss is how you can use promotion as a motivator. This is a cornerstone of policy here at XYZ. We believe in positive recognition and reward to motivate performance.

Of course, the promise of promotion has always been a good motivator. Most of your people will work harder if they believe there

→ Tip: Be certain that
your audience recog-
nizes when you are
issuing a policy state-
ment and when you are
giving advice or guide-
lines. The tone of your
text should shift from
formal to informal.

is an upward career path here. Growing companies, like XYZ, which are rapidly opening new offices and promoting people to management positions, have an easier time keeping staff than is the case with many more mature outfits.

Just don't be in a panic or rush to promote. Assess the management possibilities of your people, and let *them* know what traits and qualities merit promotion. Of course, you should not give false hope to people you just don't judge promotable, but do continue to outline for them the desirable characteristics. Who knows? Even some of these folks may find the motivation within themselves to meet your expectations.

You will sometimes find yourself tempted to hold back a promotion because you believe the person would be difficult to replace. This is a mistake, as well as a violation of at least the spirit of company policy on promotion. Besides, one of the ways for you as managers to move up the corporate ladder is to acquire a reputation as a *developer* of other managers.

It is likely that, on occasion, you will find that you have at least two good candidates for promotion. You may perceive this as a difficult dilemma, but, in reality, you are fortunate.

The best strategy is to support them equally. Allow a little competition to develop between them—and reap the rewards of heightened performance as you continue, quietly, to evaluate the pair.

It is also possible that you will find yourself with a highly qualified, highly motivated, highly capable individual—but no management slot to aim him or her toward, at least not at the moment. Sometimes, you can successfully counsel patience. But you run the risk of creating a morale problem, of *de*motivating, or even losing, the employee. If you don't see management positions opening in the near term, consider consulting with senior management to create an intermediate, semi-management position—in effect, a supervisor position. The availability of such positions could serve as a motivator for the entire sales staff.

As I mentioned earlier, avoid dangling promotion opportunities that do not reasonably exist. Level with your people about what they can expect. As Abraham Lincoln said, "You can fool all of the people some of the time, and some of the people all of the time, but can't fool all of the people all of the time." Illusory promises may serve as temporary inducements, but, sooner or later, your staff will become bitter, disappointed, cynical, and disloyal.

➜ Tip: The speaker makes a transition from advice/guidelines back to policy. Note that he states this shift clearly.

Now, let me proceed to third aspect of promotion policy here at XYZ.

Senior management most highly values office and field managers who cultivate personnel and who groom them for management positions. This is firm policy.

It is, therefore, in your best interest to ensure that there is someone qualified to fill your shoes. I know this idea may seem a bit disturbing, but it is a big part of your job to train someone to take your place!

Remember: your job security is *not* based on an *absence* of rivals, but on the level of performance, and part of that performance is developing other managers.

What should you be looking for in a potential successor? Here's a list:

➜ Tip: Lists are often necessary, but don't let them get too long. If you must provide a long list, print it up and distribute it—preferably after the conclusion of the speech.

- Someone well organized.
- A top performer in his or her present position.
- Someone enthusiastic.
- Someone with ambition.
- Someone who not only knows his or her job, but also how it relates to the bigger picture.
- Someone who commands respect—not just affection.
- Someone you trust.
- Someone who *really wants the job!*

In all of this, remember two things:

First: You are responsible for creating the leaders this company needs—and by "this company," of course, I mean you, me, all of us.

Second: On a more immediately personal level, the candidates you groom for promotion are a reflection of you—a very direct reflection. Choose carefully, then commit yourself to a high degree of mentoring. If all goes as it should, everyone wins: you, the candidate, and this firm.

OUTLINE

Opening

- Our company offers opportunity for employee growth
- Promotion ensures that our company has leaders

- Promotion fosters a cohesive team

Discuss three aspects of promotion

- Promotion policies
- Promotion as motivator
- How managers benefit from promoting appropriate employees

Equal opportunity and affirmative action

- Speaker sets out policy in these areas

Motivation

- Promotion is cornerstone of company policy
- Importance of positive recognition
- People work harder if they have an upward path
- Exercise caution in promoting
- Be honest
- Don't give false hope

Holding back promotion

- Why it is a mistake
- Why it is a violation of policy
- Benefit to managers of promoting employees

Problems

- Two employees equally deserving
- What you should do
- No management slot available
- What you should do
- Creating intermediate positions
- Honesty

Grooming your successor

- Why you should do it

- Don't be threatened
- What to look for in your successor

Closing

- You are responsible for creating the leaders the company needs
- Do it
- Do it wisely, carefully

MODEL SPEECH 113:
Recycling

Key Use of Speech:	To define corporate policy on recycling.
Style of Speech:	Informative and authoritative.
Audience:	Company employees and managers.
Time:	10 to 12 minutes.

→ Tip: An announce-
ment that you are
correcting false or mis-
leading information
usually attracts and
holds the attention of an
audience.

→ Tip: Don't suffocate
your audience in figures
and statistics, but do
present them with well-
chosen, highly revela-
tory figures.

Recently, recycling has been getting a bad rap. We've seen stories in the newspapers and on television about an *over*supply of recycled materials, and we've heard about municipalities that are having a hard time selling the materials they recycle as part of their sanitation programs.

Well, let me set the record straight.

Recycling continues to be very important to this company. For us, recycling exists on three levels. There are materials such as **[speaker lists the materials],** which we recycle internally for our own reprocessing and reuse. We've invested **[$ amount]** in **[processing equipment],** but each year save **[$ amount]** because of the value we are able to recapture and reuse as a result of our internal recycling program.

Make no mistake: the internal recycling program is significant for our bottom line. Managers and others who are assigned responsibility for recycling the materials I mentioned must remain vigilant and continue the scheduled pick-ups and dumps.

The second tier of our recycling policy is municipal. Office materials, such as **[speaker lists materials],** are regularly transported to the recycling center at **[location].** This is not in compliance with any laws, but is voluntary compliance on our part. XYZ has always been a good citizen and a good neighbor in this community, and the city continues to request our help in its recycling efforts. We support this, and we do not believe it is productive to rely on anecdotal reports in the media that municipal recycling is unproductive. Here, in [location], it remains an important priority of city government.

Finally, we do produce or use certain substances, namely [speaker lists them], which we must, by local, state, or federal law, recycle in prescribed ways.

It is vitally important that managers and employees ensure that these substances are recycled in accordance with all applicable regulations. If we fail to do this, we risk hefty fines, we risk varied liabilities for potential damage, and, most of all, we risk our lives and health as well as those of our friends and neighbors. XYZ fully supports the current regulations with regard to recycling the mandatory materials.

If anyone has questions about recycling at any of the three levels I mentioned, please contact [speaker gives in-house contact information].

For a variety of reasons—ranging from protection of the environment and our collective health, to risk management, to actual cost savings and bottom-line increase—recycling makes good sense for XYZ. I ask that we work as a team to give it our continued support.

Political Affairs

Openings

——*It is my pleasure to introduce a distinguished leader, who, fortunately, has also shown himself to be a great friend of this industry.*

——*Ladies and gentlemen, I've come here to talk about our future—and an important step we can take now to help ensure that that future will be a bright one.*

Closings

——*Please join me in welcoming John Doe, our next United States Senator!*

——*Next week, then, get out, go to the polls, and vote yes on Proposition 1234. It will make a difference—for all of us.*

MODEL SPEECH 114:
Support of Political Candidate

Key Use of Speech:	To endorse a political candidate.
Style of Speech:	Informative and persuasive.
Audience:	Industry group.
Time:	4 to 5 minutes.

I have been given the honor and the pleasure of introducing to you Stella Spiel, candidate for U.S. Senator. Stella is a longtime friend of business in general and of our industry in particular. As early as . . .

> ➔ Tip: Make the candidate's position and relevance clear from the start.

[The speaker briefly reviews the industry-related highlights of the candidate's career.]

This is all great for us in the **[industry];** however, Stella's record on issues relating to our industry is not a good enough reason for supporting her. To be worthy of this industry's support, a candidate must have a broad and deep understanding of the many pressing economic and social issues so important to our nation. Furthermore, a candidate must be able to look beyond the borders of our state and even of our nation. He or she must be able to take a global view of political affairs. A candidate worthy of our support must have demonstrated compassion, honor, judgment, and integrity. The candidate must be willing to work hard for us, yes, but also to represent *all* of the people.

Stella Spiel is such a candidate. If she had *no* record relating to *our* industry, she would still merit our support. But—fortunately for us—she has such a record, she is our friend, *and* she is a great legislator for the people of this nation.

> ➔ Tip: Beware of backlash. If you make the candidate's appeal too narrow, your audience may reject him or her.

Please welcome Stella Spiel, our next U.S. senator!

MODEL SPEECH 115:
Support of a Single Referendum

Key Use of Speech: A speech seeking support for a referendum important to an industry.

Style of Speech: Informative and persuasive.

Audience: Civic group.

Time: 8 to 9 minutes.

→ Tip: If you have been *invited* to speak, behave like a guest. Express gratitude and pleasure for the invitation.

Good morning, ladies and gentlemen. I'm delighted that you have given me this opportunity to talk with you about the United States airline business, which has reached a crisis in international competition.

The airline industry is very complex, of course, but the key to success is really very simple: offer a comprehensive route system with service in many origin–destination city pairs. This is the key to success, whether you fly domestically or internationally. The problem is that our government has largely neglected the competitive import-ance of international route structures—whereas foreign governments have been busy enacting regulations intended to sharpen the compet-itive edge of their national carriers. For a variety of reasons, the United States government has negotiated a long series of treaties with many nations effectively conceding substantial competitive advantages to non-U.S. carriers. Although U.S. airlines are willing and quite able to compete worldwide, our government has not used its negotiating leverage either to secure as many route rights as it could or to help U.S. carriers reap the opportunities to optimize the rights they do have. This means that those of us who operate international routes must deal with such issues as inadequate airport facilities, disadvantageous arrival and departure slots at foreign airports, prohibitions on the use of proprietary computer systems, and even, in some cases, requirements that we hire our competitors to provide customer services. And, as prejudicial as many of our treaties are, the U.S. is often reluctant to hold other nations even to the agreed terms, feeble as they may be.

[The speaker provides a few examples.]

For two decades, U.S. carriers have lost crucial opportunities. And what may happen in the next twenty years is even worse.

We are not permitted to fly beyond most foreign hub cities to the many points in other nations served by our foreign competitors. Even if the needed route rights could be secured, many foreign countries are unwilling to provide the takeoff and landing slots and facilities required to compete effectively with their national carriers.

Inevitably, ten, fifteen, or twenty years from now, all U.S. carriers will be either foreign owned or will be effectively excluded from international competition. It's that bad.

What must be done to head off this consequence?

The first key step is for the House and Senate to pass the Open Skies referendum.

[The speaker explains what this is and how it will help.]

Write or e-mail your congressman and your senator—today—and voice your support for the Open Skies referendum. If we can enact this legislation, we will have taken the first step toward becoming truly competitive in the international air travel market. If the referendum fails, I strongly believe that there will be no U.S.-owned airline that will fly internationally—if there are any U.S.-owned airlines at all. I think that you will all agree that, from a political standpoint, the loss of international routes, not to mention the loss of airline ownership, would be terrible. From a consumer's point of view, the consequences are even worse: sharply rising airfares, both nationally and internationally, in a market with greatly reduced competition.

Thank you for time, and I hope this American industry can count on your support.

Public Relations

Openings

—*My friends, I am always so very pleased to speak with you, especially about a subject as important as tonight's.*

—*Ladies and gentlemen of the Rotary Club, I am greatly honored that you have asked me to visit with you this afternoon.*

Closings

—*Thank you, ladies and gentlemen, for this opportunity to talk with you about a subject that is important to us all.*

—*This has been a real thrill for me. The work your organization is doing is very valuable, and it has been a pleasure to speak to you.*

MODEL SPEECH 116:
Business Associations or Chambers of Commerce

Key Use of Speech:	About the future of business.
Style of Speech:	Authoritative.
Audience:	Business group.
Time:	10 to 12 minutes.

→ Tip: Bid to get your audience on your side from the outset.

A lot of folks—*too* many—think of the Chamber of Commerce as a haven for the status quo, for "business as usual." Well, I know business people better than this. I know that you haven't invited me here to talk about business as usual, but, rather, about challenge and change. During the past half-decade, 150 companies have disappeared from the *Fortune* 500. This figure is a powerful incentive to change.

We are in the throes of a transition between the kind of country we have been for the last half-century to the kind we will be—or want to be—for the next fifty years and beyond. We are facing a world with less sharply defined political boundaries on the one hand and an economy driven by fiercely competitive regional alliances on the other. We are facing a world in which all nations will have to shoulder shared responsibility for the environment and for the maintenance of human health and well-being. Are we equal to these and other new tasks that lie before us?

→ Tip: You are not obliged immediately to answer the questions that you pose. Let the question hang there for a time, creating suspense.

A decade ago, I could have described a great many American companies as top-heavy, with a management firmly entrenched and quite uninterested it its employees. These companies often delivered products of mediocre quality at substantial prices.

Where are these companies today?

Changed. Or gone.

Most of the top-heavy and bloated institutions we find surviving today are, unfortunately, related to the government. As the American consumer—and the international consumer of American goods—demanded change in the private sector, so Americans are demanding change in their government.

Government, at this point, could profitably look to business to see how to put an end to "business as usual," to change, to change for the better. The current unresponsiveness of our public institutions did not happen overnight. The phenomenon occurred because the American political system has been historically geared to the principle of "more is better." We have evolved into a nation without limits. Whenever there has been a choice between resolving a problem through efficiency or numbers, the numbers have won: numbers of people, numbers of dollars, or both. Corporate America long followed this path, too. Then we ran into such problems as

➡ Tip: In speeches, keep lists specific and short. Listeners have a difficult time retaining verbal lists.

- the globalization of markets, which seriously eroded our competitive advantage and threw the balance of payments into a tailspin;
- bloated size and unwieldy structure, which isolated the top and overexpanded the bureaucratic middle, while demotivating the mass of workers;
- a decline in productivity and product quality, which eroded our customer base.

We in business have made a very good start at responding to all of these challenges. Those of us who failed to respond—well, we probably aren't here in this room, because we aren't in business any longer. The threat to our survival forced the necessary changes in our thinking. We became and are becoming more cost-effective by improving productivity, leveraging our physical and human resources, and reducing the size of our managerial bureaucracy. We are creating new opportunities by becoming more customer-driven, more responsive to our customers. We are becoming more quality conscious and more aggressively competitive—not only in our traditional markets but in new markets as well. We have consciously rejected the conventional, hierarchical command structure in favor of moving responsibility and authority to the office and factory floors.

→ Tip: Set off your main points with sharp, staccato clarity.

→ Tip: Look for natural opportunities to create memorable phrases, such as this play on "out of touch . . . out of time."

→ Tip: The speaker not only closes on a note of optimism, he gives reasons for that optimism.

Our businesses are engaging our employees more directly, recognizing them more quickly, and rewarding them more adequately. The results have been impressive. For trust, if well placed, liberates creativity, encourages, and motivates.

American business today still has a long way to go, but it has come very far. It is leaner, more limber, more global, and more competitive.

To us, the message was clear: *Change or be changed.*

To our government, it must be the same.

Government must acquire, as we in business have, a drive to get closer to and better understand the needs of people. Our public institutions still have the capacity for greatness, but they have lost touch with the basic values that drive the *people* of this country. Out of touch, many major governmental institutions are perilously close to being out of time.

What can government learn to get closer to the needs of its "customers"—the people? It must begin to:

- downsize the bureaucracy, through privatization and other means;
- move authority and responsibility downward, thereby creating opportunities for individual enterprise;
- improve the quality of government service by paying attention to the needs of the "customer."

Having witnessed and taken part in the revolution in business during the last decade or so, I am very optimistic about the ability of government to undergo the same kind of change.

The tasks we *still* face in business are, of course, *still* formidable, and the tasks the public sector faces are even *more* daunting. But confronting the *challenge of change* is what made this country great in the first place, and it is a willingness so deeply ingrained in our character as a nation, that I have full confidence in its capacity to help us regain our leadership position. All of us, the people who own and manage American business, must commit ourselves to aid and guide our public institutions in making the journey we have already fairly begun. Together, we can create a brighter future.

OUTLINE

Opening

- You've invited me to talk about the challenge of change

We are in a transition period

- Between what we've been for the past half-century and what we will be—or would like to be
- World's political boundaries are less sharply defined
- All nations fiercely competitive now
- All nations concerned about the environment, too

The past

- American companies were top-heavy
- Management wasn't interested in employees
- Quality was a matter of indifference
- This has changed
- Companies that failed to change are gone

The government

- Could learn a valuable lesson from business
- Needs to put an end to "business as usual"
- Unresponsive to the people
- Blindly believes more is better
- While business is becoming more efficient, government remains inefficient
- While business has learned "change or be changed," government has not
- Government must learn to be more in touch with the people

What can government do to get closer to the needs of the people?

- Downsize the bureaucracy
- Move authority and responsibility downward
- Pay attention to the "customer's" needs

Closing

- I am optimistic that government can change
- Task is formidable, however
- Country has successfully faced the challenge of change in the past
- We can do it now

MODEL SPEECH 117:
Civic Associations

Key Use of Speech:	Making common cause over a community issue.
Style of Speech:	Sincere, persuasive, inspiring.
Audience:	Civic group.
Time:	8 to 10 minutes.

➡ Tip: It is usually *not* a good idea to begin a speech combatively—but, in this case, the battle is a well-chosen one, and the speaker understands the impression she is trying to create on this audience.

They say *you can't fight city hall.*

If we accept this mindless cliché as fact, I'll lay claim to the shortest speech in history—beating the two minutes President Lincoln spent on *The Gettysburg Address* by a good minute and forty-five seconds. Because I can now shut my mouth, and we can all go home.

And we'd better get to those homes fast, while they're still worth living in.

Because, ladies and gentlemen, friends and neighbors, if we allow the city to build its incinerator facility in our backyard, few of us will *want* to live here any longer. Certainly, XYZ Corporation, which has been a member of this community for **[number]** years, will not *want* to do business here. Just as all of you want to keep your homes beautiful and pleasant, so XYZ wants to continue to provide its employees and customers with a beautiful and pleasant environment in which to work and do business. We owe this to our staff and to our customers. We—*all* of us—owe it to ourselves.

➡ Tip: The speaker makes clear her common cause with her audience.

Now let me pause a moment. Perhaps some of you are saying to yourselves that *our* problem is nothing like *yours*. There is a certain truth to that thought. We are a business. It is easier for us to move out of this community, lock, stock, barrel, than it is for most homeowners, who have invested so much of their treasure in their homes, to take a

397

huge loss and turn their backs on a blighted community. So, yes, you *are* in an even tighter spot than we are. However, my friends, XYZ *likes* this community. We think of it as our home. We have invested in it in many ways. **[The speaker gives examples of civic programs, etc., which XYZ has funded.]** I admit: this proposed incinerator will cost you, individually, more than it will cost us. But, folks, we *are* in this together.

Now, what about this nonsense that you can't fight city hall?

Well, what else is city hall is for?

Each and every day, a legion of lawyers and lobbyists make their living fighting city hall. Certainly, we can do the same. The question is, will we fight loudly but fruitlessly, attacking the problem individually? Or will we make common cause, and, this very evening, begin to develop a plan?

Like each of you, XYZ Corporation generates lots and lots of garbage. That much is a fact—indeed, a product—of life. It is also a fact that something has to be done with it. What our city proposes to do is to take not only our garbage, but garbage from twelve other districts, and burn it here, in a new plant to be built on a site bounded by State, Central, Nelson, and Hardy Streets. Now this is only five blocks from our neighborhood's main business district, six blocks from Nelson Middle School, and, only three blocks from our headquarters.

None of us wants it here.

But let's be honest. *Every* community says that. It's the so-called "NIMBY" response: *not in my back yard.* Quite understandably, then, our city has told us, *"We've got garbage and we've got to get rid of it—if not in your neighborhood, then in someone else's."*

This sounds like a real dilemma. It doesn't change the fact that we don't want the incinerator here, but it does put us in the position of selfishly saying, *"We* don't want the problem. Let somebody else have it." None of us is eager to pass the buck to someone else.

We don't have to.

The fact is that the city's assessment of the situation is inaccurate, short-sighted, and just plain wrong.

On behalf of ourselves and this community, and entirely at our expense, XYZ funded a study, which we filed with the city authorities, demonstrating that at least four locations, zoned exclusively for manufacture, reasonably remote from residential and retail areas, offer ample acreage for the proposed incinerator.

→ Tip: Having established her company's connection with the needs of the audience, the speaker returns to her original point.

→ Tip: Indicate a radical change in the direction of thought with a short, clear declarative sentence.

→ Tip: The speaker articulates not only the problem, but the choices that are faced.

The truth of the matter is that we don't *have* to give this problem to someone else. The truth of the matter is, there does not *have* to be a problem.

Neighbors, friends, our choice is starkly simple: We can walk away from a fight with city hall and allow the administration to build the incinerator precisely where it will do the most harm, where it will threaten our health and our children's health, and where it will burn up not only garbage, but the investment each and everyone of us has made in a home, a business, a life here. Or we can work together to ensure that an alternative site is chosen.

You know, we're not just fighting to save our neighborhood, we're really fighting for our entire city. This town cannot afford to destroy one if its greatest neighborhoods.

We at XYZ are willing to provide the following facilities and support to mount an effective campaign against building the incinerator in this neighborhood. **[The speaker lists the support his company will provide.]** Even with our support, however, the fight may require a some financial commitment from many of you. XYZ is willing to assist in organizing an appropriate fund-raising effort.

XYZ has always tried to be a good neighbor. Part of being a good neighbor is just being friendly, day to day, but you and I know that a good neighbor is more than that. A good neighbor is someone you can count on when your home and family are in trouble. Well, you can count on us. On behalf of the **[number]** employees who work in our headquarters here in **[neighborhood]**, I ask: *Can we count on you?*

OUTLINE

Opening

- Can't fight city hall?
- Incinerator crisis
- We *must* fight city hall

Our common cause

- Company and neighborhood homeowners both have a stake in this
- We are in it together

How to fight city hall

- Separately?
- Together?
- Develop a plan together

The problem

- The city's proposal
- We don't want the incinerator
- We don't want to foist it on anyone else, either

The truth

- We funded a study
- Alternative sites *are* available
- We are fighting not just for ourselves, but for our city

Our company will help

- What company can do
- We must all make a financial commitment

Closing

- We will be good neighbor
- Will you?

MODEL SPEECH 118:
Service Clubs

Key Use of Speech: To a service club.

Style of Speech: Informative, persuasive.

Audience: Service club.

Time: 10 to 15 minutes.

Ladies and gentlemen, it is a pleasure to speak to you today because, by reason of your membership in **[name of service club],** you have amply demonstrated that you are compassionate, sensitive, and concerned citizens. This makes me feel particularly optimistic, then, that my comments today will be received with thoughtfulness—by people who can act on the issues I raise.

You see, ladies and gentlemen, a very important part of our society—our civilization—is broken, and we need to fix it. I'm talking about our civil justice system.

Let's take apart that phrase, *civil justice.* The terrible truth is that our "civil justice" system is neither civil nor just. Staggering costs and mind-boggling, heart-breaking delays deter the average citizen from using the system—and that, I submit, is hardly "civil." And the fact that merely being sued costs so much that, even if you are guilty

of nothing, it is often cheaper to settle than to fight can hardly be called "justice." *Terrorism* is a better word.

How did we get to this point?

About half a century ago, a small group of academics and jurists, led by Roger Traynor, a California judge, pioneered the idea that, in the absence of appropriate legislation, it was up to the courts to bring about individual justice through social change. Specifically, Traynor et al. proposed the principle that victims of accidents should be

401

➔ Tip: Nothing is more persuasive than fact. The speaker has clearly done his homework on this subject. Perhaps everyone feels dissatisfied with the civil justice system, but the speaker manages to tell the audience something they don't already know.

➔ Tip: Build a persuasive case by progressing from bad to worse—from near-extreme to extremely extreme.

compensated for their misfortune, not based on who was at fault, but on the basis that the costs of injury should be assigned to those who could best afford to pay. Who were these parties? Insurance companies were the providers of goods and services, who (the theory ran) could best afford to pay because they could recover their costs by raising prices, if necessary. In effect, it wasn't the providers who would pay, but society—through mildly increased prices. Thus *social* change would be effected by the courts deciding *individual* cases. It was a kind of redistribution of wealth.

It wasn't a *bad* idea. In many ways it was a *noble* idea. But has it proved to be an *efficient,* let alone *just,* idea?

Most everyone today—this includes legal experts, business people, and the proverbial person in the street—say no. The fact is that **[percentage amount]** of the dollars awarded in civil cases *never* reach the injured parties. The bulk of the damages—some **[percentage amount]**—goes to lawyers, for the most part, and to other workers in the legal system. This is the very definition of inefficiency, at the very least, and injustice at the worst.

But there is much more to the inefficiency and injustice. The system is agonizingly slow. This is understandable on the basis of case load alone: in **[year],** state and federal courts were burdened with **[number]** liability suits. The system eats money. Individuals, businesses, and local, state, and federal governments spend upward of **[$ amount]** annually on direct litigation costs.

Did I say **[$ amount]**?

Staggering as that number is, it does not represent the *real* cost of litigation. The *real* cost is in what I might call "business deterrence"— the volume of potential enterprise that has either been aborted or has simply not occurred because companies were fearful of liability. Please ponder this:

- **[percentage amount]** of U.S. manufacturers have withdrawn products from the market at some time during the past five years;
- **[percentage amount]** have stopped some form of product research for fear of liability problems;
- **[percentage amount]** have laid off workers in direct response to "business deterrence";
- for U.S. firms, insurance rates are **[number]** times higher than those of their foreign counterparts and competitors.

The sad fact is that, in the area of product liability, the merest *threat* of lawsuit is often all that is needed to get a lucrative settlement. **[The speaker gives one or two particularly egregious examples.]** Rather than go through the time and expense of defending themselves, many companies pay **[$ amount]** to **[$ amount]** just to get out of the litigation.

This fear of lawsuits does not affect businesses alone. Each of us, as a consumer, pays higher prices because of it—and not just the *slightly* higher prices Traynor had envisioned. For some products, **[percentage amount]** of the retail price goes to cover projected liability.

I could, of course, go on and on. But I believe the point is clear: the civil justice system needs reform.

As I see it, the most promising reforms fall into two basic categories:

1. Making trials more efficient and less costly.
2. Avoiding trials altogether through alternative dispute resolution, such as binding mediation.

[The speaker gives examples to support both reforms.]

Ladies and gentlemen, as dreary and hopeless as the situation may seem, the civil justice system is actually, in essence, surprisingly sound. Our goal is to *fix,* not tear down, the system, to make its incentives positive. Instead of exploiting ways to "work the system," we must find ways to make the system work. The modest reforms I have suggested are a step in that direction, and they will take the support of intelligent people of good will, people such as the members of **[name of service organization],** to see them put into practice. Keep the faith, and keep up the pressure. Thank you.

→ Tip: After building from bad to worse, the speaker brings the problem home to each of us, as a "consumer."

→ Tip: Having established the existence of a problem, the speaker refuses to wallow in it, but instead proceeds to suggested directions for a solution.

OUTLINE

Opening

- Compliment to the audience
- You are compassionate, thoughtful
- The subject: our civil justice system is broken

The civil justice concept

- Our system is neither civil nor just
- Costs are staggering
- Threat of lawsuit has become a terrorist weapon

How did we get to this point?

- Chronology of developments
- Idea behind current system wasn't bad
- But execution of the idea has been faulty
- System wasteful, unjust
- Most damages are awarded to lawyers, not clients

Consequences of inefficiency and injustice

- Slow
- High case load
- Crippling costs
- The "real" costs = "business deterrence"
- Definition and examples of business deterrence
- Consumers pay higher prices

Civil justice clearly needs reform

- Two types of reform
- Make trials more efficient, less costly
- Use alternatives to trials

Conclusion

- Sounds hopeless, but isn't
- Basic system is sound
- Fix, don't tear down

MODEL SPEECH 119:
Trade Associations (Customers)

Key Use of Speech: To a customers' trade association.

Style of Speech: Informative and helpful; "free advice."

Audience: Customers' trade association members.

Time: 15 to 20 minutes.

→ Tip: Nothing creates good will more effectively than giving away free advice, provided that advice is perceived as valuable.

It is a great pleasure speaking to **[name of association],** especially because so many of you are clients of XYZ Public Relations. As you know, my firm specializes in international public relations, and while I hardly have to sell you on the idea of international trade as good business, I do think that we could spend a profitable few minutes talking about some of the marketing and communications challenges of the current international business environment.

While the American business stake in international trade has risen sharply over the past decade, many firms continue to make errors that are a lot more than a decade old. Here are some examples:

- A giant firm planned an international satellite news conference, originating in New York, only to forget about the time differences between the U.S. and Europe!

→ Tip: Analysis is drawing general conclusions from specific events or examples. Audiences appreciate this as an exercise in genuine thought. It tells them something they don't already know.

[The speaker mentions several more examples.]

There is a common denominator in the mistakes I've just listed. In every single case, the company in question failed to take into account some aspect of the culture and customs of the target market. You can't always export American marketing methods along with American products.

Now, mistakes such as these are almost the rule rather than the exception. While world trade is expanding, marketers tend to lag behind. If you are going to compete internationally, you must have people who are prepared to reinvent marketing to meet global needs. So far, most employees, even in firms targeting international markets, lack the understanding to be truly effective on the international scene. A **[year]** survey found that the vast majority of American managers— **[percentage amount]**—do not speak a language in addition to English. In contrast, our counterparts in other countries *have* had educations that emphasize languages, cultures, and international business issues.

> ➤ Tip: After analyzing the problem, the speaker offers some solutions.

So what is to be done? I wish I had all the answers—though I have one: Until you have the in-house expertise you need, hire companies like mine. But that's a commercial, and I'm an invited guest. So here's some "free advice:"

First: Don't make uniform assumptions about our target markets. It is not so much that we often *misinterpret* the culture of a target market, but that we fail to interpret it at all.

[The speaker gives an example of a company that made unwarranted assumptions.]

The moral: Don't *assume; find out.*

Second: Use international agencies with a local presence—not domestic agencies that try to run international advertising and public relations by remote control.

> ➤ Tip: The speaker is careful to avoid turning the speech into blatant self-promotion.

[The speaker gives examples.]

My third point: Much as I would like to take maximum advantage of the in-house gaps of the firms I serve—after all, filling those gaps is my business—I advise you to start a program to build international skills among your employees. And do it *now.*

Fourth: Hire internationally. It is difficult, perhaps impossible, to run a multinational business without a multinational management team. You need "native" viewpoints and insights. There is no substitute.

Finally, many of us must profoundly alter the way in which we approach problems. Americans think serially, sequentially, whereas Europeans and Asians tend to approach issues and problems from several angles at once. For example . . . **[The speaker develops this point.]**

America's international business is booming, but don't let this cheer you into complacency. We have a lot of catching up to do. *Everyone's* international business is booming.

We—you and I—are marketers and communicators. We have the opportunity not only to make greater profit, but also to promote international understanding through international trade. Let's do both of these jobs as well as they can possibly be done. The opportunities are boundless—without borders.

Thank you.

———————————

MODEL SPEECH 120:
Trade Associations (Suppliers)

Key Use of Speech: To a suppliers' trade association.

Style of Speech: Informative and helpful; helps the suppliers know what the customer wants.

Audience: Suppliers' trade association members.

Time: 8 to 10 minutes.

→ Tip: Light humor at the outset can establish a pleasant, low-pressure rapport with your audience.

Good evening, my friends. I am delighted to be here with all of you, many of whom are our suppliers or, I hope, potential suppliers. I am delighted because this speech affords me the opportunity to tell you something about what our firm wants in suppliers of **[product type].** Moreover, I've gotten a free dinner out of it, too!

I can tell you in a single word what XYZ looks for in its principal suppliers: innovation.

But what is "innovation"?

Let's begin to answer that by saying what it is *not*.

Innovation is not synonymous with invention. "Invention" is a term of technology, whereas innovation is a term of economics. As management guru Peter Drucker says, innovation "allows resources the capacity to create wealth."

→ Tip: Identify what interests your audience, then deliver it. The speaker here is addressing a group whose members are interested in selling things to his company. The speaker begins from that fact.

In short, we are looking for technology we can use—profitably, or, more to the point, to achieve new kinds and levels of profit.

Sometimes invention and innovation do happen simultaneously, but, often, they do not. Many times in history an invention has appeared without apparent purpose until, years later, a purpose is found or created. That second phase is innovation.

Now, this is not the time for the technologists in the audience to develop an inferiority complex. A common reason why some inven-

408

→ Tip: Investigating the causes of something important is always interesting to an audience.

tions don't instantly become innovations *is* technological: the supporting technologies may not yet exist to make the invention fully functional. Look at so many of Leonardo da Vinci's inventions—the helicopter, for example. His principles were sound, but a host of supporting technologies were centuries in the future.

Sometimes it isn't a question of *supporting* technologies, so much as it is giving the new technology—the invention—a certain additional technological twist. The transistor was invented by Bell Laboratories in 1947, but it took Sony, in 1956, to use the invention in the first transistor radio sold in America.

Innovation building upon invention also requires the right market conditions—that is, social and economic conditions. The forerunners of the computer have been traced to the early nineteenth and even eighteenth centuries, but it wasn't until the United States census became so complex, in 1890, that Herman Hollerith was moved to create a fairly sophisticated punch-card tabulator, which was bought, sold, and marketed by the direct predecessor of IBM. After this, calculating machines and computers were rather rapidly commercialized.

→ Tip: Stepping back to get the "big picture" is a dramatic highlight of any speech.

If innovation is critical to the success of a business such as my company, XYZ Corporation, it is vital to nations and to all of humanity. Most human activity consists of shifting and rearranging what we already have. Innovation, in contrast, is dramatic, raises productivity, spurs economic growth, and actually increases wealth.

If innovation is so crucial, it follows that it would be a valuable thing to know just what drives innovation. I can't provide a full answer. I know that you need a supply of good ideas, plus an environment in which they can develop. On a company level as well as a societal level, this means fostering a high level of education, supporting risk taking, tolerating diversity of all kinds, and maintaining an openness to new ideas. Extreme need and crisis also drive innovation. Unfortunately, wars have spurred many periods of intense innovation. If necessity—even in the form of war—is the mother of invention, it is the father of innovation as well.

How can we all, in our businesses, foster a spirit of innovation?

→ Tip: The speaker shifts to practical "how to" considerations.

We might well have to begin by shucking some outworn ideas about management. Instead of putting a high premium on narrowly specialized skills, we probably should be cultivating the generalists—who also excel in certain areas, while maintaining a *general* excellence. We need to develop flexible, fast-moving structures to replace the rigid, glacially paced management hierarchies that are our legacy of the 1950s. We need to give our people as much autonomy as they can handle. The term management experts would use is "cross-functional teamwork."

Cross-functional teamwork requires the willingness of the organization as well as the individual. The company has to see the importance of climbing over the walls that form between functions, and the individuals have to be willing to make the climb—repeatedly and routinely. It's a lot of work—and very exciting.

Now, here is something I can assure you of from my point of view as a customer. Innovation also requires staying in close contact with your customers, because that's how you know which of your inventions has the potential to become an innovation.

When all is said and done, a company is its people. Staff your firms for innovation. Look for people of wide breadth—generalists first, specialists second. Remember, time and again, innovation has come from crossing from one discipline to another. Staff your firm with people who excel at analysis and problem solving, at persuasion, and who have vision. For these qualities are not only the ingredients of innovation, they are the very qualities your customers—us, for instance—are looking for in a supplier of technology.

Thank you.

OUTLINE

Opening

- Happy to tell you what our firm wants from suppliers
- Express it in a single word: innovation

What is innovation?

- First, what it is not
- It is technology we can use
- Compare and contrast innovation and invention
- How inventions become innovations—or fail to

Innovation is critical to company and to nation

- Innovation is rare
- Innovation dramatically raises productivity

What drives innovation?

- Good ideas
- Environment that encourages development of ideas
- High degree of education
- Willingness to take risks
- Embracing of diversity
- Openness to new ideas
- Sometimes extreme need drives innovation

How can business foster innovation?

- Jettison outworn ideas
- Hire generalists, not just specialists
- Adopt flexible, fast-moving structures
- Give people autonomy
- Develop cross-functional teamwork
- Maintain close contact with customers

Closing

- The ultimate key is personnel

MODEL SPEECH 121:
Trade Associations
(Industry Competitors)

Key Use of Speech: To an industry trade association.

Style of Speech: Informative, seeking common ground.

Audience: Industry trade association members.

Time: 10 to 11 minutes.

→ Tip: Good-natured banter takes the edge off of speaking to competitors.

It's good to see so many of my friends—especially here with me in one room. If you're here, you can't be somewhere else, talking to one of my customers!

The subject of my speech this afternoon may make you laugh. So let's get the laughter over with quickly. I'm going to talk about something that could benefit all of us: a partnership between industry and government. Funny—or unbelievable—as this idea might sound, I think that such a partnership is essential for our global success. After all, many countries—*capitalist* countries—throughout the world already enjoy such partnerships. And this is making it increasingly difficult for your companies and mine to compete in the world arena.

→ Tip: The speaker prepares his audience for something they may consider outrageous.

Don't get me wrong, friends. "partnership" doesn't mean government control or the government setting industrial policy. Partnership means cooperation. For example, the government would refrain from taking action affecting our industry without first consulting us about it, while we would continue to work to ensure that what we do in no way harms the public interest.

[The speaker goes on to site other areas of potential cooperation.]

→ Tip: The speaker begins to show how his vision is not just pie in the sky.

Can this relationship actually come about?

412

Well, it has—in the past. Unfortunately, it has always taken a war to forge a positive bond between government and industry. But it *has* worked. Come peace, however, we tend to become the adversary of government, and vice versa. I have to say, quite honestly, the fault lies mainly with the government, which tends to take a know-it-all approach, an attitude that everything begins and ends with government. We cannot assume and maintain an international leadership position if change is merely dictated from Washington. Remember, our government is *representative* government. It embodies and reflects the attitudes of the people. We in this industry must work with the public to change attitudes in five areas, if we want to win in this global economy.

Number one: The American people have to change their understanding of the nature of business. Business is the creation and production of goods and services to meet the demands of everyday life. The products of business raise the standard of living for all Americans. Yet, in America, business is often demonized as the enemy—and government (or, at least politicians) fosters this image. Well, government, politicians, and special interest groups don't create wealth. Business does. We aren't the enemy. We're the *engine* that drives *everything.*

This leads to the second point. We are being taxed—not to death, but to the brink thereof. And this goes not only for business, but for the individual customers we serve: the people—ourselves!

Taxes, as Ben Franklin said, are as certain as death. And, yes, they are necessary, too. But government needs to work on establishing limits and priorities.

So let's go to point number three: Government is an area about which public opinion needs to change. The public has to stop complaining about runaway spending and start holding responsible the politicians they elect. The federal deficit is absorbing **[percentage amount]** of the net *savings* of all individuals and businesses in America. This is bad for business, and it is bad for the nation.

Why can't we get a handle on spending?

Here's point number four: The spirit of American politics is selfishly divisive, not collaborative and cooperative. We managers in business learned long ago that the only truly effective way of running a complex business is through teamwork. No business is more complex than government. But where is the teamwork in government?

→ Tip: The speaker makes his principal points clearly, in numbered paragraphs, pausing, as necessary, to point out the relationships among these points.

Diverse as we are, we have to get back to thinking and acting like a single nation. We have to begin working more for the common good.

But while we're harmonizing ourselves and reshaping discordant policies for the common good, we have to stop trying to remake the *rest* of the world in our image. This is my fifth point: We have to stop being so eager to slap other nations with economic sanctions while the *rest* of the world goes on with business as usual. Sanctions generally do not hurt governments. They hurt the people under the thumb of those governments—and they hurt us, American business.

America is a great nation, and American business is a great and mighty force. But neither the nation nor business is immune to economic realities. We're *not* unstoppable.

However, we could be *almost* unstoppable if we would unite with government—and government with us—as coequals rather than adversaries. Is this possible?

➔ Tip: The final phase of the speech is a call to action.

Well, was it "possible" for the Berlin Wall to fall?

And, let me tell you, even if we're too often adversaries, relations between government and business are not nearly as nasty as they were between democracy and communism. If the Wall can fall, so can the walls dividing business from government. Business has a vital stake in effective government and in evenhanded taxes and regulations coming out of Washington and our fifty state capitals. The more government officials work with us, the more they will be surprised at what we *can* do together. Besides, we're already on the same team! Whether we like it or not.

Thank you.

OUTLINE

Opening

- Greeting
- Subject of my speech may make you laugh
- Partnership between industry and government

Defining industry–government partnership

- Doesn't mean government control
- Cooperation
- Example

Is this partnership possible?

- Has happened in the past
- Government needs to take the initiative

Business must help change public and government attitudes

- Help people change their attitude toward business
- Reform taxation
- People must hold government responsible for its spending
- Politicians must cooperate, not fight
- We need to stop levying trade sanctions all over the world

Closing

- America is great—but is vulnerable to economic crisis
- We will be strong if the business–government partnership is developed
- It *is* possible

_____

EXAMPLE SPEECH

Finding Someone to Sue:
Regaining Control of the Tort Law

Speaker: Robert J. Eaton, Chairman and CEO, Chrysler Corporation

Thanks, Herb, and good afternoon. I'm honored that you asked me to be here. I was particularly flattered when I was told that Colin Powell spoke in this slot a year ago. Then I found out he got $60,000, and nobody offered me a dime. Somebody must have heard one of my speeches before.

That's fine. Actually, I jumped at the invitation because I have a lot to get off my chest. So, if you don't mind, I'm going to vent a little today. And I'm going to vent about lawyers.

I know that you're the good guys in your field, however, so don't take anything I say personally, okay?

I respect the knowledge and the talents of the lawyers I work with every day. They are indispensable. No business could function without them.

I'm going to talk about what I think is a distinct minority of lawyers. But this minority, unfortunately, is driving the public perception of your profession. That's not fair, but only you and your colleagues in the profession can change it.

I was always told to start a speech with a joke. It helps to make friends with the audience, and get them used to the sound of your voice. And, of course, the nice thing about talking to a roomful of lawyers is all the material you have available.

What do you have when you bury six lawyers up to their necks in sand?

Not enough sand.

I got that from one of our lawyers at Chrysler. He has a running file of lawyer jokes. It's 17 pages long, in agate type, and there are almost 200 of them.

Why does California have the most lawyers and New Jersey the most toxic dumps?

New Jersey got first choice.

Polish jokes came and went. That's because Polish people don't fit the stereotype, so pretty soon the jokes weren't funny. Dumb blonde jokes have pretty much run their course, too. I guess we all know too many smart blondes. But lawyer jokes . . . lawyer jokes have legs! They keep going and going and going like the Energizer Bunny.

Source: Robert J. Eaton, Chairman, CEO, Chrysler Corporation. Delivered to the American Bar Association, Business Section, Orlando, Florida, on August 6, 1996. Reprinted by permission of Robert J. Eaton and *Vital Speeches of the Day.*

How many lawyers does it take to screw in a light bulb?

How many can you afford?

Let me tell you my favorite recent lawyer joke.

A woman was killed in a car accident. (That's a tragedy, the joke comes later.) A trailer hitch fell off a vehicle and started a chain reaction that ended in the woman's death. Her estate sued Chrysler.

The car she was driving was not one of ours. The truck that hit her was not one of ours. The trailer hitch did fall off a Jeep, but the hitch itself was not one of ours. The original factory-installed towing bar had been removed and replaced by a trailer hitch bought at a flea market!

Here comes the joke, and it's a bad one: A jury hit us with an $8.8 million verdict!

It was obviously another case of "find someone to sue." And whoever heard of suing a flea market? No profit potential in that. So they sued Chrysler!

Let me tell you another joke, a one-word joke: Alabama!

Alabama, the land of the $4 million BMW paint job!

Alabama, the place where a jury awards a drinking driver who was not wearing his seat belt $150 million after he falls asleep at the wheel, runs off the road, has an accident, and gets thrown from the car.

Alabama's court system is a laughing stock throughout the country.

Forty years ago, Alabama's courts were a joke, too, because of the way those courts trampled all over human rights.

Today, they do the same thing to property rights. Today, there's a widespread feeling in the legal and business communities all over the country that Alabama is a place where you can arrange a "hometown" jury or get a class action certified with a phone call.

Now, that may be a slight exaggeration of the facts but it's not an exaggeration of Alabama's reputation. And I have to believe that the decent people and honest lawyers in that state must be awfully embarrassed about it.

The sad part is, some other states like Mississippi, Louisiana, Texas, California, and New York seem headed in the same direction as Alabama.

We're expanding Chrysler internationally. We're looking at a number of new places to invest. One thing we look at is the legal system because we don't want to sink capital into a third world country whose legal system is corrupt and won't help us protect that investment. But guess what? We now steer away from investing in some states . . . in our own country . . . for the same reason.

The best place to find lawyer jokes is in the daily paper.

Texas lawyers win $1 for client, collect $1.5 million in fees.

Mugger shot by cop, sues cop, collects . . .

Little leaguer misses pop fly, gets hit in eye, parents sue coach . . .

Girl Scouts sell 87,000 boxes of cookies just to pay liability insurance . . .

Student falls backward out of dorm window while "mooning" friends, sues university. And on and on, day in and day out.

In Montana, a court ruled that a marshmallow should have a warning label because it could be harmful if swallowed by children.

I know that most of the outrageous awards get reduced on appeal, and I know that the actual number of awards isn't as high as the headlines seem to indicate. But people are still laughing.

And that's the problem.

You see, I don't think lawyer jokes are funny anymore. I really don't.

I think something very dangerous happens to a society that laughs at its legal system.

I'm a layman who's a businessman. Most of you are lawyers who are also business people.

But I've got a much cleaner perspective than even you do. That's because I am unencumbered by a legal education, or the professional need to face off with all the specious sophistry used to justify those abuses.

I have the luxury of seeing the issue as black and white, right and wrong. And I am, I think, in this regard, fairly typical of most of the people in this country.

You don't have to spend a day in law school to understand that the concept of joint and several liability was devised by someone who had no interest at all in the concept of justice.

Nobody with a normal ration of common sense can defend the idea that I could be one percent at fault and one hundred percent liable. If that level of intelligence prevailed in the engineering profession, we'd have square wheels on our cars.

The same with the notion of unlimited punitive damages. In criminal law, you have to spell out the penalty beforehand so that if you make a conscious decision to commit the crime, you know the time you'll face.

But on the civil side, even if you don't make even a conscious decision at all . . . even if it's simply an accident that happens to take place on your sidewalk . . . you have no idea what the penalty can be. That decision is usually left to a group of people who have no background at all to make it.

The concept of class action litigation, on the other hand, does make some sense to me. A responsible application of it can be good for both the plaintiffs and defendants. The operable adjective, of course, is responsible.

I think, just for starters, that a lawyer ought to have a client before he files a class action suit. At least one client. We sued three lawyers in Washington earlier this year who didn't.

Class action has become a bonanza for lawyers who do virtually nothing for their clients and get millions for themselves. A few examples:

In a class action suit against Intel, lawyers got $6 million and the plaintiffs got access to four toll-free telephone numbers.

In another one against General Mills, the lawyers got $1.8 million and the plaintiffs a coupon for a free box of cereal.

In one against Ford Motor Company, the lawyers collected $4 million and the plaintiffs got a safety video and a roadside warning light.

The one I like is the Bank of Boston case where each of the consumers collected between $2 and $8, but got billed an average of $90 each for legal fees.

I'd like to see the letter those lawyers sent their clients:

Dear Sir or Madam: (These cases tend to be very impersonal, as you know.)

You'd be happy to know that we were successful in obtaining justice for you. We have negotiated a settlement on your behalf, and you have been awarded $2.00. Your share of our fees is $90.00. Please remit, and congratulations on your victory.

The Wall Street Journal ran a story last November about rival law firms in Tennessee trying to get their mitts on a juicy class action. They had a bidding war for clients that involved direct mail solicitations, press releases, and even TV ads. I had visions of lawyers with sandwich boards parading in front of the courthouse and passing out business cards.

Again, we can laugh at these examples. But they're not funny anymore. Especially if you are trying to run a business.

If you're in business, you are frankly intimidated by all these stories. Without any confidence that you'll get justice in the courts, and with the possibility that some screwball jury will tag you for a hundred million bucks, you're tempted to make a simple business decision and settle, as distasteful as that is.

When a lawyer shows up with a certified class action, and makes it clear that he'll settle it if you give his clients a few coupons and him $10 million, that's not funny. It's extortion. If he had any pride, he'd turn in his pin-striped suit for a mask, a gun and a getaway car.

Our tort system costs about $152 billion a year. (Theodore Olson, who I'm told most of you recognize as one of the leading commentators on tort reform, estimates the cost as high as $300 billion.) Even if you take the low number, that's two-and-a-half times what we spend on police and fire protection in this country every year. That works out to $1,200 per American. You could call it a hidden tort tax.

If you have a pacemaker for your heart that costs $18,000, $3,000 of it is a tort tax. If you have a wheelchair that costs $1,000, $170 of it is a tort tax. Half the price of a football helmet goes to cover the liability insurance. The Little League spends more on liability insurance than it does on bats, balls, and gloves.

The self-appointed consumer advocates say all these hidden taxes (all paid by consumers, of course) keep big business honest.

Actually, what they do is keep these folks and the trial lawyers who bankroll them alive.

Sorry to say, but our court system has become less a vehicle for the distribution of justice than for the redistribution of wealth. But it's a lousy way to do it. Any economist will tell you that an efficient transfer mechanism has to have three major attributes.

It has to be fast.

It has to be fair.

And it has to be low cost.

So much for that idea!

If the object is to redistribute the nation's wealth, then piracy makes more sense.

And come to think of it, the trial lawyers of today have at least one big thing in common with the buccaneers of old: They stay in business by sharing their booty with compliant public officials.

Blackbeard and the boys paid off the authorities with pieces of eight. The trial lawyers do it with political contributions. Massive political contributions.

The trial lawyers have taken tithing to new heights. In just three states, Alabama, Texas, and California, they gave about $20 million to candidates between 1990 and 1994. That's more than local candidates in all 50 states received from either the Democratic or Republican National Committee.

The Washington Post reported earlier this year that the lawyers had put more money into President Clinton's election campaign than all the retired people in the country, all the doctors, all the teachers, all the civil servants, and all the media and entertainment people, all of them combined! That's why they're called "America's third political party."

They do it for only one reason, because President Clinton has promised to protect them against tort reform. And he's delivered. When he vetoed tort reform in May, even some of his friends were embarrassed.

Senator Lieberman called Clinton "dead wrong." Senator Rockefeller said, "special interests and raw political considerations in the White House have overridden sound policy judgment." And *The Washington Post* called it a "cave-in" to the trial lawyers.

One survey shows that up to 85 percent of Americans want some kind of civil justice reform. No significant constituency opposes it, except for the trial lawyers, the Naderites, and the American Bar Association.

I'm obviously no expert on tort reform, but my general counsel at Chrysler sent me a piece by David Bernstein of George Mason University which compares the American tort system with those of other common law countries.

I didn't know that the United States was the only country that routinely uses juries for civil cases . . . the only country that doesn't have some kind of "loser pays" rule to discourage frivolous suits . . . and virtually the only country that allows unlimited use of contingent legal fees.

I spent four years running GM of Europe and could count the number of lawsuits on both hands. I've been at Chrysler four years and sometimes I think it would take the hands of our entire work force to count the suits.

Bernstein basically recommends something that we do in industry all the time, benchmarking. Take a look at the civil justice systems around the world that work a lot better than ours does, and learn from them.

Nowhere else do they let juries decide, first, whether real damages took place, and second, the value of those damages.

More than anything else, this is what has turned our courts into lotteries.

On the issue of frivolous lawsuits, I think we first ought to get rid of the term. There is no such thing as a "frivolous" lawsuit. A court in California threw out a suit against a car dealer as "frivolous" and reprimanded the lawyer who brought it, but the car dealer still had to pay his lawyer $23,000. That's pretty expensive frivolity.

Other countries make the losers pay, and they don't have their courts clogged with silly suits, or people just looking for an easy buck.

The contingency fee issue is probably a little more complicated. We don't want to close off the availability of legal help to people who can't afford it. The British use something called a "conditional" fee. As I understand it, the lawyer can charge up to twice his regular hourly fee instead of a percentage of the award, and then waive the fee altogether if the plaintiff doesn't recover damages.

At least that method ties the lawyer's take to the hours he actually works.

Again, I don't claim to be an expert. Every one of you in this room is more capable than I am to recommend how to reform our civil justice system.

The question I keep asking, and most other Americans as well, is "When will it start?"

And I have another question: "Who's going to lead it?"

A woman and her son were walking through a graveyard. They came upon a tombstone that said, "Here lies a lawyer and an honest man." The little boy said, "Mommy, why did they put two men in the same grave?" Lawyers don't fare well in the "most admired" polls. They're always near the bottom, along with, I hate to say it, car salesmen.

I have a theory about why Americans have so little respect for lawyers. It's because they have so much respect for the law. Or, at least they used to. And they still want to.

I remember when lawyers built reputations for things like guaranteeing people the right to vote, or to live where they wanted, not for forcing McDonald's to give us cold coffee.

Most people, like me, still have high expectations. We believe, naively maybe, that the law is there to protect us, and that it has some fundamental grounding in morality.

We have the innocent idea that the law is about fairness.

We know right from wrong, usually with absolute certainty, and that's enough for us to judge whether the law is working or not.

People believe doctors use their medical training to help them. A doctor might hurt them by mistake, or out of incompetence, or even carelessness, but never on purpose.

That's not how they see lawyers. That's also why there are lawyer jokes, and why so many of them are cruel.

As I said, I happen to believe that the low esteem in which your profession is held is not a joking matter. I think it's very, very dangerous. Where the law and those who administer it are not respected . . . where they are laughed at . . . you have a declining civilization.

The evidence in the O.J. Simpson trial last year was overwhelming, and the public saw all of it, even more of it than the jury did. That verdict came soon after the first Menendez trial and after the trial of the men who nearly killed the truck driver, Reginald Denny, during the L.A. riots.

If we get enough of those, and people lose all faith in the courts, we risk seeing the ugly specter of vigilante justice.

On the civil side, the consequences may be less dramatic, but they are insidious nevertheless.

Ten-year-old kids are taught that the law is absolute, and to respect and obey it because it's the right thing to do.

Fifty-year-old business executives hire platoons of lawyers to figure out how to use the law, or to get around it, or to protect themselves. Nobody ever talks about right and wrong. Nothing is absolute. "Absolute"as been replaced by "possible."

There's a disconnect between what we were taught in civics class, and the way the adult world really works. And the word for that disconnect is cynicism.

People laugh at lawyer jokes, but they laugh even harder at anyone who doesn't get them because it is sophisticated today to be cynical about the law.

It's not funny. It's sad.

It's sad that, in a nation built by risk-takers, a company stops doing AIDS research because the legal risks are too high.

And it's sad that our litigious society has changed the way we relate to one another as human beings.

Think about this: You can't say "I'm sorry" anymore.

If your tree falls on your neighbor's house, you can't say, "I'm sorry." That's admitting guilt. Better let your lawyer handle it with his lawyer.

If we make a mistake and we ship a car with a defective paint job, we can't simply say, "I'm sorry," and then make it right. Instead, we're forced to treat our friends and customers as potential litigants.

It's a crowded world we live in, and we're going to bump into each other sometimes. We're going to offend one another once in awhile. We'll even hurt one another. Not because we set out to do it, but because . . . well, just because it's crowded.

There's something wrong with a system that robs you of the catharsis and the simple civility of saying, "I'm sorry. What can I do to make it right?"

There's something wrong when being intellectually honest makes you dead meat for people who aren't.

There's also something wrong with a system that encourages people who would never think of stealing from a store to steal through the courts because their lawyers tell them it's okay . . . that they're entitled . . . even if they haven't been harmed in any way.

Your profession is better than that. You know it, and I know it. Somehow, somewhere, sometime, we lost control. I hope you in the Business Section of the ABA get a louder voice in helping all of us to regain that control.

Almost every state in the country has an automobile lemon law. It's embarrassing to get that kind of special attention. But the lemon laws are our own fault. Too many of the honest people in our business didn't speak up when a few others were cheating the customers. The lemon laws are our punishment for not policing our own industry.

You don't want lemon laws for lawyers. Think of the bad jokes that would start. You also have a thing called a "Constitution" that makes it harder to regulate your profession.

But some kind of significant tort reform is coming. I hope it comes from within your profession. I think it would be more effective for everyone if it did. And maybe then the jokes will stop, too. Thank you very much.

Sales and Marketing

Openings

——*I'm here to tell you how not to make sales. I don't want you to make sales. I want you to create customers.*

——*You'd have to be dead not to have heard the buzz. Well, as of March 3, that buzz will be a product—the newest, best, most exciting widget on the market today. Let me tell you about it.*

Closings

——*Thanks for listening to me, ladies and gentlemen. Now go out and start creating customer satisfaction.*

——*The new widget is exciting, isn't it? About the only thing it can't do is sell itself. That will take hard work from you. But I know that we'll all be rewarded. Thanks.*

MODEL SPEECH 122:
Advertising on Radio

Key Use of Speech:	To talk about radio advertising.
Style of Speech:	Informal and informative.
Audience:	Sales and marketing staff.
Time:	10 to 12 minutes.

When Louis Jacques Mandé Daguerre invented the first practical camera and photographic process in 1837, the French painter Eugène Delacroix declared: "Painting is dead."

He was mistaken.

And so were the folks who started performing funeral services for radio when TV came in during the 1950s. However, it *would* be foolish not to admit that television changed radio forever, just as photography transformed painting. After photography became popular, painters started making "non-realistic" pictures. Similarly, television pushed radio away from the dramatic and comedy shows it had carried in the 1930s and 1940s, and prompted it to be exclusively a medium for music, news, and talk. For advertisers, there is even better news. While television tried to be all things to all people, individual radio stations began to specialize, cultivating loyal audiences interested in a particular kind of music (classical, country, rock—various kinds of rock, at that—easy listening, and so on), those interested in continuous news reports, and those interested in talk. This means that radio is *not* an obsolescent medium, but, in fact, a very forward-looking medium: the forerunner of what we now call *narrow*casting, doing what cable TV does, targeting precisely defined and specialized markets.

What this means for a company like ours is that we can target

➔ Tip: If you have a lengthy introductory paragraph, be certain to end it with a sentence that ties the meaning together.

427

➤ Tip: The speaker says why he is giving his audience the information he is giving them.

customers very precisely with radio advertising. And that is exactly what we have begun to do. Since, as salespeople, your success is in part dependent on the kind of advertising we do, I want to fill you in about what's behind the radio campaign.

If you sell a product that appeals to teenagers, you will want to advertise on the rock station that offers the music that group listens to most. If you are selling, say, a monthly investment guide, you will want to advertise on the continuous news station—and most specifically during the financial segment of the news. If you want to personalize your product or service to build customer loyalty—and this is *us*—you will want to advertise on a show that has a popular, personable, and credible DJ. That's why we have bought time on the following shows: **[the speaker lists them].**

As important as what shows you choose to buy time on, choosing the "daypart"—the time of day—to put most or all of your ads is probably even more crucial. We have a choice of six dayparts:

- A.M. drive (6–10 A.M.)
- Midday (10 A.M.–3 P.M.)
- P.M. drive (3–7 P.M.)
- Evening (7 P.M.–midnight)
- Late night (midnight–6 A.M.)
- Weekends (all day Saturday and Sunday)

Our customers . . .

[The speaker quickly profiles the company's typical customer and mentions the most appropriate "dayparts" or advertising to that customer.]

Now just what is a radio spot? What *kind* of advertising are we going to support you salespeople with?

Spots are generally thirty or sixty seconds long. A half-minute to a minute is, believe me, a *lot* of time to fill—*creatively.* We have to create spots that capture and hold the attention of our target customer. Unlike print ads or even television ads, which, of course, have strong visual components, radio ads are exclusively sound. In thirty seconds, we can deliver only about sixty to ninety words. Roughly double that for a full minute spot. Not a lot of words to get our message across.

Radio spots present another challenge. A good print ad only needs to run once or twice to produce measurable results. Run a radio ad once or twice, and it's as if nobody hears you. Broadcast advertising thrives on repetition. We will air no fewer than twenty spots per week during the upcoming campaign, and we will cluster the spots during **[speaker specifies time and dates]** to maximize the impact on our target listeners.

In just a minute or two, I'll shut up and let you listen to the new spots. But let me say just a word about the voice we have chosen. **[The speaker talks about the celebrity spokesperson.]**

And—I want to prepare you for this one—we've *commissioned* music. XYZ Brands now has its own jingle. You'll hear it in just a moment. We've agonized over it, as we should, since a catchy jingle will give us visibility, while an obnoxious one will create negative associations we may never shed.

Ladies and gentlemen, I'm excited by these new radio spots, and I think you'll be, too. They'll give you the support you need to get out there and move XYZ's newest and greatest line of widgets.

Now—let's give a listen.

→ Tip: The speaker indicates that he is approaching the conclusion of his speech.

OUTLINE

Opening

Historical anecdote: "death of painting"
Not dead at all

Is radio dead?

People thought TV would kill radio
TV changed radio, but didn't kill it
Remains a viable advertising medium
More precisely targeted audience than broadcast TV

Why is radio the right advertising medium for our company?

We can target our customers
We must choose the right show
We must choose the right "daypart"

What is a radio spot?

- Defines it
- Explains challenge of writing an effective radio spot
- Need for repetition
- Need for right voice
- Need for right music

Conclusion

- Excited by the new radio ads
- The ads will support the efforts of the sales staff

MODEL SPEECH 123:
Customer Satisfaction

Key Use of Speech:	To encourage good customer service practice.
Style of Speech:	Informal and motivational.
Audience:	Sales and marketing staff.
Time:	10 to 15 minutes [with anecdote].

→ Tip: You may begin with a proposition, which you demonstrate and illustrate in the course of the speech.

How many times have you heard an exchange like this?

"Their product is good, but their customer service is just a joke."

"Well, then, who would you recommend?"

The implication is obvious: In today's competitive marketplace, good product is not enough. People are buying customer service.

Is it hard to please a customer?

Well, compared to what? Compared to *finding* new customers, pleasing the ones you already have is easy.

Let me tell you a true story about two friends of mine who recently moved. I think it will mean something to you.

My friends Ted and Alice applied for a loan with a mortgage outfit that guaranteed approval within thirty days. Now, Ted's a careful, prudent guy and asked what he should do to get the approval process moving on his end. Ted's self-employed, and he understood that this could complicate things.

"Don't worry about it," the loan officer said. "Just furnish your own statement. No problem."

→ Tip: Thought-provoking statements are always effective.

Ten days later, the loan officer called to tell Ted that he needed a CPA to prepare a statement.

Ted scrambled, but got the statement prepared . . .

[The speaker continues with a story that illustrates a series of customer service failures, culminating in Ted and Alice's *nearly* losing the house they wanted to buy.]

431

➜ Tip: Want to generate interest among your audience? Tell a story.

This was, I'm sure you'll agree, the proverbial nightmare. Were Ted and Alice singled out for persecution?

I see by some of the looks out there that this is an all-too-familiar scenario, isn't it? The frustration of getting products that don't work is compounded by appealing to a company that just doesn't care that its product doesn't work. In fact, usually, the *problem* is less of a problem than the company's *attitude* about the problem.

What's *our* attitude about our products and our customers?

➜ Tip: The speaker takes the opportunity to define his company's mission.

It is simple. Whatever it takes to create customer satisfaction, we'll do it. That is our attitude. We don't want to be another one of those "couldn't-care-less" companies, the kind that Ted and Alice ran into. We don't want to be a company that thinks—stupidly—that selling is enough.

Selling is important—so important that it is our number *two* priority.

Number *one* is customer service.

➜ Tip: Putting customer service ahead of sales is a bold statement.

We don't want our customers thinking, let alone saying to themselves or to others, "This isn't really the color I wanted." Or, "This really will be difficult to use." Or, "I wonder if that sales rep's going to be here if I have to return this thing." Or, "The salesperson didn't have the foggiest idea how this works."

How will we achieve a high level of customer service?

Well, it's both harder and easier than you think.

It's very hard work, customer after customer—though also very satisfying and rewarding. But, I can tell you this, it does *not* take some kind of company-wide revolution. Just think about the experience of Ted and Alice. If any *one* employee had stopped to care about them, their experience would have become positive rather than the near-nightmare it was.

One employee could have turned the tide.

Why not make that *you*?

➜ Tip: Directly addressing your audience can make a powerful impact.

Our customers shouldn't have to be hassled to get what they need when they phone us or walk into our place of business, and *you*—each of *you*—are on the front lines. Every day, you see problems like Ted and Alice's just waiting to happen.

Why don't they happen?

Because *you* care enough to stop them from happening.

And that is the way it works. One employee at a time dealing with one customer at a time.

I'm asking you to think of yourself as the customer's advocate.

Start doing this by thinking of the Golden Rule: If you wouldn't want it done to you, don't do it to our customers.

Usually, this requires nothing more than taking a little extra time and practicing a little extra courtesy and thoughtfulness. Sometimes it's an extra phone call or two. Sometimes it's a little overtime. Usually, customer by customer, it's not much—but, customer after customer, it does amount to a lot of work.

I never said customer service was easy.

But I *do* know that it's a lot easier than trying to collect all new customers

Customer service is an idea whose time has come. It keeps us in business and lets us grow this business, through great word of mouth. We may be making widgets here, but we're *selling* attitude—yours— one day and one customer at a time.

Thanks for hearing me.

→ Tip: The speaker repeats the theme of comparative effort— maintaining customers, difficult as this task is, is easier than getting new customers.

OUTLINE

Opening

- Anecdote
- Good products are not enough
- People are buying customer service

Is it hard to satisfy a customer?

- Finding new customers is harder than satisfying those you already have

True story

- Narrates anecdote
- Customer service nightmare
- Rare? No

Our company's attitude about our customers

- Commitment to satisfaction
- Selling is not enough
- Customer service is #1, selling #2 priority

How will we achieve high level of customer service?

- Each employee must be dedicated
- Why not you?
- You are customer's advocate
- Do unto others as you would have them do unto you
- Take extra time
- Extend extra courtesy
- Be thoughtful

Closing

- Customer service—an idea whose time has come

MODEL SPEECH 124:
Developing Brand Loyalty

Key Use of Speech: To explain the need to develop brand loyalty.

Style of Speech: Informal and motivational.

Audience: Sales staff.

Time: 5 to 6 minutes.

➜ Tip: In a plain-spoken, direct manner, the speaker shares a prob- lem with his audience.

I don't have to tell you that the XYZ widgets are stellar performers. We get consistently high marks in all the industry publications, and we get high marks from our customers as well. Yet what we don't get is the kind of repeat business we *should* be enjoying.

We haven't yet succeeded in creating brand loyalty.

Our advertising people are working on developing a campaign designed to build brand identity and, ultimately, brand loyalty. The ad campaign will help, but it is your sales skills, face to face with the customer, that will ultimately turn the tide. So far, repeat sales have been flat, but I don't believe in failure. I *do* believe in feedback, and our feedback from last quarter is that the market's just not beating down our door for second- or third-time-around purchase of our widgets.

I am optimistic and enthusiastic about the prospects for *eventually* generating good, strong repeat sales—that is, brand loyalty.

Here's what we need you to do.

First of all, you need to present to the customer the following special benefits of our brand:

➜ Tip: The speaker tells his audience that their role in resolving the current problem is critical.

[The speaker explains these.]

Second, we don't believe most customers are aware of the *lack* of certain features in our competitors' brands. We need to make them aware of these.

435

[The speaker lists and explains them.]

Once you have presented this information verbally, give the customer the new brochure we have created. It highlights **[the speaker lists the highlights].**

→ Tip: The speaker is specific about what he needs his sales staff audience to achieve.

Brand loyalty will not sell itself—not with this line of widgets, anyway. With some of our product lines, we *do* command brand loyalty, but this area is so new and unfamiliar to many of our customers, that you front-line sales people will have to do some educating. Be prepared to present these products with your feet on the ground while your customer's head is still in the clouds on the issues he doesn't even know he needs to deal with.

I can't *promise* instant gratification on this one. By definition, creating brand loyalty is a matter of time. But it is not a random accident, either. *We can* make it happen, one customer at a time. Once this groundwork is laid, your job with this product line will, I promise you, get progressively easier. The line will begin to sell itself.

MODEL SPEECH 125:
Developing New Markets

Key Use of Speech: To encourage the opening of new markets.

Style of Speech: Informal and motivational.

Audience: Sales staff.

Time: 6 to 7 minutes.

➔ Tip: The speaker makes a straightforward announcement of his subject.

As you very well know, **[date]** is the rollout date for the new ABC Widget. We are counting on you to push this product into new markets.

So put a shine on your shoes, knock on the customer's door, and tell 'em: "Hey! It's *new*!"

And maybe you'll infect the folks with your enthusiasm.

"We've gotta have it!" they'll shout.

➔ Tip: The routine sales talk is full of optimism and enthusiasm. This talk injects a dose of realism as well.

Then again, maybe your "Hey! It's *new*!" will get a "Hey! So what?" in response.

What are you going to do?

See, the ABC Widget is certainly new and exciting to us, and it will probably be new and exciting to our established customers, but these things are no guarantee of acceptance in *new* markets. It is even more likely that you'll encounter prospects who use other products they feel are satisfying their needs. Either way, the customer may not be moved to purchase the ABC Widget.

➔ Tip: The speaker makes it clear that the sales task here is one of consumer education.

Of course, there is no limit to the amount of money we could spend on studying new markets—unless, of course, we want to make a profit somewhere along the line. What I'd rather do is get you folks out there *creating* markets, not studying them. While some new products really do succeed according to the build-a-better-mousetrap formula—*If you build it, they will come*—the ABC Widget requires educating the market.

437

Here's the message you need to deliver.

[The speaker proposes a sales pitch to facilitate opening new markets.]

Now, I've just reviewed the features and benefits of the ABC Widget, but you also need to use fundamental salesmanship. Do you remember *AIDA*? No, I don't mean the opera by Giuseppe Verdi, but that old standby acronym:

> *A* for get your prospect's **Attention**,
> *I* for develop your prospect's **Interest**,
> *D* for build your prospect's **Desire**,
> and another *A* for move your prospect to **Action**.

➤ Tip: It is more effective to explain orders than merely to give them.

It would be wonderful if the new widget just slotted itself right into a bundle of new markets, but, as the old saying goes, *Humankind has few needs, but many desires.* Ladies and gentlemen, we need to make new customers aware of a hitherto undiscovered *desire* for the ABC Widget. Put the emphasis on the third letter of AIDA.

Folks, I hope this little talk has created positive anticipation and excitement about going out into the field to sell the new widget. It's easy to sell the tried and true, but we need push the envelope beyond that. With all the risks, why pioneer new products and new markets? The answer is simple: In this business—in this *world*—nothing stands still, not our business, nor our customers, nor our competitors.

If you find new markets initially unreceptive, work at transforming those markets by educating one customer at a time. A product like the ABC Widget, with all its potential, is worth that kind of effort.

You know, pioneering these new markets is not only important for the ABC Widget, but for our company's image as an innovation leader. Even more, pioneering like this diffuses throughout our organization, improving the speed and efficiency with which everyone works. The spirit of pioneering will, ultimately, build us into a better, stronger company.

MODEL SPEECH 126:
Developing Export Markets

Key Use of Speech:	To announce planned penetration of export markets.
Style of Speech:	Informative and motivational.
Audience:	Sales staff.
Time:	6 minutes.

Beginning with the new year, XYZ Corporation will actively promote selected products in international markets. The first products include **[the speaker lists them]**, which will be marketed in **[the speaker lists several countries].** I am gratified that so many of you have shown interest in working with our in-country field representatives to make the first phase of the export campaign a success.

We have chosen to penetrate the new export markets slowly and carefully, using "native" field reps, who understand the culture of the new markets. I am not asking the sales force here at home to take formal direction from the field reps, but to be prepared to follow their lead when it comes to deciding what product features and benefits to push.

I know that some of us like to believe that "selling is selling"—whether in the United States or in Timbuktu. Well that "selling is selling" phrase has a nice, solid ring to it—kind of reassuringly old-fashioned. In the broadest sense, I suppose that statement has a good deal of truth to it. No matter where you are, selling is still about getting attention, creating interest, developing interest into desire, then prompting your customer to action—to making that purchase. But you can only go only so far on broad generalities. To implement the fundamentals of salesmanship, you have to know the market and

→ Tip: Concede a degree of truth to the opposing side, then show how the position you advocate is superior.

know the customer. Only someone on the front lines can do that. So I am asking you to communicate freely and fully with our in-country people—and give full ear to their advice. Weigh and measure what they have to say against what you know, but always be aware of the cultural realities operating in international markets.

Let me tell you a little story.

Back in **[year]**, the WXY Wax Company launched a massive campaign to sell its highly successful floor polish in the Japanese market. Initially, the product was *very* well received, and there was a hearty round of back slapping.

"We did it," they crowed. "And we did it with our *own* people—from right here. No problem."

Unfortunately, that assessment proved premature.

Within weeks of the initial rollout, Japanese men, women, and children were showing up in hospital emergency rooms with broken legs, broken arms, and a variety of strains and sprains.

Nobody at WXY Wax had stopped to consider the fact that the Japanese take off their shoes indoors and would be walking on their now highly polished hardwood floors in their stocking feet.

WXY ultimately withdrew from the Japanese market—at substantial cost, to be sure. Had they studied the market before exporting their product, studied it with the help of people actually *in* the country, they would have formulated a special export product, one that was designed with stocking feet in mind.

Ladies and gentlemen, we have consulted in-country people every step of the way. The export products we are introducing *will work*. Now I ask that *you work with* the field representatives to organize big, efficient, and exciting campaigns, campaigns driven from right here in the home office, but guided by the cultural insights of our field people.

With this combination, we can't lose.

→ Tip: An amusing illustrative anecdote can be an effective aid to getting your point across.

→ Tip: To obtain willing compliance, explain the reasons for the compliance request. Don't just issue arbitrary orders.

MODEL SPEECH 127:
New Product

Key Use of Speech: To introduce a new product to the sales staff.

Style of Speech: Informative and motivational.

Audience: Sales staff.

Time: 4 to 5 minutes.

→ Tip: Show confidence in the people from whom you seek cooperation and hard work.

You are the most enthusiastic and skilled sales force I've ever had the pleasure of working with, and I am proud and confident about putting the new ABC Widget in your hands.

Now skill and enthusiasm are essential drivers of salesmanship, but those qualities need solid information for fuel. And that's why we're here this morning: to give you that information. I want to outline the key features and benefits of the new widget.

Benefit number one: The ABC Widget is the first product on the market to **[the speaker explains the unique benefit or feature].** This is in *very dramatic* contrast to what our competitors offer. **[The speaker develops the comparison and contrast.]**

→ Tip: The speaker makes it clear that she is briefing the sales staff on the product—not telling them how to do their jobs.

Now I don't want to send you off into the field armed only with a negative comparison. I want you to approach the ABC Widget, first and foremost, positively—*then* bring in the contrast with the competing products. Don't dwell on those competing products, and don't focus on the negative, but do underscore that we're a whole lot better!

Remember, the competition can offer only products that will **[speaker reviews benefits or features],** while ours **[speaker reiterates key features].**

Preliminary market tests have generated lots of *enthusiasm,* but not much *information* about why our customers are buying. I think that if you educate the consumers, demand will exceed our already impressive market-test data.

You will be amply supported in this rollout with an ad campaign **[speaker describes]** and the availability of sample units. We are also offering free demonstrations and Q and A sessions at **[speaker lists locations].** We also have created some terrific brochures.

Now you have the facts. Educate the customers. Bring back orders. Thanks!

———————————

Sales and Marketing Support

Openings

——*I don't have to tell you how important the XYZ Widget is to us, but I do want to make certain that you in Customer Service know just how important you are to the successful sell-through of the XYZ.*

——*Thank you. I am grateful for your attention. It is a pleasure being here.*

    I hope these three statements make you feel good. That's the way we need to make our customers feel: appreciated and respected.

Closings

——*Thanks for your attention. Please remember that the ultimate success of this new product depends on you and how well you educate the customers with whom you come into contact every day.*

——*Be kind to our customers. Never forget that they are the only reason we are in business.*

MODEL SPEECH 128:
Support of Sales Campaign

Key Use of Speech: To generate sales support.

Style of Speech: Informative and team-building.

Audience: Customer service staff.

Time: About 5 minutes.

➡ Tip: The theme of teamwork is presented forcefully from the beginning of this speech.

Here at XYZ, we've got offices, we've got a few *corner* offices, and we've got cubicles (*lots* of cubicles), but we don't have pigeon holes. *You* do *this. I* do *that.* It just isn't our style. We are a team. We value teamwork. We profit, together, as a team.

In that tradition of teamwork, then, I'm asking you in Customer Service to work more closely with Sales than ever before as we launch our new ABC Widget campaign.

Here's what Sales needs from you.

➡ Tip: "Teamwork," by itself, is an abstract concept. It needs definition. The speaker spells out precisely what he wants.

First: Information. Even more than the sales force, the Customer Service reps have frequent and thorough contact with our customers. You have an opportunity to find out what they want, what we're doing right, and what we're doing wrong.

Second: Upselling support. When you deal with customers who have issues with . . . **[The speaker explains how Customer Service can upsell customers and promote the new widget.]**

➡ Tip: The speaker comes on as a leader, telling his audience just what his expectations are.

Here at XYZ, we don't divide the world into front office and back office operations. We don't talk about "revenue producers" and "support people." We are *all* in the front office, and we are *all* support people *and* revenue producers. I don't care whether it's Customer Service or Sales that makes the sale and creates customer satisfaction, I just want that sale and want that customer to be satisfied.

445

During this campaign, Fred Silverberg will serve as the special liaison between Sales and Customer Service. He will expedite communication between these two functions and will see to it that information from Customer Service gets to Sales and is translated into action. So, folks, we're serious about this. I'm not asking you to politely drop notes in the suggestion box. *Look, listen, upsell,* and, above all, *communicate.*

MODEL SPEECH 129:
Treatment of Customers

Key Use of Speech:	To encourage behavior that creates customer satisfaction.
Style of Speech:	Informative, team-building, motivational.
Audience:	Non-sales employees who have customer contact.
Time:	8 to 10 minutes.

My name is Claire Silver, and I'm director of Sales. I'm here to say a few words to you about how each of you can help us do our job.

First, you may be asking, *Why should I* help sales do their job? I've got my own problems in shipping, customer service, tech support—whatever.

➤ Tip: Anticipate resistance and preempt it.

I have a number of answers to that:

Number one: We're all in this together. We're a team. We're all working toward the same goal—season after season of success. And we all benefit from achieving that goal.

Number two: To the customer, XYZ Industries is *not* a single salesperson. Nor is it a company. It's *people.* It's every member of the XYZ team that customer comes into contact with.

➤ Tip: Define key terms—such as "word-of-mouth"—and define them vividly.

Number three: Customer contact either creates or destroys customer satisfaction. Customer satisfaction not only means making a particular sale, it means making a *customer*—creating a long-term relationship of repeat business and positive word-of-mouth advertising. Word-of-mouth advertising: that's advertising so good that you can't even buy it. Which doesn't mean it's free. Creating positive word-of-mouth takes hard work from *all* of us.

But is it worth all that hard work? The extra time we spend with

447

each customer? The trouble we go through to find an answer to a customer's question? The effort it takes to get to know our customers, so that they are made to feel like more than a "prospect" or a "target" or a "consumer"?

Well, my friends and colleagues, I have to tell you that the days of the one-night stand are over. Today's selling relationship is a marriage, a commitment for the long haul, and *both* partners have to make that commitment. Today, customers are buying *relationships*. We cannot afford to sell them mere *products*.

➔ Tip: The speaker puts the focus on developing customer relationships.

Gone with that one-night-stand sales philosophy—at least in *this* industry—are the theories and practices of mass marketing. Today, customers want custom solutions.

Nothing fails like success—if you carve your definition of *success* in stone. To compete today, we must listen to our customers and make changes, continual changes, to satisfy the customer.

➔ Tip: Punctuate your speech with memorable phrases: "Nothing fails like success."

How do we know what changes to make?

We get to know our customers. We cultivate an intimacy with them. And we need *everyone's* help in doing this.

Use customer-contact time to exchange a few words. Share with them something of our service, technology, products, future plans. Tell them what we can do for them *now*. Tell them what plans we have—and *you* have—to meet their needs tomorrow and during the next decade.

Our sales force works by *educating* customers. But the more educators we have, the more effective the education process will be. Given a choice between a bargain-priced, stripped-down widget and a higher-priced widget that comes complete with knowledgeable support from everyone the customer speaks to, today's customer goes with the know-how and the knowledge. The more our customers know about our products, the more likely they are to buy.

➔ Tip: Revealing "trade secrets" is one sure way to capture the attention of your audience.

I probably shouldn't tell you this, but we in sales are *not* magicians. I *really* shouldn't tell you *this*: There is nothing all that special about us. Nothing mystical and magical about making a sale.

It all begins with knowing your customer and knowing your product. If you don't know your customer and your product, you're being irresponsible in your relationship with the customer. That relationship will fall apart. Guaranteed.

In sales, we have found that the relationship with the customer is built on more than self-talk. To get intimate with your customers, you have to help them disclose self-knowledge. You ask questions. It's amazing what a few minutes spent with a customer will tell you about what needs she or he has. Find out what motivates your customer. Find out what benefits the customer wants, not just the features.

For those of you who may be unfamiliar with these terms, let me explain. A product's *features* are its basic attributes. *Benefits* are how those attributes make the customer feel. For example, you may remember some years back that an overnight courier service developed a persuasive ad campaign built around an important benefit. The product *feature* of overnight delivery is simple: delivery *overnight!* But the *benefit* the ad campaign sold was confidence and relief from worry. *Ship with us, and you can relax and feel good. You've done the job.*

Find out everything you can about what benefits the customer wants—how he wants to feel. To stay competitive, we're going to have to turn our customers' wants-and-needs list into next year's products and services. We can all help in that process. Lead your customer to disclose self-knowledge. Then pass it on to Sales.

[The speaker concludes by telling her audience the simple mechanics of communicating information to Sales. She assures her audience that they will find a receptive ear.]

Let me end with a quotation. My sales staff is familiar with this one, because it is a favorite of mine.

I knew a sales manager once who was fond of saying that sales was really quite easy once you learned to remind yourself that customers are *not really people*—they're only *customers.* **[The speaker turns and begins to walk away from the podium.]** That sales manager hasn't had a job for years.

→ Tip: Make certain that you and your audience speak the same language; define key terms.

OUTLINE

Opening

- Speaker identifies herself
- Announces subject

Why you should help Sales do their job

- We're all in this together

To the customer, every member of team is important
Customer contact either creates or destroys customer satisfaction

Is it worth the hard work?

Today, selling is a long-term relationship
Requires commitment
Customers buy relationships
Customers want custom solutions, personal attention

Listen to customers, make changes

Get to know our customers
This requires everyone's help
Use customer contact time constructively
Educate your customers
Know customer
Know product
Get your customers to tell you about themselves

Closing

Quotation from salesman who failed to treat customers as people
He's out of work

———————————

MODEL SPEECH 130:
Upholding Image of Company

Key Use of Speech: To encourage pride in the company image and the communication of a positive image.

Style of Speech: Informative, team-building, motivational.

Audience: Non-sales employees.

Time: 8 to 10 minutes.

→ Tip: Begin with a positive message.

I'm very proud to be speaking to you today, because I am proud of you and all that you have accomplished. You have been and continue to be critical to our continued success. You have built and you maintain what I believe to be the best firm in our industry.

I believe that. I *know* that.

But not everybody outside of this company knows it, and that's what I want to speak with you about this morning.

XYZ Industries needs you to talk us up. Senior management often talks *you* up. You make us all look good, and we talk to securities analysts, investment managers, and the press. Now we need more of you—middle management, supervisors, everyone—to spread the good word about XYZ generally. We're asking you to take on this "bragging" task in addition to your regular assignments. We're asking that you preach our message from your desk every day when you talk to visitors and telephone callers. And we're even asking that you take it on the road as well.

→ Tip: The speaker outlines the task ahead.

Today, I am inaugurating a new program in which we'll ask for volunteers to take a seminar or two to become official spokespersons in the local community. We'll ask you to speak to large audiences and small, to friendly audiences and maybe a few unfriendly ones. We need to spread the word about us, to develop our good image.

451

→ Tip: The speaker carefully explains the new program—what it is meant to accomplish and what degree of extra work it calls for.

Misinformation and partial information as well as outright lies are communicated one on one. Let's take that same one-on-one approach to spread the good word and develop the positive image.

Those of you who volunteer as spokespersons will receive ongoing briefings on finances and future plans for products and services. You will learn the ins and outs of the complex problems that face us, and you'll learn how to explain those problems in ways that the community at large understands and appreciates. Most people accept a *clear* statement as a *true* statement, and that's what we're counting on. If you learn the facts about the complex issues that face us, then pass those on to others, our story will be told, our image will develop positively, and our business—every aspect of our business—will be the better for it.

→ Tip: Anticipating a "why us?" response, the speaker explains why middle managers and supervisors are the ideal spokespersons for the firm.

Look, no one can tell our story better than you, the people who *make* that story each and every day. You are the eyes, ears, hands, and feet that make this company work. You create the impression of competence and quality and sound management.

What is the message we want to convey?

We want you to explain how our products contribute to the quality of life. We want the community to know how we operate internally to cut costs and then to pass those savings on to our customers—to the community. We want the community to understand the hard realities of our costs, of what it costs to provide the quality of products and service we are known for.

→ Tip: Anticipate the questions or objections your audience may have.

Shouldn't PR and Sales do this kind of thing?

Well, they do, and they do it well. But we feel the message will be even more effective coming from diverse parts of this company. It will impress the public as spontaneous and sincere, not slick and canned.

We know that we need to communicate more effectively and to more people. Recent studies we've undertaken indicate that the public has a grossly distorted and generally inadequate perception of who we are and what we do.

[The speaker reviews the highlights and conclusions of the study.]

Ignorance brings about fear, suspicion, and resistance, whereas knowledge creates trust and favor. The better the community gets to know us, we believe, the better they will like us.

Let's get the facts out. Let's demonstrate the *fundamental* fact that we are interested in making a reasonable profit for our stockholders and we are just as concerned to create high-quality, high-value products and services to the communities we serve.

All this, I know, sounds perfectly rational. The trouble is, people aren't always rational. You can't count on them hearing the facts, then coming to logical conclusions. If it were all just a question of facts, we could take out a few big newspaper ads. But we have to make the community *feel* as well as hear the truth. The people you speak to should sense your emotion and sincerity. We need *your* words and *your* emotions to convey the message to everybody you come in contact with as a representative of this company or as a volunteer speaker.

What's in it for you, taking on this PR job?

Those of you who hold stock in the company should benefit quite directly, of course, but we should all also benefit from increased security and increased profits to share. We are all in this together.

> → Tip: Explain the reason behind the request for "extra mile" effort. If you can make your reasons clearly understood, you are more likely to obtain cooperation and

OUTLINE

Opening

- Expression of pride in employees
- You are critical to our success
- You are why we are the best firm in our industry
- Insufficient public awareness of our quality
- My subject

Company needs spokespeople

- Management talks about you employees
- Now we ask you to spread the good word about the company
- Take on a "bragging" task

New program

- Need volunteer spokespeople
- Counteract misinformation and partial information

- We will teach you how to make presentations
- No one can tell our story better than you

What do we want to convey?

- Explain how our products contribute to quality of life
- Explain how we cut costs
- Explain the realities of our costs

Isn't this a job for PR?

- They do this, but we want something more spontaneous and sincere
- Need speakers from all parts of the company

Need to communicate more effectively and to more people

- Studies indicate we aren't coming across
- Public's view of us distorted, inadequate
- Ignorance breeds fear, suspicion, and resistance
- Knowledge creates trust and favor
- Let's get the facts out

Closing

- What's in it for you?
- Enjoy the fruits of increased profits
- Increased job security
- We're all in this together

Solicitations

Openings

——*I'm here to tell you about some people who need your help. More important, I'm here to tell you how you can help them.*

——*Can I see a show of hands of those people who don't care what happens to their children?*
    I don't see any hands, so I know I'm speaking to the right people.

Closings

——*Thanks so much for listening to what I had to say. I am confident that you agree with me: this project is vitally important, and it deserves our support.*

——*Please, look into your hearts. Find the time, find the cash, and find the imagination to help.*

MODEL SPEECH 131:
Charitable Gifts

Key Use of Speech: To raise money for charity.

Style of Speech: Informal, sincere, persuasive, without coercion or pressure.

Audience: Company employees or business organization members.

Time: 8 to 10 minutes.

→ Tip: Asking for money is difficult. Why not tell your audience just how difficult it is?

I spent a good deal of time thinking about this speech. Part of it, the main part of this speech, was easy. It's about the **[name of charitable program],** which I have supported for **[number]** years and whose great good work I know very well. I could talk to you for hours about it. (Don't panic. I'll take only a few minutes!)

The hard part, though, was thinking of a clever way to begin the speech—you know, to get your attention and gently, subtly to lead into the fund-raising part of things.

I devoted a great deal of thought to this. I tore up and threw away one opening paragraph after another before it finally occurred to me: just begin this way.

We need money.

→ Tip: Skip the flowery language. Just say how much you need and what you need it for.

We need money for **[the speaker states some overall goals and lists a number of projects].**

That's the heart of the matter.

We know exactly how much we need: **[$ amount].** We know that those of you here will be generous, but we also know that a sum like this will require appealing beyond this group.

It will be hard work—impossible, some might think—to raise that much money by **[date].** But I know that I can count on your help, your

457

contacts, your energy, to reach out to the people who have money to give to a cause such as **[name of program]**. You are giving people, and I suspect that your friends and families and colleagues are, too.

You folks are not pessimists. I can see that much in your faces. I see energy, enthusiasm, confidence—and *will*. Today is but the first step in what will have to be a success story.

It *has to be* because **[name of program]** counts on us to make its vital work possible.

We did it last year, ladies and gentlemen. Perhaps you recall what we accomplished.

[The speaker relates past successes.]

Before you write your checks and before you start calling on your contacts, let's just *visualize* what these funds can do for us:

[The speaker picks a few vivid aspects of the program to explore with his audience.]

Now is the time for action. There's a place for each of you on the team—a place for your dollars and for the dollars you raise.

Now, it is my pleasure to introduce Sarah Williams, who will tell you how you can contribute and who will distribute information packages you can share with your own contacts.

➺ Tip: Express confidence in the group's generosity— but don't take their contributions for granted.

➺ Tip: Recall past successes for a we-did-it-before-we-can-do-it-again response.

MODEL SPEECH 132:
Donation of Labor for Charity

Key Use of Speech: To encourage the contribution of labor to a project.

Style of Speech: Informal, sincere, persuasive, without coercion or pressure.

Audience: Company employees or business organization members.

Time: 8 to 10 minutes.

→ Tip: Engage your audience by asking questions. This interactive approach is especially effective when you are soliciting money or other things from audience members.

Childhood. What does that word conjure up for you? Rollerskating, hopscotch, the ol' swimmin' hole, and other visions of sugar plums?

These days, the word all too often evokes images of fear and vulnerability and brings to mind *drugs, gangs, dropouts,* and *delinquents.*

What should *any of this* have to do with the world of children? *Should?*

None of this *should* get anywhere near our children, but I see by the looks you are giving me that all of you know only too well how crime, despair, and drugs threaten our children, our legacy, our future.

What has gone wrong with the world?

Perhaps that is what you are asking yourselves.

You feel helpless to change the world and helpless even to protect your own children.

→ Tip: The speaker skillfully creates an identification between his experience and that of his audience.

I don't want to stand here and tell *you* what *you* are feeling. Actually, I'm projecting exactly what I felt when, **[number]** years ago, I agreed to work for the XYZ Neighborhood Association. I volunteered, but, to tell the truth, I didn't think I could do much to help the world. I hoped I could at least make an effort to protect my children, my family.

459

I wasn't and am not a wealthy person. I own no mighty business, and I hold no great elective office. But I *do* work here, in this community, with the rest of you. No matter where we live in this city, this is our neighborhood for at least eight hours a day, five days out of the week. We have a stake in this place and in the people of this place.

Most of you, I'm sure, are familiar with the empty lot on Johnson and Gilbert Streets. It's a real jungle, isn't it? A wasteland.

Those of us in the XYZ Neighborhood Association have been looking past that lot and toward its future. In its future, what we see is an oasis, a haven, a place of fun and safety.

At the conclusion of this meeting we will distribute to each of you a proposal for a supervised playground to be built on the lot at Johnson and Gilbert. The plan is detailed, though it is open to creative suggestions. I hope that you will study the plan for yourselves, but let me, right now, jump to the bottom line.

We can pay professional landscapers to clean up and plant the playground, and we can pay for professional installation of the play equipment. The cost will be **[$ amount].** In addition, we need **[$ amount]** for paid, professional supervision of the playground.

That's a lot of money.

We can raise part of it, I know that. We already have sufficient funds to purchase the parcel of property. Perhaps given time, we can raise all that we need to develop it. Raising the ongoing funding for supervision will be harder, but maybe we can manage. Given time.

But in that time, what will happen? How many more children will go unsupervised? Unguided? How many will drift—drift into trouble, into drugs, simply into wasted, dangerous time?

How can we accelerate the fund-raising process?

The answer is to do the work ourselves.

[The speaker explains what work volunteers can do and how much money this will save.]

But it's not just a matter of getting together for two months of weekends to clean up the lot, plant it, and install the equipment. If some among you are willing to commit over the next year—or the next few years—to part-time supervision of the playground on an ongoing basis, we can save an addition **[$ amount],** and here's the

> ➤ Tip: The speaker quickly proceeds to specifics. In solicitation speeches, it is important to provide adequate and persuasive information, but also to move quickly to the action request.

> ➤ Tip: The speaker brings in the dimension of time, giving his request an air of urgency.

exciting thing: *that* makes this project feasible, not as an eventual goal, but right now, right now, when it's needed most.

[The speaker details how volunteers can get further information and/or sign up.]

→ Tip: Convert requests into offers of opportunity.

Friends, most things we do because we have to do them. And, even then, most things that we do are done and over with and gone. We are blessed to have an opportunity now to do something because we *want* to and because it is the *right thing to do.* Even better, what we do now will not be over and done with. It is doing for the future, for our community, for our children.

OUTLINE

Opening

- Threat to our children
- Drugs, gangs, dropouts, delinquents—all dangers

What can we do?

- You feel helpless
- I also felt helpless
- Now work for XYZ Neighborhood Association
- No different from you, but now empowered

The empty lot

- Identify and describe empty lot
- XYZ Neighborhood Association has plans for the lot
- The proposal: supervised playground

Funding

- We can pay professionals
- Cost
- A lot of money, but we can raise it over time
- We don't have time

- How to accelerate fund-raising?
- Do the work ourselves—now
- How to sign up

Closing

- This is an opportunity to do something we want to do and that is the right thing to do

---

Strategies

Openings

——*These are tough times, and I'm supposed to come before you with a pep talk about how tough times build character. Well, I have all the character I need, and I'd rather be able to take it easy. But the fact is that we are facing certain challenges, and we might as well take advantage of them by letting them build our strength.*

——*The subject for this afternoon is very exciting: it is our plan for growth over the next five years.*

Closings

——*Ladies and gentlemen, not only am I confident that we will merely* survive *the challenges I have outlined, we will grow and develop as a result of successfully dealing with them.*

——*Thanks for your attention this afternoon. I am very excited about entering into—with all of you—this momentous new phase of our development.*

MODEL SPEECH 133:
Downsizing Program Strategy

Key Use of Speech: To explain a downsizing strategy.

Style of Speech: Informational, authoritative.

Audience: Company employees.

Time: 10 to 12 minutes.

➡ Tip: An anecdote eases the way into a painful subject.

Abraham Lincoln was famous for keeping his office in his stovepipe hat, but Albert Einstein went him one better for reducing "overhead." "My mind is my office," he declared.

I wish it could be just as easy for us.

During the past three years ... **[The speaker explains how costs have risen while market demand has shrunk.]** Now this reduction of market demand has not been universal. Certain markets, including **[speaker lists them],** have actually expanded for us during this period, while others—**[speaker lists these]**—have retreated significantly.

You've heard a lot in the last two decades about increasing productivity, and you have been doing more with fewer people for several years now. You're not alone in this practice. It's a trend, from the smallest firms in the U.S. to the *Fortune* 500. It's called belt-tightening. It's what you do as long as you still have a belt. But, the fact is, we've tightened our belt down to the last notch, and if we don't do something soon, we'll have no belt. Eventually, the pants will be gone, too.

It's not our fault, but it *is* our problem.

Cutting overhead just isn't enough anymore. If we want to hang on to our pants, we have to begin to withdraw from the nonproductive markets. Here's the plan:

[The speaker lays out a phased schedule for pulling out of various markets.]

→ Tip: The speaker avoids emotionalism and apology; instead, he asserts maintenance of control and adherence to a plan.

Obviously, this will not be a painless process. In Phase 1 . . .

[The speaker outlines the phased cutbacks in employee numbers by department.]

To the extent that we can, we are handling the layoffs by attrition augmented with inducements to take early retirement. Of course, wherever possible, we are shifting employees from the departments we're closing to those that are still active.

I only wish we could handle *all* the layoffs this way. We cannot. **[Number]** employees will be laid off between now and **[date]**. We intend to carry out this strategy humanely.

[The speaker explains the layoff process and the provisions made for the laid off employees.]

There is not a great deal I can do to put this downsizing program in a rosy light. I *can* tell you, quite truthfully, that I am confident the downsizing will reverse the downward revenue spiral and make this company profitable again. I can also tell you that the downsizing program will preserve as much of the talent we have here as possible.

→ Tip: This is a time for honesty—not grim pessimism, but an honest assessment of the situation.

But this is adversity, and it's time to stand up to it. By reducing the size of this enterprise, we will rebuild it, and we will build in ourselves character. We've had rough times before, and we've stood up to adversity before. That's why I'm confident that we will hold together, survive this, and emerge as a company strongly adapted to the new market conditions.

To many of you, I know that, right now, this may sound hollow: But thank you for your hard work, for your commitment, and for your support. To those who will, in the course of the year, be leaving us, rest assured that we will support you as you find work suitable to your great skill and intelligence.

MODEL SPEECH 134:
Decision-Making Process Strategy

Key Use of Speech:	To call for a streamlined decision-making process.
Style of Speech:	Informational, persuasive.
Audience:	Company managers.
Time:	10 to 12 minutes.

→ Tip: A beginning that questions the status quo is almost always of great interest to an audience. You have their attention.

Can we ever be *too* careful?

The knee-jerk response to that question, of course, is *no*. And here at XYZ Publishing we have always prided ourselves on our system of checks and balances, which help to ensure that when we acquire literary properties for publication, we have a clear picture of the market, we have a clear picture of costs, we have a clear picture of any liability exposure.

→ Tip: Self-generated questions and answers can be used to drive a speech forward, to raise the key issues.

How could there be a downside to such a system?

Well, ladies and gentlemen, I'm here to tell you that there *is* a downside to our decision-making process, and that downside is cost.

Cost!? But it is precisely to reduce costs that we have so rigorous a decision-making process! Besides, the process itself doesn't cost much.

In a sense, both of these responses are true. The reason we are so careful is to avoid *costly* mistakes, and it is also true that the mechanics of the decision-making process are not particularly expensive.

→ Tip: If possible, encapsulate the thrust of your message in a short declarative sentence.

So where is the cost?

It's in missed opportunity.

This year alone, we failed to acquire what proved to be for other publishers two best-selling books. Why? Because it took us too long to decide whether to acquire the projects or not.

→ Tip: It takes courage to deliver a frank review of errors.

This year alone, we published three books at precisely the wrong time—well *after* the events that would have boosted sales.

[The speaker goes on to give the details of this snafu.]

While it is true that we cannot afford to make costly mistakes, there is nothing more costly than missed opportunity, and our hyper-careful, glacially slow decision-making process is, indeed, causing us to miss opportunities.

Beginning in the next quarter of this year, we will be introducing a new strategy of accelerated decision making. Let me outline it for you.

[The speaker paints the broad strokes of the new procedure.]

As you can see, there are still rational steps involved, with many fail-safe points built in; however, we also have the option of fast-tracking selected projects when current events or other considerations call for us to move with agility. To be sure, the new system involves risks, but they are risks that we can see, *controlled* risks. Missed opportunities, however, are invisible risks, cannot be controlled, and, once lost, can never be recovered.

MODEL SPEECH 135:
Growth Strategy

Key Use of Speech: To explain a growth strategy.

Style of Speech: Formal, informational, persuasive.

Audience: Stockholders.

Time: 10 to 15 minutes. [Depends on the level of
                       detail.]

→ Tip: The speaker
quickly welcomes the
stockholders, then digs
into business, thereby
projecting an image of
great efficiency.

It is my pleasure to welcome you today to our annual meeting of XYZ Company stockholders. Your copy of this year's annual report should now be in your hands. The report reviews our **[number]** years of continued growth. Let me say at the outset that our strategy calls not just for continued growth, but for accelerated growth, with the object of penetrating **[number]** new markets: **[the speaker lists the new markets].** We believe this strategy is essential to maintaining our leadership position in this industry.

I realize that some of you may have concerns about our growth strategy. After all, last year was certainly one of the most turbulent in the history of our industry. Negative impacts ranged from **[the speaker lists the negative impacts].** Yet XYZ not only weathered these challenges, we even grew substantially. In view of our fundamental strength, we believe that we can leverage our growth far beyond the rest of the industry by expanding *now,* precisely when conditions among our competitors are unsettled.

→ Tip: Speeches to
stockholders include lots
of numbers. Render
them as meaningful as
possible by emphasizing
before-and-after
relationships, trends,
and cause-and-effect.

The year started off flat, but because of our **[name of campaign]** campaign, we achieved sales of **[$ amount]** and revenues of **[$ amount],** setting a record for the **[number]** year in a row. Our earnings totaled **[$ amount],** a record surpassed in only **[number]** years since we started business. We saw new investments of **[$**

469

amount] in the future growth of the company, our total assets being **[$ amount].** The price of our shares has risen from **[$ amount]** to **[$ amount]** during this year, a direct reflection of our steady growth, even in troubled times.

With numbers like this, it would be a tragic mistake to pass up the opportunity to expand and to dominate **[number]** new markets, all of which look so promising. We are especially excited about our ongoing research into the field of **[type of field].**

[The speaker details the research and its potential for profit.]

→ Tip: Never fail to appeal to the stockholders' self-interest.

We have a clear picture of the potential of these new technologies, and we owe it to the consumer and to you to continue to move ahead with our quest into them. What's taking place in our laboratories today will create a better world tomorrow—especially for our stockholders.

On the regulatory front, Congress has **[speaker explains legislation favorable to growth].** So the stars are aligned as occurs few times in history. *Everything* tells us to move forward. We are also encouraged by recent tax legislation … **[speaker hits the highlights].** We anticipate seeing a positive impact from this new regulatory legislation and the tax changes in the last quarter of the year.

→ Tip: Don't avoid the negative, but do put it into perspective.

While we are eager to proceed with our program of expansion, I do have some discouraging news about our expedition into the **[type of market]** market. We are discontinuing our line of **[product]** because of disappointing sales. Yet I don't want to write this experience off as a failure, because it did teach us several things. **[The speaker details these lessons.]** We will use this experience to help guide our growth in other areas.

The big picture?

The price of our stock has gone from a **[year]** low of **[$ amount]** to this year's high of **[$ amount],** an accumulative return of **[percentage amount].** Obviously, XYZ's performance during this past year has demonstrated a sound financial foundation and an efficient operation. Combine this with a will to pioneer and to grow, and we can all anticipate exciting new directions and new rewards.

MODEL SPEECH 136:
Hedging Strategy

Key Use of Speech:	To explain a hedging strategy.
Style of Speech:	Informational, persuasive.
Audience:	Company managers.
Time:	5 to 6 minutes.

➜ Tip: Sometimes you can reinvigorate a cliché. Here, the horns of a dilemma become a "real" place to sit.

Few perches are more painful than the horns of a dilemma, and that is precisely where we currently find ourselves. As you know, it is critical to our strategic plan to introduce **[product]** before the end of the year. But, as you are also aware, two technical standards for this **[product]** are currently contending for domination of the industry. If we go with the wrong standard for our **[product]**—well, it will be Beta and VHS all over again. We'll be stuck with a warehouse full of unsalable machines.

The rest of the industry is taking a wait-and-see attitude, which, of course, leaves us with a tremendous opportunity to cream the market, to be the first with the most.

But which way should we go? Which technology should we adopt?

We could flip a coin and hope for the best. We could go with what our R&D department believes is the better technology—but there is no guarantee that the better technology will prevail. (Again, think of the battle between the VHS and Beta video formats. All the experts agreed that Beta was superior—but just try to find software for a Beta machine in your local video store!)

➜ Tip: A strategy speech can be quite simple: present the problems and the objectives, then lay out a strategy to overcome the problems and attain the objectives.

When you find yourself on the horns of a dilemma, the best thing to do is get off. This is how we propose to do that.

We are going to adopt a hedging strategy with regard to the introduction of **[product]**. We will produce a machine compatible with technology A, and we will offer an optional conversion kit to technology B. This will get the customer off the fence and prompt him to buy just as soon as we get the drop on the rest of the industry by bringing out **[product]** on **[date].** And if the worst *does* happen, if technology B becomes dominant, we can consider deep discounts on conversion kits.

So, folks, go ahead and take this potentially very profitable plunge—but let's hedge it with a conversion kit parachute, just in case.

———————————

MODEL SPEECH 137:
Mergers and Acquisitions Strategy

Key Use of Speech: To explain a proposed acquisition.

Style of Speech: Informational, persuasive.

Audience: Trade association members (customers).

Time: 5 to 6 minutes.

Good afternoon, my friends.

XYZ Corporation has always aimed to be your one-stop source for all your **[type of product]** needs. This principle guides our strategy year after year. You, our customers, have let us know on a number of occasions that you would be very interested in purchasing **[type of product]** from us, since this **[product]** is so closely related to the line of widgets that we offer.

I am pleased to announce, therefore, that XYZ has entered into talks with WXY Company for the purchase of its **[type of product]** unit. You, our customers, were—as usual—right: It makes perfect, rational sense for XYZ to integrate **[type of product]** with our current widget line. We are, after all, the leading total-solution provider of **[type of technology]** and, therefore, can most effectively coordinate **[type of product]** into our large-system offerings.

Our plan is to incorporate the WXY unit and its **[number]** employees into our **[name of division]**. Over the past year, as you know, XYZ has taken steps to provide customers with packaged, off-the-shelf **[type of product]** solutions. Once the acquisition of the WXY unit is complete, we will be able to take the final step toward this integrated approach.

The advantage to XYZ is obvious: more business for us!

The advantage to you, however, includes reduced cost of ownership of **[type of product]** and a system that requires no tweaking and

→ Tip: The speaker uses the occasion of an acquisition announcement to demonstrate responsiveness to customers.

→ Tip: The speech shows how the acquisition benefits the company's customers.

very little maintenance. This acquisition is really a step toward firming up our partnership with you, our customers. By means of more thoroughly integrated products, we can be more responsive to your special needs, thereby lowering not only your direct costs, but your indirect costs as well.

Our acquisition of the WXY unit, upon completion, will also strengthen our business and marketing alliance with that firm. We believe that this will also allow us to serve your needs more effectively, especially where whole-system support is concerned. The continuing evolution of integrated approaches to the needs of our customers is a strategy to which we are absolutely committed. We intend to remain open to future acquisition of companies or their technologies whenever such acquisition promises to make us a stronger, more agile, more responsive business partner to all of you.

Thank you.

OUTLINE

Opening

- Greeting
- We want to be your one-stop source
- You, our customers, have told us you want **[type of product]** from us
- We are acquiring **[type of product]** unit from WXY Company

Our plan

- Incorporate WXY unit into our company
- Provide customers with off-the-shelf **[type of product]** solutions

Advantages

- Advantage to company: more business
- Advantages to customer
- Reduced costs
- Increased convenience
- Firmer partnership with us
- We can be more responsive

Closing

- Acquisition will allow us to serve you better

MODEL SPEECH 138:
Reinventing Business

Key Use of Speech:	To outline a strategy for rethinking business.
Style of Speech:	Informational, persuasive.
Audience:	Industry trade association members.
Time:	10 to 15 minutes. [Depends on the level of detail.]

➡ Tip: Beginning a speech with momentous news is a sure way to capture the attention of your audience.

➡ Tip: Don't be afraid of teaching your audience something; just make certain that the lesson is truly relevant to their interests and needs.

"Business as usual" is not a phrase many of us hear these days—and with very good reason. We are at a momentous turning point in the international economy—involving changes every bit as profound as the transformation of the nineteenth-century agricultural economy into the twentieth-century industrial economy—and it's taking place *right* now.

Our fathers and mothers were part of the last generation that lived in an industrial economy of mass production and mass consumption.

The meaning of this statement would have simply bewildered mom and dad—at least at the beginning of their careers. For them, mass production was still a given, an absolute brought to the world by such demigods as Henry Ford and the industrial engineer Frederick Taylor. Not only did mass production make mass consumption possible, thereby profoundly shaping American life, it also shaped *work* itself. All important decisions were centralized around a small managerial elite, and *planning* or *thinking* was deliberately separated from *doing.* As for the *doing,* it was usually broken down into repetitive, mindless tasks—tasks admirably suited to robots, except that none were available at the time, so managers made do with people. These people had few decisions to make and were obliged to adhere to a rigidly defined standard of quality. *Flexibility* was an obscene word.

→ Tip: Drive home the point of complex statements with short, simple, sweeping summary statements.

Rigid structures buckle and break if enough force of change is applied to them.

Today's emerging economy is that force of change.

In the past, we measured economic health by the value of the gross domestic product and by growth and unemployment rates. Today, the *key* indicator is standard of living, as this is measured by comparative productivity versus that of other industrialized trading regions. Our high standard of living already requires higher productivity than the rest of the world, and the old industrial mass production economic model is being displaced by *customization* of goods and services and the *decentralization* of work.

Business is reinventing itself.

Today, new products are developed in a fraction of the time it took in the old industrial economy. Moreover, services and products are being custom built to order, quality is dramatically improving, and such technologies as computer systems and robotics are drastically lowering costs.

→ Tip: Support broad statements with more specific facts.

Above all, companies are reinventing the nature of work. It is the workers who are interacting with customers, and it is the front-line workers on the factory floor who are empowered to make decisions. Centralization and customization just do not go together.

→ Tip: Create dramatic structure by raising the ante: "If you think X is difficult, with until you see Y."

As if reinventing the nature of work weren't a sufficiently formidable task necessary to meet the promise and challenges of the new economic realities, we are also faced with having to redefine key strategic resources. These used to be such commodities as oil, coal, iron, and so on. Today, the key strategic resources are ideas and information. They come out of our minds rather than out of the earth. This profound shift not only requires rethinking business, but also the entire system of education—and even the way business works with that system. And I have to tell you, ladies and gentlemen, that many of the world's industrialized nations are doing a better job than we are of preparing their workforce to make decisions and to generate the natural resource of ideas. We need to reinvent business in order to integrate it more closely with our culture and our society. We need to recognize the goals of business and the goals of society as *common* goals, common goals for the common good.

Can we reinvent business so profoundly?

The answer is, we *have* to.

Low-skilled manual work will be rewarded less and less, which means, among other things, that the United States cannot afford to continue to rely on other nations to do our high-skilled work. If we become a nation of low-paid workers, we will not be able to purchase the products and services of foreign high-paid workers. Reinventing business, beginning with a far-seeing reinvention of work itself—decentralizing it, raising the bar of skill—is vital to our economic future, to the standard of living that our children and their children will enjoy—or suffer with—for a long, long time.

MODEL SPEECH 139:
Reinventing Government

Key Use of Speech:	To propose a new approach to government, especially as it relates to business.
Style of Speech:	Informative and authoritative.
Audience:	Civic group.
Time:	12 to 15 minutes.

→ Tip: Make certain your audience understands your key terms. Here, the speaker slips in a formal definition of "strategic planning."

Over the past twenty or thirty years, business began discovering what our government has known about for more than two centuries: strategic planning. You know what strategic planning is—the process of rationalizing a business in order to achieve defined goals in the context of defined strengths, weaknesses, resources, and needs. That is precisely the function of the U.S. Constitution. In fact, the Constitution was the government's *second* strategic plan. The first, the Articles of Confederation, proved a failure; so the government reinvented itself, revised the strategic plan as the Constitution, and went on to the most successful launch of a government in all history.

So government had a two-century lead on business as far as strategic planning is concerned.

Then something happened.

→ Tip: Examining a crisis or problem is almost always an interesting subject for a speech—provided that you can demonstrate the relevance of the crisis or problem to the needs and interest of your audience.

Somewhere along the way, this great idea began to fall victim to a kind of mass amnesia. Slowly, somehow, government drifted away from its strategic plan. Means and ends became increasingly confused, and sometimes we had ends without means and, even more often, means without ends: processes and procedures that have little productive point.

Let's take an often-publicized example. Let's audit the IRS. Now, let's not debate the necessity of taxation. It's necessary. End of

478

discussion. Second, let's not debate the nature and amount of the various taxes—though, goodness knows, these offer plenty of opportunity for debate. No, for the purposes of this discussion, let's just consider how the IRS operates and why it operates that way.

[The speaker discusses a number of all-too-typical cases of IRS abuse, insensitivity, and unresponsiveness.]

➜ Tip: Examples are powerful and necessary features of a speech; provide them, then interpret them.

All of this, of course, is enraging. Thankfully, lawmakers are becoming increasingly aware of problems like this as hot-button issues. These abuses are truly frightening—but what's really scary is that they aren't aberrations. They are the norm—the *worst* of the norm, to be sure, but the norm nevertheless. That is, these abuses flow from a fixed attitude of government.

➜ Tip: The speaker develops his analysis of government's chief problem by focusing on the concept of customer focus.

It is *not* the attitude of a totalitarian dictatorship or of power-hungry dictators or monarchs. Rather, it is the attitude of a *business* that has forgotten to put the focus on its customers. And *that* is an extraordinary state of affairs where the "business" known as the United States of America is concerned; for customer focus is item number one in *this* company's strategic plan: "We the people . . ." the Constitution begins, not "We the politicians . . ." or "We the legislators . . ." or "We the policymakers. . . ." As Abraham Lincoln said in the Gettysburg Address, this is a "government of the people, by the people, and for the people." *He* understood the basis of the strategic plan.

Lincoln understood it. But our lawmakers and our regulators seem to have lost that understanding.

In the 1950s and earlier, most U.S. businesses ran pretty much the way government runs now: with the focus on the business —making things, administering things, counting things, managing employees, and so on—rather than on relations with customers, serving customers, satisfying customers. The result of this was a consumer shift, in full swing by the 1970s, to foreign companies, which *did* focus on the customer.

Well, American business changed. It reinvented itself. Faced with disaster, it shifted the focus to its customers and, in a process that continues today, has become and is becoming increasingly customer driven.

Government?

Politicians often claim to have the interest of their "customers" at heart, but, so far, the actual results in government have been disappointing. Take, for example . . .

[The speaker discusses various aspects of government that are arbitrary and inefficient and obviously not focused on the needs of the governed.]

→ Tip: The speaker shifts the focus to the relation of government to business.

Among government's many "customers," none is more important than business itself. I didn't say that business was the only important "customer" of government. I said that none is *more* important. This is because business generates wealth. Business sets our standard of living. Business provides employment and provides goods. Business drives the economy. Yet government often operates as an adversary of business.

→ Tip: An elaborate illustration of a problem is useless if it does not greatly clarify or dramatize the problem. This question—"How long would we last as businesses if we behaved as the adversaries of our customers?"—drives home the speaker's point.

How long would we last as businesses if we behaved as the adversaries of *our* customers?

In the process of reinventing itself, of refocusing on the creation of customer satisfaction, government must also look to its key customer known as business.

Now, those of us in business know that creating customer satisfaction does *not* mean simply doing everything the customer says and acting on his every desire. A customer may want a Mercedes for the price of a Ford Escort. Well, it won't happen. It *can't* happen. And it *shouldn't* happen. If a business loses money on every product it sells, it will soon cease to exist and, obviously, relinquish all ability to satisfy *any* customer.

→ Tip: A good analogy is capable of considerable development. It illustrates a point in depth.

No, customer satisfaction is about relationships. It's about being responsive. It's about being rational. It's about making common cause with the people you serve—not regarding them as dupes to be fleeced or enemies to be regulated. The U.S. Constitution sets out a strategy intended to avoid these very pitfalls—the problems that have plagued arbitrary, nonrepresentative governments since the beginning of government itself.

Fundamentally, the Constitution is a sound strategic plan. Government needs to rediscover it and reinvent itself in accordance with it. Here's how we can support our government in this process.

[The speaker discusses participatory strategies to help government change.]

We *are* the people of the United States. And we *are* the customers of its government. Let's help this great business satisfy us all. Again.

Thank you.

OUTLINE

Opening

- Business has begun discovering what government knew years ago: value of strategic planning
- Government's strategic plan = Constitution

Something happened to government

- Seems to have abandoned its strategic plan
- For example, the IRS
- Typical cases of IRS abuse
- Point of this: government has forgotten to put the focus on its "customers"

Business used to run like government

- Focused on things and money, not customers
- Result: customers drifted away from American business, sought imports
- Business reversed this situation by reinventing itself
- Government hasn't reinvented itself—yet

One of government's most important customers = business

- Why?
- Business creates wealth
- Business sets our standard of living
- Business provides employment
- Business drives the economy
- Yet government is often the adversary of business

What creating customer satisfaction means

- Not doing everything the customer wants
- Customer satisfaction is about relationships
- It's about common cause and partnership

Closing

- Constitution = sound strategic plan
- Government needs to rediscover this and reinvent itself
- Here's how we can support this effort

MODEL SPEECH 140:
Research and Development

Key Use of Speech:	To lay the foundation of an R&D strategy for a firm.
Style of Speech:	Informative, authoritative, and exciting.
Audience:	Company managers.
Time:	10 to 12 minutes.

→ Tip: Starting off on an apparently irrelevant, off-the-wall note is an effective attention grabber.

This is a speech about establishing an R&D strategy for XYZ Industries, but let me begin by telling you the stupidest thing that somebody from *Sales* can do. It's just this: setting their sights on *making the sale.*

Fortunately, *our* Sales Department cares about tomorrow as much as today and knows that it is never enough just to make *a* sale. Their goal is to make *customers.* For our Sales Department, a successful sale is one that is leveraged into a satisfied customer who will be the source of *many more* sales—now and over the years. The core of our R&D strategy takes its cue from our own Sales Department. We want to leverage each new product success into one success after another. To accomplish this, we need to answer three key questions:

→ Tip: You may start off on a discordant note, but you must quickly demonstrate the relevance of your opening. Make yourself perfectly clear within the first few sentences of the speech.

1. What markets should we be in?
2. What products should we create?
3. What technologies should we work on?

The answers to these questions may be formulated in what consultants like to call a "product innovation charter." I have a simpler name for it: "the game plan." Either way, it's a strategy.

So far, we've operated as a small, upstart company—and we've

483

been pretty successful. But we're now too big to be cowboys.

→ Tip: The speaker uses a dramatic illustration from history to make clear the need for a strategy.

Let me tell you about another "cowboy," one who lived more than 250 years B.C. in northwestern Greece. His name was Pyrrhus, and he was king of Epirus. He decided to fight the Romans and led 25,000 men and 20 elephants against the Roman legions at the Battle of Heraclea. He had not bothered to make a plan, but he did know how to fight bravely, and he and his men won a victory—though at a tremendous cost. Congratulated on that victory, Pyrrhus shook his head and replied, "One more such victory and I shall be lost."

→ Tip: Don't rely on analogies to make your point. Reel off the hard facts—the consequences of an action or of a failure to act.

Without a sound strategy, even a *successful* new product launch can be a Pyrrhic victory—a gross triumph and a net defeat. A poorly thought-out launch could strangle cash flow and can lead us into an area of technology we cannot afford to develop sufficiently to remain competitive. It could take us into distribution channels that prove to be dead ends. It could even bring about our own defeat—if it knocks out our existing product line.

And *that's* a success!

If we deliver an out-and-out flop, well, the disaster becomes a whole lot quicker and bloodier.

There's no guarantee of avoiding these highly unpleasant scenarios, but developing a sound R&D *strategy* will minimize the risk.

Let's go back to our three questions. We need to answer them with two *whats* and a *how:*,

The first "what" is this: In the long term, *what* role will new products play for XYZ?

→ Tip: Illustrate the problem vividly, but put the focus on the remedy, not the problem.

The second "what" is this: Into *what* arenas do we want to venture? ("Arenas" include such things as markets, market segments, products, technologies, and so on. We'd better decide where we want to go.)

Finally, the "how": Just *how* will we achieve our goals?

Let's turn for some help to a marketing professor by the name of Robert G. Cooper, who identified five basic strategies for innovation among more than a hundred corporations he studied. Let's take a look at them:

First, there's what Cooper calls "Type A." It's technologically driven, and it is the most popular innovation strategy around. Essentially, R&D runs the show. The idea is like that movie *Field of Dreams,* "if we build it, they will come." Sometimes they *do* come. But, actually, this strategy is pretty inefficient. There are a lot of unknowns here and, therefore, a lot of risk.

This brings us to Type B, the "balanced strategy." This approach weighs technological factors against market orientation. The results are better than the average. While the average new product success rate is about 66 percent, firms using the Type B strategy enjoyed a 72 percent success rate.

There's still more. Type C is the "me too" approach to new products—little technology, but a lot of imitation. Results are not only below average, they make for a boring company—and one we don't want to work in.

The Type D research and development strategy is superconservative. It works for some companies who are content to keep making the same thing over and over. That's not us, and it's not our marketplace.

→ Tip: Present your audience with a range of possibilities, then point them in the direction you want them to go.

Type E is what I call a nonstrategy strategy. A lot of money is thrown at R&D, which is let loose without direction, and the results typically range from disappointing to disastrous.

It seems pretty obvious that we need to go with a Type B balanced strategy for our R&D program. Here are what Professor Cooper sees as the principal characteristics of the approach:

- The Type B approach seeks markets with high potential growth.
- It avoids competitive markets.
- It avoids markets new to the firm.
- It is technologically sophisticated and innovative, but always market oriented.
- It is not afraid to price premium products at a fair premium.

Beyond these guidelines, I also want us to think about our objectives in developing new products. We need to set a percentage of company sales to be derived from new products by a certain time. We need also to set a profit target and a growth target. We should decide what role we want our new products to play—to hold our market share, to expand it, to exploit our strengths more effectively, and so on.

→ Tip: The speech concludes with a specific call to action.

These questions and issues are the foundation of an R&D strategy. You will find in your mailboxes by this afternoon a set of assignments for working groups to formulate the details of the strategy—to build on this foundation. This will be difficult, but also exciting work. I look forward to our first meetings on the subject, beginning on **[date].**

OUTLINE

Opening

- Subject: establishing an R&D strategy for company
- Mistake some Sales Departments make: they focus exclusively on making the sale

R&D can learn from Sales

- Our Sales Department focuses on cultivating customers and repeat business, not just sales
- Our R&D strategy will emulate this
- Leverage each new product success
- Ask what markets we should be in
- Ask what products we should create
- Ask what technologies we should work
- Create a product innovation charter

We need a plan

- We're too big to be without an R&D strategy
- Example of Pyrrhus
- Plan will minimize risk

How to begin the plan

- Answer what role we want new products to play in our company
- Answer into what arenas we want to venture
- Answer how we will achieve our goals
- Five basic strategies
- Types A through E

Type B as strategy of choice

- It seeks markets with high growth potential
- Avoids competitive markets
- Is technologically sophisticated as well as market oriented
- Willing to set a fair price on products

Objectives in developing new products

- Percentage of sales
- Profit target

Conclusion

- Answering all these questions creates a foundation for our R&D strategy
- Work on this
- I look forward to your ideas

———————————————

MODEL SPEECH 141:
Spin-off Strategy

Key Use of Speech: To outline a new-product strategy of developing spin-offs.

Style of Speech: Informative, authoritative.

Audience: Company managers.

Time: 8 to 10 minutes.

→ Tip: The opening of this speech asks the audience to think in a new direction.

XYZ Corporation has always been known as an innovator—and that is a very good thing, as far as it goes. But, sometimes, it just goes *too* far. We spend so much time fathering and mothering new "children" that we risk neglecting the children we already have. I am proposing that we take a new approach to innovation. I am proposing that we begin a review of our current product line with the goal of spinning off a series of products from it.

I am aware that this strategy is not without risk. If we aren't careful, we'll create perceptions in the trade as well as among our customers that improvements and additions were necessary because our original products were somehow flawed. But we're a high-tech company, and I believe that we can create a program of regular, routine upgrades without raising eyebrows and *with* great revenue in-flows.

→ Tip: Anticipate problems and objections, and address them. Preempt resistance.

Another spin-off strategy I want us to consider is taking some of our products into new markets. We'll have to think about using a special sales force, creating some special advertising, innovative displays, new packaging, and creative promotions, but products such as **[the speaker gives examples]** don't have to be stuck in **[type of store]**. We can get them out in **[another type of store]**, too.

And we don't have to explore new domestic markets only. At least **[number]** of our current products, with some modification, should enjoy success in such market countries as **[the speaker lists them].** It is true that translating a product from one country to another is not necessarily a *short* short cut to developing a new product. It will require a commitment to research, design, and marketing, and we will have to be prepared for substantial repackaging and fresh directions in promotion. But we cannot afford to let these international opportunities simply evaporate.

Finally, we need to review—intensively—our current product lines and look for line-extension opportunities: spin-off products that are a continuous, logical development of the products we currently offer. This approach will not only give us the opportunity to leverage our technological assets, but also our reputation. We are known for our **[list]** lines. Let's work toward extending these.

The next avenue I want to explore may be more controversial. Let's look at creating some multiple or alternative brands in such product lines as **[list].** I think that this approach could stir up action in some of our slower-moving lines.

Finally, let's analyze our slow-movers with an eye toward repositioning some of them. We will have to create advertising campaigns aimed at *educating* dealers, wholesalers, and retailers, as well as end consumers, and I think we might encounter certain pockets of resistance in the trade. But in the following product categories—**[list]**—I feel we might benefit from exploring some new positioning strategies.

I want to begin moving on these initiatives before the end of the year. I ask that you give these matters thought, and that we reconvene on **[date]** for preliminary spin-off development discussions. We have a number of high-profile, high-quality product lines. Let's extend, develop, and more thoroughly exploit them all.

→ Tip: Vary your presentation to keep the speech from being a monotonous list.

MODEL SPEECH 142:
Strategic Planning

Key Use of Speech:	To state the need for strategic planning and outline an approach to it.
Style of Speech:	Informative, authoritative.
Audience:	Company managers.
Time:	8 to 10 minutes.

→ Tip: The speech begins with apparent cynicism—then turns the tables on the speaker as well as his audience.

Democracy is a wonderful thing. Turn on the television during an election year in a boom period, and you'll hear the incumbent take credit for the economy. In a recession year, he'll blame the problems on "business cycles."

We all laugh.

Then we go to work and start talking about "product life cycles," as if these were a law of nature. We're being just as silly as the candidate on TV. An unquestioning belief in the theory of product life cycles leads to unnecessary, resource-wasting product proliferation. Blind faith is not an adequate substitute for clearly articulated corporate goals and a new product development program based on strategy. Ladies and gentlemen, it's about time that we at XYZ Corporation created a strategic plan.

→ Tip: A strong paragraph ends with a definite conclusion that opens up the rest of the speech.

We need to begin by defining our mission in precise terms: what we want to attain and what we may and may not do to attain it. Our mission defines the boundaries of our business activity in terms of specific goals. Formulating this definition will require from all of you an exercise in vision. Just what do I mean by *vision*? It is the quality that allows definition of our boundaries that are neither too narrow nor too broad. Our vision must simultaneously stimulate and focus—filter and limit—the direction of our development, growth, and introduction of new products.

→ Tip: Be precise in your definitions, especially when you are making an assignment.

→ Tip: Acronyms or similar mnemonic devices make it easier for your audience to digest and retain your message.

I suggest that we begin to define both our vision and our mission by a review of the "three C's":

First, our *Customers:* Who are they now? Who else would we like to attract?

Second, our *Competitors:* How do *they* attack the market? What gaps in the market have they failed to fill? What values do they provide that we do not? What values do they fail to provide that we can supply? And How will our competitors react if we grow and if we introduce some major new products?

The third C—our *Company:* We need a thorough review of our strengths and weaknesses, and then we need to brainstorm on strengthening the weaknesses and exploiting our present strengths.

Once we get our Three C's under control, let's start setting some goals—some *strategic* goals. What is a strategic goal? It's a carefully, clearly defined statement of what we want to be, to do, and to achieve in the relative long term—say the next three years.

Now, to get us started down the road to setting some doable and worth-doing goals, let me tell you what *I've* been doing lately. I've been studying our current business and our current customers, and I've reached the following tentative conclusions:

1. XYZ Industries is the leader and innovator in the **[type]** industry.
2. XYZ has invented a better way to do **[some key operation].**
3. XYZ products provide quality and value.
4. XYZ has excellent name and brand recognition; consumers think of us when they think of **[product].**

This is the good news. Now, the not-so-good:

1. High production costs are cutting into our margins.
2. Our chief competitor, WXY Company, is beginning to achieve comparable name recognition in our markets. This has me nervous.

Now, what I've just run by you is a very rough Market Position Statement, and I'd like to use it to suggest a few goals:

Number one is to become a higher-volume manufacturer so that we can generate greater margins through production efficiencies.

This leads to the second goal—leveraging down the cost of sales as volume increases.

Number three: Let's harvest our reputation for innovation by

➔ Tip: This speech, one in which a professional is speaking to other professionals, pushes the limit of using lists as ways to structure what you have to say. The speaker would do well to distribute a printed version of his various lists as an aid to retention and action.

continuing to be *the* great innovator in this industry. We need to affirm our commitment to developing new products.

Number four: We need to remain the dominant company in the **[type]** industry.

Doubtless, after discussion, many of you will want to add to this list of basic goals. Let's do so. Let's evaluate them. Then let's let the rest of the company in on them.

Here's what I propose as the next step.

I want each department head to prepare a simple, single-page statement of our corporate goals. And I also want the heads to prepare a two-column list. Put company strengths on one side, weaknesses on the other. Next, each of you should prepare three *concise* statements:

First: Where has the company been? Second: Where is it now? Third: Where will it be three years from now? There's more for you to do, too.

Each department head should formulate two mission statements— one for the company and one for his or her department.

➔ Tip: Carefully specify what you want from your staff.

By **[date]** I want to meet to discuss this work and to decide, collectively, on the best management system for achieving our goals.

Ladies and gentlemen, I realize that few things are more difficult than thought, and I further realize that this exercise requires a process of very intense thought. But this is also your opportunity to make yourselves heard in the most direct and effective way possible.

OUTLINE

Opening

- Apparent cynicism regarding politicians
- But business too often suffers from the same delusions as politicians

Our business needs a strategic plan

- Blind faith in product life cycles leads to waste
- Faith is not an adequate substitute for strategy
- We need a plan—we're overdue for one

Define our mission

- What we want to attain
- What we may and may not do to attain it
- Requires an exercise in vision
- Vision defined
- The "Three C's"
- Customers
- Competitors
- Company
- Set goals

My conclusions and suggestions

- We are the leader and innovator
- We have invented a better **[product]**
- We provide value and quality
- We enjoy excellent name and brand recognition
- However, we have high production costs
- Our chief competitor is closing in

Goals

- Become higher-volume manufacturer
- Leverage down cost of sales as volume increases
- Harvest our reputation
- Remain dominant in industry

Invitation to add to these goals

- The next steps
- Answer what, how, and when

Closing

- Thinking is difficult
- This is an opportunity to make yourselves heard, to influence the future of the company

MODEL SPEECH 143:
Turnaround Strategy

Key Use of Speech: To outline a strategy for recovery and turnaround.

Style of Speech: Authoritative, persuasive; exhibiting leadership.

Audience: Stockholders.

Time: 12 to 15 minutes.

Good evening, ladies and gentlemen. I am Patricia Small, president and chief executive officer of XYZ Corporation. It is a pleasure to welcome you to the company's annual shareholders' meeting. Let me first introduce our Board of Directors.

[The speaker introduces the members.]

We are fortunate to have a board of great dedication, integrity, and professional judgment. As you know, they stand today for re-election to another one-year term.

Before I speak to you about the events of this past year, our corporate secretary, Michael Schroeder, will observe our legal requirements.

[The secretary performs his function.]

Thank you, Michael.

Now, let's review the year.

[**Year**] began at the trough of the biggest downturn in our industry in recent history.

→ Tip: Speeches to stockholders usually have legally mandated preliminaries.

494

[The speaker details the problems in the industry and the economy.]

Those of us in management were uncertain what the year would bring, and so were the investors, who kept our shares at **[$ amount]** for **[number]** weeks—the lowest share price in **[number]** years. To be sure, we faced a difficult environment, but, I think you'll agree, XYZ became stronger, not despite these difficulties, but because of them. "What doesn't kill me," the philosopher Nietzsche said, "makes me stronger."

Let's detail some more of the things that *didn't* kill us.

[Having talked about general problems in the economy and the industry, the speaker details some specific problems relating to his company.]

Despite these difficulties, we did attain several milestones. More accurately, we built a strong foundation on which the future will stand—and that future, ladies and gentlemen, will begin immediately. Here's what we've managed to do during this most challenging year:

First, in the area of international marketing, we have . . .

[The speaker highlights accomplishments.]

Second, we have revised customer service procedures to make them more efficient and more responsive. We are featuring our new "customer service advantage" in the coming season's ad campaign. Customer service is perceived in the marketplace as a very high-value item, and we intend to communicate to the consumer our high-value commitment to it.

Third, we are not cutting back on new product development. Other firms in our industry are. This is a knee-jerk, panic response, and we won't let ourselves fall prey to it. More important, the fact that our competition is reining in their new product development efforts creates an opportunity for us. Part of our turnaround this year will result in our significantly surging ahead of the pack with new products.

Although we will invest in new product development during the coming year, we will also reduce operating expenses in the following areas: **[list]**. We will be a leaner organization in **[year]**, but by no means an organization in retreat. We are, in fact, moving ahead.

→ Tip: It is always best to express matters positively. This does not mean ignoring problems, but it often means translating those problems into challenges and even into opportunities.

→ Tip: The speaker emphasizes positive achievements—not responses to crisis.

→ Tip: The speaker shows how the hard times represent an opportunity to gain a competitive edge.

And at the lead of our advance is a superb new management team.

[The speaker introduces the new managers, highlighting the special qualifications and accomplishments of each.]

→ Tip: In presenting a self-appraisal, keep the focus on your firm and on the context in which it operates.

The new team will work to build on the foundation we have already laid. Look at us in the context of industry performance this past year. We look good. Of course, we are all disappointed in the way that context looks—but, within that context, we look good. Not that "good" is ever good enough. Our aim is to turn this company around to greatness once again. With the advantages we have over our competitors, with the management team we have in place, and with your support, we *can* do this. We have a plan. We're committed. We're stronger than ever.

May I take your questions now?

Technology

Openings

——*Are you tired of hearing about the Internet and our industry? Well, let me assure you, that we will all be a lot more tired if we ignore this technology and watch our competitors stream past us one by one.*

——*I am hear to talk with you about getting the most out of our new high-speed Internet connection. This technology has been installed to make us more productive, and it requires remarkably little understanding from us.*

Closings

——*It is understandable that we feel a bit threatened by the new technology. Let's recognize those feelings, then get beyond them. The new systems we have put into place will help us all do our jobs faster, better, and with greater reward.*

——*Thank you for your attention this morning. If you have any questions about the new system, first consult the manual. If you still have questions, call Technical Support at extension 1234. No question is irrelevant. And the only "dumb" question is the one you don't ask.*

MODEL SPEECH 144:
Communications Technology

Key Use of Speech:.   To outline the opportunities and challenges of communications technology.

Style of Speech:.   Authoritative, informative, thought-provoking.

Audience:.   Company managers and supervisors.

Time: 10 to 12 minutes.

➜ Tip: A radically off-the-wall opening commands attention. Your audience wants to find out where in the world you're going.

All in all, the War of 1812 was a pretty bad idea. Supposedly, we got into it because the British were abducting U.S. citizens on the high seas and forcing them to become sailors in the Royal Navy. But that matter was settled a few days before war broke out. No, we got into that war because we *wanted* to—thought it would make us stronger and get us more land.

We almost lost.

But there were a few impressive U.S. victories against the British and their Indian allies. Certainly the most impressive was the Battle of New Orleans, which Andrew Jackson won on January 8, 1815. The victory was cause for great jubilation on our side, and it made Jackson's political career for him.

There was only one nagging detail about that glorious victory. **[Pause.]** The war had ended two weeks earlier.

British and American diplomats had signed a treaty in Ghent, Belgium, but, in those days, news traveled so slowly that Jackson didn't hear about it before or during the fight.

Today, of course, with instantaneous communication almost a universal fact, the Battle of New Orleans would never have been fought. Many lives would have been saved. On the other hand, the political career of Andrew Jackson might have been very different, and we might just have a picture of John Quincy Adams on the twenty-dollar bill.

Given the choice between instantaneous communication and long-delayed communication, I'm sure we'd be unanimous in opting for what we have today: dependable voice-phone service; conference calling, which allows us to convene meetings without everyone having to be physically in the same room; video teleconferencing, which makes those far-flung remote meetings that much less far-flung and remote; e-mail, which threatens to make the posted letter obsolete; voice mail, which means we don't have to worry about missing our calls; cell phones and pagers, which keep us in touch wherever we are . . . and so on.

→ *Tip: The speaker sets up one side of his argument.*

Technology makes communication easy—*if*, by "communication," you mean sending words and pictures to somebody.

In the 1950s, when the writer Truman Capote was told that the novelist Jack Kerouac had written his *On the Road* in a matter of a two or three weeks, Capote quipped, "That's not writing. That's typing." Similarly, merely sending words and pictures isn't communicating. It's data transmission.

→ *Tip: Here's the other side of the argument.*

Communicating—conveying ideas, conclusions, and opinions in a way that shapes the thoughts and feelings of others—remains at least as difficult in our technological age as it was, say, in Andy Jackson's time. Maybe technology has even made real communication *more* challenging than ever.

In the pre-electronic age, people communicated more slowly, and that certainly created problems. On the other hand, folks had more time to think back then. Using pen, ink—and mind—they pondered and carefully composed their messages. If it took an hour or two to write an important letter, well, that was little enough time, seeing that it would consume a week, two weeks, a month, or more to "transmit" that letter. Even after the advent of the telephone, you could always hire a secretary to intercept calls, to buy the yourself time. And you *could* leave the office and be blissfully out of touch for long periods. After all, a telephone cord could only reach so far.

Then came the relatively early days of technology. Let's say you needed to communicate with someone overseas. You could put in an expensive international telephone call, and hope that time zones and luck were on your side. Or you could send a telex, which required a trip to the "Telex Room," and even that exercise stimulated thought and economy of expression before you or the telex operator put fingers to keyboard.

Today, as my grandfather would have put it, data transmission is as "easy as rolling off a log." And that does two things: First, it relieves some of the pressure to *think* before you start transmitting. Technology has made all communication more like casual conversation. That may lead to more honest, open communication—or it may prompt some fairly thoughtless, careless communication.

Second, however, technology also puts the pressure *on*. We are expected to communicate more, more often, and more quickly than ever before. Faxes pour in, e-mails pile up, people want answers—*now*.

There is a third challenge.

Electronic communication technology gives us access to huge amounts of information. That's wonderful—in some ways. In other ways, it's a problem. We find ourselves awash in a *sea* of information—and that's almost as bad as the old way of getting your information, in a mere trickle. If you are sending information, your challenge nowadays is to present it in such a way that somebody reads it, interprets it, responds to it, and acts on it. If you're trying to take in information, the trick is to escape drowning.

One thing is certain: electronic technology has shot down the usual excuses for failing to at least *try* to communicate. Everybody is reachable, and everyone can reach you. The tools of communication are available as they never have been before. As with any other tools, this technology can be used to accomplish great things, can be squandered on the trivial, or can even cause substantial harm. Technology makes it easy to transmit data. It is still up to each of us to shape it into meaningful, positive, constructive communication.

→ Tip: This speech is structured like a balance —weight is put on one side and then the other.

EXAMPLE SPEECH

The PC Platform: Computers Now Affect Every Age Group and Room of Your Home

Speaker: Eckhard Pfeiffer,
President and CEO, Compaq Computer Corporation

Good morning, everyone. I believe that five-year-olds should get behind the wheel and drive. They should pilot mini submarines among exotic sea creatures. They should travel to distant planets. And they should hang out with characters named Frogmella, Clump the Grump, and Dave the Wave.

Now you may be wondering whether I lost not just my money but also my marbles at the roulette table. But when we at Compaq think about computers, we think of their power to transport not only data and images but also the mind and the imagination—especially the imaginations of the very young.

With our partner Fisher-Price, the preeminent brand for play and learning, we will soon be making these journeys of the imagination possible for preschoolers. Last night, our two companies announced a new line of intuitive, highly interactive computing products that allow kids to get behind the wheel and steer, honk, joystick, and throttle their way through animated, educational words. And that's key because kids love to drive. They love the sense of freedom and physical interaction of using a steering wheel.

We call this new line of computer products Wonder Tools. To quote English author Lewis Carroll, they are designed for: "Child of the pure, unclouded brow And dreaming eyes of wonder."

That's how he described children in his classic, Through the Looking Glass. And I can tell you Alice in Wonderland never had it so good. We think these Wonder Tools will make learning fun, exciting, even irresistible to kids.

We're convinced these interactive digital tools will strike a chord with the needs and the interests of young children and their families, mothers and grandmothers, fathers and grandfathers.

Now, I've drawn your attention to these tools—the first of what will be an extensive product line—for several reasons. First, they open a new chapter in interactive education

---

Source: Eckhard Pfeiffer, President and CEO, Compaq Computer Corporation. Delivered to the Winter Consumer Electronics Show, Las Vegas, Nevada, on January 5, 1996. Reprinted by permission of Eckhard Pfeiffer and *Vital Speeches of the Day.*

and play as well as a new chapter in consumer electronics for the home. Second, they confirm that the PC is in a state of perpetual transformation. And third, they underscore how today's PC has evolved to the point of fundamentally redefining experience for people of all ages.

In fact, the PC has progressed so far and so fast along the inventive continuum that it now defines the computer industry. And it will come to define the consumer electronics industry as well.

As computing and communications have fused, we've seen the PC evolve from a stand-alone personal productivity device to a communications tool—a connector and coordinator. And when combined with the Internet, the PC can radically transform personal and business communication, commerce, education, healthcare delivery, home automation, entertainment and play, and perhaps even government.

The PC's life-changing power is not lost on people. While personal computers are in just one third of American homes today, many, many more people aspire to owning a PC, mostly because of its educational value. A recent survey found that more than 80 percent of people who plan to buy one soon say it's mainly for their children's education. We know that a majority of all computer purchases are influenced by a child in the household.

So by 1998, we expect half of American homes to have at least one PC. In fact, households with more than one computer will become as common as households with more than one TV, VCR, or phone.

According to market researcher Link Resources, 11 million U.S. homes already have two or more working PC's. New users tend to spend more time on the PC than in front of the TV.

Why is this happening?

Well, the PC's become so versatile and such a magnet for more and more functionality that the entire family wants to use it at the same time. And who can blame them? Can you think of any other mass market product that has proved so adaptable, so multiform, so elastic in function, definition, and price?

The same PC can be used today as a telephone, a fax machine, a modem, a scanner, copier, and TV. It can be used as a connection to the increasingly commercialized and ubiquitous Internet. It can be used as a node on the office network. A tool for managing personal finance or educating and entertaining children. A vehicle for telecommuting and videoconferencing. A place to play audio and video CD-ROMs. As well as an intelligent command center for controlling your major appliances and monitoring your home's energy use and security systems.

What's more, the PC can connect to nearly every kind of communications infrastructure. You can hook it up to analog and ISDN lines, to Ethernet, cable, infrared, and wireless communications of all kinds.

And that's essential because people want to connect—to one another, to the Internet, to on-line services, to businesses, to the ocean of information in cyberspace. Little surprise then that last year the two-phone-line household became a common fact of life. The connection machine par excellence is the PC. And this gateway device keeps getting more and more powerful.

Compaq's Presario PC's for the home are 200 times more powerful than the first x86 PC introduced in 1981. Here at CES we are demonstrating several intriguing, new technologies that may find their way into the new 96 Presario line.

One of these technologies is a first for any PC. It's a scanner incorporated into the PC's keyboard. With this scanner, your home PC could become an intelligent filing cabinet that lets you scan tax statements, school records, medical forms, and other important documents into your system.

Once scanned, these documents can be annotated with "electronic sticky notes," grouped in electronic folders, and faxed or E-mailed to others.

Another home PC technology we are demonstrating is a rewritable optical CD drive. You can copy files to or from these CDs. Each one equals 450 standard floppy disks. So you can easily shuttle large amounts of data back and forth between your home and the office.

Now, as you probably know, our Presarios already provide one of the industry's richest multimedia experiences.

Given these features, who would want to share his PC? And who would want to be excluded from using one? Certainly not preschoolers now that Wonder Tools are here. And certainly not senior citizens, who rely on PCs to manage their personal finances and to send E-mail to their children and grandchildren. A sophisticated toy for one family member. A sophisticated communications device for another.

But it doesn't stop there. Because I see the PC as a universal tool for home and business. By universal tool I mean it does many things well. And its features, form factor, and price can be tailored to suit the activities that go on in the different rooms of your home. I believe the PC now has a place in nearly every room of your home. And yet it won't be the same kind of computer in each room.

We've put this idea into practice by helping design what we call the Information Highway House. It's a real four-bedroom house located just north of San Francisco in Corte Madera. Inside are five different Compaq PCs linked in an Ethernet-based local area network.

With these PCs, family members can schedule a doctor's appointment, buy stocks, or pay bills electronically from the den. They can research a school project or listen to interactive books from the bedroom. They can look up a recipe on the kitchen PC, and laugh at comedy routines in the living room. This cyberspace house represents just the earliest stages of what will be possible before the turn of the century.

I say that because today's PC has only just entered its adolescence. Its hormones are just kicking in. Its major growth and the realization of its full potential lie ahead. In fact, it's as far from a commodity as a product can be. To know that's true, just consider how many really different versions of the PC are emerging. Everything from high end clustered multiprocessor servers for the datacenter, to room-specific devices for the home, to light-weight, mobile PC companions that combine data transmission and voice recognition capabilities.

No single commodity motherboard can meet all these form factors or all customer needs cost effectively. I think the PC is about where the automobile was back in the 1920s. While we're past the equivalent of drivers needing to crank and choke their cars by hand, we're not yet to the point of automatic transmission—let alone antilock brakes and air bags. In short, PC advances in the next two decades will dwarf those of the past two.

Now, there are other reasons for my optimism. Given the momentum behind the Internet, we're going to see a major increase in communications bandwidth to the home. This bandwidth will be delivered by ISDN, broadband over copper wires, cable modems, direct digital satellite services, and ultimately all-optical networks.

What's more, we at Compaq are convinced there's enormous opportunity to integrate the PC far more completely into the home. Your home can have far more diverse and interactive links to the outside world. That way you can pull in digital content on demand along with a wealth of information and services. And you can engage in full-blown electronic commerce, telemedicine, and distance learning.

Equally important, I believe your home itself can become a far more intelligent and automated environment and as programmable as a PC.

These developments are pulling us toward the Intelligent Networked Home of the very near future. I know the idea of a "smart home" has been around for decades. Back in the 1950s, science fiction writer Ray Bradbury offered a memorable vision.

In one of his short stories, he described a 21st century house where the front door recognizes visitors and lets them in, the kitchen ceiling "speaks," reminding you which bills are due today. And tiny robot mice roam the floors collecting dust.

In another story, we read about a family whose house has a special room built just for the kids. It's a virtual reality nursery that brings to life in three dimensions whatever scene the kids are thinking about, whether it's the cow jumping over a very realistic moon, lions prowling an African plain, or more to the point, parents turning over their car keys and credit cards to their kids.

Compaq's vision of the intelligent home is a bit more down to earth and it's available this century!

With that in mind, let's consider the following scenario. Suppose it's four years from now—January 5th in the year 2000. It's a weekday, 6:30 in the morning. You shuffle to the kitchen in search of coffee and turn on your voice and touchscreen-activated kitchen PC-TV.

With its advanced digital display system, this PC can handle the spectrum of bandwidths, aspect ratios, and scan rates depending on the content you've selected. And it's linked to a multichannel, multipoint distribution system whether wireless digital broadcast, wireless cable, or digital satellite video and data.

You select CNN Headline News, which reports that the Winter Consumer Electronics Show is under way. You notice a live satellite feed of CES is available and watch a few minutes of the opening keynote. With a touch of the PC's keypad, you check for any pressing phone, fax, or E-mail messages delivered overnight.

Software agents that act on your behalf by knowing your interests prioritize your messages and point out a conflict in your schedule for the day. These agents interact with you on your monitor through animated facial expressions.

While this is happening, your wife is in the bedroom seated by a large-screen PC connected to wide-area ATM-based, broadband services. She's flying to China this afternoon for an extended business trip. But before leaving the country, she wants to consult with her doctor to make sure her vaccinations are up to date.

While waiting for her scheduled 7 A.M. telemedicine appointment, she reads her personalized electronic newspaper, which was compiled overnight by her software agents scanning the network. This morning's lead stories notify her of a delay in her flight's departure, Beijing restaurant reviews, and an acquisition just undertaken by the Chinese customer she's visiting.

She also logs on to the Compaq/Fisher-Price Web site to browse for computing toys for her daughter. This Web site allows her to watch videos and read customer reviews of new toys. And since this site is connected to these companies' strategic partners, she can access information and services related to toys and computers, clothing for kids, and even bulletin boards devoted to child development issues.

At 7:00 sharp a chime sounds, and her doctor's face appears in a high-quality video tile on her PC. She touches the tile with her finger, causing it to fill the screen. During this personal video-conference, her doctor reviews her medical record and the latest health advisories from China.

Meanwhile, your teenage daughter starts her day as she always does, by jumping on the I-phone (the Internet phone) to talk to a friend in Germany. She also logs into a video rental store on the Net, looks at a dozen movie trailers, and selects the one she'll watch that evening on the living room PC-TV, which has a 60–inch screen.

The laughter from your twin four-year-olds' bedroom suggests they are thoroughly enjoying the 4th generation Wonder Tools. This newest version allows kids to navigate by voice commands as well as by steering. Software agents constantly refresh the animated worlds they visit.

After your wife leaves for the airport, and the kids head off to day care and school, you drive to the office for a quick meeting. Your house, sensing it's now empty, automatically switches to "away mode," turning off lights, closing drapes, dialing back the thermostat, and resetting the security system. In fact, your home network is constantly monitoring its subsystems, ready to page you if there's any change from the normal settings.

Later that morning while you're at work, your home security system sends you an urgent page with the message: "Front window broken. Security company called." With voice commands directed at your desktop PC, you dial into your home remotely. You speak your personal ID code and then say: "Activate control console. Activate security camera."

You take a quick pan of your front yard and notice a tree limb leaning against your house, and a crack running the length of your living room window. Relieved that no one has broken in, you send an "all-clear" signal to your security company. And then you say to your computer: "Find a nearby glass repair service and dial the number."

Two hours later, a technician from "Window Doktor" arrives in your driveway. Your security system senses someone approaching your front door and pages you again. The technician holds his badge up to the security camera for verification, and you remotely unlock the front door.

A couple of hours later, he sends a page that the window has been replaced and the bill comes to $485. And over the Web, you send a secure electronic payment to "WindowDoktor.com."

When you get home that evening, you decide to call up the energy management program on your PC. This gives you an up-to-the-minute look at your phone and utility bills It also lets you save money by shifting your peak power consumption to times of day when rates are significantly lower.

Now I could continue with this scenario, but you get a sense of the wealth of convenience offered by an intelligent Networked Home. Perhaps you're thinking if this is not complete fantasy, then it must require the resources of a Warren Buffett. Well, we believe this scenario is not only feasible but affordable. Most of the technology needed to fully implement home automation and provide valuable services is here today.

Compaq has put the weight and influence of our Fortune 100 computer company behind an industry standard home networking technology known as CEbus, the consumer electronics bus. The CEbus will do for homes what the local area network did for offices. It will help bring automation and networks to everyone.

The concept is to put intelligence in thermostats, stereos, TVs, and other consumer appliances so they can communicate over the home network with PC's, and so that in-home local area networks can connect to outside services. And since it communicates through existing power lines, phone wiring, and radio signals, most consumers will find no need for expensive rewiring.

When combined with the PC, CEbus holds so much promise that we've made an equity investment in Intellon Corporation, a leading provider of the technology that will link computers with household appliances. CEbus will be incorporated in some computers and appliances later this year, and on a wide range of products in 1997.

If you'd like to see this technology at work, why not come over to the Compaq booth? With the help of AMP, which is supplying CEbus-compliant controls, we will be demonstrating our Presario PCs controlling lighting, thermostats, appliances, a TV, a security system, and much more.

Through the centuries, the focal point of the house has changed several times. Early on, it was the fireplace. People gathered around it to keep warm and cook their meals. Over time, that focal point switched to the kitchen. And then it seemed to switch to the TV. But now, I believe the home's new focal point is becoming the PC.

The PC platform is now at the center of consumer electronics technology.

And no one knows more about the PC than Compaq. Over our 14 years of existence, we have shipped more than 19 million PC's to customers around the world.

Our forte is extending this versatile platform, humanizing the personal computing experience, and integrating the PC into a variety of home environments. It's this expertise that has propelled us to the No. I worldwide marketshare in PC's for the second consecutive year. At the same time, we've become a highly successful consumer electronics company with tremendous brand loyalty and brand recognition.

Our vision is to transform computing into an intuitive experience that extends human capability on all planes—communication, education, work, and play. We know that for PC's to become part of the very fabric of society, they must become much easier to use, behave more like personal assistants, and delight consumers over the entire life cycle, from initial purchase to replacement.

In support of this goal, we are pursuing useful innovation on all fronts. For example, we're hard at work creating speaker-independent, continuous speech recognition for PC's. We're striving for a system that, with little or no training, can recognize any person's voice, deal with continuous speech, and dynamically adjust the size of its vocabulary to meet the user's needs.

In time, we believe you'll be able to talk to your PC, with the emphasis on the PC understanding you rather than you having to understand it. We also know that consumers are overwhelmed by the avalanche of digital data rushing at them from the Net, on-line services, E-mail, and ever larger bundles of pre-installed software.

As one economist noted, "A wealth of information creates a poverty of attention and a need to allocate that attention efficiently." So we're developing new ways to help consumers locate, filter, and organize all the information on their PCs, and even preview and sample software, so they'll know ahead of time just what they're buying.

In addition, we're building home networking infrastructures as well as the array of devices that will work within these networks. As you'd expect, we're experimenting with devices like large-screen PC-TVs, home mobile PCs, edutainment peripherals, and much more. We see the PC at the center of an expanding universe.

Now, there's a key platform I haven't mentioned. And that's the much-discussed, low-cost Internet appliances. I'm sure you've heard about them. We believe these devices have merit. In fact, they will expand the market by offering lower functionality at lower price points. They will appeal to consumers whose prime interest is in a communications device that surfs the Web, and enables E-mail and electronic commerce.

Of course, the infrastructure needed to make these appliances work isn't here yet. Missing, for example, are specialized hardware, the rich applications that will reside on the network, and higher bandwidth to the home. These hurdles will be surmounted given the absolutely huge financial investment flowing into this opportunity, and the major development programs that a broad base of companies, including Compaq, have under way.

As to the cost and pricing of these devices, the goals are certainly aggressive. However, until concepts and related costs are defined, we won't really know what price points these appliances will sell for.

It could well be in the $500 to $1,000 range. And this would open up a huge new market opportunity, which we see as an addition to the current PC demand, demand that will most definitely continue to grow.

In closing, I believe all of us have at our disposal today an information-linking, knowledge-manufacturing, people-connecting technology that may well dwarf every communications system the world has seen to this point.

I'm talking about the powerful combination of the constantly evolving PC and Internet. A combination with the potential to completely reinvent commerce, human collaboration, and leisure. And I can assure you that Compaq intends to bring the wonders of this capability to the greatest number of the world's workplaces, homes, and schools.

MODEL SPEECH 145:
Computer Utilization

Key Use of Speech:	To lay ground rules for computer usage.
Style of Speech:	Authoritative, informative.
Audience:	Company employees.
Time:	4 to 5 minutes.

→ Tip: When you recognize that your audience may be familiar with some of the material you are presenting, be careful to avoid talking down to your listeners.

A little while ago, this would have been a long speech. To most of us just a few years ago, desktop computers looked like a strange mutant breed of television set grafted onto a keyboard. We needed a lot of help learning how to make use of this little monster. Today, however, most of us have computers at home—and if we aren't fully comfortable with them, our kids certainly are.

So this will be a *brief* talk about some fundamentals concerning the use of your computer.

First: turn it on.

→ Tip: Give instructions simply and clearly.

Easy enough? Well, I mean turn it on *first* thing. Make certain it completes the boot-up process without any problems. If you do experience a problem, turn the computer off, wait twenty seconds, then turn it on again. If the computer still fails to boot properly, put in a phone call to the Tech Support Center at **[extension number]**.

Once you are up and running, check your e-mail. This should be part of your morning routine.

In day-to-day computer operations, please observe the following:

Do not eat or drink anywhere near the computer. These machines are super dependable. If something is going to kill them, it's almost always "human error"—and "human error" is almost always coffee, hot, black, cold, with sugar and cream, it doesn't matter, it's almost always coffee spilled either on the keyboard or on a floppy disc. If

510

you do experience a spill, shut off the computer immediately and don't turn it back on until it's been serviced by Tech Support.

There is another computer killer out there: the virus.

Most computer viruses come from loading unauthorized programs onto the computer. Most viruses are carried on floppy discs, though they can also be downloaded from the Internet. Viruses can destroy data, and, if they are carried across our network, can do great harm. We can defend against viruses in two ways:

Number one: Use the anti-virus program loaded on your computer. You will find complete instructions for its use in the program's "Help" file.

Number two—and this is even more important: Make no unauthorized downloads. Accept no diskettes unless you can fully vouch for their source.

Speaking of unauthorized programs, avoid them altogether. Only the software loaded on your machines is authorized for use on the machines. Do not copy other software. The use of unlicensed software can result in very heavy civil penalties for us.

Finally, do shut down your computer at night. We do not leave the machines on overnight. In general, you should turn the machine on in the morning and turn it off when you leave. This will prolong the life of the equipment.

If you have any questions, don't hesitate to contact the Tech Support Center at **[phone number]**. Answering your questions is a big part of our job, and we love doing it.

———————————

MODEL SPEECH 146:
Desktop Publishing

Key Use of Speech: To introduce desktop publishing.

Style of Speech: Informal and informative.

Audience: Small business people.

Time: 12 to 15 minutes.

Mark Twain was once reported dead. The humorist, very much alive, learned of this error and cabled the *New York Times*: REPORTS OF MY DEATH ARE PREMATURE.

Similarly, during the 1980s, the demise of the printed book and magazine was frequently reported. It was widely predicted that the computer and electronic publishing would bring about the death of "paper publishing." Of course, it was also said that the widespread use of the personal computer would bring into being the "paperless office"—a business environment in which all documents would exist in electronic form only.

Picture in your mind's eye your desk. All the paper gone?

Yeah, right.

Now take a look at your bookshelves and coffee tables.

You will also conclude that reports of the death of the paper book and magazine are premature.

The fact is that our society continues to be dominated by *printed* information. No technology has yet supplanted the sheer convenience and portability of print on paper. There is also something that simply *feels* good about holding a book or magazine or newspaper and reading it at your own pace, then putting it aside. Nothing to turn on. Nothing to plug in.

Nevertheless, the *generation* of paper print has changed drastically.

→ Tip: Interact with your audience. Engage them in your speech.

512

→ Tip: The speaker is careful to distinguish between electronic publishing and paper publishing aided electronically.

You may still find some folks practicing the art of manual typesetting—for special art book projects and limited editions—but the use of computers to set type and compose pages, and the use of electronic means to acquire images for reproduction has become well-nigh universal. Furthermore, many of the most advanced electronic reproduction technologies are available to users of desktop computers, so that, potentially, just about all of us can be our own publishers.

Desktop publishing systems are able to format text and graphics interactively on a high-resolution video screen with the aid of page-description command programs. Once a page has been formatted, the entire image is transferred to an electronic printing or photocomposition device. It can then be sent, via modem or on a diskette or cartridge, to a commercial printer. The result: an instant publication.

→ Tip: In a concise manner, the speaker reviews the equipment needed for desktop publishing.

Desktop publishing requires fairly modest equipment: a personal computer, a video monitor, a high-resolution printer, a digital scanner, and capacious portable memory storage, such as a Zip-Drive or Sy-Quest disk system. You'll need word-processing software and design software, as well as software to help you acquire and edit images—if your publication is to be illustrated. The more powerful desktop publishing software programs offer full-featured word processing and graphics capabilities.

It all sounds easy. And it *is* easy to create and publish—perfectly dreadful material!

→ Tip: The speaker suddenly shifts themes and now turns to the pitfalls of desktop publishing.

Desktop publishing has put the tools of professional editors, typesetters, and designers in the hands of amateurs—some with talent, some without, some with the patience and persistence to learn, some who just want instant results.

The purpose of my introductory talk is not to discourage you from exploring the world of desktop publishing, but it is intended as a reality check.

→ Tip: The speaker uses a simple analogy to make his point: great tools don't make a great craftsman.

The reality is simple. Ownership of an advanced word-processing program doesn't make you Shakespeare. It doesn't even make you a good writer. This comes as news to no one. We all accept this. Yet many desktop enthusiasts believe that ownership of hot new computer gear and design and type programs with all the bells and whistles *does* make them master designers and typesetters.

Whether you are setting type with the equipment Johannes Gutenberg used on his Bible in the 1450s or employing the latest that Silicon Valley can throw your way, you need to master certain basics.

[The speaker reviews the basics of design and typesetting.]

This kind of skill is not acquired overnight—though you can certainly acquire enough of it, with a little practice, to produce effective reports and brochures.

The only question is: should you?

> → Tip: Be helpful. Here the speaker suggests guidelines for deciding whether or not to get into desktop publishing.

If you cannot afford to make the commitment to sufficiently mastering writing, editing, and design fundamentals to create published documents that will enhance your image, not detract from it, you are probably far better off hiring professionals. Certainly, this is the case if your publishing requirements are one-shot or occasional. If, however, your business would profit by regularly issued brochures, information sheets, and newsletters, it would be worth investing in a good desktop publishing course, such as those offered at **[speaker mentions local colleges/university]**.

Remember, desktop publishing is a tool. Its purpose is to help you present information more effectively. The purpose of presenting information more effectively is to enhance your image as a company, to show to the outside world that you may be small, but you pack the power and the professionalism of the big operators. Don't be tempted by amateur-hour desktop publishing shortcuts. Use the technology to leverage your capabilities, not to magnify—and publish to the world—your gaps and deficiencies.

OUTLINE

Opening

- Mark Twain anecdote: "Reports of my death are premature."

The printed book is not dead

- Predictions that electronic publishing would end "paper publishing"
- Ask yourself: Have these proven true?
- No

No technology has replaced print on paper but electronics is now used in paper publishing

- Capabilities of desktop publishing
- Requires little equipment

- Sounds easy, but requires training and talent
- Too much desktop publishing looks amateurish

Ownership of equipment does not confer expertise

- Need to master basics
- The basics are . . .

Is mastering the basics worthwhile?

- How to decide

Closing

- Desktop publishing is a tool
- Purpose: present information more effectively
- Enhance your corporate image
- Don't be tempted to take shortcuts

———————————

MODEL SPEECH 147:
Electronic Commuting
(Telecommuting)

Key Use of Speech: To explain your company's telecommuting policy/experience to a trade group.

Style of Speech: Informative.

Audience: Members of a trade or professional group.

Time: 12 to 15 minutes.

→ Tip: The speaker defines telecommuting as a force to be reckoned with. He also shows how it is distinct from other work-at-home situations.

Telecommuting is here. It's arrived. It's not going away. Between 8 and 9 million Americans telecommute today. Despite the popular image, telecommuting is *not* exclusively home-based. Some employees *do* work from their homes, but others work from a growing number of remote sites called telework centers (often leased space where companies share fax machines, modems, printers, video conferencing facilities, and so on) or from corporate satellite offices at least a few days a week. I want to point out that I am talking about telecommuters, not independent contractors and free-lancers—there are about 41 million of these, working from home. Telecommuters are full-time, regular corporate employees.

The numbers of telecommuting employees have increased at about 20 percent a year since the early 1980s. This has come as a shock to many who swallowed whole the predictions of such futurists as Alvin Toffler and others, who believed that management resistance—a fear of losing control and sacrificing productivity—would kill the movement. To be sure, some managers do resist telecommuting (as do certain labor unions, for that matter), but changes in technology and the climate of business, augmented by environmental concerns, are generally overcoming objections.

→ Tip: Select your data carefully and use it sparingly—but do use *it*.

Since the 1980s, personal computers and fax machines have become home appliances as much as office equipment. Voice mail, too, is becoming as commonplace as answering machines, and e-mail is within reach of virtually everyone. The Internet—who even had heard of it in the 1980s?—provides broad access to many sources of information, and it also provides a basis for e-mail. The point is this: there is no longer any need for most data-related functions to be centralized. And what is an office or a corporate headquarters but, for the most part, a centralized location for data? According to a study by **[source],** at most companies, about 60 percent of the employees spend most of their time processing information. With a fax machine and a modem, **[source]** estimates that some 70 percent of those do not need to be physically present in a central office.

But what about productivity? Home is where you sleep, eat, watch TV, play with the kids . . .

→ Tip: The speaker balances third-party data with the results of his own firm's experience.

Studies by **[sources]** document—yes, *document*—increased productivity for those who work either at home or off site. Consider these figures: **[the speaker offers some key numbers].** Our experience at XYZ Corporation suggests a **[percentage amount]** increase in productivity.

For the employee, the benefits of telecommuting are obvious: flexibility of work hours, comfort, an enhanced ability to juggle family and work responsibilities, more time devoted to work instead of behind the wheel of a car or hanging off a subway strap. But there are also big benefits for the employer: reduction of occupancy costs is number one. At XYZ Corporation, we project a **[percentage amount]** savings in real estate costs over the next **[number]** years as a result of telecommuting.

→ Tip: Know your audience. The speaker is talking to managers, so he puts the emphasis on telecommuting's impact on and benefits for the company, not the individual employee.

Beyond these direct bottom-line considerations, we have found the telecommuting option helps us meet the mandates of the federal Clean Air Act, which requires employers to reduce driving by workers. We also use telecommuting to help us comply with federal requirements for workplace access for the disabled. Of course, the concept helps us meet the needs of employees with special family situations as well.

But there is an even more exciting prospect.

→ Tip: Use good dramatic structure. Move from "interesting" to "exciting" or "even more exciting."

We have discovered that telecommuting lets us hire the *best* people *regardless* of where they happen to live. This is a major barrier that has suddenly evaporated.

→ Tip: The speaker does
not avoid the negative.

Is there a downside to telecommuting?

Sure.

Most of it comes from distrustful management—an unwillingness to empower employees, a reluctance to relinquish control. "If we don't see you," many managers feel, "you *can't* be working." And it is also true that some workers—some *people*— just don't do well in the physical isolation of working at home or working at a remote site. How can you tell if you have the mental and emotional aptitude to be a successful telecommuter? Let me offer a little quiz:

→ Tip: Take every
opportunity to introduce
interactive elements into
your speech. These really
engage an audience.

1. Are you well organized and goal oriented—a self-starter?
2. Are you good at controlling distractions? (And will your family, neighbors, and friends cooperate?)
3. Do you work well with little supervision?
4. Can you get along without the social aspects of the office environment? Can you work comfortably solo?
5. Are you an effective telephone and e-mail communicator?
6. If you are working at home, can you set aside an area for *exclusive use* as an office?

If you answered yes to all six questions, you have the potential to be a successful telecommuter.

→ Tip: Share your experi-
ence with your audience.

At XYZ Corporation, we are excited by the potential of telecommuting. We are excited by its *potential* because it is working for us *now*. I have one important word of caution, however. Don't *jump into* telecommuting. Discuss it. Plan it. Formulate a specific policy on it. Before I conclude my remarks, let me share with you some of XYZ's telecommuting policy:

First: The use of telecommuting at XYZ is a management decision; telecommuting is neither an employee entitlement nor an obligation, but a means of increasing staff effectiveness and productivity, increasing organizational flexibility, reducing costs associated with turnover, attrition, and absenteeism, supporting Clean Air mandates, and resolving employee work/personal time conflicts.

Second: Participation in the telecommuting program is voluntary. This is a crucial aspect of our policy!

Third: Since one objective of telecommuting is to increase organizational flexibility, telecommuters may use this program in combination with an *approved* flex-time schedule.

Fourth: A telecommuting agreement is developed for each telecommuter. It addresses the particulars of specific work functions and individual performance requirements.

Fifth: The employee must be reachable by telephone during the agreed upon off-site work hours. Of course, the employee must have separate home and business phone lines—*two* business lines, actually: one for voice and one for fax and data.

Sixth: The telecommuter's conditions of employment are the same as for non-telecommuting employees and salary, benefits and employer-sponsored insurance coverage (including workman's

compensation) do not change as a result of telecommuting. This means that telecommuters are responsible to ensure that their home offices are safe and ergonomically correct.

This last piece of policy is very important. Since the telecommuter's home work space is an extension of the company's work space, the company's liability for job-related accidents continues to exist during the approved work schedule and in the employee's designated work location. At XYZ, we reserve the right to evaluate the employee's home office for ergonomic considerations— placement of desk and chair, keyboard height and lighting—as well as safety considerations (especially electrical hook-ups) at a mutually agreed upon time.

Finally, while one of the great boons of telecommuting is the ability to resolve conflicts between family demands and work time, we make it clear that telecommuting is not a *substitute* for dependent care. Telecommuters with small children or other dependents must make arrangements for dependent care during scheduled off-site work hours.

With the right workers and the right policies, telecommuting can not only work, it can save costs, increase productivity, and increase employee satisfaction.

OUTLINE

Opening

- Telecommuting is here: deal with it
- Definition of telecommuting

Growth of telecommuting

- Percentage increase since 1980s
- Belies predictions of its decline
- Resistance: who is resisting and why
- Technology spurs growth of telecommuting
- No longer a great need for a centralized office for data-related functions
- Most workers don't need to be physically present in office to do their jobs

Impact on productivity

- Studies document improved productivity
- Our company's experience supports this

Benefits of telecommuting

- For employee
- For employer
- Increases compliance with federal environmental regulations
- Broadens job market

Downside?

- Yes—distrustful management
- Reluctance to relinquish control
- Some workers are not suited to remote working
- Quiz for assessing suitability as a telecommuter

Our company is excited by telecommuting

- Our policy

Closing

- Telecommuting not only can work, it can save costs, increase productivity, and improve employee satisfaction

MODEL SPEECH 148:
Electronic Libraries

Key Use of Speech: To consider the present and future of electronic information distribution.

Style of Speech: Speculative and philosophical.

Audience: Members of a professional or educational group.

Time: 10 to 11 minutes.

➥ Tip: The speaker approaches a "think" topic by allowing himself to think aloud.

I find it difficult to begin this talk without resorting to comparisons that seem to me clichés: how the electronic distribution of knowledge is a revolution that recalls the introduction of the printing press. Perhaps I shouldn't apologize. Clichés, after all, usually get to be clichés because they bear more than a grain of truth. But the trouble with clichés is that, for all their truth, they usually call a halt to productive thought. Yes, electronic distribution of knowledge will put knowledge into more hands—just as the printing press put books in more hands. So what? What are the consequences of that? There is still the fundamental question: What do we *do* with the knowledge that is put into our hands—or on our monitor screens or onto our hard disks? Will the electronic distribution of knowledge really affect how we use knowledge, how we think?

It is quite possible that what we tend to mean by "knowledge" is rooted in print technology: words on pages. Perhaps electronic libraries will alter the very form of knowledge, changing even the nature of consciousness itself.

And can we take in all that knowledge—or, rather, information? For it is information, not knowledge, that is available in electronic form. The trouble is that we can't process or think about this infor-

521

mation—can't convert it into knowledge—because we just don't have enough time.

And there will be more and more information coming at us. After all, the electronic library is not a place, it is a distribution scheme—a transmission system—the cost of which will progressively fall, so that there will be more and more of it produced and made available.

How do we cope?

How do we use this gift—*gift?*—that is being heaped upon us?

I'm going to pause here—not to catch my breath, but because the message I have been developing is not *my* message. It's something, I think, we *all* feel. But, really, it need not be a new feeling. Print libraries have been in existence for thousands of years. What if you *lived* in a print library? Would you feel overwhelmed by the presence of all those books? Where would you start? How could you read them all?

I love books, but I am very happy that I do not live in a library. I like the idea of being able to put aside a book—to close it and put it back on the shelf. I like the idea of walking in—and *out*—of the library door. I like the idea of being able to get away from all those books when I want to.

As the electronic library continues to develop, however, it will be as if we *all* live in a library. The so-called knowledge explosion is history. It's well under way. In fact, we have been swamped by what we *could* know (if only we had the time) for hundreds of years now. We became so accustomed to that feeling of being swamped that we are no longer aware of it. The emergence of the electronic library, the ability to plug into "shelf" upon "shelf" of information anywhere, anytime, has shaken us out of our habit of willful ignorance. We realize—as if for the first time—that we are, indeed, swamped.

The great secret of successfully, happily, and usefully living in this electronic library, then, is not so much one of gathering information as it is of selecting it and organizing it. The art of being in the knowledge business will increasingly be defined as the art of selection and classification.

Book-laden libraries are often pleasant, even beautiful places. But, essentially, they are simply places: architectural enclosures for shelves. Similarly, the electronic library is basically a means of data storage and transmission. These two functions are by no means synonymous with communication, for to communicate implies trans-

→ Tip: The style of the presentation reflects a sense of information overload.

→ Tip: The speaker steps back to put his speculations into perspective.

→ Tip: The rhythm of an effective speech is often one of presenting information and emotions, then drawing conclusions from what you've presented, then proceeding to the next set of information and emotions.

mission as well as reception. It implies thoughtful, intelligent people at both ends of the transaction. Everything else is just noise—like the whistles and hisses your modem makes when it connects or is searching for a connection.

➜ Tip: Again, the speaker provides perspective on his subject.

Electronic libraries give us—and, in the years to come, will increasingly give us—access. But access to what?

With so much cheap information pouring out at us, how will we separate the knowledge from the noise?

Essential for the future of knowledge are information tools:, filters and classifiers. Electronics is coming to the rescue here to some degree. Computer programs to filter and classify information have become a major software category. But this is only a partial solution. To use the electronic library effectively, people will have to develop their own brain-borne filters and classifiers. I suspect that the thrust of education in the years to come will be less toward the acquisition of information than toward the acquisition of the mental equipment necessary to sort and pick through the stream of information cheaply and abundantly available. If we don't begin to learn how to use the electronic library, we will become a people increasingly informed yet decreasingly knowledgeable.

➜ Tip: The speech does not simply complain about information overload. It suggests a solution to it.

Perhaps some of you in this audience recall an episode of "information" transmitted via another electronic medium: television in the early 1960s. The show was Rod Serling's *Twilight Zone,* and the episode was one in which Burgess Meredith is a bank teller who could never find enough time to read the many books he wanted to read. One day at lunchtime, he is curled up deep in the bank vault, stealing time to read. There is a nuclear attack—this is the Cold War era, after all—and everyone is wiped out in an instant—except for Meredith, down in that vault. For the misanthropic bank teller, this is a happy ending! At last he has time enough to read! He is alone with mountains of books! However, while venturing out among the rubble, he trips, falls, and breaks his glasses.

If we fail now to equip ourselves and, especially, our children with the mental tools required to select, classify, evaluate, and filter the flow from the electronic library, we will find ourselves a race of myopic tellers, wallowing amid all those books, but lacking the vital lenses needed to read them.

OUTLINE

Opening

- Knowledge revolution
- Consequences of the knowledge explosion
- Will electronic distribution of knowledge affect how we think?

What is knowledge?

- Electronic libraries may alter the form of knowledge
- May change consciousness
- How to take in all the available knowledge?
- How do we cope?

Knowledge explosion is history

- It's a long process
- Electronic library has made us suddenly more aware of it
- We now realize we are swamped
- Realize need to select and organize knowledge more effectively

How will we separate the knowledge from the noise?

- Need tools: filters and classifiers
- Computer programs
- Mental equipment

Closing

- Require education for classifying and filtering knowledge
- If we don't prepare ourselves, we will find the electronic library to be of little use

---

EXAMPLE SPEECH

Growth and the Road to Cyberspace

Speaker: Dana G. Mead,
Chairman and CEO, Tenneco, Inc.

Today I'm going to talk about the transition of our economy to the Cyber-Age (or the knowledge economy as some label it) and some of the challenges we face on what I call the Road to Cyberspace.

As many of us have observed, there is sometimes a crossover between what's virtual and what's real.

By the virtual reality of the future—for example that we will be able, using our computers, to buy tickets for a trip to say, San Francisco to book a meal at a Greek restaurant on a Saturday night, to look at the menu, the dining room, to read the food critics' review, pick a table, order ahead, even talk to your waiter—all of it in the virtual world of Cyberspace.

It sounds wonderful, but I'm an industrialist and also a realist.

I keep thinking someone has to manufacture the tables, the silverware and the napkins; someone has to produce the food; someone has to put the wine in the bottle, and someone has to get the product to the customer.

The transition to the Cyber-Age is proving to be a painful process. The *New York Times* had a seven part series on it. And the latest issue of *Foreign Affairs* has the following on its cover: "The world may be moving inexorably towards one of those tragic moments that will lead historians to ask, 'why was nothing done in time?'"

These articles and many like them point up the fact that our transition to the Cyber-Age holds huge potential for problems, big problems—economic insecurity, worker anxiety, social displacement and disruption—and the very damaging political repercussions that may well result.

This issue is not immune from political demagoguery witness the campaign of Pat Buchanan, an old acquaintance of mine from my White House days.

The difficulty of this transition also has not escaped the fine political instincts of President Clinton. He now has his Labor Secretary, Robert Reich, out front as his point man basically polarizing the issue pitting managers against workers, investors against labor, government against corporations, larger corporations against small ones and so on.

Source: Dana G. Mead, Chairman and CEO, Tenneco, Inc. Delivered to The Economic Club of Detroit, Michigan, on May 15, 1996. Reprinted by permission of Dana G. Mead and *Vital Speeches of the Day.*

And although the rhetoric has cooled a bit, organized labor, the media and others have picked up the themes and run with them.

This transition—in all of its ramifications—is perhaps the greatest domestic challenge we face in this country over the next decade. And it's a case of "how we get there" being just as important as "being there."

If we do not do it right, we are going to end up with all the things I've mentioned earlier—paying a hard political, economic and social price and causing historians to question "why we didn't do something."

Despite all the talk of our "virtual future," the Road to Cyberspace has to go through places like Newport News, Virginia, where ships are built; through Cozad, Nebraska where they make shock absorbers . . . through Racine, Wisconsin, where they bolt tractors together . . . Counce, Tennessee where they make linerboard, and of course, through this city of Detroit and its environs.

That's just an oblique way of saying that we must find some way to use the vast experience and talent of a "non-knowledge economy workforce" while we move to one with workers and managers who are "cyber-ready"—and to do so without losing our competitiveness.

To get to the knowledge economy of the future is going to require huge resources, huge amounts of money—in people, time and effort.

That is why economic growth is so important to our transition. Unless we can achieve growth at high enough levels to generate the revenues that both government and business need—and it may not matter if it is government or the private sector that is spending the money—we won't be able to pay for the dislocations in our labor force . . . to pay for the training and retraining we need to equip our workforce with skills for jobs in the Cyber-Age . . . to establish effective safety nets for the inevitable dislocations and economic hardships.

We also have to pay for all the new Cyber-systems that will raise productivity—but which are already proving to be tremendously costly.

Has anybody here lately put in a new software system? Is there anybody here who thought it was cheap? Is there anybody here who does not believe that the next time is going to be even more expensive and complex?

And regarding the growth issue, we are facing big time problems.

There is a phalanx of "experts"—predominantly "doctrinaire economists" who think our current 2.2 percent growth rate . . . is all we can manage without inflation.

They include people at the Federal Reserve, the OMB, the Congressional Budget Office, the blue chip forecast and respected academics throughout the country . . . this, in the face of our average historic growth (since 1870) of 3.5 percent.

In fact, I have to tell you that in the last 6 months, as we in the NAM have been out beating the drum for growth in the three percent range, there has been a disturbing closing of the ranks in the academic community around the view that the country cannot sustain a rate of growth higher than the low two percent range without triggering rampant inflation.

I find this scary.

There are, however, some growth hawks fighting the conventional wisdom . . . influential and respected people like Milton Friedman, Lester Thurow and the man who saved New York City, Felix Rohatyn.

They see the low growth argument for the eco-babble it is.

In fact, some of us have been stunned at the number of people who see growth not as a logical economic argument for more investment, greater competitiveness and ultimately, higher living standards, but as a means to an evil end.

These are the conspiracy junkies who see growth as a plot by greedy corporations and the wealthy of the world to turn the United States into a plutocracy. Felix Rohatyn's recent column on growth in the *Wall Street Journal* has elicited almost unbelievable mail—accusing him of selling out his Democratic (big D) principles and attempting to alter the whole principle of income redistribution!

On the other hand (always an important phrase for an economist), there are those who sincerely believe that higher growth will cause inflation.

With the low inflation and low unemployment to date, I think that's an unfounded fear—a little like the cat who once sat on a hot stove. The cat will never sit on a hot stove again, but he'll never sit on a cold one, either. The stove of inflation is cold.

Now I am not ready to declare the death of inflation. I think it is dangerous, I think it is a problem, I think is has to be watched.

I also am not ready to sign up with those who think zero inflation is a legitimate goal for this economy, because I think that is dangerous also.

One of the things not being fully accounted for in the inflation debate is the result of increasing productivity—gains in output from what is known as "technology deepening."

What his means is, as we drive systems and innovations deeper and deeper into our organizations, we are getting a large boost in productivity—and often we don't even know it.

For example, Tenneco has increased productivity in one of our paper mills by 9% in the last 3 years without adding a dollar of investment.

We have not hired more people to do it.

We have not inflated the cost of labor per ton of output. We have done it solely by improving our processes.

Globalization—and the fierce competition it has spawned—is another effective inflation fighter.

Most people do not understand how really global most businesses are. Last year our Newport News Shipbuilding division signed a contract with a Greek shipping firm for four double-hulled tankers . . . basically an export item.

To help build those tankers, we probably have two thousand suppliers—small to medium size shops making parts for the ships. And if you asked them if they were exporters, most of them would probably say, no, they're suppliers to Newport News.

The intensity of global price competition is greater than many people think—it's not just the big multinationals, it's many of the firms who supply to them in countries across the world.

So much of what we are fighting in the halls of government and in the Federal Reserve is the misuse and misreading of economic data that don't take into account technology and globalization.

For example, the Federal Reserve and the rest of the low-growth crowd have been using an economic indicator called NAIRU—the awkward acronym for the even more awkward phrase it stands for: the non-accelerating inflation rate of unemployment.

Stated simply, NAIRU holds that when you go below a certain level of unemployment, the cost of labor will go up, triggering price increases on products and a spiral of inflation.

This has been the single most important indicator used by the Fed in monitoring inflation.

Of course, they get very upset with me, because I have been running around the country saying that NAIRU is to economics what the Nehru jacket is to fashion: Outdated.

I say that because the NAIRU has been systematically discredited.

People once thought the NAIRU was 6.1% unemployment. When unemployment got to 6%, the economists all said inflation is coming—sort of like Chicken Little, the sky is falling.

But we had no inflation. The unemployment rate dropped to 5.8% in early 1995, and people thought, the sky really is falling this time. So the Fed jacked up interest rates.

But low and behold, there was still no inflation.

NAIRU is like predicting the End of the World (or the Red Sox winning the World Series); if you predict it long enough, you'll eventually be right.

My point is, if you're going to follow economic indicators, they've got to be the right indicators.

Another example of a dubious indicator used by the Fed is changes in inventories and absolute levels of inventories. Basically, when inventories are high, growth and inflation stay low. When they're low, growth and inflation go up. That's the conventional wisdom.

I played the skunk at the Sunday picnic the other day. I asked one of these economy watchers if he takes into consideration the fact that every business in America has tried to reduce its inventories . . . to shorten up its cycle time.

I explained, for instance, that in our auto parts business, we often build a focus plant right next to our customer's plant, so we can deliver parts for a particular platform in a matter of hours.

So I said to the inflation fighter, if you think that no inventory in the auto plant indicates runaway economic growth, you are using the wrong indicator.

My point is, nobody really understands the impact of the changes that business—particularly manufacturers—have brought to this economy.

What is the impact of massive increases in productivity? What is the impact of Just-in-Time inventory? What is the impact of reengineering—which is a fancy word for eliminating the things that customers won't pay for?

We have to begin to talk about these changes and their impact.

And it's going to be uncomfortable for everyone.

Uncomfortable for industrialists like me because frankly, it conjures up the idea that part of this increased productivity may be from eliminating jobs.

We have to stand up to that issue. If our companies are to remain competitive in a global economy, we have to eliminate jobs that are no longer delivering value to customers . . . but at the same time, prepare people for jobs that are delivering value.

There is real irony in some of this jobs-and-growth debate. I was at a dinner in Washington a couple of weeks ago and a cabinet member got up and spoke proudly of the fact that the current administration has eliminated hundreds of thousands of government jobs.

Yet when it happens in the private sector, some government leader calls it corporate greed and labels CEOs "corporate killers."

So we have to take a very hard look at our economy . . . at the impact of the changes with an eye towards making this transition to the Cyber-Age a successful one.

To do that we have to focus on real issues, not phony ones that make good political rhetoric.

For example, the Secretary of Labor (I seem to be picking on him a lot) talks about the decrease in real incomes for the average wage earner during the past 20 years. And he usually says it in the same breath as phrases like "corporate welfare" and "class warfare."

This is all very polarizing stuff, and it makes good sound bites—which partly explains why many Americans are confused and discouraged.

They might feel they're doing better than 20 years ago, but they're being told they're worse off.

A report by Michael Cox and Richard Alm of the Federal Reserve Bank of Dallas puts some perspective on this paradox.

Alm and Cox used quality of life measures to compare 1970–1990. They found some interesting things.

I'll reel off a few of them:

The average size of a new home went from 1500 square feet to 2100 square feet.

People using computers rose from 100,000 to 76 million.

Households with VCRs went from zero to 67 million.

Attendance at symphonies and concerts, 13 million to 44 million.

The amount of time worked to buy gas for a 100–mile trip, from 49 minutes to 31 minutes.

People finishing high school: 52% to 78%.

People finishing college: 14% to 24%.

And life expectancy: 71–75 years.

These figures cast into doubt the idea that life has gotten worse for most Americans. And it warrants our taking a second look at the statistics so often cited by the doom and gloomers of this 7 to 10 percent decline in wages.

When you take into account things like the CPI's overstatement of inflation by one-half to one percent; the declining size of families; the growth of non-wage compensation like health care and pensions . . . most workers have seen compensation rise by up to 23%.

You take a further look, and you see the biggest bite in real income has come from taxes. In 1955, taxes took an average 27% of household income; today the figure is 38%.

At NAM, we recommend a number of things the government can do to help this economy achieve higher growth: deficit reduction, tort and regulatory reform, paying down the national debt, many others.

But the first among equals is tax reform that will encourage investment over consumption. This will take real leadership because tax reform will not immediately produce growth.

And when it does kick in, it will probably first benefit upper income Americans more . . . which means there will be plenty of howling about the rich getting richer.

So what we at NAM have been suggesting is something that reaches well beyond tax reform, and that is a new covenant between business, labor, and government . . . a compact of mutual support to pursue pro-growth policies.

One of the ironies of the recent militancy of the labor movement is its timing, because American industry has finally figured out that within our plants, we have people with 35 or 40 years experience who know a hell of a lot more about how to run that corrugator or know how to run that paper machine than any of us wearing white shirts and suspenders.

For years we have not utilized that talent. Now that we're reaching out and doing so, we are confronting a huge backlash from unions.

Why? Well, if you think about it, when you bring labor and management together on a project, you are basically supplanting the union's conventional role . . . which was to communicate with their members, to decide what work they would do and to organize the work.

So they see the team concept as a direct threat to their existence. Making matters worse is the recent NLRB ruling that supports a 1937 labor law that forming a labor/management team in a non-union facility is against the law.

We are being challenged in manufacturing facilities all over the United States, any time we put teams together—teams that are an absolute prerequisite to our staying competitive with the rest of the world.

That's part of what I mean by forging a new covenant.

Another part of that covenant has to do with the whole notion of gain sharing. This is a huge issue.

For years enlightened managers have tried to find ways to share company gains with unionized workers, and it has been very difficult to do so because it was often looked upon as a way to circumvent the contract—and their control.

Now let me talk about worker anxiety.

Though there is a lot of misinformation and disinformation out there, the fact is, worker anxiety exists, and it's not a mirage.

There are reasons for anxiety, and here I depart from the party line, and believe it or not, I agree with the Secretary of Labor.

It is a real problem. It includes things like people losing their jobs (and no new job prospects), their loss of benefits, and being unable to pay for their children's education.

Restructuring is going to continue—in whatever name you call it—and jobs will both be lost and changed.

The reason is, the old "don't look back" syndrome—someone's gaining on you. For every business, there are a lot of someones across the globe catching up in places like India, China, Brazil and Slovenia. This is not likely to change.

One of the consequences of this intense competition is job displacement. Twenty-five years ago, if you were a lathe operator, you had a skill . . . a marketable skill.

If you lost your job, the chances of your being out of work for very long were pretty low, because there were still jobs for lathe operators being created.

Now if you are a lathe operator, 50 years old, and you lose your job, the jobs that are being created are for people who can use distributive process control, or work in computer programming, or service robotics.

The skills of the old jobs being lost don't match the skills of the new jobs being created.

So we have to change our mindset. We can no longer guarantee a lifetime job.

We must begin to do what we can to guarantee lifetime employment by changing the skill set of people as they work ftor us.

We also have to be realistic. We cannot convert every welder at our shipyard to a computer jockey—that won't work.

But we can do things to give that individual a certain skill set that will increase the probability that he or she will have the ability to land a job in this quote-unquote "knowledge" economy, if and when their current job disappears.

Business, labor and government must cooperate to provide the training . . . and also pay for it. For its part, business needs to double what it spends . . . from 1.5% to 3%.

Meanwhile, workers—organized and unorganized—must be flexible. They must look upon their careers like opera singers—every 3 or 4 years developing a new repertoire . . . because a four-year-old repertoire is ancient history.

Like the opera singer, nobody is going to hire you for a new role unless you have learned the music. And there's more and more to learn with each passing year.

What are the ramifications of employment security as opposed to job security:

Well, for one thing, it means we are fast becoming a nation of job hoppers . . . which gets me to another area of cooperation: portability of benefits.

There is no reason we cannot develop a system of benefits people can take from job to job.

There is no reason why a worker should not take the equity built up in his or her pension fund to the next job.

There is no reason we cannot cooperate on benefits to help educate our workers' children.

And there is no reason we can't give our employees a larger piece of the action in our companies—to align the owners', the managers' and the workers' interests.

When we brought our Case tractor division public two years ago, we gave every single employee—right down to the guy bolting tapping screws on a tractor, options on a hundred shares. Today those options are worth roughly $3,000.

Those are some of the things that we have to do to make this transition to the Cyber-Age—and then succeed when we get there.

But I'll remind you that the Road to Cyberspace won't be a smooth one. It has to pass through every factory, every union hall, every board room in the country—and also through Washington, D.C. and all the state capitols.

This is not just an issue of "corporate responsibility," as many would like to call it, but of "national responsibility." It is going to take true leadership in the White House, Congress, business, and labor to make the transition successful.

And I think the jury is still out on whether we have that leadership in any one or all of these institutions. . . whether our leaders are ready to step up to the challenges and the risks that lie ahead.

MODEL SPEECH 149:
Internet Successes and Failures

Key Use of Speech: An informal sharing of Internet experience.

Style of Speech: Informal and helpful.

Audience: Company employees, colleagues.

Time: 10 to 15 minutes.

→ Tip: This speech is, in part, about the digressive nature of Internet research. Appropriately, the speaker begins digressively.

There are certain universal experiences in life: birth is one, and death is another. I believe that the experience of getting on the shortest line at the supermarket checkout, even though you know deep down that, somehow, it will end up taking the longest to move, is also universal, as is the fact that the water is always colder out of the bathroom faucet than out of the kitchen faucet. Such experiences, as I say, are universal. And here's one more: Setting out to look up something specific in the dictionary or encyclopedia and ending up reading a half-dozen miscellaneous and unrelated articles along the way.

We've all done that. We all do that. Personally, I think it is one of the more endearing traits of humanity (which can use all the endearing traits it can claim).

There is a universal impulse to browse: these days we call it "surfing the Net," as if this browsing were some form of strenuous physical activity.

→ Tip: Even if you state your theme humorously, state it clearly.

Well, it *can* be strenuous—if you want to stop *surfing* and start actually *finding* the information you really need. Just as there came a point, back in school, when it was a good idea to stop browsing the encyclopedia article on salmon fishing and get to that entry on Salmon P. Chase that you needed to write your term paper about Lincoln's cabinet, so there comes a point when you need to use the Internet to get some specific work done before you surf your way past your deadline and ride the pipeline right out of a job.

→ Tip: Definition by process of elimination is often a useful device for arriving at understanding.

First of all, let's get straight what this Internet is. And, to do that, let's consider what it is not.

It is not a place, and it is not a supervised, centralized system. It is an electronic network of loosely linked smaller networks and individual computers, the users of which have agreed to share (some) information. To do this, they use certain electronic protocols that make one computer's or network's information intelligible to another's. It is a giant network—though some people have called it a cloud, because it is so hard to define and contain—and it is almost entirely unsupervised.

→ Tip: There are two sides to every story, runs the old saying. Often, this is a very useful assumption to make about the topics in your speeches. Weigh and evaluate the pluses and minuses.

This lack of supervision is both good and not so good. On the plus side is freedom, freedom of speech, freedom of choice, freedom from censorship, freedom from having to gather only that information some authority has sifted out for you. You're on your own. And that's pretty much the minus side, too: *You're on your own.* The amount of information available online is unprecedented. It is like living *in* the biggest library you can imagine. But there's no librarian to tell you to be quiet—or to help you to the right shelf or to advise you on the best reference source for that article on Salmon P. Chase.

As overwhelming as the Net can be, it *used* to be a lot worse. A very few years ago, venturing onto the Internet was guaranteed to be an exciting—and frustrating—adventure. To begin with, figuring out how to connect to the Internet was a daunting task. Then, once you connected, you had to find ways to get to where you wanted to go. Those of us who could barely use the simple DOS commands necessary to operate our desktop PCs suddenly had to cope with a flood of Unix terminology—powerful but willfully obscure commands, all in lower-case type—in an effort to reach even more obscure addresses that no one ever seemed to copy down quite right. Mere typographical errors are easy to correct, but an out-of-place "dot" in an Internet address? You might as well try to guess the winning lottery number.

Well, it's gotten a whole lot better in the past few years.

→ Tip: This is a realistic appraisal of the Internet. Using it presents challenges, to be sure, but new tools do make it easier to use.

Clearly, the most important advance in Internet use has been the emergence and development of the World Wide Web. Some people think this *is* the Internet, but, actually, it's a sort of subset of the Internet, a kind of communication system that uses the Internet. For the most part, the Web replaces the obscure, user-*un*friendly Unix commands with what computer folk call a graphical interface, which allows you to navigate to the information you want by clicking with your mouse on the appropriate words of menus you find at each Web site.

Use of the Web has been greatly facilitated by a generation of elegant computer programs called Web browsers, the most popular of which are marketed by Netscape and by Microsoft. There are two great things about a good Web browser:

First—it makes getting around the World Wide Web relatively easy.

Second—it acts as an umbrella interface for the *entire* Internet. Remember, while the World Wide Web is growing, it is *not* the whole Internet, and a good browser will help you locate and journey to information on the Web as well as elsewhere on the Internet.

Indeed, a good browser is one of the most important tools you can use to keep from either spinning your wheels on the Net or finding yourself stuck in blind alleys. One of the great things it will do for you is to make instantly available an assortment of "search engines." These are programs that take the place of the trusty reference librarian who takes your request for information, then walks back to the stacks, and retrieves just the volume you need. Type in a "keyword" into one of these search engines, and the program will retrieve what it "thinks" is the relevant information.

Let's discuss some specific browser and search engine features.

[The speaker discusses common browser and search engine features.]

While a good browser and a set of search engines are indispensable aids to uncovering the information you want, they are double-edged swords. The faithful reference librarian rarely returns with a single book, but comes to you laden with "other things you might want to read, too." Similarly, browsers and search engines usually yield a number of sources. Indeed, "browser" is an especially appropriate term for the software, because the Web is a *digressive* medium. It turns up fascinating tangents and exotic byways—even when you are trying to do very finite, hard-core, specific research.

Now this isn't all bad. The digressive nature of the Web can turn up information you didn't even know you needed, and if you are doing preliminary research on a subject—if you're at the "fuzzy front end" of a project—the digressions can really trigger new ideas and new directions. In fact, in a perfect world, digression would be the ideal, because there would be no such thing as wasting time. No knowledge

→ Tip: The speaker explains an array of Internet tools.

would ever be wasted. Then again, in a *perfect* world, none of us would have to earn a living. So we're stuck with finding more efficient ways to use our time on the Web. Here are some suggestions:

First, create bookmarks. The browser software will let you do this easily—to mark sites you encounter that are interesting and to which you would like to return at a future time. If you don't create the bookmark *now,* you may never find the site again.

Second: Rigorously separate your business from your educational or entertainment use of the Web.

Third: Know where you *think* you want to go. Discipline yourself to head for the information you need—when you really do need that information. When you are doing fuzzier research, well, then it is best to give yourself over to the digressive nature of this medium, at least to some extent, and let it take you where it will. To borrow Microsoft's oft-repeated ad line, the question you have to ask, each time you use the Web, is where do you want to go today? If your work calls for you to reach a specific destination by a certain time, use discipline and cut through the extras that the medium dishes up. If your work on this day calls for the generation of preliminary ideas, let the medium carry you.

Happy hunting.

> ➜ Tip: Remember, you don't always have to come down on one side or the other of an issue. Your conclusions may be a matter of degree.

OUTLINE

Opening

- "Universal experiences"
- One universal experience: browsing the dictionary or encyclopedia
- Universal impulse to browse
- Surfing the Net
- Problem: how to use the Internet to get *specific* work done

What is the Internet?

- Begin by what it is not
- Not a place
- Not a supervised system
- Electronic network of loosely linked computers
- Lack of supervision is a plus and a minus

Using the Internet has become easier

- World Wide Web = most important advance
- Web browsers also an advance
- How a browser functions as a tool
- Search engines: what they do
- Specific browsers and search engines

Browsers and search engines have an upside and downside

- Yield a number of sources
- Makes the Web especially digressive
- Leads to exotic byways—even when you are searching for specific information
- Need more efficient ways of searching the Web
- Suggestions

Conclusion

- Decide where you want to go before logging on to the Internet
- Exercise discipline if you need specific information
- Let the medium carry you if you are looking for general ideas or inspiration

MODEL SPEECH 150:
Machines Replacing Humans

Key Use of Speech: A brief speech on a familiar topic.

Style of Speech: Authoritative and reassuring.

Audience: High school job fair attendees.

Time: 6 to 7 minutes.

When I was your age, and, for that matter, when my parents were your age, TV, radio, and the press were full of dire discussions about how computers and robots were going to throw millions of people out of work. The job market, we were told, would shrink, shrivel, and disappear.

Today, unemployment is at a **[number]**-year low. In many regions, including here in **[location]**, companies are *hunting* for qualified people to staff thousands of positions.

What went wrong with all those predictions?

To begin with, in their preoccupation with the future, pundits sometimes overlook the lessons of history. This is what history teaches: With each advance in technology, a certain number of jobs were lost, but far more were created. For example . . . **[the speaker gives an example].**

Technology creates more jobs than it eliminates.

This is not mere hopeful propaganda. It's a fact of life. If it were *not* true, there would be no such thing as technological progress.

Think about it a moment.

If technology eliminated jobs, it would also eliminate consumers, because you need a job to get the money to be a consumer. Without consumers, there would be no need for technology, because there would be no market for the things technology produces. The fact is

→ Tip: The "what happened?" or "what went wrong?" approach can be a very effective way of driving your speech.

→ Tip: Contrary to what many may believe, the force of logic is very powerful in a speech— often as powerful as the force of feeling and emotion.

that technology creates new jobs, creates new markets, and creates new consumers.

Let's look at personal computers, for example.

➜ Tip: Avoid abstraction wherever possible. Make your main points with specific examples.

Pundits predicted that desktop computers would wipe out the position of secretary—eliminate a whole class of office workers. Well, if by *secretary* you mean *typist,* the prediction is pretty accurate. But if by *secretary* you mean *executive assistant,* personal computers have helped to *create* a whole class of jobs, promoting mere typists to far more challenging roles. Not only was a new class of job created—or expanded—but it is a *better* job, a job with higher pay, far more challenge, far less tedium, and far more opportunity for advancement, for growth.

Of course, personal computers also created many more jobs in addition to upgrading secretaries to executive assistants. Jobs directly supporting computers and computer use, for example, are legion.

➜ Tip: The speaker reveals that the job benefits of technology also entail demands for education.

Technology opens rather than closes doors. There is a catch, however. Technology does not wrap up a new job and deliver it to your doorstep. Instead, technology creates new opportunities for *learning* a job. That is, while technology creates new jobs, it also creates new knowledge vacuums that require filling.

I dare say that, shortly after Henry Ford introduced his Model T in 1908, the number of automotive engineers surpassed the number of buggy-whip designers. After a time, many buggy-whip designers were out of work, while many empty positions for automotive engineers went begging. Those buggy-whip designers who could reeducate themselves for the new industry found new jobs—and much better and more exciting jobs than they had before.

Technology does not cost jobs, but it does create obsolescence of skills even as it creates demand for new skills.

How do we keep ahead of this curve? After all, how many buggy-whip designers could afford the time and money necessary to reeducate themselves as automotive engineers?

The answer is to learn all you can *now.* Learn *how* to learn. Acquire a load of skills that are not related to any particular job, but may be applied to any number of jobs. Acquire portable, *transferable* skills— skills that belong to you, not to your position. This is the best preparation for the new, very rich, but very challenging technological job market.

EXAMPLE SPEECH

Taming the Technological Monster

Speaker: Dominic Tarantino,
Former Chairman, Price Waterhouse World Firm

I'd like to introduce you to a five-year-old girl named Megan. Megan was scared of a monster that lived under her bed. That's not unusual. Most five-year-olds have a monster lurking somewhere. What's unusual is what Megan did about hers. She used her computer and a software package for children her age to create a story about how she got rid of the monster. She sent it to live under her brother's bed. Megan even drew pictures to illustrate her story. Then she sent it over the Internet to an electronic bulletin board for pre-school age children. Her story was picked up by a CD-ROM multimedia magazine. That's where two gentlemen named Stan Davis and Jim Botkin saw it. It was their inspiration for a book on the interaction between technology, business and education entitled, you guessed it, The Monster Under the Bed.

Unlike Megan, we can't send technology anywhere. For good or ill, it's here to stay. Our challenge is to keep it from turning into the monster under all our beds. No one is better equipped than Jesuit business schools to lead in meeting that challenge. And I know of no better set of guidelines to follow than the Caux Round Table's Principles for Business. These principles are a truly global effort that unites respect for human dignity with the Japanese concept of kyosei, living and working together for the common good. And they go beyond merely not doing wrong to encompass doing right and doing good.

When uncontrolled and misused, technology poses serious ethical threats. But technology is also a powerful ethical tool. It can prevent wrong. It can do right. It can do good. Let's use Megan to explore some of technology's threats and some of its possibilities. Then I'll offer my thoughts on how you and your colleagues can help technology reach its full ethical potential. Obviously, my suggestions will barely scratch the surface. I'm hoping they'll act as a catalyst for your ideas.

Megan has yet to attend school. She doesn't know how to write, at least not in the traditional sense. But she knows how to use a computer. As a result of that knowledge, her monster story circled the globe, reached an audience of millions, and ended up

Source: Dominic Tarantino, former Chairman, Price Waterhouse World Firm. Presented to the Fourth World Forum—Internaional Association of Jesuit Business Schools, Loyola Marymount University, on July 28, 1996. Reprinted by permission of Dominic Tarantino and *Vital Speeches of the Day.*

immortalized in print. That's a lot of power in the hands of someone so young. And it raises unsettling questions. Technologically, Megan is a grown-up. Ethically, she's still five years old.

On the positive side, technology has given Megan access to a rich array of educational and cultural resources. On the negative side, it has given some very potent ethical threats access to Megan. More important, the constant presence of technology in Megan's life will shape her ethical development in ways we can't fully comprehend.

The debate is raging over who will shield the Megans of the world from the most blatant threats roaming the Internet. These include pornography, violent or frightening material, and various types of predators. At one extreme in the debate are those who believe government must act in loco parentis. This view recently produced the Communications Decency Act. The Act, however, has been ruled unconstitutional in federal district court. And like any purely national approach, it is probably impossible to enforce. At the other extreme are the "Netizens." They view the Internet as the last frontier of pure freedom, and they want government to stay out. Their solution is "Netiquette," a loose fabric of implicit rules and informal agreements. Netiquette is an appealing concept. But it is effective only for those who willingly obey rules and have nothing to hide.

Between the two extremes, I believe there are very sound reasons why business should and will become chief regulator on the Net. Business is the primary creator, producer and distributor of technology. It has a responsibility to control what it has created. The Net is global. Business is global. Governments are constrained by their boundaries, by their own agendas and by other countries' resistance.

While the Net originated in the public sector, it is rapidly becoming a commercial entity.

The Net's commercial potential is enormous. But commerce can be conducted only in an orderly and secure environment. That requires rules. It is very much in business's interest to create those rules. But in doing so, business must be guided by sound ethical principals that ensure adequate protection of all stakeholders. As one example, there is the privacy issue. There is a mind-boggling amount of information about individuals sitting in databases all over the world. Its commercial possibilities are equally mind-boggling. But so are the risks of abuse. A line must be drawn between legitimate business use and invasion of privacy. In resolving this and other difficult issues, I believe the Caux Principle of respect for human dignity is very much on point. The third principle is also applicable. It talks of going beyond the letter of the law to foster a spirit of trust.

Models for the business regulation of cyberspace are beginning to emerge. One idea that's being explored is the development of "on-line communities." These communities would be composed of companies or service providers in similar lines of business. Or they could be entities that act as gateways to other communities. The forerunners already exist, Compuserve, Prodigy, America on Line, and Motley Fool. But they don't even begin to tap the potential of this approach. Members of on-line communities would have to abide by certain rules in exchange for receiving certain privileges. Those privileges could include copyright and trademark protection, access to customer databases, marketing support, and security for data transmissions or commercial transactions. Communities could serve businesses, individuals, or groups of individuals. Single communities could band together in networks. At some point, joining a community might be the only way to do business on the Net. And individuals might be able to access the Net only through a community, even for something as simple as sending e-mail. Both members and users of communities would have identifiers that are far more secure than today's passwords. Lack of anonymity would shut out many who want to use the Net for unwholesome or dishonest purposes.

This network of specialized communities has been compared to the medieval guilds. The guilds created order out of the chaos of the Dark Ages. On-line communities would help create order out of the chaos of cyberspace. And the catalyst in both cases? Business. I'm sure this audience would be quick to remind me that the other major source of order in the Dark Ages was the Church. In the IAJBS and the institutions you represent, we have the fusion of these two influential forces. And your influence is going to be more important than ever. Let's return to Megan to see why.

Internet communities can help protect Megan from the most obvious challenges to her ethical development. But other challenges will defy easy solution. One of these is the ability of technology to redefine distance. In this case, I mean emotional, social and psychological distance. Technology has made it possible for Megan to interact with countless individuals, groups of individuals, public institutions, and business institutions anywhere in the world. They are as close as her computer screen. At the same time, they are nothing more than blips on that screen. This has a depersonalizing and dehumanizing effect. The real becomes unreal.

It is far easier to rob, exploit, cheat and otherwise abuse those who do not seem real, and when personal confrontation is not a risk. To quote one observer, "You never have to face someone with a gun as you would if you were stealing from a Seven-Eleven." And courtesy of technology, a thief and victim thousands of miles apart can be as close as the thief and victim in the Seven-Eleven. We don't have to guess about the results of this phenomenon. They are all around us. Technological theft. Technological espionage. Technological fraud. Viruses. Hackers.

I'm not suggesting that Megan is about to start raiding brokerage accounts, yet. But her generation is being exposed to technology almost from the cradle. This exposure could create a very different ethical "mind-set." We're all familiar with the saying, "Power corrupts. Absolute power corrupts absolutely." Technology is close to absolute power. If the problems it's creating are serious now, how much more serious will they become as Megan's generation grows up?

One possible solution to this problem is the cause itself—Technology. Technology is a powerful educational tool. It should be used to the fullest extent for ethical education. The so-called "edutainment" industry is thriving because it disguises learning as entertainment. Technology can be used to make ethics come alive for children Megan's age and up through high school. The possibilities include multimedia presentations, games, and interactive quizzes. And while we're at it, why use technology only in a defensive manner, to prevent wrong doing? Why not use it to promote the positive value embodied in the Caux Principles, knowledge of and respect for other cultures, and a sense of responsibility for the well-being of people half a world away?

That kind of positive ethical education can help meet another challenge created by technology. Technology's power to redefine ethical distance is not confined to individuals. It also applies to corporations, countries and cultures. We're quickly reaching the point where technology really will permit the development of virtual corporations. A company may physically be located in one country. But it will be able to carry out many of its functions in distant locations via telephone and computer screen. To quote *The Economist,* "Services as diverse as designing an engine, monitoring a security camera, selling insurance or running a secretarial paging service will become as easily exportable as car parts or refrigerators." This is already happening. For example, the back office functions of Swissair and British Airways are now located in India. Heating, lighting, elevators and security operations in office buildings in Pacific Rim countries are monitored from Perth, Australia.

Virtuality by wire has some significant advantages. Companies can expand globally without expensive fixed investments, without relocating people, and without the other risks, costs and headaches of establishing foreign facilities. Workers in countries on the receiving end may have far better jobs and higher incomes than they ever thought possible, and there will be positive ripple effects on the local economies.

But the flip side of economic expansion by wire is economic exploitation by wire.

Companies will have no physical presence in communities where they exert enormous influence. They can implement decisions in the blink of an eye, without understanding the full impact, and without having to face the consequences. We could see the technological equivalent of plant openings and closings. One day there are lots of new jobs, and a booming economy. A long distance dependency relationship is created. Then suddenly the "plant" closes, leaving an economic black hole.

Companies that expand by wire must make a special effort to ensure that "out of sight" does not become "out of mind." The Caux Principles call on companies to be good citizens in all communities in which they operate. Nothing is said about physical location.

There's another way in which technology is redefining distance, and it may represent the greatest challenge of all. This is the economic and social distance that technology is creating between "haves" and "have nots" on both a national and global scale. We are even facing this dilemma in the United States, where lately we've been congratulating ourselves on recapturing global economic leadership.

Let's return to Megan. Megan is a "have." Her early access to technology has already created a wide gap between her and children who lack that access. Children below the poverty line are not the only ones ending up on the wrong side of the gap. All children from families who either cannot afford technology or choose not to afford it are vulnerable. Parents who believe their children will get sufficient exposure to technology in school are wrong. U.S. public schools are woefully behind both in teaching techno-logical skills and in using technology as an educational tool. By the time Megan graduates from high school, the gap between her and classmates who lack her advantages could be unbridgeable. This, unfortunately, includes the one-quarter of her classmates who won't be able to read their diplomas. Technology-based teaching methods might have helped such students, or given teachers extra time to devote to them. It didn't happen. It's not happening.

The have/have not problem isn't confined to new and future members of the work force. People currently in the work force who lack technological skills and the means to acquire them are being forced into low-paying jobs no one else wants. Even those who have technological skills can't afford to be complacent. They could become obsolete at any time. Lifelong learning is no longer nice-to-have. It's essential.

Business has recognized the problems and is trying to solve them. Many companies are involved in developing and funding technology programs in public schools. Business commitments to remedial education, retraining programs, and lifelong training are massive and growing. The authors of The Monster Under the Bed suggest that these initiatives and the private consumption of technology-based education are making business the country's primary educator. Is that far-fetched? Ask yourselves this. Will Megan be any less competitive in the job market if she never goes to public school? Of course, the public schools are supposed to do more than prepare people for gainful employment. They have a social role as well. Many critics say they're not meeting that responsibility either. In fact, business devotes more time and resources to value educa-tion than the public schools do.

Botkin and Davis believe business will have to consciously assume the educational role it has acquired by default. It will have to forge a working partnership with the public schools, define a division of responsibility, and give the public schools the technology they need to meet their obligations. This is a tall order, but Botkin and Davis warn that the alternative is "a third world country within our country."

Technology can create "have" and "have not" classes in a single country. And it can create "have" and "have not" countries. The world is on the threshold of developing a global telecommunications network. Countries that are not part of this network will be so shut out of the global economy that they might as well be on another planet. They will be cut off from the world wide web of information, education and business resources that others can access by tapping a few keys. These countries will not be able to attract businesses that need to access that web. They won't be able to create a world class work force. Their own businesses won't have a prayer of competing in world markets.

It's been estimated that the "worldwide" telecommunications network could actually bypass half the world. The least likely candidates for being wired to the network are developing countries who could benefit the most from the connection. Many of these countries offer the least potential for immediate economic return in comparison to high costs and huge practical and technical headaches. Most lack solid "ethical infrastructures," by this, I mean the rule of law, coherent and transparent regulatory frameworks, and acceptable standards of public accountability and corporate governance. Much of Africa, for example, falls into this category. Africa has been called the lost continent of telecommunications. African countries have two percent of the world's telephones. Their telecommunications operations are heavily state controlled, poorly managed, and riddled with corruption.

I urge the companies and consortia developing the global communications network to take a longer term economic view, as well as an ethical view. Many developing countries have valuable resources waiting to be tapped. That includes their people resources. And is it ethical to deprive these people of the benefits of technology because they were born inside the wrong set of borders? Why not go to developing countries and offer a quid pro quo? Access to the global telecommunications infrastructure in return for developing an ethical infrastructure, as well as assistance in developing that infrastructure?

A world that is 50 percent "have" and 50 percent "have not" is unacceptable, economically, socially, politically and ethically. Giving every country the power to communicate is part of the fabric of Principle Two of the Caux General Principles. It declares that businesses have a responsibility to contribute to the economic and social development, not only of the communities where they operate, but of the global community.

Some emerging nations are more fortunate than many in Africa. Their economic potential is so great and their market so huge that business and technology are rushing in with a vengeance. But they are also rushing in with little regard for the condition of the ethical infrastructure. The Republic of China is probably the best example. There, a modern market economy is being grafted onto an authoritarian society in which the rule of law and respect for human rights have a ways to go, to put it charitably. To me, this is analogous to placing the unbridled power of technology in the hands of a five-year-old, with no thought of the ethical implications.

Some suggest that trying to make China accept Western social and political ideals is cultural imperialism at its worst. I would argue that the market economy and the legal and cultural environment in which it developed are not severable.

A market economy cannot thrive without the order and certainty provided by rule of law. It is impossible for businesses to operate effectively and efficiently when they must contend with a tangle of corrupt bureaucracies and conflicting and illogical rules. Direct and portfolio investment may initially be attracted to China because of the economic potential, but the flow will likely dry up in the absence of stability, transparency and accountability. Protection of both tangible and intellectual property is not an issue only for foreign companies doing business with China. The domestic entrepreneurship and creativity that must ultimately fuel the Chinese economy cannot flourish if the results are inadequately protected. An economy that depends on individual initiative and energy and a sense of security will stagnate in an environment where encroachments on human rights and freedom are sudden and arbitrary. If the Chinese want a vigorous, self-sustaining market economy, they need an ethical infrastructure. It might be uniquely Chinese in certain respects, but there must be one.

That's the practical argument for developing an ethical infrastructure in China. Here's an ethical argument. Let me read you an amazing statement from an article I encountered. To quote: "The United States condemns China for the Tiananmen Square massacre and crackdowns on dissidents without recognizing that the Chinese have never shared Western views of democracy and individual rights." Am I missing something? If at least some Chinese don't believe in individual rights, who were those protestors in Tiananmen Square? And why are there dissidents to crack down on? Respect for the dignity and rights of the individual are basic to the human condition, whatever the culture.

Culture and the ideals and attitudes it generates are not immutable. They respond to changes in the environment. The Chinese environment is definitely changing. Privatization is proceeding at a fairly rapid pace. Certain elements of an ethical infrastructure are being developed. Commercial accounting and financial reporting standards are emerging. This seems like a purely technical achievement, but it's far more than that. It's a leap from secrecy to transparency.

China is being changed by technology and the outside contacts and communication technology makes possible. It is being changed by the presence of Western companies and their expatriate employees, and by the training programs these companies offer. It is being changed by the introduction of relative affluence and exposure to Western products. When McDonalds can attract record crowds in the middle of Beijing, can other Western influences be far behind? I say that only partly tongue-in-cheek.

Should Western companies in China actively work for the development of an ethical infrastructure? Absolutely. I realize this is a difficult proposition in an authoritarian state that cherishes its cultural heritage. But I am not proposing confrontation or preaching. I am suggesting dialogue, education, and leading by example, in line with the Caux Round Table's emphasis on kyosei, and on identifying shared values and reconciling differing values. Western companies that conduct training programs could develop modules on business ethics, from both the Western perspective and the Chinese perspective. Ethics programs could include discussions of human rights. I realize this is a modest beginning. But the Chinese themselves are fond of saying that a long journey begins with a single step. And it was not long ago that any type of change in China was beyond imagination.

In line with these comments, I was delighted to hear that a group of the Jesuit business schools are involved in establishing an MBA program in Beijing. This program could become a prototype in combining ethical education with business education. And it could also become an instrument of ethical outreach. It could act as catalyst for ethical activism by the expatriate business community, and for a dialogue between government and business on ethics and human rights issues.

That brings me to my more general comments on the role of Jesuit business schools and all business schools in defining and confronting the ethical challenges of technology and globalization.

I firmly believe that nothing less is called for than the complete integration of ethics into MBA courses and programs. Business ethics should not be crammed into a single course that may be an elective. It should not be on the periphery of MBA programs. It should be at the core. At the very least, the very least, I would argue strongly for a mandatory, special module on the ethical implications of technology. At a minimum, it would address all the challenges I've talked about today. The Caux Principles might serve as the framework for the module. I urge your organization and its member schools to consider developing such a module, in cooperation with high technology companies.

The globalization of the MBA is making the full integration of ethics, technology and business education even more necessary. More and more foreign students are enrolling in American business schools. Business schools are developing foreign programs, just as your organization hopes to do in Beijing. Some business schools are experimenting with "virtual MBA" programs. They are beaming business courses all over the world. Your organization could be a leader in ensuring that ethics education and ethics outreach are not left behind when MBA programs go abroad. The program in Beijing could be a model in this respect.

Let me briefly suggest three other initiatives your organization might pursue or encourage. First, research on the effects of technology on ethical development. Second, the development of technology-based ethics education for school-age children. And finally, I've mentioned two solutions to the have/have not dilemma, expanding the educational role of business, and trade-offs between ethical infrastructures and telecommunications infrastructures. These ambitious approaches clearly need a lot of spade-work, not to mention a lot of missionary work.

You may find these suggestions and others I've made radical, or even unrealistic. But technology is making the radical commonplace and the unrealistic real. And we haven't seen anything yet. When a five-year-old girl can get rid of the monster under her bed by launching it into cyberspace, we've entered a realm that used to be reserved for science fiction.

Training Employees

Openings

——*On behalf of the entire XYZ Corporation team, welcome to our new colleagues. This is the first of three orientation programs you will, I hope, find interesting and useful. We put the single most important subject first: ethics.*

——*Welcome to our Computer Training Seminar. Let's face facts. Many of you don't want to be here. You are afraid that the material presented will be too technical, that it will be over your head, that you'll never master it. I understand your feelings, but let me assure you, we will see you through to the successful completion of this program.*

Closings

——*Thank you for your attention today. I look forward to seeing you tomorrow for the second talk in the orientation series. The subject then will be Employee Benefits.*

——*This concludes the first session in the seminar. As you can see, we have all come through this first hour uninjured. I trust that fact gives you the necessary confidence to face tomorrow's session, which will deal with word processing.*

MODEL SPEECH 151:
Corporate Ethics

Key Use of Speech:	An orientation speech about a company's policy concerning ethics.
Style of Speech:	Authoritative and informative.
Audience:	New employees.
Time:	10 to 12 minutes.

→ Tip: The opening of the speech is the ideal place to define the importance and the scope of your topic.

Some of our most important corporate policies concern ethics. Far too many businesses find their way into the news for the wrong reasons: in stories about unethical behavior rather than new technology or record earnings.

What is unethical behavior?

It ranges from executive extravagance at the expense of shareholders, to insider trading, to industrial espionage, to overcharges kickbacks, to illegal disposal of toxic waste, to bad warranties, to making hollow promises to customers just to make a sale.

Why do we have policies and procedures governing ethics? Isn't it sufficient just to be honest?

→ Tip: The problem with most corporate policies is that they are presented arbitrarily, without explanation. If you explain the rationale behind policy, you are more likely to secure cooperation and compliance.

Honesty—personal honesty—is a good place to start. But the issues we deal with are often more complex than matters of simple honesty. Our policies are intended as guidelines. We have formulated them not just because we believe in conducting an honorable business of which we can all be proud, and not just because we believe we should treat others as we would like to be treated, but also because of our bottom line. It has been our experience at XYZ Corporation that unethical behavior corrupts and erodes the entire organization. Sure, there may be some isolated, short-term gain in cheating here or there, but the price, ultimately, is destructive demoralization. Given enough time— and it doesn't take very long—shoddy ethics are reflected in a shoddy bottom line.

→ Tip: Remain grounded in reality. Demonstrate the importance of ideals to maintaining a healthy business.

So there are two principal reasons for our company's concern with ethics: A basic moral code that we value and subscribe to, and a common-sense law of business that stresses credibility with our customers in order to create long-term profitability.

In your *Employee Manual,* on pages **[numbers],** you will find a guide to ethical business. Please let me highlight some of the key areas where we have concerns:

[The speaker highlights some areas.]

Our ethical policies are specific and stringent. They are intended to combat the kind of fuzzy thinking and hedging of bets that are all too typical where so-called corporate ethics are concerned. Many managers tell their staffs to "Do whatever you have to; just don't tell me about it." Here at XYZ, we don't practice management by "plausible deniability." We keep our heads out of the sand here, and we ask that you make those individual decisions that involve ethical matters based on the company's guidelines. If you find yourself in a situation that you feel uncomfortable with, ask about it. Seek advice. Go to your supervisor. Don't keep quiet. What we don't know *will* hurt us, if not now, then sooner or later.

→ Tip: Provide guidelines for action—not just ideals.

Andrew Jackson said, "One man with courage is a majority." Be that majority. Here at XYZ Corporation, we're committed to making sure the ethical decision becomes *the* majority position. That's what the ethical guidelines in this *Employee Manual* are all about—not just to *dictate* policy, but to support your common-sense honor and decency and sound judgment.

→ Tip: The speaker strives for a balance between individual and collective ethics.

Please remember that policy in and of itself is meaningless. *You,* as our agents and operatives and representatives, write the final line to every piece of business we do. *You* are this company's signature. For our customers, *you* are XYZ Corporation. Policy means nothing if you, our front-line representatives, make the wrong decisions, take the easy way out, go for the short-term, ethically bankrupt easy fix. Ours are not one-shot ethics. We're here for the long haul, and we need your help.

Do you want to be in step with the organization? Then value integrity. Infuse integrity into all of your professional decisions.

Rules are not to be broken and not be bent. Instead, embrace them. As Mark Twain said, "Always do right. This will gratify some people and astonish the rest." Here at XYZ Corporation, we're pleased with either result.

MODEL SPEECH 152:
Introduction to Technical Training Program

Key Use of Speech:	An orientation speech introducing a training program.
Style of Speech:	Friendly, confidence-building.
Audience:	Company employees.
Time:	8 to 10 minutes.

→ Tip: Make your audience feel welcome.

Welcome to the first day of a **[number]**-day seminar designed to give you all the technical background you need to sell and help your customers effectively use our fine line of widgets.

→ Tip: Address the feelings of your audience. Do what you can to reduce apprehension and anxiety.

I know that many of you are nervous—a bit apprehensive—because you are salespeople and customer service professionals, not technicians. We understand that, and, believe me, this seminar makes no assumptions of technical expertise. We'll give you what you need, and I am confident not only that all of you *can* handle this material but also that you will find it interesting and exciting. Certainly, technical knowledge about our product line will help you sell that line and will make it possible for you to ensure the creation of customer satisfaction.

→ Tip: Paint the big picture. Show how attending the seminar will benefit the company.

Modern market-driven economies are becoming ever more technically complex. Sales and Customer Service are taking on increasing levels of responsibility for educating consumers. This not only benefits the customer, it is also essential to the long-term welfare of our company. Helping the customer to use our products more effectively leads to higher levels of customer satisfaction and future sales. Failure to instruct him invites disastrous customer reactions, leading to long-term customer dissatisfaction and negative word-of-mouth advertis-

553

ing. Growth in applied technical knowledge in the world economy is nothing short of phenomenal, and the teaching role of Sales and Customer Service is becoming more critical.

As Sales and Customer Service professionals, you will be asked to apply technical training expertise any time you need to get your customers to:

> → Tip: Motivate your audience by showing them how the seminar will enable them to do their jobs more effectively.

- Know something intellectually or conceptually they did not know before. Years of practical field observations have convinced us that most customer contact calls do not concern problems or malfunctions, but are simply requests for knowledge of some sort.
- Do something that couldn't be done before, such as operate a device, implement a procedure or install a system.
- Use a different combination of existing skills, knowledge, and concepts to form a more productive new behavior.
- Rearrange what they currently know about some thing or idea to develop a new understanding of that thing or idea. This is what it means to be a *consultative* salesperson

> → Tip: Give the audience credit for their skills and knowledge. Make them feel that they bring valuable assets to the table.

This seminar will equip you with the technical knowledge you need to help your customers in the ways I've just outlined. However, just because a person knows all about a product, procedure, or system, he is not necessarily qualified to teach others what he knows. Training skills are different from technical skills. Fortunately, as Sales and Customer Service professionals, you have already demonstrated communication, presentation, and sensitivity skills, which are all vital for effective trainers. The seminar will help you hone these skills—but they are skills you already possess and we all highly value.

Similarly, your ability to deliver messages convincingly is very important in customer education. That education is complete and successful when the customer has understood the message, not merely when we have sent the message. Persuasion—selling—is a big part of the customer education job, even as customer education is a big part of selling. Once again, you folks bring selling skills to the table. The seminar will address these, but we'll certainly be building on skills and knowledge you already possess.

> → Tip: Define the limits of the training.

There is one thing this seminar cannot give you: patient persistence. Customer education can be hard work because most people just don't get it when first told. Multiple deliveries using varying approaches, repetition, and reinforcement are all necessary for learning to occur. And that takes patient persistence.

Ladies and gentlemen, I began this talk by acknowledging that many of you may be nervous about the seminar. This may be an unpleasant feeling, but it is a useful one. Remember how you feel right now, because this memory will help you to empathize with your customers. Confronted by technically sophisticated equipment, many of them actually fear the product or, at least, lack confidence that they can use the product effectively. Fear and lack of confidence inhibit the customer's ability to use and, importantly, to receive maximum value from the product. In this seminar, we will learn not only to overcome our own fear of technology, but how to help the customer overcome his fears as well.

Thank you for your commitment to your profession and to our customers. Now, let's begin the first day of the seminar.

OUTLINE

Opening

- Welcome

We know that many of you are apprehensive about the training program

- We understand
- We make no assumptions about your technical expertise
- Program will prepare you
- Program will help you perform even better than you already do
- Training essential to long-term welfare of the company

Situations requiring technical training expertise

- To educate customers
- To train them to use our products
- To show them new approaches to old problems
- To consult usefully with customers

Seminar will equip you with the technical knowledge you need

- You already have many skills
- You have communication skills
- You have selling skills
- These skills give you a great advantage
- Seminar will help you hone these skills and apply them

Seminar cannot teach you patience

- You need to be patient in dealing with customers about technical matters
- Patient persistence required
- Repetition required

Closing

- Just as you may be apprehensive now, customer may be apprehensive about product
- Needs to overcome anxiety to receive maximum benefit from product
- Your job is to help
- Thank you for your commitment to this task

Index

Achievement
  civic award, 47–49
  employee award, 52–53
Action, calls to, 265–72
Affirmative action/EEO policy, 351–52
Agenda presentation, 75–76
Anecdotes, 70–71, 82, 214, 229, 298, 334, 347
Anniversaries
  before and after approach to, 86
  of building, 89–90
  of company, 81–83
  of employment, 86–88
Announcement/explanation, 2–42
  of crisis/emergency, 33–40
  of customer/client loss, 25–26
  of departure, employee, 14–16
  of downsizing decision, 17–20
  of health plan change, 5–8
  of merger and acquisition, 27–28
  of outsourcing decision, 12–13
  of plant/facility construction, 31–32
  of relocation, 3–4
  of reorganization, 41–42
  of retirement benefit change, 9–11
  of sales campaign, 21–24
Arguments
  anticipating, 6, 110, 168
  concession to opposing, 7
Associations
  business, 393–96
  civic, 397–400
  See also Trade associations
Award presentation
  for civic achievement, 47–48
  for employee achievement, 52–53

Benediction, farewell, 129
Bennis, Warren, 141–45
Birthday, employee/colleague, 84–85
Browning, Robert, 61

Celebrations, 66–72
  of citizenship (naturalization), 67–68
  of engagement/wedding, 69–70
  opening of new facility, 71–72, 121–23
  See also Holiday celebrations

Chairperson, 74–78
  agenda presentation, 75–76
  introduction of distinguished guest, 78
  introduction of speaker, 77
Challenges, meeting, 273–74
Chambers of commerce, 393–96
Chanukah, 232
Charitable gifts/donations
  corporate, 96–104, 121–23
  solicitation of employee, 457–62
Christmas, 232
Christopher, Warren, 134–38
Citizenship celebration, 67–68
Civic associations, 397–400
Civic awards, 47–48
Clichés, 63, 96
Client. *See* Customer
Clinton, William J., 134–36
Closings
  announcement, 2, 8, 11, 16, 20, 24
  celebrations, 66, 70
  chairpersons', 74, 76
  commemorations, 80, 83, 88, 95, 100, 104
  competitiveness, 109, 112, 115, 118
  congratulations, 44, 49, 56, 62
  corporate history, 212, 216
  corporate goals, 166, 173, 176
  dedications, 120, 123
  farewells, 128
  financial reports, 148, 153, 156
  funeral eulogy, 158
  gifts, 162
  government regulation, 178, 185, 192
  graduation, 196, 200
  holiday celebrations, 222, 230
  informal events, 234
  introductions, 238
  legislative testimony, 244, 248, 252
  media, 254
  motivating, 264, 268, 290, 294, 322, 327, 331, 337
  policies, 350, 360, 369, 381
  political affairs, 386
  public relations, 392, 396, 400, 404, 411, 415
  sales and marketing, 426, 430, 434, 444, 450, 454
  solicitations, 456, 462
  strategies, 464, 474, 482, 487, 493

Closings
   technology, 498, 515, 520, 524, 537
   training, 550, 556
Collaboration, motivating employee, 283–85
Commemorations, 80–106
   anniversary of company, 81–83, 91–92
   anniversary of employment, 86–88
   birthday of employee/colleague, 84–85
   history of building, 89–90
   scholarship endowment, 96–104
   of tragic events, 93–95, 105–06
Commencement address, high school, 197–200
Commitment, motivating employee, 286–90
Communications technology, 499–501
Company. *See* Corporate; Corporate history
Competitiveness program, 109–18
   domestic, 109–12
   foreign, 113–15
   new product, 116–18
Computer technology, 502–11
Congratulations, 44–64
   civic achievement award, 47–49
   employee academic achievement, 45–46
   employee suggestions, 50–51, 63–64
   employee work performance, 52–56
   on goal attainment, 57–62
Cooperation, motivating employee, 283–85
Corporate
   anniversaries, 81–83, 89–92
   awards, presenting, 47–48, 52–53
   change in benefits, 5–11
   downsizing, 17–20, 465–66
   ethics, 310–12, 551–52
   gifts, 96–104, 121–23
   goals, 166–76
   growth, 167–69, 372–73, 469–70
   image, 338–339, 451–454
   mergers and acquisitions, 27–28, 473–74
   mission, 332
   relocation, 3–4, 130–31
   reorganization, 41–42
   See also Employee; Manager;
      Plant/facility; Policies; Sales
      and marketing; Strategies
Corporate history, 212–19
   of building, 89–90
   of employee relations, 217–19
   of founding, 91–92, 213–14
   of products and services, 213–16
Cost-saving suggestion, 50–51
Creativity, motivating employee, 319–22
Crisis management, 33–40

Customer
   acquisition of, 29–30
   loss of, 25–26
   service, 54–56, 291–94, 431–34, 447–50
   trade association, 405–07

Death, memorialization of, 93–95, 105–06
Deavenport, Earnest W., Jr., 361–65
Decision making
   company strategy, 467–68
   motivating employee, 295–97
Dedications, 120–25
   of corporate-donated facility, 121–23
   of memorial, 124–25
Definition of terms, 5, 201, 286
Desktop publishing, 512–15
De Vink, Lodewijk, J.R., 275–82
Downsizing, 17–20, 465–66

Eaton, Robert J., 416–23
Education
   employee development, 45–46, 300–02, 353–54
   graduation, 196–209
   new facility dedication, 121–23
   scholarship endowment, 96–104
   See also Training program
Employee
   anniversary of employment, 86–88
   birthday of, 84–85
   citizenship celebration for, 67–68
   contracts, 374–75
   development, 45–46, 300–02, 353–54
   empowerment, 355–56
   engagement/wedding of, 69–70
   farewells from, 129, 137–38
   farewells to, 14–16, 132–36
   gift presentation to, 164
   history of relations, 217–19
   introduction of new, 239–40
   performance recognition, 52–56
   promotion, 378–82
   solicitations from, 456–62
   suggestions by, 50–51, 63–64
   See also Motivating employees; Training program
Empowerment program, 355–56
Endowment, scholarship, 96–104
Engagement celebration, 69–70
Environment
   company policy on, 357–65
   government regulations on, 182–85
Ethics, corporate, 310–12, 551–52
Eulogy, funeral, 158–60

Excellence, motivating employee, 313–14
Explanation. *See* Announcement/explanation

Facility. *See* Plant/facility
Farewells, 128–45
    from employee, 129, 137–38
    to employee, 14–16, 132–36
    to nonmoving employees, 130–31
    from retiree, 139–45
Figures of speech, 318
Financial reports, 148–56
    to executives/management, 149–50
    to financial analysts, 151–53
    on outsourcing decision, 12–13
    to stockholders, 154–56
Fourth of July, 226–27
Free speech policy, 370–71
Funeral eulogy, 158–60

Gifts, 162–64
    presentation to employee, 164
    thank you from manager, 163
    See also Charitable gifts/donations
Goals
    congratulations on attainment, 57–62
    motivating employee, 315–18
Goals, corporate, 166–76
    growth, 167–69
    quality, 174–76, 340–41
    during recession, 170–73
Government, reinventing, 478–82
Government regulation, 178–94
    affirmative action/EEO, 351–52
    environmental, 182–85
    pricing, 186–87
    reform, appeal for, 179–81
Graduation, 196–209
    college, 203–09
    employee training program, 201–02
    high school, 197–200
Growth, corporate, 167–69, 372–73, 469–70

Health plan, announcement about changes, 5–8
Hedging strategy, 471–72
High school graduation, 197–200
Holiday celebrations, 222–32
    Christmas/Chanukah, 232
    Fourth of July, 226–27
    Memorial Day, 224–25
    New Year's Day, 223
    office party, 236
    Thanksgiving, 231

Holiday celebrations *(continued)*
    Veteran's Day, 228–30
Humor, 9, 52, 77

Imagination, motivating employee, 319–22
Informal events, 234–36
Internet research, 533–37
Interview
    print media, 255–57
    tv/radio, 258–59
Introductions, 238–42
    of distinguished guest, 78
    of new employee, 239–40
    of new manager, 241–42
    of speaker, 77
Irony, 57

James, Henry, 48

Leadership, motivating employee, 328–31
Legislative testimony, 244–52
    before investigation committee, 245–48
    in support of bill, 249–52
Lidstad, Richard, 268–72

Manager
    farewells of, 129, 137–38
    farewells to, 14–16, 132–36
    financial reports to, 149–50
    gift presentation by, 164
    gifts to, 163
    introduction of new, 241–42
    motivating leadership, 328–31
Marketing. *See* Sales and marketing
Mead, Dana G., 525–32
Media, 254–261
    advertising, 427–30
    news conference, 260–61
    print media interview, 255–57
    tv/radio interview, 258–59
Medical benefits announcement, 5–8
Memorial Day, 224–25
Memorialization
    anniversary of civic tragedy, 105–06
    anniversary of death, 93–95
    of company founder, 124–25
    funeral eulogy, 159–60
Mergers and acquisition, 27–28, 473–74
Mission, corporate, 332
Motivating employees, 264–47
    to action, 265–67
    in challenges, meeting, 273–74

Motivating employees *(continued)*
  in commitment, 286–90
  in corporate image improvement, 338–39
  with corporate mission, 332
  in customer service, 54–56, 291–94
  in decision making, 295–97
  in educational development programs, 300–02
  in ethics/values, 310–12
  examples of, 268–72, 275–82, 303–09
  in excellence of R&D, 313–14
  in goal setting, 315–318
  in imagination and creativity, 319–22
  in leadership, 328–31
  in optimism/positive thinking, 333–34
  in perseverance, 298–99
  in procrastination avoidance, 335–37
  in productivity, 323–27
  in risk taking, 342–43
  in teamwork, 283–85, 346–47
  in workplace safety, 344–45

News conference, 260–61
New Year's Day, 223
Numbers, quoting, 31

Office party, 236
Openings
  announcements, 2, 7, 10, 15, 19, 23
  celebrations, 66, 70
  chairperson's, 74, 76
  commemorations, 80, 83, 87, 94–95, 99,
    103
  competitiveness, 109, 111–12, 115, 118
  congratulations, 44, 49, 56
  corporate history, 212, 215
  corporate goals, 166, 172, 176
  dedications, 120, 122
  farewells, 128
  financial reports, 148, 153, 155
  funeral eulogy, 158
  gifts, 162
  government regulation, 178, 184, 191
  graduation, 196, 199
  holiday celebrations, 222, 230
  informal events, 234
  introductions, 238
  legislative testimony, 244, 247, 251
  media, 254
  motivating, 264, 266, 289, 293, 322, 326, 330, 337
  policies, 350, 360, 368, 380–81
  political affairs, 386
  public relations, 392, 395–96, 399, 403, 410, 414
  sales and marketing, 426, 429, 433, 444, 449, 453

Openings *(continued)*
  solicitations, 456, 461
  strategies, 464, 474, 481, 486, 92
  technology, 498, 514, 519, 524, 536
  training, 550, 555
Optimism, motivating employee, 333–34
Outline
  announcements, 7–8, 10–11, 15–16, 19–20, 23–24
  celebrations, 70
  commemorations, 83, 87–88, 99–100, 103–04
  competitiveness, 111–12, 115, 118
  congratulations, 49, 56
  corporate goals, 172–73, 176
  corporate history, 215–16
  dedications, 122–23
  financial reports, 153, 155–56
  government regulation, 184–85, 191–92
  graduation, 199–200
  holiday celebrations, 230
  legislative testimony, 247–48, 251–52
  motivating, 266–67, 289–90, 293–94, 322, 326–27,
    330–31, 337
  policies, 360, 368–369, 380–382
  public relations, 395–96, 399–400, 403–04, 410–11,
    414–15
  sales and marketing, 429–30, 433–34, 449–50,
    453–54
  solicitations, 461–462
  strategies, 474, 481–82, 486–87, 492–93
  technology, 514–15, 519–20, 524, 536–37
  training, 555–56
Outsourcing
  announcement/explanation of, 12–13
  policy on, 376–77

Performance analysis, 60
Perseverance, motivating employee, 298–99
Person-to-person communication, 9
Pfeiffer, Eckhard, 502–09
Picnic, company, 235
Planning, strategic, 490–93
Plant/facility
  announcement of construction, 31–32
  foreign, 366–69
  opening/inauguration of, 71–72
Policies, 350–84
  on affirmative action/EEO, 351–52
  on employee development, 353–54
  on employee empowerment, 355–56
  on environmental protection, 357–65
  on foreign facility, 366–69
  on free speech, 370–71
  on growth, 372–73

Policies *(continued)*
  on labor contracts, 374–75
  on outsourcing, 376–37
  on promotion, 378–82
  on recycling, 383–84
Political affairs, 386–89
  candidate endorsement, 387
  referendum support, 388–89
Positive reinforcement, 57, 60
Pricing regulation, 186–87
Print media interview, 255–57
Procrastination avoidance,
    motivating
  employee, 335–37
Product
  brand loyalty, 435–36
  new, 116–18, 441–42
  safety regulation, 188–92
  spin-off strategy, 488–89
Production goals, 57–58
Productivity, motivating employee,
    323–27
Promotion policy, 378–82
Pronouns, 7, 12
Public relations, 392–423
  business associations/chambers of
      commerce, 393–96
  civic associations, 397–400
  example, 416–23
  service clubs, 401–04
  trade associations, 405–15

Quality goals, 174–76, 340–41
Questions, 133
Quotations, 9, 50, 57, 61

Radio
  advertising on, 427–30
  interview, 258–59
Recycling policy, 383–84
Regulation. *See* Government
    regulation
Relocation announcement, 3–4
Reorganization announcement, 41–42
Research and development
  motivating excellence in, 313–14
  strategy for, 483–87
Retirement
  farewell by retiree, 139–45
  plan, announcement about changes, 9–11
Risk taking, motivating employee,
    342–43
Rumors, handling, 25

Safety
  product, 188–92
  See also Workplace safety
Sales and marketing, 426–54
  announcement of campaign, 21–24
  brand loyalty, 435–36
  company image, 451
  congratulations on goal attainment, 59–60
  customer service, 54–56, 291–94, 431–34,
      447–50
  foreign markets, 439–40
  new markets, 437–38
  new product, 116–18, 441–42
  radio advertising, 427–30
  teamwork, 445–46
Scholarship endowment, 96–104
Self-interest
  admission of, 62
  appeals to, 6, 117
Sentences
  declarative, 29
  selling point in, 22, 23
  transitional, 110–11, 190, 324
Solicitations, 456–62
  of gifts, 457–58
  of labor, 459–62
Speaker introduction of, 77
Sports events, company, 235
Statistics, 31, 114, 194
Stockholders
  financial reports to, 154–56
  growth strategy explanation to, 469–70
Strategies, 464–96
  decision-making process, 467–68
  downsizing, 465–66
  growth, 469–70
  hedging, 471–72
  mergers and acquisitions, 473–74
  planning, 490–93
  reinventing business, 475–77
  reinventing government, 478–82
  research and development, 483–87
  spin-off, 488–89
  turnaround, 494–96
Suggestions
  cost-saving, 50–51
  safety improvement, 63–64
Sullivan, James N., 35–40

Tarantino, Dominic, 203–09
Teamwork, motivating employee, 283–85, 346–47,
    445–46
Technology, 498–547

Technology *(continued)*
  communications, 499–501
  computer, 502–11
  desktop publishing, 512–15
  examples of, 525–32, 540–47
  information distribution, 521–24
  internet, 533–37
  labor market impact of, 538–39
  telecommuting, 516–20
Telecommuting, 516–20
Television interview, 258–59
Testimony. *See* Legislative testimony
Thanksgiving, 231
Thank you, for gift, 163
Tone, 3
Technology
Trade associations
  competitor, 412–15

Trade associations *(continued)*
  customer, 405–07
  supplier, 408–11
Training program
  corporate ethics in, 551–52
  graduation from, 201–02
  introduction/orientation, 553–56
Turnaround strategy, 494–96

Values, corporate, 310–312, 551–52
Veteran's Day, 228–30

Wedding celebration, 69–70
White, Thomas W., 303–09
Workplace safety
  employee suggestions, 63–64
  government regulations, 193–94
  motivating, 344–45